*To the soul of my father, Mohsen, who gave me his **ring** as a message and a lifelong souvenir.*

Table of Contents

About the Author

Mansour Ayouni is one of the leading contributors to the Ring programming language. He wrote his first BASIC computer statement in the mid-80s, using only pen and paper, when he was 10 years old. It wasn't in a California garage, though, or under the lights of the prestigious Eiffel Tower of Paris; it was in the rural village of Regueb in the center of Tunisia (North Africa) where there was no electricity or computers at all. Over the years, programming took him on an otherwise impossible international journey. From Tunisia to Niger to Canada, he contributed to the development of dozens of software applications ranging from lawyer office management solutions to banking to nuclear waste management systems. During his career, he has overseen programmers from three cultures and led software teams in various companies such as Whitecape, Keyrus, and Webgenetics. Now, he is a member of the Ring core team and runs Kalidia Consulting, helping businesses to make effective software.

About the Technical Reviewer

 **Bert Mariani** has worked on mainframe hardware as a field engineer for Univac and Amdahl, where machine language coding was used to debug and fix hardware problems when the OS would not boot. He supplements his coding skills with Assembler and C Code.

Bert currently resides in Montreal, Canada, where he works for Bell Mobility, helping to migrate 4G technology to 5G. Along with his team, he tests and implements many different types of network equipment from various hardware vendors to support mobile communications and cell phones.

Acknowledgments

To Cherihen, Teeba, and Haneen for their love, encouragement, and unbounded sacrifice.

To Mahmoud Fayed, Bert Mariani, and the Apress team (Mark, Matt, and Steve) for their support, patience, and dedication.

To those who inspired and taught me something during my programming career.

Introduction

In Tunisia, a nation that's more than 3,000 years old and my motherland, ancient building engineers left us the second biggest Roman theater in the world (Al-Jam), the first Islamic university (Al-Zaytoona), and the prestigious Cathedral of St. Vincent de Paul in the heart of the capital, Tunis. They are all beautiful and still functional, and they continuously inspire architects and artists alike. They are civilizational achievements that convey intellectual supremacy, design elegance, and timeless rays of spirituality.

In this book, I try to keep track of my grandparent's footsteps, and make a modest contribution to the building of Software Civilization, by providing a new learning experience of the art of programming, for a new programming language called Ring...

Ring

Like a beautiful star, Ring shines in the sky of the new generation of programming languages because of its outstanding learnability, expressiveness, and extreme flexibility. The language is remarkably dogma-free and embraces declarative and natural programming in an effective new way. Yet it is a serious tool, with powerful features and extended portability. It is ranked in the top 100 most popular programming languages (https://www.tiobe.com/tiobe-index/) and has been used to develop the PWCT open source visual programming project, which more than 21 million downloads from SourceForge.

The Book

The main goal of *Beginning Ring Programming* is to help you gain a gentle yet rigorous introduction to the world of Ring programming with clarity as the first concern, rich visualizations, and a lot of practical code examples.

In this book, Ring is used more as a computational thinking medium than a programming language. Its simple pseudocode-like footprint will help you focus on the underlining logic and ideas instead of the code itself. Its flexible syntax allows anyone, whatever language programming language they use, to feel at home when reading and writing computer code. Several programming paradigms (structured, object-oriented, functional, declarative, natural language, and metaprogramming), all allowed by Ring, are used in combination to compose specific designs to address specific problems in different situations.

Part I shows you how to install Ring and gives you a bird's-eye view of the language by exploring its features. I explain how Ring rigorously structures programs, and then you'll learn about the type system of the language by exposing its four native data types (number, string, list, and object) and how you can augment them by crafting your own user-defined types.

Part II is where you will learn how Ring manages inputs, outputs, and what is in between. The basic constructs of computer logic (sequence, selection, and iteration) are used in isolation and then combined to show more complex logic flows. I will discuss real-world scenarios and common mistakes leading to code complexity and present several strategies of refactoring, code cleansing, data modeling, and variable naming. Then, I will explain how Ring deals with the scopes of variables, at the local, object, and global levels.

In Part III, you will master the two conceptual constructs every programmer truly needs: functions and objects. You'll discover how they can be composed to solve a problem and how more advanced programming paradigms, such as declarative and natural, are beautifully implemented on top of them. Then I will introduce game programming as one of the domain applications of Ring. You'll learn how you can design a game declaratively, in Ring code, like you were designing it in visual software. Finally, I'll deliver 30 years of experience in writing code in the form of a gamified Ring-oriented fantasy world called Ringorialand. You'll learn how much of programming is complex, both technically and socially, and how gaming can be a good metaphor to reign over it.

The book was written over a period of nine months, with a lot of patience, consideration, and love of sharing. It is not intended to be a clinical user manual of Ring, though, but rather a passionate alchemy of technical knowledge, real-world programming experience, and critical personal reflections. So, use it to build your technical programming skills in Ring while developing a *cultural consciousness of programming* from the intellectual conversation it contains between you, the reader, and me, a seasoned programmer questioning today's code complexity via an emergent programming language that provides elegant and unprecedented answers to those questions.

Beginning Ring Programming is for those who are passionate about the craftsmanship culture in writing code, thinking in code, and solving algorithmic problems in a beautiful, expressive, and learnable programming language. You'll gain beginner-friendly knowledge about Ring and benefit, at the same time, from a one-stop container of lessons learned and valuable returns on experience, all distilled into real-world, customer-facing programming projects.

What You Will Learn

Specifically, in this book, you will do the following:

- Get started with the Ring programming language

- Master data types, I/O, GUI widgets, events, functions, and classes, including how they can be composed

- Carry out structural, object-oriented, functional, declarative, natural, and metaprogramming with Ring

- Quickly design professional-grade video games on top of the Ring Game Engine and enjoy a new declarative gaming programming experience with Ring

- Use the full power of Ring to refactor program code and develop clean and flexible program architectures

- Deploy visual thinking techniques in pragmatically solving complex algorithmic problems in Ring

- Embrace the Ring language culture founded on syntax freedom, programmer responsibility, hackable transparency, and dogma-free multiparadigm programming.

Foreword

Ring was created with a goal: to be a new language for a new programming experience.

Developing a programming language that we can rely on when we are thinking about the problems we need to solve instead of being constrained by the syntax and the rigidity of the programming paradigm is not an easy endeavor. The general mindset cultivated by the programming domain so far has proliferated the establishment of a set of technical dogmas. Obviously, this narrows the window of innovation and constitutes a serious barrier to entry for many people who could be great programmers but are demotivated by the complexity of today's programming tools.

Facing such a cultural and technological challenge, I was aware from the beginning that I should develop a programming language for the long term. Although Ring, as you will discover in this book, is designed to deal pragmatically with any situation that a general-purpose programming language can manage, my focus was to enable new ways of thinking in code, which I believe will be required from any programmer in the foreseeable future. Writing programs *visually* while leaving the tedious code generation task to the machine, designing programs *declaratively* with the semantics of the application domain, and talking with the code in a *natural* language written by the programmer inside that code are just three domains of innovation the new generation of programming languages should embrace.

In this regard, what makes the Ring language so important is that it naturally emerged as a solution for these strong requirements when I tried to solve them in existent programming languages and couldn't. Every feature of the language finds its origin in a problem I faced when I was working on the PWCT project,[1] and every decision I made on its design, even if it breaks the norm and sometimes shocks the common sense, forms an answer to a practical problem that was unsolvable or hard to solve in other languages. In fact, most of them focus restrictively on conventional programming paradigms such as procedural, object-oriented, and functional programming. In Ring, our message is to *connect* between those paradigms and others, such as declarative and natural language programming, in a new programming experience.

---

[1]http://doublesvsoop.sourceforge.net/

The beauty of the book in your hands is that it embraces the *culture* of the language while presenting its powerful features in a practical way. Mansour really shows how Ring can be an option in developing small or large programs and in enabling a programming journey based on prototyping, experimentation, iterative design, clean architecture, and code craftsmanship. Nevertheless, the author, who I consider to be a master of Ring and programming in general, has revealed the secrets of the great programmers in thinking, analyzing, modeling, and writing code. Many technical constructs famously known to be complex in programming, such as MVC architecture, data-oriented modeling, scope management, function and object composition, event-driven systems, real-time applications, and even game programming, are all introduced in an innovative visual way, with tons of examples and many engaging stories to tell.

By contemplating the strategies and real-world situations in this instructive, well-organized book and how they are solved nicely in Ring, I can say with confidence that the message behind the language has been delivered. That said, I hope that this book will help you gaining an *emotional* connection with Ring as a thinking tool, as a hackable learning environment, and, ultimately, as a friendly programming language built around the core values of syntax freedom, programmer's responsibility, technological transparency, and multiparadigm programming.

Welcome to Ring, and welcome to *Beginning Ring Programming*.

Mahmoud Samir Fayed
Creator of Ring
Egypt, January 2020

CHAPTER 1

Getting Started with Ring

"Barka da zuwa"[1] to the wonderful world of Ring!

In this chapter, you'll come face to face with a relatively new and promising programming language created to be accessible, learnable, and expressive.

- *Accessible* from the first moment since Ring is installed within seconds

- *Learnable* due to its quality documentation, rich examples, and clear error messages

- *Expressive* by its clean and flexible syntax, exceeding the rigid barriers of most classical programming languages

My objective in this chapter is to get you set up with Ring for the next chapters of the book. I'll also connect you emotionally to the beauty of the language by showing how Ring is an accessible, learnable, and expressive tool for *thinking* in computer code.

First, I will guide you to install Ring and get it up and running. Then, we will jump into using the language by writing a simple helloring program. During the process, you'll discover the date() and time() functions, the List data type, and how you can

---

[1]As you might suspect, "Barka da zuwa" means welcome. Welcome to Hausa! Spoken by 60+ million humans across Africa, the language of the Kingdom of Kano is still alive with dozens of local dialects. Because of its extreme flexibility, the language has formed a cultural platform for civilizational and religious cohabitation. A nice illustration of such a mutual influence with the Arabic language is how Hausa people name their children: *Lawali* for the first (*Al-awal* in Arabic), *Sani* the second (*Athani* in Arabic), *Salisou* the third (*Athaleth* in Arabic), *Rabiou* the fourth (*Arrabee* in Arabic), and so on. In its modern form, several writing systems are available in Hausa, including the Latin Boko, the Arabic Ajmi, and the Braille system. I would argue that Ring is the Hausa of programming languages.

© Mansour Ayouni 2020
M. Ayouni, *Beginning Ring Programming*, https://doi.org/10.1007/978-1-4842-5833-0_1

easily define your own functions, all with a goal of writing expressive code. Finally, I will introduce you to the rich set of available Ring documentation by presenting its high-level overview and showing three of the most common use cases of the help system.

What You Will Learn

Specifically, you will learn the following in this chapter:

- How to install Ring and access the content of the installation folder
- How to use Ring Notepad, the Ring integrated development environment (IDE)
- How to have a conversation about time with Ring
- How to refactor Ring code to enhance its expressiveness
- How to contribute to the official Ring codebase
- How to say hello in Ring to the console, to a window, on a web page, and even inside a game
- How to use the Qt library in Ring
- How to write multilingual text in Ring programs
- How to efficiently use the rich documentation of Ring

Download and Installation

In this section, you'll learn how to install Ring and how to use it for the first time. To do so, let's go to the official web site at `www.ring-lang.net` (see Figure 1-1).

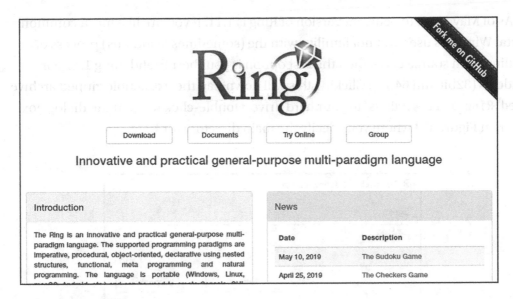

Figure 1-1. *Ring home page*

Selecting the Appropriate Installer

Click Download on the left of the screen. You'll see the screen in Figure 1-2.

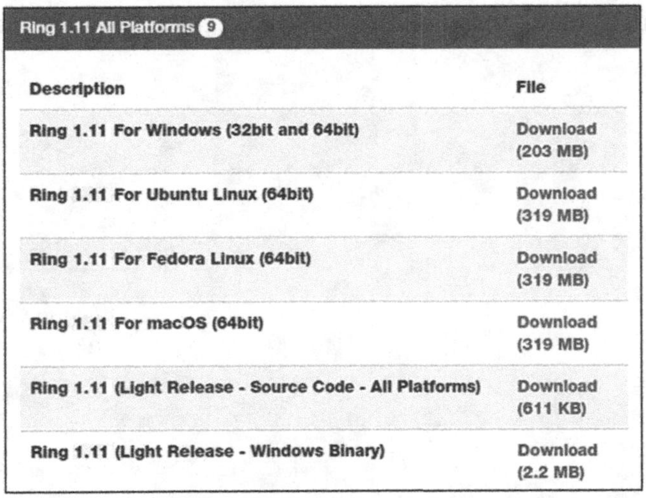

Ring 1.11 All Platforms ⑨	
Description	**File**
Ring 1.11 For Windows (32bit and 64bit)	Download (203 MB)
Ring 1.11 For Ubuntu Linux (64bit)	Download (319 MB)
Ring 1.11 For Fedora Linux (64bit)	Download (319 MB)
Ring 1.11 For macOS (64bit)	Download (319 MB)
Ring 1.11 (Light Release - Source Code - All Platforms)	Download (611 KB)
Ring 1.11 (Light Release - Windows Binary)	Download (2.2 MB)

Figure 1-2. *Available options for downloading Ring*

As of May 2019, the current version of Ring is 1.11. If you are like me, a common mortal Windows user and not familiar with the (sometimes fastidious) process of building from source code, then the first option is your best friend: Ring 1.11 For Windows (32bit and 64bit). Clicking this will download the extractible zipped archive Fayed_Ring_1.11_Windows[2] to your hard drive. Double-click to open the dialog box shown in Figure 1-3 where you specify the main directory for Ring.

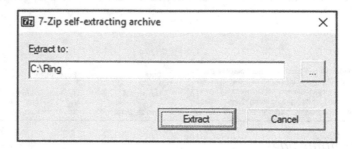

Figure 1-3. *Extracting Ring*

Discovering the Ring Installation Folder

Congrats! You are only a few steps from having Ring up and running. Before doing so, let's look at the content of the installation folder (c:\ring in my case), as shown in Figure 1-4.

---

[2]Fayed at the beginning of the executable name stands for Mahmoud Fayed, the language designer.

Figure 1-4. *Content of the Ring installation folder*

Unlike other common tools where you might feel like a "stranger in Moscow,"[3] you can do a lot with the Ring installation folder.

- You can jump directly into writing Ring code in the Ring Notepad tool by launching the rnote.exe file (you can do this now and skip to the next section if you'd like, but if you stick with me here, you won't be disappointed).

- You can open a PowerPoint presentation about the language from the presentation subfolder.

- Go to the samples folder to find more than 500 code snippets and instructive tutorials.

- In the applications folder there are dozens of real-world applications made by the community along with many funny games you can play (such as chess, cards, game of life, gold magic, flappy birds, and many others).

---

[3]The same sentiment Michal Jackson felt in his hotel room while composing the song.

- You can see the "internals" of Ring by skimming the `tests` folder where you will find a complete yet knowledgeable testing suite for every Ring function (composed of both test scripts and test examples).

- You can learn about the code editors that Ring supports by reading the listing in the `editor` folder (there you will find the instructions to use Ring with your preferred editor; Ring Notepad will be our choice for this book).

- You will find many other informative details[4] and get an idea about the scope and reach of the strong tool in your hands.

Launching Ring Notepad

Launch `rnote.exe` to see how familiar the user interface looks (see Figure 1-5).

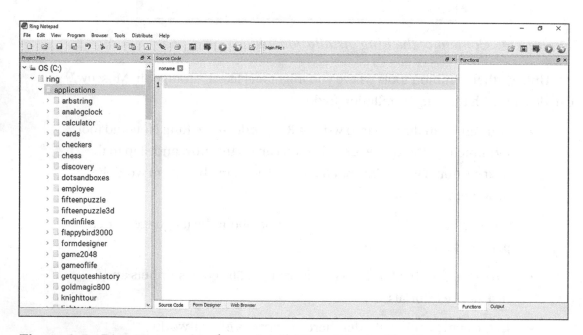

Figure 1-5. *Ring Notepad, a (nostalgic?) Visual Basic–like IDE*

---

[4]You'll find the 2,000-page *Ring Reference Book* in the doc subfolder, but please forget about reading it for now.

Not only is Ring installable in minutes, whatever your platform is, but also Ring programs are distributable[5] nearly automatically to any platform your users are on (desktop, mobile, or server) no matter what operating system they use (Windows, macOS, or Linux). In addition, because Notepad is just a Ring application, nothing prevents you from running it on your Android or iPad tablet, so you can craft your code wherever you are.

Your First Ring Program

My objective in this section is not to just print some "Hello World!" text on your screen but rather to take you on your first trip around the Ring garden, plunge your eyes in its colorful basin of floating flowers (the Ring functions), and take a deep breath of its reanimating air surrounding the place (the Ring syntax).

This is not gratuitous poetry[6] but a reality I live with every day as a Ring programmer who has (*finally!*) found in Ring a flexible tool to express the way he thinks.

Ready?

Organizing Yourself

First let's create a folder under c:\ to host all our code snippets for this book. Name it ringbook. Then create a subfolder for every chapter we are working on, such as chap1 for the current one. Inside that c:\ringbook\chap1 folder, create a Ring file called helloring.ring that we are going to use to craft our first Ring statements.

To do so, execute the following steps:

1. In the file browser, select the c:\ringbook\chap1 folder to tell Ring Notepad that this is your active work folder.

2. In the main menu of the Notepad application, select File ➤ New.

---

[5]The Ring2EXE tool automates the building of multiplatform Ring applications. You'll learn more about this later in the chapter.

[6]As a hobby, I use Ring to make visual poetry essays that combine shapes, colors, animations, and sounds (thanks, Ring Game Engine!) with a sole and ultimate objective: designing for beauty! This has influenced my style of writing code as you will observe in the several snippets we are going to produce together in the book.

3. In the "New file" window, enter helloring as a name of your
    new file.

4. Click Save, and you are done!

Asking Ring Questions

Let's ask Ring what time it is. See Figure 1-6.

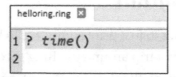

Figure 1-6. *Our time question*

As you can see, we just need to type ? time() and press Ctrl+F5.[7] The answer is
shown in the output window to the right of Ring Notepad (see Figure 1-7).

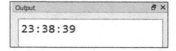

Figure 1-7. *Ring's answer*

Now let's ask Ring about the current date. It's easy too: we type ? date(). Figure 1-8
shows the result.

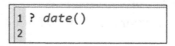

Figure 1-8. *Our date question*

---

[7]You can also use the main menu to run your code by selecting Program ➤ Run GUI Application.

Ring returns the current date. Figure 1-9 shows the answer I got.

Figure 1-9. *Ring's answer*

What if we try a different question, like asking about the date tomorrow? I think we can agree that tomorrow is nothing but today plus one day. This is exactly how Ring thinks. We need to use date() and call the addDays() function on top of it (see Figure 1-10).

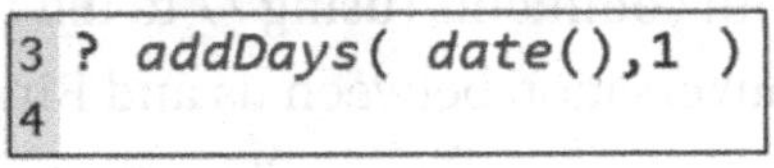

```
3 ? addDays( date(),1 )
4
```

Figure 1-10. *Asking for tomorrow in Ring*

What about yesterday?

Yes, you are right. We say this:

```
? addDays( date(), -1 )
```

What will be the exact date after a whole century?[8] Well, we need to compute the number of days in a century. Let's make it simple by multiplying 365 days a year by 100 years. Put the result in a nice n variable and call addDays() again (see Figure 1-11).

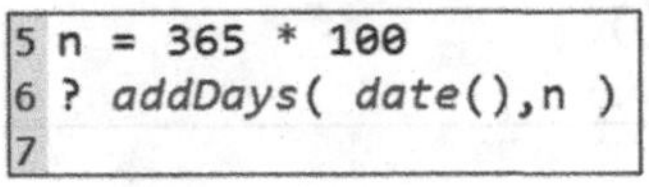

```
5 n = 365 * 100
6 ? addDays( date(),n )
7
```

Figure 1-11. *What is the exact date 100 years from now?*

I'll leave you to get the answer from Ring.

---

[8]This addDays() function is a lot of fun for me and Teeba, my 7-year-old daughter, especially when we use it to ask questions about the past and future.

From Date to Time

Enough with Date. Let's taste some Time fruits from the Ring garden and ask about the current time using the `time()` function, as shown in Figure 1-12. In my case, the answer is a late 00:44:28 (yes, I am a nocturnal programming owl[9]).

```
8  ? time()
9
```

Figure 1-12. *After Date, it's time for Time*

If we decorate our code with comments (using `//` to tell Ring to ignore a line), we end up with a nice piece of conversation between us and Ring (see Figure 1-13).

```
helloring.ring  ☒

1   // What is the current date?
2   ? date()
3
4   // What is the date tomorrow?
5   ? addDays( date(),1 )
6
7   // What is the date in a century?!
8   n = 365 * 100
9   ? addDays( date(),n )
10
11  // What time is it now?
12  ? time()
13
```

Figure 1-13. *The dialogue with Ring about date and time*

---

[9]In early Indian folklore, owls represent wisdom and helpfulness and have powers of prophecy. By the Middle Ages in Europe, the owl had become associated with witches and was the inhabitant of dark, lonely, and profane places, a foolish but feared specter. With superstitions dying out in the 20th century, the owl has returned to its position as a symbol of wisdom. —From Owls in Mythology and Culture (`https://www.owlpages.com/owls/articles.php?a=62`)

A Ring Flower: timeList Function

Undoubtedly, *time* is, was, and will be the first concern of all humanity, programmers included. Let's imagine some basic questions about time in the context of writing computer programs, as shown here:

- What are the time and date now?

- What is the full weekday name?

- What is the full name of the month?

- What is the number of the current day in the year?

- What is the number of the current month?

- What is the current week of the year?

- What is the current day of the week?

- What is the number of the current year of the century?

- Can you show only the minutes after the hour?

- What is my current time zone?

Ring has all of these questions covered; you need just to use timeList() to get the answer to any of these questions. As you can probably understand from its name, this function is a list containing the answers. To get the answer, you just need to specify its index inside the list. So, in my case:

- timeList()[2] gives Saturday.

- timeList()[4] gives May.

- timeList()[19] gives 2019.

We can add these lines to our code, as shown in Figure 1-14.

```
14  // Play with timelist()
15
16  ? timelist()[17] // time
17  ? timelist()[7] // hour-24
18  ? timelist()[8] // hour-12
19  ? timelist()[11] // minutes
20  ? timelist()[13] // seconds
21
22  ? timelist()[16] // date
23  ? timelist()[2] // day long
24  ? timelist()[1] // day short
25  ? timelist()[4] // month
26  ? timelist()[19] // year
```

Figure 1-14. *Some values of the timeList() function*

Making timeList Expressive

At the end of this section, you will get a complete reference of the numbers you should use as an index for every answer to the previous questions. This is great, but the issue with those index numbers is that there are plenty of them, and you have to learn 'em by heart! My objective is to avoid them altogether so we can write something like this instead:

- timelist()[:time] instead of timelist()[17]
- timelist()[:minutes] instead of timelist()[11]

Figure 1-15 shows the ideal replacements.

```
14  // Play with timeList() : Expressive
15  ? timelist()[ ti[:time] ]
16  ? timelist()[ ti[:hour_24] ]
17  ? timelist()[ ti[:hour_12] ]
18  ? timelist()[ ti[:minutes] ]
19  ? timelist()[ ti[:seconds] ]
20
21  ? timelist()[ ti[:date] ]
22  ? timelist()[ ti[:day_long] ]
23  ? timelist()[ ti[:day_short] ]
24  ? timelist()[ ti[:month] ]
25  ? timelist()[ ti[:year] ]
```

Figure 1-15. *timelist() revamped for the sake of expressiveness*

Add those lines at the end of the helloring.ring file and comment out the old lines with the basic timeList() syntax so they look like Figure 1-16.

```
16 /*
17 // Play with timelist()
18 ? timelist()[17] // time
19 ? timelist()[7] // hour-24
20 ? timelist()[8] // hour-12
21 ? timelist()[11] // minutes
22 ? timelist()[13] // seconds
23
24 ? timelist()[16] // date
25 ? timelist()[2] // day long
26 ? timelist()[1] // day short
27 ? timelist()[4] // month
28 ? timelist()[19] // year
29 */
30
```

Figure 1-16. *Note the use of /* and */ to comment a whole block of code*

Listening to Ring When It Complains

If you were attentive enough to Figure 1-15 (and I am sure you were[10]), you will have noticed the strange ti[ ] before the natural :time, :date, and :year that we haven't talked about yet. If you try to execute the code (Ctrl+F5), Ring complains with an error, as shown in Figure 1-17.

```
Line 15 Error (R5) : Can't access the
list item, Object is not list !
in file C:/ring/ring-book/hello ring.ring
```

Figure 1-17. *The error message you will get in the output window*

---

[10]And if you weren't, then don't blame me for being courteous.

Ring was clear enough about the problem at hand: it can't access a given list item. This list is definitely ti[], and the item to be accessed is defined by its index, :time in our case (because the error is first raised in line 15 containing the :time index). You might ask where is the root cause of the error exactly, and is it related to the object ti[] or the index :name? Ring clearly says "Object is not list!" expecting it to be a *list*, but it wasn't. Let's *listify* it to save the world.

Playing with Lists

To create a list in Ring, type the following:

Mylist = [1,2,3,4,5]

or equivalently:

MyList = 1:5

By analogy, you can do this:

Mylist = ["A","B","C","D","E"]

or equivalently:

MyList = "A":"E"

Tip   Create a file called tempo.ring to use for your own experimentations that are not part of the current code we are working on. For now, try the examples of declaring lists shown earlier and try to access them using not only MyList[1] and MyList[2] but also MyList[999], MyList[-88], and MyList[] without any index.

Let's get back to dealing with our error message. The ti[] list we need to declare is the list of names I want to bind to every index of the timelist() function. I called it ti as an abbreviation of *time info*, but the code explains it better (see Listing 1-1).

Listing 1-1. Time info in a ti[] list

```
// Declaring the time info (ti[]) list

ti = [
        // Time info
        :time = 17,
        :hour_24 = 7,
        :hour_12 = 8,
        :minutes = 11,
        :seconds = 13,

        // Date info
        :date = 16,
        :day_long = 2,
        :day_short = 1,
        :month = 4,
        :year = 19
]
```

Immediately, you can do the following:

- You can print the content of the whole list with ? ti.

- You can read the content of the :time field in the list with ?
  ti[:time]. The result is 17.

- You can read the content of the :year field in the list with ?
  ti[:year]. The result is 19.

- You can also read the pair of values (index, value) contained in the first
  field of the list: ? ti[1]. The result will be a list containing time and 17.

- You can return the name of that first field with ? ti[1][1]. The result
  will be just a string of text containing time.

- You can get the *value* of that first field with ? ti[1][2]. The result
  will be 17, of course, and this is the same as saying ? ti[:time].

> **Note**   Without a lot of hype, we've played with one of the most advanced data structures in all programming languages: *hash maps*. (They are sometimes also called *dictionaries* or *indexed lists*.) You saw how easy it is to implement them in Ring, but this is not important right now. What we achieved was to produce more expressive Ring code for using the timeList() function.

Expressiveness: First Round

You are inside open tempo.ring, containing the code in Listing 1-1 that we just wrote. Let's save it to a new file called timeinfo.ring in the c:\ringbook folder by selecting File ➤ Save.

Now, to make the data defined in this list a citizen in our main program, we need to invite it by adding load "timeinfo.ring" in the head of the helloring.ring file. Listing 1-2 shows the full listing.

Listing 1-2. timeinfo.ring

```
load "timeinfo.ring"
// Play with timelist()
? timelist()[17] // time
? timelist()[7] // hour_24
? timelist()[8] // hour_12
? timelist()[11] // minutes
? timelist()[13] // seconds

? timelist()[16] // date
? timelist()[2] // day long
? timelist()[1] // day short
? timelist()[4] // month
? timelist()[19] // year
// Play with timelist() : Expressive

? timelist() [ ti[:time] ]
? timelist() [ ti[:hour_24] ]
```

```
? timelist() [ ti[:hour_12] ]
? timelist() [ ti[:minutes] ]
? timelist() [ ti[:seconds] ]
```

Execute your program (Ctrl+F5) and you're done: the error message has disappeared!

To be honest, I'm still not satisfied with the result. The remaining ti[ ] inside the code is disturbing my expressiveness paranoia and should be fixed (see Figure 1-18).

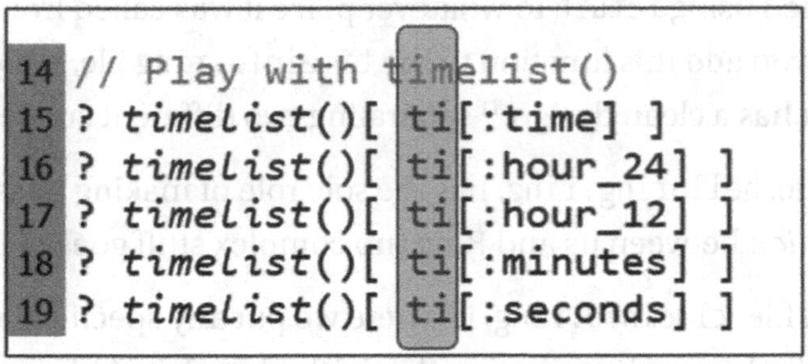

```
14  // Play with timelist()
15  ? timelist()[ ti[:time] ]
16  ? timelist()[ ti[:hour_24] ]
17  ? timelist()[ ti[:hour_12] ]
18  ? timelist()[ ti[:minutes] ]
19  ? timelist()[ ti[:seconds] ]
```

Figure 1-18. We need a solution to avoid those ugly ti[]s!

timeList() is a true flower; still, its use in this particular context lacks some semantic versatility. In fact, it is named after an implementation detail: a list data type containing some information about time. That *information* is what we're looking for, so why don't we talk directly about timeInfo() and hide timeList() from being visible in the first place? In a better world, we would be able to just type what's shown in Figure 1-19.

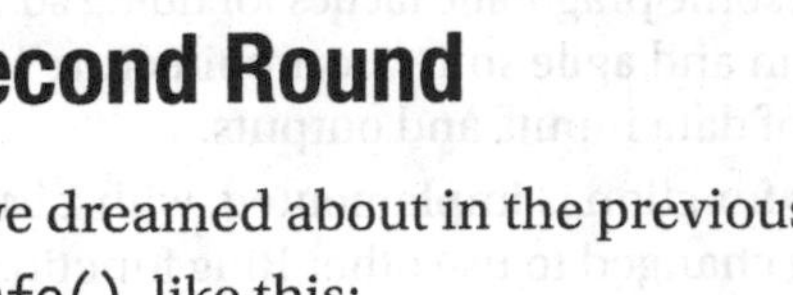

```
? timeInfo(:date)
? timeInfo(:month)
? timeInfo(:year)
```

Figure 1-19. This is expressive code

Expressiveness: Second Round

To build a better world like we dreamed about in the previous section, we need to define a new function called timeInfo(), like this:

```
func timeInfo( item )
    return timeList()[ ti[item] ]
```

17

The first line constitutes the syntax we will be using in our main `helloring.ring` program (and any other program we could write in the future based on that `timeInfo()` function), while the second line stays internal to the function and hides its complexity from the rest of the world (sorry, I mean the rest of the code).

When invoked with an `item` equal to `:date`, for example, this value is used inside the function, so the following expression is executed:

```
timeList()[ ti[:date] ]
```

It is then returned using `return` to whatever place it was called from.

Now, I suggest you add this function to the `timeinfo.ring` file, which is not only straightforward but has a clean design,[11] separating two different concerns.

- A main file, `helloring.ring`, has the sole role of making possible the *conversation* between us and Ring (no complex stuff goes here!).

- A second file, `timeinfo.ring`, is where we put any specific data (like the `ti[]` list) or implementation detail (the `timeInfo()` function) that serves to boost expressiveness and alleviate the complexity[12] of writing (and reading) code in our first file.

The list `ti[]` in the `timeinfo.ring` file looks like Listing 1-3.

Listing 1-3. ti[] list code in timeinfo.ring

```
// Declaring the time info (ti[]) list

ti = [
    // Time info
    :time = 17,
```

---

[11]Beautiful code cannot be achieved by just writing expressive statements (which we focus on here) but also and mainly by crafting a clean architecture. I'll be doing my best to show you, whenever possible in this book, some pragmatic tactics for doing so. In particular, Chapters 3 to 5 show you how you make a clean and agile software architecture for enabling your program to easily deal with various types of data inputs and outputs.

[12]By *complexity* I mean how this function is implemented, with `timeList()` for now, but nothing prevents it from being changed to use other Ring functions or external libraries. Even `timeList()` indexes can be subject to change, when for example their order is changed or new information about time is added in future versions. In such cases, `timeInfo()` doesn't change, and even if we have used it 1,001 times around in our program, nothing is required other than adapting the single `timeList()` implementation.

```
        :hour_24 = 7,
        :hour_12 = 8,
        :minutes = 11,
        :seconds = 13,

        // Date info
        :date = 16,
        :day_long = 2,
        :day_short = 1,
        :month = 4,
        :year = 19
]

// Hiding the complexity of timelist()
// inside an expressive timeinfo()
func timeInfo(item)
    return timelist()[ ti[item] ]
```

The Final Listing of the "Hello Ring!" Program

Go back to the main helloring.ring file and replace every timeList()[ti[item]] with the corresponding timeInfo(item) to get the final listing of our program, as shown in Listing 1-4.

Listing 1-4. timeInfo(item)

```
load "timeinfo.ring"

// What is the current date?
? date()

// What is the date tomorrow?
? addDays( date(),1 )

// What is the date in a century?!
n = 365 * 100
? addDays( date(),n )
```

```
// What time is it now?
? time()

// More questions!
? timeInfo(:time)
? timeInfo(:hour_24)
? timeInfo(:hour_12)
? timeInfo(:minutes)
? timeInfo(:seconds)
? timeInfo(:date)
? timeInfo(:day_long)
? timeInfo(:day_short)
? timeInfo(:month)
? timeInfo(:year)
```

The "Very Final" Listing: One More Adjustment!

I can't help but to think there is one more problem of expressiveness in the previous listing. Let's fix it.

When we say that we are having a *conversation* with Ring in the scope of the main helloring.ring file, we mean the following:

- ? time() looks like a natural, unequivocal question that we asked Ring.

- However, ? addDays(day(),1) doesn't!

I do not pretend to be an expert in neuroscience and cognitive processing, but when my lazy brain reads the first line, it sees ?, replaces it with What, and then reads time() and replaces it with time?. The result is obviously that What time? means What time is it now?.

But when I read the second line, the result is a scrambled sentence resembling Figure 1-20.

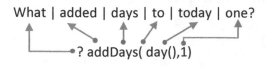

Figure 1-20. *Disconnected dots inside my brain*

My brain is expecting to read "What is tomorrow?" This question, if reverse-engineered according to the logic we agreed on in the first line, leads to such the concise Ring code of ? `tomorrow()`.

Without further ado, let's make it happen, through yet another set of `functions` we construct and add to `timeInfo.ring` like this:

```
func tomorrow()
    return addDays( date(),1 )
```

Add the following also:

```
func dateAfter1Century()
    n = 365*100
    return addDays ( date,n )
```

Why not add the following?

```
func yesterday()
    return addDays( date,-1 )
```

Then in the main file `helloring.ring`, leave room for a true conversation as natural as shown in Listing 1-5.

Listing 1-5. Final Listing

```
// Dialog on time with Ring

load "timeinfo.ring"

// What is the current date?
? date()

// What is the date tomorrow?
? tomorrow()     // In stead of : addDays( date(),1 )

// What is the date in a century?!
? dateAfter1Century()    // Instead of :
                         // n = 365 * 100
                         // ? addDays( date(),n )
```

```
// What time is it now?
? time()

// More questions!
? timeInfo(:time)
? timeInfo(:hour_24)
? timeInfo(:hour_12)
? timeInfo(:minutes)
? timeInfo(:seconds)
? timeInfo(:date)
? timeInfo(:day_long)
? timeInfo(:day_short)
? timeInfo(:month)
? timeInfo(:year)
```

Section finished! And because I'm happy with our achievements,[13] I won't forget my promise. Figure 1-21 shows the list of all the index numbers available for the timeList() function.

index	value			
1	abbreviated weekday name		10	Month of the year
2	full weekday name		11	Minutes after hour
3	abbreviated month name		12	AM or PM
4	full month name		13	Seconds after the hour
5	Date & Time		14	Week of the year (sun-sat)
6	Day of the month		15	day of the week
7	Hour (24)		16	date
8	Hour (12)		17	time
9	Day of the year		18	year of the century
10	Month of the year		19	year
			20	time zone

Figure 1-21. *timeList() indexes*

---

[13]Let's challenge ourselves by sending a proposal to the Ring mailing list to accept timeInfo() as a standard function in the language! Mahmoud will react (quickly, for sure!), and I'll share his answer with you as soon as I receive it.

Documentation and the Help System

In this section, I'll show you the best path you should take among the vast materials provided for you to learn Ring.[14] Before this, let me bring you some good news: our proposal for integrating our `timeInfo()` function (see the previous section) to the Ring standard library has been accepted🎖! On May 24, 2019, I wrote the message shown in Figure 1-22 in the Ring Google Group.

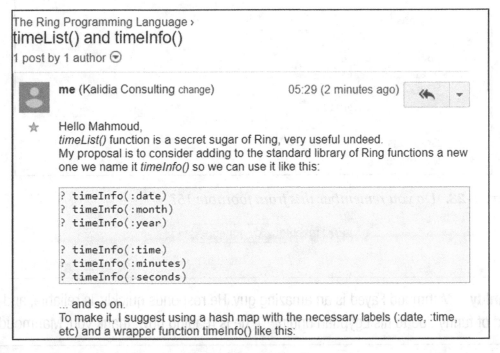

Figure 1-22. *I've shared the code we've written together in the previous section*

In just a few hours, Mahmoud reacted positively (see Figure 1-23)!

---

[14]Ring has impressive documentation for such a young project. It also has a rich number of working examples you can experiment with.

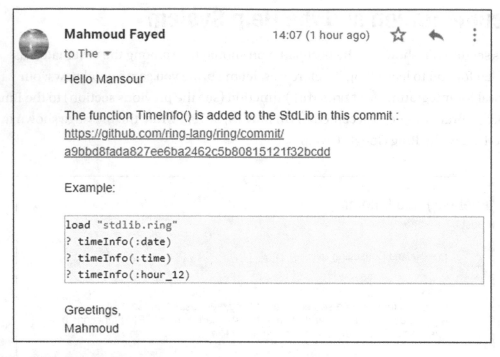

Figure 1-23. *Do you remember this from footnote 15?*

Mahmoud will react (quickly, for sure!) and I'll share

Frankly   Mahmoud Fayed is an amazing guy. He responds quickly, is reliable, and is kind of funny due to his Egyptian origin.[15] If he is reading now, thank you, Mahmoud!

In this section, I'll give you the big picture of the available Ring documentation and provide you with practical and quick answers to the following questions:

- Is there a "Hello World" tutorial I can start with?

- Where can I read an introductive article about Ring written by Mahmoud Fayed?

---

[15]Known for their proverbial sense of humor, Egyptians resort to comedy as a safety net in everyday life and as a creative tool in many cultural productions. Among Arabs, they are (recognized to be) awlād al-nukta (sons of the joke) for their passion for jokes and their ability to laugh even in hard times. —From "Egyptian Sense of Humour: Characters, Strategies and Context" by Cristina Dozia, 2015/2016

- How is the help system structured in Ring, and how can I use it in practice?

- Where can I ask questions when I am struggling?

- Are there any critics and reviews of Ring out there on the Internet?

- Are there any videos tutorials about the language on YouTube?

- Is there any FAQ I can consult?

I will answer these questions in the following sections.

Any "Hello, World!" Tutorial?

The first article I suggest you read is "Different styles for writing Hello World program in the Ring programming language" by Rub Lu on Code Project[16] (published in December 2017).

The beauty of this article is that it gives you a first taste of Ring's capabilities while saying "Hello, World" in the console, in a window, inside a game, in a web page, and as a natural language expression. We will explore some of the code snippets provided and comment on them briefly. Sometimes, I will change them by adding to or simplifying them. There is similar material to this article in the help system available in Ring.[17]

Say Hello in the Console

There is nothing magical to get Ring to say hello; just type `? "Hello, World!"`. Other options are also provided, as shown here:

- `see "Hello, World!"`

- `put "Hello, World!"`

- `load "stdlib.ring" Print("Hello, World!")`

Why are there four options for doing the same thing?[18] The answer is: expressiveness. You can stick to only one, but, in my case, I take advantage of the flexibility of the language to use every option in its convenient context.

---

[16]https://www.codeproject.com/Tips/1222859/Different-styles-for-writing-Hello-World-program-i

[17]http://ring-lang.sourceforge.net/doc1.10/getting_started.html

[18]There is a minor difference, though: ? automatically adds a new line after the string, but the other options don't.

- If I'm REPLing[19] or dialoguing with Ring (remember `helloring. ring`?), then my choice is : ?.

- If I'm in the context of describing what a user would see, I use `See`.

- If I'm describing to the computer what steps it must follow to solve a problem, then I use `Put`.

- In a large program involving a large team and rigorous standards, I use the `Print` function from the `StdLib` library.

This kind of freedom offered by Ring is not a side effect but a foundational feature for writing expressive programs.[20] Expressiveness is the door to all other quality criteria of well-written code (efficiency, speed, safety, maintainability, etc.). It's all about being clear about your intent so others can read your code without a hassle, connect to your train of thought, and add new features without transforming your codebase into a hot dish of shakshuka.[21]

Say Hello in a Web Page

Try saying hello in a web page by writing this code in the `tempo.ring` file:

```
load "weblib.ring"
import System.Web

new page { text("Hello, World!") }
```

---

[19]REPL stands for *read-eval-print-loop*, a kind of interactive tool to script your programming language. Ring's REPL can be fired from the main menu by selecting Tools ➤ RingREPL – Console or Tools ➤ RingREPL – GUI depending on your preference for a console or graphical user interface.

[20]An illustration of writing expressive code is provided, in practice, by Jonathan Boccara in his Fluent{C++} blog: `https://www.fluentcpp.com/2016/12/19/can-you-write-expressive-code-christmas-break-challenge`.

[21]Shakshuka is a well-known dish in Tunisia, Algeria, and North Africa consisting of a dish of eggs cooked in tomato sauce, chili, and onion, often seasoned with cumin. It's delicious indeed! People in Tunisia use the word *shakshuka* to describe complex situations and things lacking clarity and organization.

The first two lines import the necessary library[22] (`weblib.ring`) and package[23] (`System.Web`) to deal with web pages in Ring. Then, in the third line, a new page object is created. Inside that object (between the two braces[24]), text is created with the value "`Hello, World!`" (see Figure 1-24).

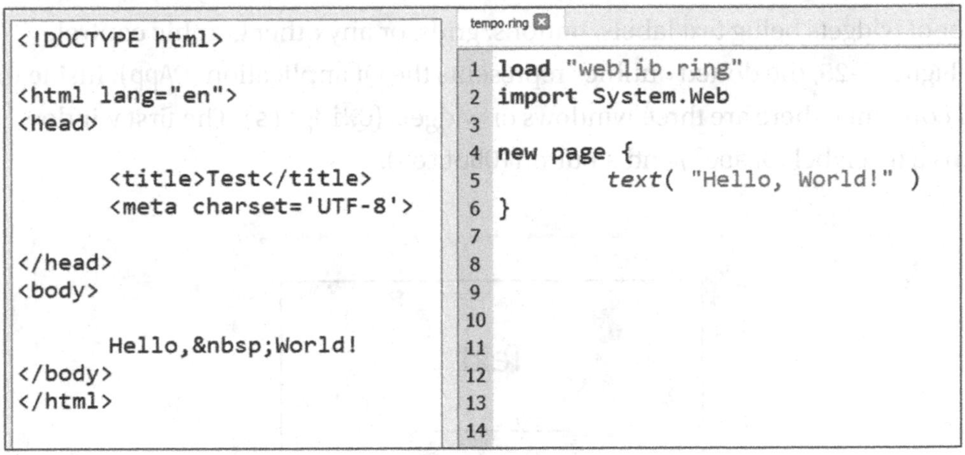

```
<!DOCTYPE html>

<html lang="en">
<head>

        <title>Test</title>
        <meta charset='UTF-8'>

</head>
<body>

        Hello, World!
</body>
</html>
```

tempo.ring ❌

```
1  load "weblib.ring"
2  import System.Web
3
4  new page {
5          text( "Hello, World!" )
6  }
7
8
9
10
11
12
13
14
```

Figure 1-24. Saying "Hello, World!" in a web page

We're not going further now into web programming.[25] Just take note that every aspect of HTML and web pages are modeled in Ring, which means you can design your whole front-end (and back-end, of course) web application using the functions provided by the WebLib library.[26]

---

[22] A *library* is a set of Ring code placed in a text file with a name and a `.ring` extension. The library can be loaded from other Ring code by using the `load` command.

[23] In object-oriented programming with Ring, a *package* is a set of classes bundled together to make possible the design of modular programs.

[24] This is a cool feature of Ring allowing the access of an object context (attributes and methods) without the need of making a separate instantiation of the object (using the `New` command) and then invoking its members (using the *dot* syntax) like this: `oPage = New Page()` and then `oPage.setTex("Hello, World!")`.
It comes in handy when you need to perform a visual XML-like organization of your code using braces. You will become familiar with this declarative approach in many places when you are programming in Ring (GUIs and web applications, games, natural language, and so on).

[25] We will come back to some web examples in the upcoming chapters, but please note that web programming is not covered like it deserves in this book due to space limitation. I have selected game programming as a domain application of Ring to talk about n more detail in Chapter 9). Luckily, the documentation of the language has extensive tutorials about the other domains: web, desktop, and mobile programming.

[26] The other classical way of programming web applications à la PHP, by writing Ring scripts inside HTML code (CGI and FastCGI scripts), is also supported.

Say Hello in the Window

Ring doesn't reinvent the wheel and relies on the popular Qt Framework[27] for designing graphical user interfaces. In this section, I'll give you a basic idea of how Qt works.

In a nutshell, Qt models your program as a set of windows. Every window contains a number of widgets being text labels, buttons, grids, or any other graphic control.

In Figure 1-25, the dotted outlines represents the Qt application (QApp). Inside this logical container, there are three windows or widgets (QWidgets). The first window contains a text label (QLabel) and a button (QButton).

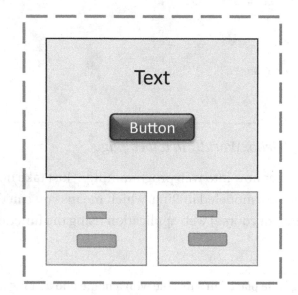

Figure 1-25. *Structure of a Qt application*

To use the power of Qt inside Ring, you can load the guilib.ring library in the header of your code. Then instantiate a new QApp application through new qApp{}. Inside qApp{}, instantiate a text widget using new QLabel. Finally, provide the text itself by a call to the method setText(). Figure 1-26 shows the result.

---

[27]Qt is the de facto C++ framework for building portable modern user interfaces and more; see https://www.qt.io.

```
tempo.ring ✕

1  load "guilib.ring"
2
3  new qApp
4  {
5          win = new qWidget()
6          {
7                  label = new qLabel(win)
8                  {
9                          setText("Hello, World!")
10
11                 }
12
13                 show()
14         }
15         exec()
16 }
17
```

Figure 1-26. *A nice declarative way of describing GUIs in Ring*

Note here the use of exec() to run the Qt application and the use of show() to display the window and its children (a text label in our case) on the screen. Finally, if you run the code (Ctrl+F5), don't be disappointed in the result. This was just an example, and later we will develop a fancier window using Ring Form.

Say Hello on Your Mobile Phone

It is possible to port the same window[28] we made in the previous section to your mobile phone. To do so, Ring provides an automated solution to generate a Qt project folder from the last option of the Distribute menu, as shown in Figure 1-27.

---

[28]To be usable on a mobile phone, the screen must be enlarged automatically to cope with 100 percent of the phone screen. This is possible by using showMaximised() instead of show() in the code sample.

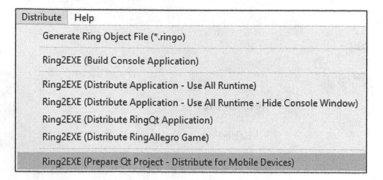

Figure 1-27. *Calling the Ring2EXE distribution tool*

You need to open the generated folder under Qt Designer and generate your mobile application from that.[29] Try it.

Say Hello in a Game

Ring and gaming are in love! Like graphical user interfaces, games can be developed declaratively by describing the game stage and its components (graphics, sounds, collisions, and so on). We'll develop this idea in detail in Chapter 8. For now, we will just show how we can display "Hello, World!" inside a game application. The code is self-explanatory.

```
load "gameengine.ring"
func main
    oGame = new game {
        title = "Hello in Game"

        text {
            x = 10 y = 50
            animate = false
            file = "pirulen.ttf"
            text = "Hello, World!"
            color = rgb(0,0,0)
        }
    }
```

---

[29]Qt Designer is the standard IDE for Qt. You will get it by installing Qt. I think Ring needs to allow the direct generation of Android APKs (like iOS requiring you to go through Apple Xcode) without going through an external tool.

Before you run your game, you need to make a copy of the font file `pirulen.ttf` from `c:\ring\samples\fromdoc` and put it in the current folder, `c:\ring\ringbook\chap1`. The code declares a `main` function[30] and instantiates a game object called `oGame` inside it. The game stage is defined then by what is enclosed inside game `{ ... }`. In our case, there is just one component, a text object containing "`Hello, World!`", along with some attributes defining its look and feel and its behavior.

Now run it. Then let's get back to the code: change `animate = false` to `animate = true`. Run it again. We're moving along so smoothly!

Say Hello in Plain Arabic

Natural language programming is a killer feature of Ring. Its implementation is simple, and it's fun. We will have the chance to dig into the magic sauce created by Mahmoud Fayed to make Ring speak like humans, but for now, we will just use it to accomplish the following use case:

- Instead of writing any structured code, we will talk to Ring in plain English, right in the code editor, saying this:

  "`I want to say hello world but in Arabic.`"

  or this:

  "`Can you tell me hello world in Arabic?`"

  or any other sentence that comes to mind containing "hello world."

- Ring understands what we wrote and responds with elegance, as shown here:"مَرْحَبا أَيُّها أَلْعَالَم.".[31]

How do we turn this into Ring? Simple. Take a look at Listing 1-6.[32]

---

[30]The `main()` function is the first fragment of code run by Ring. Unlike other languages such as Java and C#, this function is optional in general programs in Ring, but it is compulsory when you are writing games based on the Ring Game Engine (you'll learn more about this in Chapter 8). `main()` functions are particularly useful to avoid the use of global variables. (You'll learn more about this in Chapter 6.)

[31]This is "Hello, world!" in Arabic.

[32]Save it as `natural-short.ring` in the current work folder (`c:\ring\ring-book`).

31

Listing 1-6. Natural

```
new Natural {
    // The following is natural
    // but Ring code!
    can you tell me hello world
}

class Natural
    // Key attributes
    hello world
    // Words to ignore
    can you tell me

    // Escape function
    func getHello ? "مرحبا"
    func getWorld ? "أيّها العالم"
```

Before we explain it, run it by pressing Ctrl+F5. Figure 1-28 shows what you get.

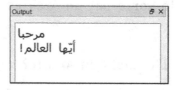

Figure 1-28. *You asked, you've got it*

What is this? It's a programming language accepting a plain English statement, understanding it, and reacting to it! Let's add a requirement: I want to *thank* Ring by writing this down in the first Natural block. And I want Ring to understand that I'm thanking it and respond accordingly. Do the following:

- On line 5 (before the end brace), insert the following:

  I will be really thankful

- At the end of the line 9 (after "hello world"), insert a space and type the following:

  thankful

- On line 12 (after "can you tell me"), insert the following:

  I will be really

- Finally, on line 16 (at the end of the file), add the following:

  func getThankful **?** "You are welcome!"

Run it and watch what Ring says (see Figure 1-29).[33]

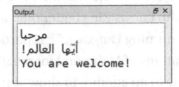

```
Output                                          ⊟ ×
┌──────────────────────────────────────────────┐
│ مرحبا                                          │
│ أيّها العالم!                                   │
│ You are welcome!                               │
└──────────────────────────────────────────────┘
```

Figure 1-29. *You are welcome!*

The power of this paradigm as imagined by Mahmoud Fayed is that it is built upon a deterministic foundation (object-oriented programming), but it is not deterministic at all. We are free to say it in our way, with our own words or in whatever our writing style is. We can ask all the question our program has been taught to answer or just a portion of them. Imagine when this feature is offered to our users in a graphical user interface or in a voice-based conversational bot. That's empowering!

Technically, the principle is simple. We can tell Ring to compute anything it is capable of by binding a *statement* we write in natural language to a *function* written in standard Ring, while ignoring all the rest of that natural statement.

---

[33]Save this new version as `natural-long.ring` in the current folder (`c:\ring\ring-book\chap1`).

But Ring goes far[34] in this domain by providing us with the first-ever *natural language programming* framework inside a general-purpose programming language. You'll learn more about that in Chapter 7.

Introductory Article by Mahmoud Fayed

There are plenty of articles written by the language designer that I invite you to read. They are hosted on the Code Project web site and will offer you the benefit of listening from the mouth of the person who knows Ring better than anyone else.

The article "The Ring Programming Language"[35] is particularly well written. You'll find the background and motivations of Mahmoud for creating Ring. Then, you will be invited to put your hands in code in an attempt to show you the key differentiators of the language.

---

[34]To be frank, this is the piece of Ring that breaks my heart. I do see its potential in alleviating the digital divide between the common mortal programmer and the cloud-APIfied-serverless-pay-on-the-go-vendor-locked advancements in programming today. Think of someone in Ayourou, a village on the Niger River, who wants to develop a conversational bot, by turning on his Android mobile phone and speaking his local language, just to help farmers predict the cyclic invasion of farms by hippopotamus depending on weather conditions, water flow, season of reproduction, past invasions in other villages, average number of victims over the past 10 years, and so on.

There is no API or paid cloud service capable of doing this, no matter the amount of intelligence put into it and the ease of use offered by its REST endpoint. Google Home and Amazon Echo and their respective clouds are just unusable gadgets. What is needed is a programming language, like Ring, that is self-contained in term of intelligence, conversational capacity, and multilingual support and that is deployable easily across platforms including Android phones. The potential of Ring to alleviate the digital divide is huge. Particularly, schools, governments, and opinion leaders in the developing world should take the strategic opportunity of embracing a programming language, like Ring, as a main tool for educating the next generation of computer programmers. Those future programmers are the only asset I see, not oil and minerals, to help them defeat the threat of poverty, unemployment, and underdevelopment.

[35]https://www.codeproject.com/Articles/1089887/The-Ring-Programming-Language

Dynamic Transformation of Types

Among many other useful details, Mahmoud stresses that Ring uses dynamic typing[36] and lexical scoping.[37] You can use the + operator for string concatenation, and the language, because it is *weakly typed*,[38] will convert automatically between numbers and strings based on the context. To show this, let n be of value 2, as shown here:

```
n = 2
```

When I need to add it to the number 3, then Ring understands it is a number and gives us the sum of 5.

```
? 3 + n      // Gives 5
```

But when I use it in the context of a concatenation with another string, Ring will dynamically change its type from Number to String, as shown here:

```
n = 2
? "I have " + n + "lovely daughters"
# Gives : I have 2 lovely daughters // Note: # is same as //
```

In the other direction, if we start from a string variable that happens to contain the value "2" (returned as is from a web service, for example) and we play the same code (3 + n) again, a magical thing happens.

```
n = "2"
? 3 + n      // Gives 5 also, although n is a string!
```

Great, but wait. Try to inverse the order of 3 and n around the + operator.

```
n = "2"
? n + 3      // Gives 32 instead...
```

---

[36]A language is dynamically typed (versus statically typed) if the type of variables is not necessarily known at compile time but inferred by the language at runtime.

[37]Lexical scoping (versus dynamic scoping) means that the scope of your variables (the portion of code in which they are alive) are defined at author time and are therefore known in advance by the compiler. You'll learn more about this subject in Chapter 2.

[38]In a weakly typed language, like Ring and Python, variable types can be automatically cast from one type to another depending on the context, where in strongly type languages, like Java, such transformation must be explicitly described by the programmer inside the code.

Think about it: Ring analyzes the context by identifying the type of the first member (n is string in our case) and automatically transforms the second member from its original type of number to the same string type of n. Internally, our ? n + 3 expression is "understood" by Ring as follows:

```
? "2" + "3"      // Which leads logically to "32".
```

It becomes a tradition in the Ring community to use this feature of dynamic casting to make rapid transformations from strings to numbers, and vice versa, like this:

```
n = 0+ "1250"      // n contains the Number 1250
n = "" + 1250      // n contains the string "1250"
```

Using Lists During Their Definition

Back to the article, Mahmoud shows an awesome feature of Ring: using the content of a list *during the time of its definition*. Here is the code he suggested, quietly minified for the sake of simplicity:

```
aList = [ [1,2,3] , aList[1] , aList[3] ]
see aList // Print 1 2 3 1 3
```

While aList variable (of type list) is being declared, we can read its nth member (aList[n]) and use it to make whatever computation we need. It seems obvious,[39] but in reactive real-time systems and sensor-based data harvesting, this solves critical issues otherwise requiring hundreds of lines of code.

Exiting from More Than One Loop

Why should we be constrained in the vast majority of programming languages to exit from just one level of a loop? Ring beaks this dogma[40] and allows us to easily exit from one or more loops.

---

[39]Obvious for the rest of us, but for seasoned conservative programmers, this is crazy!

[40]This feature is not advisable for use in large programs. It's up to the programmer then to decide when to take advantage of this Ring flexibility and when to adopt a more conservative and, therefore, safer approach.

```
for x = 1 to 10 // First loop
        for y = 1 to 10 // Second loop
                see "x=" + x + " y=" + y + nl
                if x = 3 and y = 5
                        exit 2      # exit from the 2 loops
                ok
        next
next
```

The article contains some other advanced information we are not going to care about for now. But bookmark it and go back to it any time you feel yourself progressing in the programming of Ring. You won't regret it.

Using the Ring Help System

In this section, I will show you how you can access the Ring documentation. Then I paint its big picture to help you comprehend its vast scope. Finally, I expose some practical uses cases of the help system that will become handy in the daily life of a Ring programmer.

Three Ways to Access Ring Documentation

There are four ways to access the extensive Ring documentation.

- In Ring Notepad, select Help ➤ Language reference ➤ CHM file. This will open a desktop application conforming to the Microsoft CHM standard, but you can use the available PDF version if you want. See Figure 1-30.

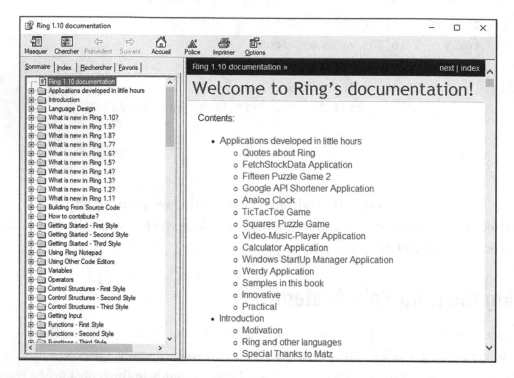

Figure 1-30. *Desktop help system of Ring*

- In Ring Notepad, select Browser ➤ Local help. This will open an
  HTML version of the help system inside a browser tab in Notepad.
  See Figure 1-31.

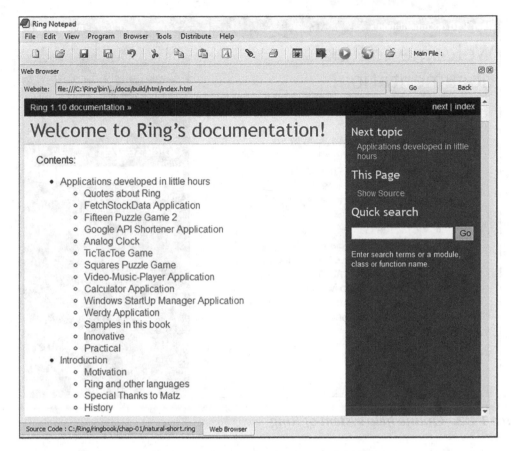

Figure 1-31. *The help system displayed in a tab inside Notepad*

- From the Ring home page,[41] click the Documents button. This will open the HTML online version of the help system. See Figure 1-32.

---

[41]http://ring-lang.sourceforge.net/doc1.11/index.html

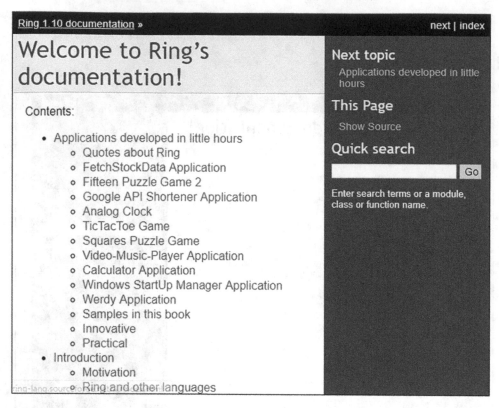

Figure 1-32. *Online help system of Ring*

- Go to the menu provided at the bottom of the same home page (see Figure 1-33).

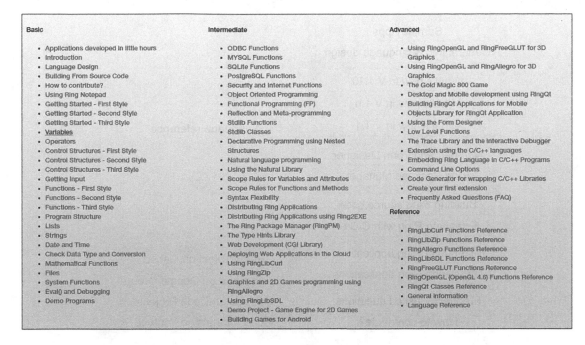

Basic

- Applications developed in little hours
- Introduction
- Language Design
- Building From Source Code
- How to contribute?
- Using Ring Notepad
- Getting Started - First Style
- Getting Started - Second Style
- Getting Started - Third Style
- Variables
- Operators
- Control Structures - First Style
- Control Structures - Second Style
- Control Structures - Third Style
- Getting Input
- Functions - First Style
- Functions - Second Style
- Functions - Third Style
- Program Structure
- Lists
- Strings
- Date and Time
- Check Data Type and Conversion
- Mathematical Functions
- Files
- System Functions
- Eval() and Debugging
- Demo Programs

Intermediate

- ODBC Functions
- MYSQL Functions
- SQLite Functions
- PostgreSQL Functions
- Security and Internet Functions
- Object Oriented Programming
- Functional Programming (FP)
- Reflection and Meta-programming
- Stdlib Functions
- Stdlib Classes
- Declarative Programming using Nested Structures
- Natural language programming
- Using the Natural Library
- Scope Rules for Variables and Attributes
- Scope Rules for Functions and Methods
- Syntax Flexibility
- Distributing Ring Applications
- Distributing Ring Applications using Ring2EXE
- The Ring Package Manager (RingPM)
- The Type Hints Library
- Web Development (CGI Library)
- Deploying Web Applications in the Cloud
- Using RingLibCurl
- Using RingZip
- Graphics and 2D Games programming using RingAllegro
- Using RingLibSDL
- Demo Project - Game Engine for 2D Games
- Building Games for Android

Advanced

- Using RingOpenGL and RingFreeGLUT for 3D Graphics
- Using RingOpenGL and RingAllegro for 3D Graphics
- The Gold Magic 800 Game
- Desktop and Mobile development using RingQt
- Building RingQt Applications for Mobile
- Objects Library for RingQt Application
- Using the Form Designer
- Low Level Functions
- The Trace Library and the Interactive Debugger
- Extension using the C/C++ languages
- Embedding Ring Language in C/C++ Programs
- Command Line Options
- Code Generator for wrapping C/C++ Libraries
- Create your first extension
- Frequently Asked Questions (FAQ)

Reference

- RingLibCurl Functions Reference
- RingLibZip Functions Reference
- RingAllegro Functions Reference
- RingLibSDL Functions Reference
- RingFreeGLUT Functions Reference
- RingOpenGL (OpenGL 4.6) Functions Reference
- RingQt Classes Reference
- General Information
- Language Reference

Figure 1-33. *Menu of the Ring documentation at the bottom of the home page*

The four options get you to the same content. Personally, I used to go to the online version, but sometimes when I am not connected to the Internet, the offline options (first and second in the previous list) come into rescue. For you, as a beginner to the language, I suggest you begin with the list provided at the bottom of the home page (the third option then) because it is well structured. Then continue by making your path as shown in the next section.

High-Level Overview of Ring Documentation

Ring has extensive documentation covering every aspect of the language. To help you comprehend the scope of the documentation and find your way around, see the following two images.

- Figure 1-34 represents the high-level structure of the available documentation and resource.

- Figure 1-35 zooms in to the language reference, the one you will be using most of the time.

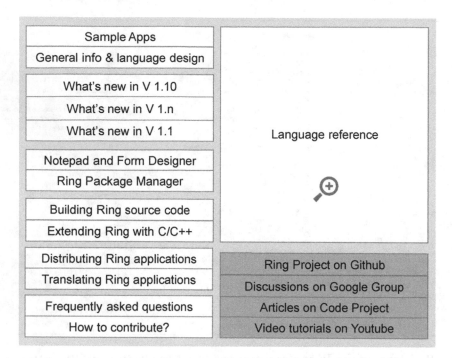

Figure 1-34. *High-level overview of Ring documentation*

The documentation contains a core region (language reference) and a number of complementary subjects (samples, new features in every version, use of Ring tools, and so on).

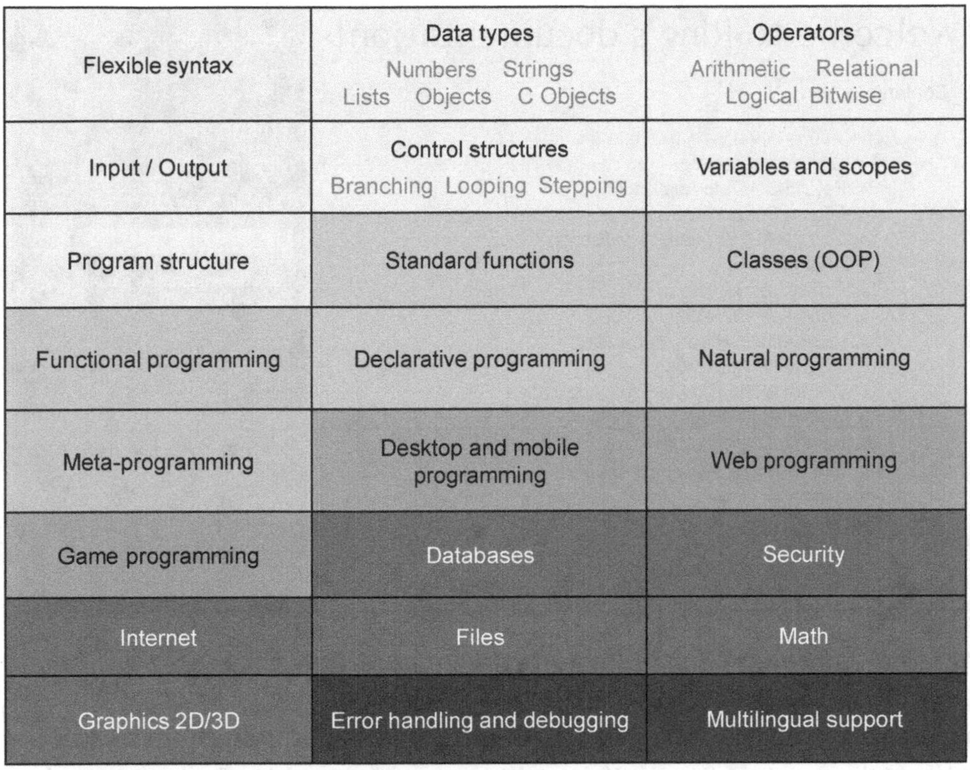

Flexible syntax	Data types Numbers Strings Lists Objects C Objects	Operators Arithmetic Relational Logical Bitwise
Input / Output	Control structures Branching Looping Stepping	Variables and scopes
Program structure	Standard functions	Classes (OOP)
Functional programming	Declarative programming	Natural programming
Meta-programming	Desktop and mobile programming	Web programming
Game programming	Databases	Security
Internet	Files	Math
Graphics 2D/3D	Error handling and debugging	Multilingual support

Figure 1-35. *High-level overview of Ring documentation*

Practical Use Cases of the Help System

On a daily basis, you will be using the Ring documentation to learn new things or find information about a specific feature. There are three common use cases. I will cover the first two options, leaving the third one for your own discovery.

- Discovering a new topic

- Searching for how to use a specific function

- Finding an example of code

Start by opening the documentation center at http://ring-lang.sourceforge.net/doc1.11/index.html (see Figure 1-36).

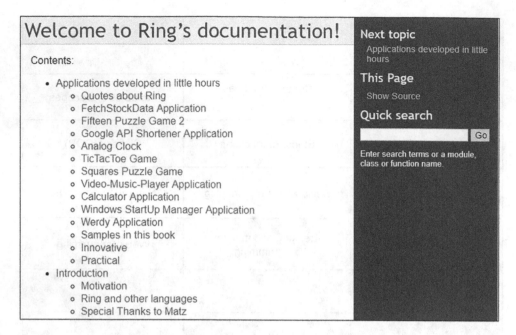

Figure 1-36. *Online version of the Ring documentation*

To read about any new topic (say object-oriented programming, for example), start by looking at the previous figures. If the subject you are searching for is present there (which is the case for object-oriented programming), then you can find it by skimming the menu on the main page. In my case, I prefer using the search feature of my browser to quickly find it (Figure 1-37).

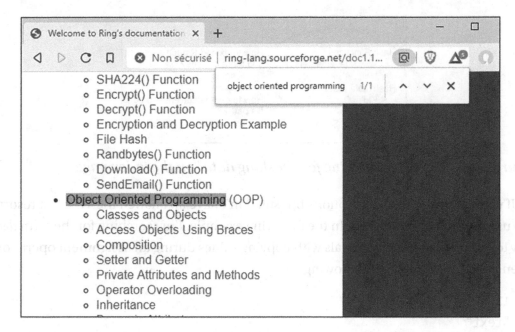

Figure 1-37. *Searching for a subject on the main page of the documentation*

If the topic does not exist in the main menu (say "Hashing data," for example), then you have one of two options.

- Using the index by clicking Index in the top-right corner

- Searching directly for your subject in the Quick Search field

In the first case, a list of letters is displayed (see Figure 1-38).

Figure 1-38. *List of letters on the index page*

Click H and then select one of the two subjects related to "hashing data" (see Figure 1-39).

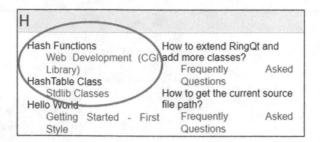

Figure 1-39. *Result of searching for "hashing data" on the index page*

If you're done with all the options but still don't have an answer, then the last resort is to use the Quick Search field. In the following example, I'm searching for the term *deep copy* to learn about how Ring deals with copying values during an assignment operation. When I say, for example, the following:

```
A = 12
B = "text"
c = [1,2,3]
```

are the values 12, "text", and [1,2,3] copied inside the variables A, B, and C? Or do they keep their initial value in memory and the = operator just references them?[42] In the top-right corner of the page, I enter **deep copy**, as shown in Figure 1-40.

Figure 1-40. *Searching for "deep copy" in the Quick Search field*

The help system displays the results of the research, as shown in Figure 1-41.

---

[42]This is a common discussion in the programming language landscape. Whether you make deep copies or just reference the initial values is seen differently by language designers. In Chapter 2 (Data Types in Ring), you will see in detail the pragmatic answer provided by Ring and the flexibility you have to force your own deep, weak, or something-in-between copy strategy.

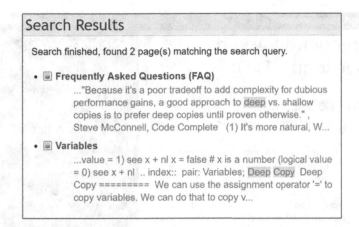

Figure 1-41. *Results of searching for "deep copy" in the online help*

By clicking the second search result, which better corresponds to my request,[43] the next result page is displayed with my search terms underlined (see Figure 1-42).

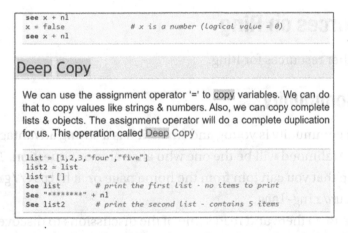

Figure 1-42. *The help page about "deep copy" in the online help of Ring*

Frequently Asked Questions

To end our tour of Ring documentation system, let's look at the FAQ page. You can find it at the bottom of the main page of the help system or quickly search for *faq* in the Quick Search field. Figure 1-43 shows the result.

---

[43]Although the first one is worth reading because it gives the why of the story.

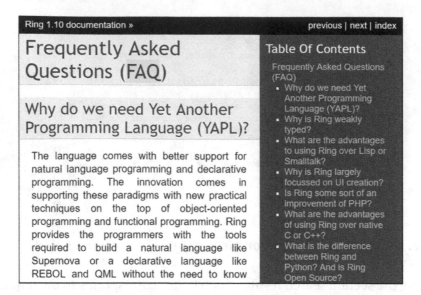

Figure 1-43. *Learning about the difference between Ring and Python*

Other Resources on Ring

Here are some other resources for Ring.

Asking the Community

Because the Ring community is young and small, it has a strong advantage: reactiveness! Most of the time, Mahmoud will be the one who answers your question. This takes place in a Google Group that you can join from the home page or at `https://groups.google.com/forum/#!forum/ring-lang`.

Don't hesitate to go there and read some of the discussions to discover new things or enhance your understanding of what you are learning in this book.

Video Tutorials About Ring

There is a lot to do as part of the Ring community to spread the word about the language, especially in the form of video tutorials on YouTube. In addition, you can view high-quality tutorials made by Mahmoud Fayed[44] and Mohamed Hassouna[45] (in Arabic only). Rushan Ali has recorded a short but instructive tutorial in English.[46]

Critics and Reviews of Ring

Go to Quroa.com, search for *Ring programming language*, and you will be provided with dozens of opinions about Ring. While some are simply erroneous or lacking knowledge of the language, some are worth considering. Some reviews are compiled on the Ring web site here:

```
http://ring-lang.sourceforge.net/doc1.11/ringapps.html?highlight=Quotes
```

I'm not going to comment on these reviews; you can use your experience from this book to forge your own fact-based opinion about Ring.

Summary

So far, you have learned how to install Ring and how to write a first program. Most of our focus has been put on expressiveness and how Ring can empower us to write clean code. We had a first meeting with the Notepad code editor and saw the best way to organize our application into separate Ring files. We wrote our first Ring function we named `timeInfo()` and succeeded to integrate it into the standard function library of Ring. While playing with a "Hello, World!" example, we discovered how to say hello to the console, to the window, to a web page, inside a game, and even in plain natural language. Finally, we looked at the Ring documentation and saw common scenarios to use it in practice.

"Taya murna!"[47] You are ready now to delve into the fascinating Ring code and start with exploring its powerful basic data types (number, string, list, and object). Let's rendezvous in the next chapter.

---

[44]https://tinyurl.com/t2r2459

[45]https://www.youtube.com/watch?v=3YsdVicFv3Q

[46]https://www.youtube.com/watch?v=7BqoQldxOPk

[47]This is the second word in your personal Hausa dictionary. Ask Google Translate for its meaning: https://translate.google.fr/#view=home&op=translate&sl=ha&tl=en&text=Taya%20murna

CHAPTER 2

Data Types in Ring

In the course of my career as a programmer and a manager of programming teams, I have observed a common symptom of low-quality code: poor mastery of data type systems. Data types are the foundation of any programming language. They are part of a "language inside the language,"[1] and they define the nomenclature of what is possible to say in the language and the range of what is possible to do through its features. Unfortunately, data types are not deeply addressed in the majority of programming books and documentation. Decidedly, that won't be the case of this Ring book.

In this chapter, I will take you on a tour of the Ring data type system, merging conceptual material with practical code to help you acquire the necessary skills to use the language to its full potential. Everything starts with meeting the Gang of Four, which in this book are the simple yet powerful data types in Ring: numbers, strings, objects, and lists. I will show how you can use them to write clean code and how to craft natural language applications. Next, I will expose the details of the type system so you can use the native types, define new types, and convert between types. Then, I will focus on each data type separately and reveal techniques, sometimes unprecedented, for how to use them in modeling your program world. Finally, I will explore an effective mindset for approaching the pros and cons of dynamically typed programming languages like Ring.

Nine Things You Will Learn

Specifically, you will do the following in this chapter:

- Understand the importance of a data type system in learning programming
- Visualize a reference architecture of the data type system of Ring

---

[1] This is not an abuse of language but a technical reality so common in computer language study and compiler design theory that it is well understood by programming language designers.

© Mansour Ayouni 2020
M. Ayouni, *Beginning Ring Programming*, https://doi.org/10.1007/978-1-4842-5833-0_2

- Discover the four main data types in Ring and write code with them

- Experiment with operations on those types

- Check the types of variables and convert between types

- Solve several algorithmic problems using the most convenient types

- See how Ring undertakes the implicit conversion between types

- Learn how Ring uses lexical scoping to define the visibility of variables inside code

- Understand the dynamic advantage of a programming language like Ring

How Ring Sees the World

How does Ring see the world? This is an existential question you can ask of any programming language, not only Ring.

Since they are algorithmic factories for transforming inputs to outputs, programming languages need to store their data in memory along with information about their type. Otherwise, they would just be a sequence of raw numbers without any particular meaning. See Figure 2-1.

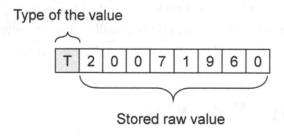

Figure 2-1. *Types define the meaning of data*

Having the value 20071960 in a given place in computer memory can be interpreted by the language as a national ID if it is of type number, as the independence day of Senegal (July 20, 1960) if it is of type date, and as a decent amount of money if it is of type money.

Therefore, *types* are what convey meaning to data so programming languages can compute them in a consistent and valuable way. In practice, they form a set of rules that define the correctness of the language syntax and, later, the correctness of the program when it is executed.

Types and Type System: A First Flavor

Types are governed by the language type system. Mainly, the type system enforces the rules of classifying data living inside the program world. But also, the type system defines the set of operations[2] the language can perform on top of each data type.

In the following sections, you will see how this applies to Ring. I will show the main four types of the language (I call them the Gang of Four[3]) and give you a snapshot of how they work.[4]

Meet the Gang of Four

First, create a new folder under c:\ringbook and call it chap2. In Ring Notepad, create a new file called tempo.ring to use for the following experimentations with Ring code.

In the eyes of Ring, every piece of data you can deal with in your program code drills down to a fundamental set of four[5] types: numbers, strings, objects, and lists. The values of n1 to n5 shown in Listing 2-1 are all of type number.

Listing 2-1. Values of n1 to n5

```
// Some numbers
n1 = 12
n2 = 2.08
n3 = 12/8
n4 = -5201300
n5 = 0
```

[2]Call them features if you want.

[3]In music, the Gang of Four is an English post-punk group formed in 1976 (the same age as me, and I particularly love their new single "Change the Locks"). In computer science, the Gang of Four are the authors of the ultimate reference book in design patterns. In Ring, the Gang of Four is composed of...well...read the section.

[4]This is just an overview of the Ring features for every type. You'll get a more elaborate idea about every type in its dedicated section of this chapter.

[5]In reality, they are five, but we won't discuss the Object C type in this beginner's book.

In the last line, n5 = 0, the n5 variable contains the number 0, but it is also considered by Ring as the Boolean FALSE, while any number other than 0 will be considered as the Boolean TRUE. You'll learn more about this in the section "Missing Members of the Gang."

Some of the possible operations on numbers are the arithmetic + for calculating the sum of two numbers, * for multiplying them, < and > for comparing between them, and if for logical verification (to see whether the value is TRUE or FALSE), as shown in Listing 2-2.

Listing 2-2. Possible Operations on Numbers

```
// Some operations on numbers
? n1 + 8    // Gives 20
? n2 * 3    // Gives 6.24
if n1 > n2 { ? "It's bigger" }   # Gives "It's bigger"
if n5 = FALSE { ? "It's FALSE" } # Gives "It's FALSE"
                                 # because n5 = 0
```

The values of c1 to c5 shown in Listing 2-3 are all of type string of text.

Listing 2-3. Type string

```
// Some strings
c1 = "Cairo"                    // simple text
c2 = "is the capital of Egypt"  // 2 lines string
c3 = "12/05/2019"               // A date inside the string
c4 = "10:24AM"                  // A time inside the string
c5 = ""                         // This is an empty string
```

In the last line, the empty string hosted in c5 is considered by Ring as a NULL value that you can identify using the isNull() function. You'll learn more about this in the section "Missing Members of the Gang."

Some of the possible operations on strings are concatenation, date calculation, and logical evaluation through the use of isNull(), as shown in Listing 2-4.

Listing 2-4. Operations on Strings

```
// Some operations on strings
? c1 + " " + c2          // Gives "Cairo is the capital of Egypt"
? addDays(c3,1)          // Gives "13/05/2019"
if isNull(c5) = true {   // Returns TRUE because c5 = "" SEE "Oh, this is
                             empty!" + NL }
```

The value of o1 in Listing 2-5 is of type object.

Listing 2-5. Value of o1

```
// Creating a new data object of type Person
o1 = new Person { name="Foumakoye" country="Niger" }?
o1.whois() // Gives "Foumakoye Niger"

// Definining the data object
class Person
     name country      // The object attributes
     def whois()       // You can use def or func⁶
          return name + " " + country
```

As we saw in the first chapter, when we said Hello! to a web page (see Figure 1-24 and footnote 24), an object can be accessed with the dot operator or with braces, {}. Add this before the line where the Person class was defined (remember, classes must always go to the end of a Ring program), as shown in Listing 2-6.

Listing 2-6. Object Access with Braces

```
? o1.name                // Dot operator: gives "Foumakoye"
o1 { name="Saadetto" } // Braces: modifies name attribute
```

Finally, the values of a1 to a5 in Listing 2-7 are all of type list.

---

⁶Don't be surprised when Ring gives you more than one option to do the same thing. This is done for a good reason: flexibility. Usually, I use func to define a function and def to define a method inside an object.

Listing 2-7. Type list

```
// Some lists
a1 = [1,2,3]           // could be written a1 = 1:3
a2 = ["A","B","C"]     // could be written a2 = "A":"B"
a3 = [1,"B",o1]        // list of mixed types
a4 = [0, [1,2,3], 4]   // nested list (list in list)
a5 = [ :name = "Foumakoye", :country = "Niger" ]  // indexed list (hashmap)
```

Some possible other operations are expanding the list using the + operator and measuring the number of its elements using the Len() function, as shown in Listing 2-8.

Listing 2-8. Operations on Lists

```
// Some operations on lists
? a1 + 4           // Gives [1,2,3,4]
? a1 + a2          // Gives [1,2,3,["A","B","C"]]
? Len(a1+a2)       // Gives 4 with ["A","B","C"] as 4th item
? a5               // Gives:
                   // name
                   // Foumakoye
                   // country
                   // Niger
```

Save the whole program in tempo.ring in another file in c:\ringbook\chap2 by selecting File ➤ Save as from the main menu of Ring Notepad and entering typeop.ring as a filename. Now clear the contents of the tempo.ring file so we can use it for other stuff in the following section.

Missing Members of the Gang

There is a legitimate question that arises here about two absent members of the gang: the Boolean and NULL types. Aren't they compulsory players in any programming language? Of course, yes. Without True and False types and the NULL value (the value of nothing), a programmer wouldn't be able to create a successful program with any code.

Let's talk about Booleans first.

In Ring, the Boolean type doesn't stand for itself as an explicit type but is articulated by the number type according to the value it receives. This is shown by these two simple rules:

- true is a variable of type number, and its default value is 1.

- false is a variable of type number, and its default value is 0.

Therefore, the statements in Listing 2-9 will lead to "It's false."

Listing 2-9. Boolean Types

```
n = 0
if n = true { ? "It's true" else ? "It's false" }
```

Listing 2-10 will lead to "It's true."

Listing 2-10. Boolean Types

```
n = 1      // Try also n=12 and n=-7
if n = true { ? ? "It's true" else ? "It's false" }
```

Therefore, Ring evaluates the following:

- Any number that is equal to 0 to false

- Any number that is different from 0 to true

But be careful and note the following:

- true and false are just two variables.

- Ring gives them the default values 1 and 0, respectively.

- Those default values can be changed!

This means that if we use the same code snippet we have previously and we change true to 0, which is crazy and goes against the Ring assumptions but nothing prevents us from doing it,[7] then the result will be the inverse, as shown in Listing 2-11.

---

[7]This level of control is unique in Ring. You can change everything, including the standard keywords of the language (using the ChangeRingKeyword instruction), the default values of the main logic arguments (true and false), and many other things. Some people would say this is risky, but if you adopt the Ring mindset, this is the spirit of the language made with extreme freedom *and* responsibility. Many applications become possible: crafting your own programming language with your own syntax and programming style without learning how to fight with the compiler theory, writing serious code in your native human language, explaining the internals of programming languages to your students by looking transparently at what happens under the hood (only Ring allows such a transparency), to cite just a few! But this should be used *with responsibility* to protect your program from unwanted critical threats.

Listing 2-11. Gives False

```
true = 0
n = 1
if n = true { ? "true" else ? "false" }    # Gives false!
```

Be careful to pay attention to this detail, especially when you are using external code written by a crazy programmer[8] who would turn `true` to `0` and `false` to 1. In this case, all the logic you made inside your program can go completely topsy-turvy!

Agreed? Great.

Anyway, the use of Booleans is what constructs your logic, the story you are telling in your program. A particular sense of expressiveness is then needed in naming your variables so your code can seem natural and really comprehensive.

Under any circumstances, *If you want me to play* with you the unforgettable Scary Maze game,[9] I must *have time* and be in *good mood*. See Listing 2-12.

Listing 2-12. Scary Maze Game

```
# Try this in the "tempo.ring" file
true = 1    false = 0    // To avoid any surprise

havetime = true
feelgood = false

if havetime and feelgood
       ? "Ok, let's play!"
else
       ? "Sorry."
End
```

Note that I explicitly set the default values of `true` and `false` to their natural configuration, 1 and 0, respectively. This will protect my code from any "crazy" change made to those values outside the code.

---

[8]Seriously, in the context of a web application, this can be a target for a seasoned hacker to break the logic of your program by stimulating a code injection attack. In this case, the solution is easy, as you'll discover at the beginning of the next code snippet.

[9]Scary Maze is a highly stimulating, exciting game requiring deep coordination between the player's eyes and hands. To complete the game, you have to pass many difficult levels, so you need to be careful, skillful, focused, and patient.

In addition, there is an important detail you should be aware of: Ring uses *short evaluation* of multiple conditions. This means that if the first condition is false, then all the condition chain is considered false. In reality, Ring breaks the chain completely and wastes no time in evaluating the remaining conditions.

To experiment with this, change havetime to false in the previous code. In this case, only the bold part of the condition statement (**if havetime**) is evaluated, while the remaining part (and feelgood) is ignored.

Good. It's time for a bit of nothingness now...

As Plato said to his student Aristotle, "There is no such thing as nothingness, and zero does not exist. Everything is something. Nothing is nothing." In today's digital era, computers form a major part of human existence, 0 and 1 are their first existential words, and NULL is their usual tag, in the majority of programming languages, for expressing the value of nothing.

In Ring terms, not only is *Boolean* absent as a native type, but the famous NULL is missing, so how the languages makes it possible to declare a variable of type NULL?

The language's rules for the NULL type[10] are simple.

- Any empty string is NULL.

- Any string containing the text "null"[11] is NULL.

We can easily verify this by using the isNull() function as shown in Listing 2-13.

Listing 2-13. isNull()

```
v = ""      # The variable v contains an empty string
if isNull(v) { ? "Null" else ? "Not null" }      # Gives Null
```

v can be set to "NULL", and we get the same result, as shown in Listing 2-14.

Listing 2-14. NULL

```
v = "NULL"  # The variable v contains the text "NULL"
if isNull(v) { ? "Null" else ? "Not null" }      # Gives Null
```

---

[10]It isn't really a type, since there are only four in Ring.

[11]Whatever form it takes (NULL or Null or nULL, etc.), remember that Ring is *not* case sensitive. Note that this particular feature is useful to identify the NULL values extracted from a database.

Don't be confused; NULL and FALSE are two different things. The first one, NULL, is the computational representation of NOTHING, an *empty* string in Ring. The second, FALSE, is a *logical* value representing the WRONG facet of the truth inside your algorithm, a well-rounded 0 in Ring.

If you want to take it from Ring's mouth, then run the code in Listing 2-15.

Listing 2-15. Null or Not Null

```
v = false
if isNull(v) { ? "Null" else ? "Not null" }
```

Now see what Ring thinks about it.

This being said, please note that NULL is just a default *variable* in Ring containing an empty string. This means you can use the code in Listing 2-16.

Listing 2-16. Default value of NULL

```
s = "text" + NULL
? s
```

You get just "text" as a result.

This also means you can change the default value of NULL to any value you want, even if it is a *crazy* one. In this case, code like the lines in Listing 2-17 would leave the Ring isNull() function confused and unable to take a decision about whether the variable v is NULL or not NULL.

Listing 2-17. Changing the default value of NULL

```
NULL = "crazy"
v = NULL
if isNull(v) { ? "Null" else "Not null" }
```

You can simplify further this and write it directly without any v variable in between, as shown in Listing 2-18.

Listing 2-18. Changing the default value of NULL - Simplified

```
NULL = "crazy"
if isNull(NULL) { ? "Null" else "Not null" }
```

Test it and you get nothing.[12]

Anyway, I'm not teaching you to be a crazy programmer. On the contrary, I want you to demonstrate a level of wisdom and responsibility by using NULL as is and change it only when this makes sense. In particular, to protect your code from any external craziness, you can reinforce the value of the NULL variable at the beginning of your program by simply saying this:

```
NULL = ""
```

or this:

```
NULL = "NULL"
```

And then you may live in peace inside your algorithm.

Again, when you work with NULL in your Ring code, think of expressiveness. So, let's end this section with a short story.

---

[12]This particular case should be reported to the Ring team. In my opinion, this is a situation that needs to be covered, so that the isNull() function, when the NULL variable itself has been shifted from its default value (the empty string), becomes able to say something about it. I've published the code in the Google Group, so join the discussion at https://tinyurl.com/ryj9awc.

In particular, you will discover in Mahmoud's answer an important feature that was totally new to me: all the standard functions that are natively written in C and used by Ring, such as isNull(), for example, can be redefined in your program using pure Ring code. Hence, any behavior you want can be implemented!

In our current case, I would add a new function called isNull() that reacts to all the cases I need, including the crazy case of putting any string in the NULL variable. In such case, I want the function to reject any craziness by ignoring any value other than the default empty string, as shown here:

```
NULL = "anything"
if isNull(NULL) { ?"It's null" else? "It's not null" }
func isNULL(value)
        if value = NULL or value = "" or value = "NULL"
            return true
        else
            return false
        ok
```

Test it, and you will find that isNull() is no longer confused. NULL (whatever value it contains), an empty "", "NULL", or a "crazy" thing will always behave as NOTHING. Satisfied? Use it. If not, change the function to cope with your needs.

Coming back with a null trawl means Maîga, the fisherman, has no importance at all in his Timbuktu[13] village. This is a bummer, but the laws of the tribe say he will be ignored without mercy. Maiga should be prepared for a supreme punishment, as shown in Listing 2-19.

Listing 2-19. Maiga the Fisherman

```
# Maiga the Fisherman and the Angry King of Timbuktu
maiga_trawl = ""        // experiment with 0, null and "null"
if isNull(maiga_trawl)
    ? "The King of Timbuktu is angry!"
else
    ? "Maiga is happy"
End
```

This fanciful story is made possible by a wise use of the isNull() function. The next section shows you how to use similar functions to identify the other types in Ring and more.

A Little Bit of Magic

With the NULL type alone, we can do a lot. In fact, we can do a bit more than one might expect from a conventional programming language.

Do you remember our natural language program in the first chapter? We are going to craft a new one using a different strategy: we'll use the null type. The idea is that our code can contain any English word we define to be null. The same that happened to Maiga the fisherman will happen to these words: Ring ignores them completely. See Listing 2-20.

Listing 2-20. Seven or Not Seven

```
its_seven = true
if its_seven
    see "It's seven!"
```

---

[13]Timbuktu is located on the southern edge of the Sahara nine miles north of the main channel of the River Niger. The town is surrounded by sand dunes, and the streets are covered in sand. The annual flood of the Niger River is a result of the heavy rainfall in the headwaters of the Niger and Bani rivers in Guinea and northern Ivory Coast. —From Wikipedia

```
else
    see "It's NOT seven."
ok
```

This can be transformed into what is shown in Listing 2-21.

Listing 2-21. Seven or Not Seven - Continued

```
its_seven = true
if its_seven in_the morning
    I want to see "It's seven!"
else
    I rather see "It's NOT seven."
ok
```

If you try to execute this code, then the following four error messages are displayed:

```
Line(3) Error(C3): Unclosed control structure, 'ok' is missing
Line (3) Error (C11) : Error in expression operator
Line (4) Syntax error
Line (6) Syntax error
```

Ring has been disturbed by the use of some undefined variables (in **bold** in Listing 2-21). The language is made for freedom, but as a serious programmer, one should assume some responsibility and tell Ring what type and values to give to those newcomers. Let's nullify them so they are all Maiga's brothers.

Listing 2-22. Nullifying Undefined Variables

```
its_seven = true
// Nullify the extra-variables
in_the=null morning=null
I=null will=null rather=null

if its_seven in_the morning
    I will see "It's seven!"
else
    I rather see "It's NOT seven."
ok
```

Execute this code by pressing Ctrl+F5. Change the its_seven value to false. Execute it again. This is a working program that is natural-language-enabled using just the null type.

Pushing this feature to its limits, we come up with a programming style for the rest of us, who dream of a humanized programming experience, free of any unnecessary complexity and bragging syntax. Ring was made to fulfill this vision of humanizing programming activity and sees the future of code to be visual, descriptive, natural, and fully gamified.

Believe it or not, Listing 2-23 shows our next listing of the Ring code.[14]

Listing 2-23. Natural Ring Program

```
Load "nullify.ring" // Nullifying the extra-variables
ChangeRingKeyword but temp // nullifying a Ring keyword
but = null        // "but" is used below
Load "say.ring"  // say and scream functions

I_am_sleeping = false
its_seven = false

if I_am_sleeping whatever the hour is
    my wife would say("Wake up, Mansour...")

else // I'm not sleeping then!
    if its_seven in_the_morning
        she will rather scream("Take your daughter to
        school, please!")
    else
        // I'm not sleeping nor its seven,
        // so in this case:
        nothing granted but
        she may offer me a hot cup of coffee()
    ok
ok
```

---

[14]Don't pay a lot of attention to the first four lines for now. We will talk about them later.

Before you play with this code and before you experiment with it in various situations by changing the values of the two variables I_am_sleeping and its_seven, do the following:

1. Save it to a new file and call it mywifesays.ring.

2. Create another file, call it nullify.ring,[15] and put this code inside it:

```
the = null
hour = null
is = null
my = null
wife = null
would = null
its = null
in_the = null
the = null
morning = null
she = null
will = null
rather = null
may = null
offer = null
me = null
a = null
hot = null
cup = null
of = null
nothing = null
granted = null
whatever = null
```

---

[15]Remember, we will always stay loyal to our precious principle of separation of concerns that was introduced in Chapter 1.

3. Create a third file, name it `say.ring`, and put this code inside it:

```
func say(something)
    ? something

func scream(something)
    return say(something)

func coffee()
    ? "Would you like to take a coffee?"
```

4. Execute, play, and play again.

Natural programming will be approached in a more formal way in Chapter 7 by discovering several features of Ring objects that make it happen. For now, I kindly invite you to share this little programming experience with your family and best friends, or maybe with your colleagues or your students if you are a programming teacher. Engage with them in a discussion about a possible future where programming can finally go natural.

Statics and Dynamics of the Ring Type System

As a "language inside the language," the Ring type system relies on four data types, which we need to further explore. It also provides us with a set of features applied to those data types that we are going to experiment with. The two are presented in a reference architecture[16] to see how they fit together in a consistent way.

A Reference Architecture

In the FAQ section of the Ring documentation, we can find the answer to the question, "What is the philosophy behind data types in Ring?" I've paraphrased the answer here.

---

[16]A reference architecture is a formal, consistent, and stable representation of the components of any system and how they interact. It is used mainly to discuss the system and explain both its static and dynamic aspects (i.e., its structure and behavior).

WHAT IS THE PHILOSOPHY BEHIND DATA TYPES IN RING?

The Ring programming language is designed to be small. The language provides the basic constructs that you need to do anything. One of the goals is to keep the basic constructs simple and as small as possible.

Using lists in Ring you can do the following:

- Create arrays (one data type)

- Create lists (mix of data types)

- Create trees (nested arrays)

- Use a string index (looks like dictionary/hash table)

The same principle is applied to numbers, as shown here:

- You can use a number for an int value.

- You can use a number for a double value.

- You can use a number for a boolean value (True/False).

The sample principle is applied for strings, as shown here:

- You can use a string for storing one character.

- You can use a string for storing text (one or many lines).

- You can use a string for storing binary data.

- You can use a string for storing dates.

- You can use a string for storing time.

- You can use a string for storing NULL values (empty strings).

In addition, we support object-oriented programming (OOP), along with *operator overloading*,[17] where the programmer can define new data types and use them as default types defined by the language.

---

[17]Operator overloading will be explained in detail in Chapter 7. So, don't take the burden of asking what they are now.

So, we have the following:

- A small and simple language that someone can learn in few days

- A fast language that provides primitive types (String, Number, List, Object)

- A flexible language that can be extended using OOP to add new types according to the application domain

From useful philosophy to the concrete topology, I came up with a visualization showing the reference architecture of the Ring data type system in the context of the general structure of the Ring language. It consists of the following:

- A first component, the Ring type system itself

- A second component, containing the C language type system

The first component is divided into three main subcomponents.

- The code layer where the programmer interacts with the Ring data types by declaring variables (this happens implicitly depending on the value you provide, so n=3 means n is number; s="Maiga" means s is a string; and a=[] means a is an empty list), checking for their types, converting them explicitly from one type to another, and defining her own data types through objects.

- The core layer is where we find the Gang of Five (they are not four anymore) with the List type installing itself at the center (simply because this is the type that helps combine all the other types and organize them in a hierarchy).

- An automatic layer of implicit type conversion and lexical scoping.

Around those components we observe an extension layer formed with two wings where new types can be created using C and C++.

Finally, at the bottom of the visual is a layer that exceeds the scope of this book where Ring is embedded in other languages and therefore takes advantage from their built-in data types.

Take a look at Figure 2-2 and tell me if this makes sense.

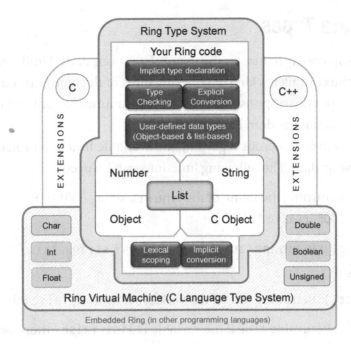

Figure 2-2. *The reference architecture of the Ring data type system*

The remaining paragraphs explain every component, except the Ring embedded layer, with regard to the flexibility provided by a dynamically typed programming language like Ring and show some examples.

Reminder   It is your responsibility as a programmer to master the type system of your language, especially when it is not statically typed.[18] The time you invest in understanding the dynamics of such a strategic piece of the language will be rewarding. The skills you gain in defining and checking types, converting them explicitly, mastering their scope, and understanding how the language automatically converts them will be your secret weapon for making efficient and bug-free programs.

---

[18]In this case, the compiler of your language would help you check the correctness of your program by raising a large number of type errors. But what you would lose is the world of flexibility and expressiveness made possible with dynamically typed languages like Ring. So, please don't leave this chapter before being confident you have the necessary understanding and have played with the several examples I provided.

Checking Data Types

Type checking is a necessity to master the *dynamics* of your code. Unlike statically typed languages where the compiler is king in checking most of the type correctness, dynamic languages like Ring put the responsibility on the programmer to control the situation. This creates freedom, but freedom has a price.

Ring has proved to be generous regarding the available functions you can use to check the type of your data. The following functions can be used:

- type(): Returning the name of the type in a string ("NUMBER", "STRING", "OBJECT", or "LIST")

- isString(): Returning true if the variable is a string, false otherwise

- isNumber(): Returning true if the variable is number, false otherwise

- isList(): Returning true if the variable is list, false otherwise

- isNull(): Returning true if the variable is null, false otherwise

Most of the time, you will need some checking with more granular detail. Depending on your needs, you probably have a Ring function that does the job. Table 2-1 highlights some examples; you can find the whole list in the documentation center.[19]

Table 2-1. *Some Ring Functions on Checking Data Types*

When You Need to Check	Use This Ring Function
If the string is alphanumerical	isAlpha()
If the string is formed of pure digits	isDigit()
If the string is in lowercase	isLower()
If the character is a punctuation	isPunct()
If the string is a hexadecimal	isXDigit()

---

[19]http://ring-lang.sourceforge.net/doc1.10/checkandconvert.html

Converting Between Data Types

The data living in your program code isn't always in the best suitable form for the meaning it is pretending to represent. As an example, suppose you are invoking a distant web service for the exchange rate between the Malian CFA Franc (XOF) and Japanese Yen (JPY). The returned value is captured in a string variable you named exchange with the value "1XOF=5.185496JPY". Clearly, you need to transform this value into a number data type (name it exchangerate) so you can calculate the 1000 XOF you have in JPY. You will write something like amount = 1000 * exchangerate.

In the same documentation page as you saw in the previous section, there are functions that are responsible for converting data from one type to another. Let's take a quick look at them.

- number(): Converts a number contained in a string to a native number[20]

- string(): Converts a number to a string

- ascii(): Converts a given character to its corresponding ASCII number

- char(): Fulfills the inverse action of ascii()

- hex(): Converts a decimal number to its equivalent hexadecimal representation

- dec(): Fulfills the invers action of hex()

- str2hex(): Converts a string of text to its hexadecimal representation

- hex2str(): Fulfills the inverse of str2hex()

In our case, number() is maybe what we need. Let's see whether this works; see Listing 2-24.

---

[20]It would be better if this function were called str2number() and its inverse were called number2str().

Listing 2-24. number() function

```
// Exchanging Malian XOF to Japaneese JPY
exchangerate = "1XOF=5.185496JPY"
exchangerate = number(exchangerate)
? exchangerate
```

When you run the code, you get an angry error message.

```
Line 3 Error (R18): Numeric Overflow!
In number() in file C:/ring/ringbook/tempo.ring
```

Before we go further, we need to be sure that exchangerate is in the form expected by number() to properly do its job: a string. Add this before the line where the error occurred:

```
? type(exchangerate)
```

Run it. It is a well-formed "STRING". Delete this line because we no longer need it.

Tunisians used to describe a person who is never absent from any social event under any circumstances: "He is like the salt, never misses any food." This is exactly the case of the unavoidable "Stack overflow error" here.

Wikipedia says, "In computer programming, an integer overflow occurs when an arithmetic operation attempts to create a numeric value that is outside of the range that can be represented with a given number of digits—either larger than the maximum or lower than the minimum representable value."

What happened then is that Ring, while trying to *convert* the value of exchangerate variable ("1XOF=5.185496JPY") to a number, was faced with some pieces ("XOF", "=", and "JPY") that are not suitable to the expected number representation. Ring gets an immediate headache and gets a *stack overflow*! Visually speaking, Figure 2-3 shows what happened.

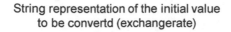

String representation of the initial value
to be convertd (exchangerate)

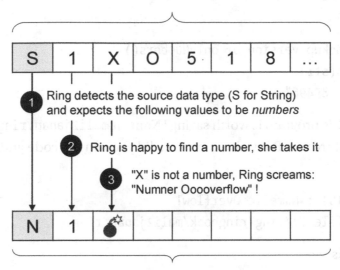

Number representation prepared by
Ring to host the result of the conversion

Figure 2-3. *Stack overflow: "the salt that never misses any programming food"*

Let's get back to our exchange rate program, and before we hope it will exchange any XOF to JPY, there is an urgent need for a function that "purifies" the string "1XOF=5.185496JPY" and extracts only its contained number ("5.185496"). In the meantime, suppose that this function exists[21] and name it onlyNumbers().

Our new code of the rate exchange program should look like Listing 2-25.

Listing 2-25. Exchange Program

```
// Exchanging Malian XOF to Japaneese JPY
exchangerate = "1XOF=5.185496JPY"
er = onlyNumbers(exchangerate) // Returns "5.185496"
// Conversion now should work
exchangerate = number(exchangerate)
```

---

[21]This function can be easily implemented in Ring through an algorithm that iterates over the string items, checks whether the item is a number, and if so, adds it to a tempo variable containing the result.

```
// Finally, we're done
amount = 1000 * er
? amount

// Defining a mockup version of onlyNumbers()
func onlyNumbers(str)
        return "5.185496"
```

Do you think this program is worth saving? Name it `mali2japan.ring` and preserve it for a potential future use. But wait a moment: did you run the code and discover this error message?

```
Line 5 Error (R18) : Numeric Overflow!
In number() in file C:/ring/ringbook/mali2japan.ring
```

Correct it, please.[22]

Never read code I give you in this book without trying it. There will always be a way of enhancing your understanding if it works and a valuable opportunity to face a challenge if it doesn't. At every stage, refer to the Ring documentation, as I showed you in Chapter 1. Use it to spot how the book translates the knowledge contained there into didactic narrations, illustrative visualizations, and practical exercises. Discover what particular subjects I left behind because I think they are not necessary for a beginner using Ring and try to paint the big picture of the language in your head. Agreed?

User-Defined Data Types

A type system worth considering should offer a way for programmers to define their own data types. Programs are intended to solve real-world problems, and these can't be modeled by numbers and strings only. In this section, we define a new data type using objects while leaving the second option of combining several data types using lists for later in the chapter.

---

[22]Just replace exchangerate with er.

Because Ring strings are coded in 8 bits for every character, they are not suitable for managing Unicode text like Arabic.[23] Let's say, for example, we have this:

```
txt = "كتاب" // "book" in arabic
```

Try Listing 2-26.

Listing 2-26. Arabic text in a string variable

```
? txt[1] // Should give "ك" since arabic is right-to-left24
? len(txt) // Should give 4 for "ك", "ت", "ا", and "ب"
```

Press Ctrl+F5 to run them. Figure 2-4 shows the result.

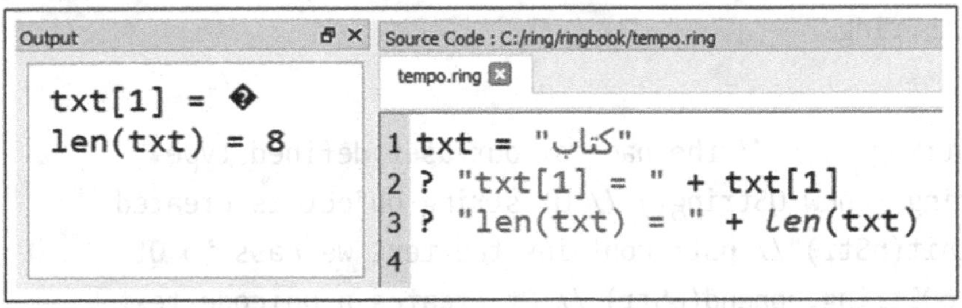

Figure 2-4. *The built-in string type in Ring doesn't support Unicode text*

Ring was unable to find the first Arabic letter ك. This is a matter of character encodings and code pages and a matter of being unable to read strings in the Unicode[25] standard. This is a typical situation in which we need to define a new data type for

---

[23]If your computer does not enable Arabic, then it is easy to find how to do it on the Internet depending on you operating system. These are some links that could help: if you are on Windows, visit `https://tinyurl.com/wja6t3b`; if you are on macOS, visit `https://tinyurl.com/sye26xr`; and if you are on Linux, visit `https://tinyurl.com/d6uadk`.

[24]The two graphemes ك and ﺱ represent the same letter *K* in Arabic.

[25]Unicode is the de facto standard of representing text universally on any language and any platform. By the way, this is a subject every serious programmer needs to understand. I suggest you pay attention to what Joel Spolsky says about it in his blog Joel on Software (`https://bit.ly/2ibBNoI`).

supporting Unicode text in Ring. To do so, we rely on object orientation and the Qt library. The steps are as follows:

1. Import Qt by loading the `guilib.ring` library.[26]

2. Create a class called `ucdString` based on the `QString` class from Qt.

3. Use the features provided by this class to initiate the string content via `QString.append()`, access a letter by its position via `QString.mid()`, and compute the length of the string via `QString.count()`.

To create the `ucdString` class, write the code in Listing 2-27.

Listing 2-27. ucdString Class

```
Load "guilib.ring"
// ...

Class ucdString       // the name of our user-defined type
    oQString = new QString() // Qt string object is created
    def init(pStr) // pStr contains the text we pass to Qt
         oQString.append(pStr) // Qt creates a unicode text
```

To use it, we should create an object of type `ucdString`. To do so, add this to the *beginning* of the code before the description of the class[27]:

```
o1 = new ucdString("كتاب")     // o1 is of type ucdString
```
[28]

At this level, try to inspect the created object by simply saying the following:

```
? o1
```

---

[26]In fact, Qt is a huge library for more than just graphic user interfaces. The GuiLib library is a complete hub between Qt and Ring. This means you can do everything Qt is capable of using only the Ring language.

[27]If you put the new lines after the class code, an error is raised. You must organize your Ring programs in this order: load and import commands, main function (if any), other functions, and finally classes. You will learn more about structuring Ring programs in Chapter 6.

[28]Use the Google Translate service from English to Arabic to get "كتاب," the translation of *book* in Arabic (and to the Panjabi and Kannada languages we will be using on the next page).

Great, the oQString object is created. How can we read its content? Because we went object-oriented, we just need to add an attribute text to the ucdString class and populate it with the text content, as shown in Listing 2-28.

Listing 2-28. ucdString class - Continued

```
Class ucdString // the name of our user-defined type
    text        // the attribute we will use to read the content
    oQString = new QString() // Qt string object is created
    def init(pStr) // pStr contains text we pass to Qt
        oQString.append(pStr) // Qt creates unicode text
        text = pStr // We initiate the attribute text
```

Try again with ? o1. You have the Unicode object and its text attribute, as shown in Figure 2-5.

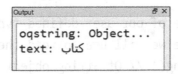

Figure 2-5. *uncString, ready to be read*

Reading the object text is as simple as writing it, as shown here:

```
? o1.text
```

So far, your new own data type has been created. Congrats, you've empowered Ring with Unicode fuel. Anywhere in your program you can now sing "Kitab, Buka, Pustaka!" in all the tunes of the world, as shown in Listing 2-29.

Listing 2-29. Book in Three Languages

```
// "Book" in three languages
o1 = new ucdString("كتاب")    // "kitab" in Arabic
o2 = new ucdString("ਬੁੱਕ")    // "buka" in Panjabi
o3 = new ucdString("ಪುಸ್ತಕ") // "pustaka" in Kannada
```

Now remember, the data type is not only data but also *operations* on that data.

Until now, the unique operation we supported in the ucdString type is reading the text content through the use of ? o1.text. Try it for the two other languages for fun!

Seriously, to really solve our initial problem, we need to augment our type with two other features.

- *Accessing letters by providing their position in the string*: ? o1[1] gives "ಕ".

- *Computing the length of the string*: ? o1.len() returns 4 and not 8 as was the case before the Unicode era.

The second one is easy to implement. Add a method to the ucdClass, name it len(), and use the Qt QString count method to count the number of letters, as shown in Listing 2-30.

Listing 2-30. Counting the number of letters in a Unicode strings

```
Class ucdString // the name of our user-defined type
      text // the attribute we will use to read the content
      oQString = new QString() // Qt String object is created

      def init(pStr) // pStr contains text we pass to Qt
           oQString.append(pStr) // Qt creates a unicode text
           text = pStr     // We initiate the text attribute

      def len()
           return oQString.count()
```

Test it by trying ? o1.len(), ? o2.len(), and ? o3.len().

For me, the result is awesome (see Figure 2-6).

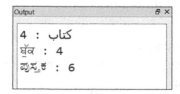

Figure 2-6. *Ring is a citizen of the world!*

If you've experienced any problem, Listing 2-31 shows a complete listing.

Listing 2-31. The Books Program

```
// Inviting Qt
load "guilib.ring"

// Creating the unicode string objects
o1 = new ucdString("كتاب") // "kitab" in Arabic
o2 = new ucdString("ਬੁੱਕ") // "buka" in Panjabi
o3 = new ucdString("ಪುಸ್ತಕ") // "pustaka" in Kannada

// Reading text and computing lenght
? o1.text + " : " + o1.len()
? o2.text + " : " + o2.len()
? o3.text + " : " + o3.len()

// Defining the unicode type class
Class ucdString # the name of our user-defined type
      text # attribute we will use to read the content
      oQString = new QString() # Qt object is created

      def init(pStr) # pStr contains text we pass to Qt
          oQString.append(pStr) # Qt recieves unicode text
          text = pStr # We also initiate the attribute

      def len() # returns the lenght of unicode text
          return oQString.count() # the hard work done by Qt
```

Save it as ucdstring.ring.

Happy? So am I.

Now let's go back to our mission and deal with the first requirement: o1[1] should give "ك," and more generally o1[n] should give the nth letter of the string. Technically speaking, we need to implement the operator [ ] on top of the ucdString class. Welcome to *operator overloading!*[29]

---

[29]Operator overloading means changing the meaning of an existing operator in the language (for example, the + operator) by a new implementation method defined by the programmer inside a user-defined class (for example, ucdString + "something" will change the + operator with the QString.append() function).

In the ucdString class, we craft the code in the standard operator() method, as shown in Listing 2-32. This method is provided by Ring by default for programming new operators inside any class.

Listing 2-32. ucdString class - Method for Accessing by Position

```
def operator(p,value)
    If p = "[]"
        return oQString.mid((value-1), 1)
        # value-1 because Qt begins counting at 0
        # while Ring begins at 1.
        # 2nd 1 is the number of letters to read
    Ok
```

Test it by inserting the code shown in Listing 2-33 at the beginning of the class.

Listing 2-33. Accessing by Position

```
// Accessing the text by position
? o1[1]
? o2[3]
? o3[5]
```

I executed it and got ك,ب, and ತ as a result, as shown in Figure 2-7.

Figure 2-7. *Ring avoids ◆ thanks to ucdString*

For the sake of clarity, in case you are still asking yourself what operators are,[30] we will add a tiny + operator to the uncString type. If you prefer to close the book and do it as an exercise, do that.

In the operator() method, add the code in Listing 2-34 to the if statement.

Listing 2-34. + Operator of the ucdString class

```
def operator(p,value)
    if p="[]"
        return oQString.mid( value-1 , 1 )
        # -1 because Qt begins counting at 0
        # 2nd 1 => read 1 letter starting
        # from value-1
    but p = "+"
        return oQString.append(value)
    ok
```

Test it by inserting the code in Listing 2-35 just before the beginning of the class. See Figure 2-8.

Listing 2-35. Using the + operator with ucdString objects

```
// Appending string text
? o1 + " <=> book"
```

You will get:

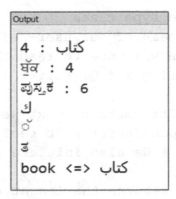

Figure 2-8. *Book is "Kitab" in Arabic*

---

[30]Don't be shy. I ask dozens of similar questions every day. And if you check out my activity in the Ring Google Group (https://bit.ly/2WnFDmp), you will find plenty of them.

Again, Listing 2-36 shows the complete listing you can refer to in case of problems.

Listing 2-36. Unicode Program - Complete listing

```
// Inviting Qt
load "guilib.ring"

// Creating the unicode string objects
o1 = new ucdString("كتاب") // "kitab" in Arabic
o2 = new ucdString("ਬੁੱਕ") // "buka" in Panjabi
o3 = new ucdString("ಪುಸ್ತಕ") // "pustaka" in Kannada

// Reading text and computing lenght
? o1.text + " : "+ o1.len()
? o2.text + " : "+ o2.len()
? o3.text + " : "+ o3.len()

// Accessing the text by position
? o1[1]
? o2[3]
? o3[5]

// Appending string text
? o1 + " <=> book"

// Defining the unicode type class
Class ucdString # the name of our user-defined type
    text # attribute we will use to read the content
    oQString = new QString() # Qt string is created

    def init(pStr) # pStr contains text we pass to Qt
        oQString.append(pStr) # Qt recieves unicode
        text = pStr # We also initiate the attribute

        def len() # returns the lenght of text
            return oQString.count()
            # the hard work done by Qt
```

```
def operator(p,value)
    if p="[]"
        return oQString.mid( value-1 , 1 )
        #-1 because Qt begins counting at 0
        # 2nd 1 => read 1 letter starting
        # from value-1
    ok
```

In the upcoming chapters, we will enhance this ucdString class by adding more features and operators (+, =, and more) and see if we can request its inclusion as a new library in the official distribution of Ring.

Implicit Conversion and Lexical Scoping

In Chapter 1, you discovered how Ring automatically converts data based on the context. Remember, n = 0+ "12" means n is a number of value 12, and s = ""+ 25 means s is a string of value "25".

What was called dynamic transformation of types is exactly what we named "implicit conversion" in the third layer of the Ring type system architecture we saw later in the chapter.

Implicit conversion shouldn't be confused with *implicit declaration* of types, where Ring infers the type of your variables from the values you provide (remember, there is no way in Ring to statically declare the type of a variable like **int** n = 5 in Java or **float** n = 23.0098 in C). Nor it should be confused with *explicit conversion*, which is a voluntary decision made by the programmer to convert between data types using the functions we saw in the previous section.

As to lexical scoping, this feature means that Ring performs a static[31] analysis of your code to identify the scope of your variables depending on their position in the code. We will be exposing this in detail in Chapter 6 (Juggling with Scopes). For now, we can just refer to the Wikipedia code sample,[32] as shown in Figure 2-9, to see how the majority of modern programming languages manage the scope.

---

[31]The wide majority of programming languages, being statically or dynamically typed, adopt this static strategy to define the scope of variables.

[32]https://en.wikipedia.org/wiki/Scope_(computer_science)#Lexical_scoping

```
program A;
var I:integer;
    K:char;

    procedure B;
    var K:real;
        L:integer;

        procedure C;
        var M:real;
        begin
          (*scope A+B+C*)
        end;

      (*scope A+B*)
    end;

  (*scope A*)
end.
```

Figure 2-9. *Lexical scoping explained by Wikipedia*

Wikipedia says, "The variable I is visible at all points, because it is never hidden by another variable of the same name. The char variable K is visible only in the main program because it is hidden by the real variable K visible in procedures B and C only. Variable L is also visible only in procedure B and C, but it does not hide any other variable. Variable M is visible only in procedure C and therefore not accessible either from procedure B or the main program. Also, procedure C is visible only in procedure B and can therefore not be called from the main program."

Under the Hood: C Language Type System

Ring is written in ANSI C.

This means that what we have as high-level constructs for managing types in Ring are themselves programmed in C and provided to us in an expressive and simple language. I have a strong temptation to help you discover the C types so you can appreciate the amount of effort made by the Ring designers to hide such complexity and provide a lightweight and flexible type system. Unfortunately,[33] I'm invited to leave you alone in that endeavor so that we can stay focused on what is possible with the Ring data types (the next section).

---

[33]I suggest you want this excellent five-minute video presentation by Kevin Lych to get a quick idea of the data types supported in C: https://www.youtube.com/watch?v=V1mBtAZxHgw.

For now, it is important to know that, as you are programming in Ring,[34] you don't need to think about int or float or double specifically but rather in a high-level way: as numbers just like you meet them in real life.

Besides that, it may be useful to note that, internally, and, again, because it is written in ANSI C, Ring relies on the standard C language data types.

- Ring always uses the Double data type to represent numbers internally for your Ring programs.

- The C int type is used by internal Ring functions.

- There are *some* internal arithmetic functions that make use of C unsigned int.[35]

- The string data type in Ring internally uses 8 bits for each character; it is good to work on binary data directly when each character is stored in 1 byte. But this limits the ability of the language to natively process Unicode strings as we saw previously when we learned how to enable them via QString of the Qt framework.

These were the main rules applied to achieve a high-level programming experience in Ring. But using the language as a programming API, and writing C/C++ *extensions* for it, gives you full control when it is really needed.

In practice, you can prepare any C/C++ code or library, not only Qt, to be managed by the Ring language. There is a dedicated tool to generate the code, the configuration files, and the build process necessary for this operationEnough internals for now. You can find more about the subject in the documentation here:

`http://ring-lang.sourceforge.net/doc1.10/codegenerator.html`

More on Data Types

This section provides you with useful techniques related to the main four data types in the Ring programming language. The focus is on the features of each type and the underlining principles governing its use.

---

[34]The following paragraph is extracted as is from a discussion between the author and the language creator.

[35]Namely, the unsigned() function.

More on Numbers

Once you have a variable n of type number, you can do a lot for it with Ring: arithmetic operations, mathematic functions, big numbers, and more.[36]

Table 2-2[37] presents all the *arithmetic* operators provided in the Ring language. Assume x=12 and y=8.

Table 2-2. *Arithmetic Operators in Ring*

Operator	Description	Example	Result
+	Add	x + y	20
-	Substract	x - y	4
*	Multiply	x * y	96
/	Devide	x / y	1.50
%	Modulus	x % y	4
++	Increment	x++	13
--	Decrement	x--	11

Ring also provides 22 mathematic functions. The following have proven useful in my career as a lambda programmer:

- ceil(12.5), which returns 13.

- floor(12.5), which return 12.

- fabs(-12.5), which return 12.5.

- random(10), which returns a random[38] number between 0 and 10.

- And many others.[39]

---

[36]I particularly love this syntax sugar: n = 12590112 + 2 can be written as n = 12_590_112 + 2.

[37]This is from the Ring documentation (https://bit.ly/2ET6QCT).

[38]You will find the random() function useful in Chapter X when we discuss game programming in Ring.

[39]http://ring-lang.sourceforge.net/doc1.10/mathfunc.html

Among them, `decimals()` deserves special attention. Consider this code to see how it works:

```
pi = 22/7      // Gives 3.14
```

But when we add `decimals(10)` just like before, we get Listing 2-37.

Listing 2-37. decimals(10)

```
decimals(10)
pi = 22/7       // Gives 3.1428571429 instead!
```

Here's a challenge: play with this code to force Ring to raise the following error:

```
Line 1 Error (R33) : Bad decimals number (correct range >= 0 and <=14) !
```

Finally, we will end our tour on numbers by talking about big numbers.

The `BigNumber` library was developed by Bert Mariani and Gal Zsolt and helps deal, unsurprisingly, with huge numbers. To use it, consider the following division of a big number bn by a small number 64, as shown in Listing 2-38.

Listing 2-38. Big Number

```
bn = 12825032019922087654Ø110
? bn / 64              # Provokes a numeric overfolw!
```

It's so natural. This is because the number type in Ring (using internally the `float` type of the C language) doesn't offer to host such a huge number. Fix it then by writing the code in Listing 2-39.

Listing 2-39. Big Number - Continued

```
load "bignumber.ring"
bn = new bignumber("12825032019922087654Ø110")
                 // Note the number is hosted in a string
? bn / "64"     # Note "64" is also a string
```

More on Strings

Ring plays well with text strings. There are 16 standard functions that cover the major scenarios you may need in real-world text processing applications. To get an idea of them, we will use the REPL tool accessible from the main menu; select Tools ➤ RingREPL GUI in Ring Notepad (see Figure 2-10). Click History to show the history panel at the bottom.

Figure 2-10. *RingREPL GUI*

In the Ring field, you will start writing code. When you press Enter, the code is evaluated interactively, and the result is displayed at the top of the window. Open the help page where the string functions are documented.

```
http://ring-lang.sourceforge.net/doc1.10/strings.html
```

Pick the functions you want and decide on a basic string to play with. For me, I selected this Chinese proverb:

```
str = "  Even tigers need to sleep   "
```[40]

Then, I tried the following:

1. Deleting extra spaces from left and right

2. Calculating length

3. Reading the five characters from the left

4. Finding the position where "Tiger" starts

---

[40]Yes, extra spaces are intentional so we can apply the `trim()` function on them.

Figure 2-11 shows my version of the game.

Figure 2-11. *I was String-REPLing. It is your turn...*

A feature I didn't cover here is the ability of a Ring `string` to host binary data such as images, sounds, and even entire EXE files by simply appending them to string variables like in Listing 2-40.

Listing 2-40. Binary in String

```
v = "myimage.jpg"
? v
```

Binary strings can also be created using `int2bytes()`, and then many operations can be done on them (`+`, `len()`, `ascii()`, etc.). If you want to get a more detailed idea, then I suggest you spend some time reading and experimenting with the examples of code provided in this entry in the Ring documentation: `http://ring-lang.sourceforge.net/doc1.11/strings.html`.

More on Objects

Objects are structured data types (data is stored in attributes) empowered by business logic (logic is created by a set of methods). They are created in real time based on their description defined in a class. Listing 2-41 shows an example.

Listing 2-41. Book Data Type

```
// Defining a book class
class Book
      // Attributes
      title
      publisher
      author

      // Methods
      def info()
              info = "Title      : " + title + NL
              info += "Publisher : " + publisher + NL
              info += "Author     : " + author + NL

          return info

      def thanks()
          return "Thank you dear reader!"
```

This is just the description of a Book class, the footprint for any book object to be created. A particular book object becomes alive when it is instantiated in the runtime using the new command. Add the code in Listing 2-42 to the beginning of your file, name it book.ring, and save it.

Listing 2-42. Book Object

```
// Creating a book object
new book {
      title = "Beginning Ring"
      publisher = "Apress"
      author = "Mansour Ayouni"

      ? info()
      ? thanks()
}
```

Run the code. Figure 2-12 shows the result.

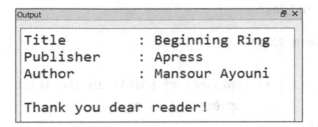

Figure 2-12. *Thank you for being an attentive reader of Beginning Ring*

The point here is how we accessed the book object *directly* using braces, which are something that we can use to craft a hierarchy of nested objects right in the Ring code. Thus, any data structure you would come across in the real life and is sufficiently complex to be represented in basic data types can be modeled using a tree of objects inside objects.

To illustrate this powerful feature of data type *composition* in Ring, let's look at an example from how the GUI library `guilib.ring` models screens. In fact, the `screen` object is a container for other objects such as buttons, text edits, images, and so on. In simpler terms, let's take the case of a screen composed of just two points. Each point is defined by a couple of *x* and *y* coordinates. We will start building from the bottom up and define a point class, as shown in Listing 2-43.

Listing 2-43. Defining a Point Class

```
// Defining a Point class
Class Point
     X = 10
     Y = 30
```

Regarding the design of a well-structured screen class, two main criteria must be met.

- For the end user, the screen `content` is none other than a `list` of `points` (in real programs, Ring expects more but stick to points to get the point).

- For you as a programmer, it is a list of points plus a mean to add new points to it.

This requirement is faithfully implemented in a few lines, as shown in Listing 2-44.

Listing 2-44. Screen Class

```
// Defining a Screen class
class Screen
     scrnContent = [] // container of points in the screen
                      // implemented using a list
     def addPoint
        scrnContent + new point // A new point added
        return len(scrnContent) // Index of last point added

     def show()
         ?"Screen content:"
         For ptXY in scrnContent
             See ptXY
         next
```

This class acts like a *factory* of points. Returning the index of the last point created with addPoint() will ensure it is added at the right place. Hence, the screen world remains in harmony.

At the top of the file (name it compose.ring and save it), add the code in Listing 2-45.

Listing 2-45. Adding Points to Screen

```
// Creating a screen containing 2 points
func main
    win = new screen {  # Now inside the screen object scope

        // Adding a first point
        scrnContent[ addPoint() ] {       # point is added
            # Now inside the point object scope
            x = 10
            y = 30
        }

        // Adding a second point
        scrnContent[ addPoint() ] {
            x = 100
```

```
        y = 180
    }

    // Show the points
    show()
}
```

Run it and take a deep breath. What you have learned will help you gain a better reading and understanding experience of Ring code whether it is from the documentation examples or the more intensive language libraries.

More on Lists

For me, lists are the most powerful data type in Ring and maybe the most influential feature in the entire language. Not only do they hold dynamic structured data but other things, as listed here:

- They can be of any basic type, including other lists of things.

- They can be functions returning any type of data and can be any number of nested functions.

- They can model any hierarchy of things, just using new[ ] inside the current list.

- They can be passed as parameters to functions and form, therefore, the Ring way to perform optional parameters.[41]

- They can be returned from functions, so it is possible for a function to provide "multiple" returns (as items of the returned list).[42]

As they are designed, Ring lists form an elegant replacement of many similar data types you find in other languages. To cite a few:

- Arrays, in their static and dynamic forms

- Stacks

---

[41]You can learn more about this in Chapter 7.

[42]If at the end of your function you say return [r1,r2,r3], then in the caller code you can obtain three values (r1, r2, and r3) returned in one list.

- Trees

- Hash maps

- And so on

As a model, lists can play the role of structures (as they are known in the majority of programming languages) and classes (because they can hold both data and functions) with a critical difference: a list is hot data you can access at runtime, by your program code itself or by any other external medium. Thus, when you build your models with them, your whole application can be dynamically changed by you, by the programmer, by an external system, or by your users if you decide it.

Still wondering? Right now we are going to remake the last object-oriented screen-and-points program in three lines (save the code in a `listmodel.ring` file), as shown in Listing 2-46.

Listing 2-46. Modeling the Screen World

```
// Modeling the screen world
aPoint1 = [ :x = 20, :y = 30 ]
aPoint2 = [ :x = 10, :y = 50 ]
aWin = [ aPoint1 , aPoint2 ]

? "Screen world created." + NL
```

Now the screen is created and populated with two points. The party just began: read the lines in Listing 2-47 and contemplate the ease by which we can *think in code* and manipulate our screen world.

Listing 2-47. Reaching Points in Screen List

```
? "Displaying all points :"
? aWin

? "Displaying Point 1 only :"
? aPoint1[:x]
? aPoint1[:y]

? "displaying Point 2 only :"
? aPoint2[:x]
? aPoint2[:y] + NL
```

```
? "Displaying X coordiantes only:"
? aPoint1[:x]
? aPoint2[:x] + NL

? "Displaying Y coordinates only:"
? aPoint2[:y]
? aPoint2[:y] + NL

? "Changing all x cordinates:"
aPoint1[:x] = 999
aPoint2[:x] = 999
? "Done" + NL

? "Displaying them after they've been changed:"
? aPoint1[:x]
? aPoint2[:x]
```

How many class declarations, method definitions, and object instantiations do you need to make this in an object-oriented style? A lot. But Ring lists do not stop here. Ring provides us with advanced features such as sorting, searching, nesting, and indexing. The exhaustive reference is available on the well-written Ring help page.[43] Here's some sincere advice, though: every section of this help page is a skill you need to acquire before you hope to go further in mastering Ring. These are the strict minimum of skills you need:

- Creating lists
- Adding items to lists
- Getting the list size
- Deleting items from lists
- Getting a list item
- Setting a list item
- Searching in lists, both linear and binary search
- Sorting lists

[43]http://ring-lang.sourceforge.net/doc1.10/lists.html?highlight=list

- Reversing a list

- Inserting items inside a list

- Designing nested lists

- Copying list content, including nested lists

- Using lists during definition

- Accessing string items by string index

- Swapping items inside a list

Then, as advanced skills, you need to learn how to do the following:

- Storing lists in variables

- Passing them as parameters to functions

- Returning them as an output of functions

Finally, the remaining features will be postponed to be introduced in the context of future chapters. In particular, you will see in Chapter 7 when lists are sent *by reference* and when they are copied depending on the scope they live in.

Capturing the Potential of Dynamic Ring

Ring is a dynamically checked, weakly typed, lexically scoped programming language. These terms should be clear to you for now since I covered them, with examples, previously in the chapter.

In his foundational book on type theory called *Practical Foundations for Programming Languages*,[44] Robert Harper from Carnegie Mellon University stipulates that "most programming languages exhibit a phase distinction between the static and dynamic phases of processing. The static phase consists of parsing and type checking to ensure that the program is well-formed; the dynamic phase consists of execution of well-formed programs. A language is said to be safe exactly when well-formed programs are well-behaved when executed."

---

[44]https://amzn.to/2WosCoO

He continues, "Dynamic languages are often considered in opposition to static languages, but the opposition is illusory. Just as the untyped λ-calculus is uni-typed, so dynamic languages are but special cases of static languages in which there is only one recursive type (albeit with multiple classes of value)."

Once and for all, we show where Ring fits in compared[45] to other languages, just to enforce your mastery of some confusing technical terms you will find when you are dealing with data types: strongly, weakly, statically, and dynamically typed. Ring sits in the bottom-right corner of Table 2-3 along with Perl.

Table 2-3. *Ring Is a Weakly Typed, Dynamically Checked Language*

	Statically Checked	**Dynamically Checked**
Strongly typed (or type safe)	Java (almost), C# (almost), Swift (almost)	Ruby, Tcl, PHP
Weakly typed	C, C++	**Ring**, Perl

Why am I talking about the dynamic aspect of Ring?

Well, because I want you to capture the opportunity of dynamic Ring, while staying away from the discussions in the programming community about "dynamic versus static" in regard to programming languages. My personal opinion is that they may lack scientific accuracy; if you have chosen a given language, by your own will or for professional reasons, then you should understand its strengths and focus on how you use its *full potential*. This is exactly what I am going to share with you about Ring.

Laurence Tratt from Bournemouth University wrote an instructive article[46] titled "Dynamically Typed Languages." In concise and clear language, she successfully demystified the technical concepts related to this domain. Then she exposed her vision of what could be the advantages and disadvantages of dynamically typed programming languages.[47]

---

[45]I am not a believer that a programming language can be better or worse than any other. But for sure, I have met in the course of my career programmers of all kinds.

[46]https://bit.ly/2QPjbwx

[47]To be fair, Laurence taught me, for the first time, that dynamic languages influenced their static sisters in adopting innovations such as garbage collection, if-then loops, just-in-time compilation, and many more.

Among the advantages she cited, I can definitely endorse the following ones based on my practical programming experience with Ring:

- Simplicity, expressiveness, and interactivity

- Reflection, dynamic code execution, and refactoring

As for the disadvantages, she highlighted mainly *performance*, which I agree with, but also want to mention debugging and code completion.

Summary

The book in your hands is a journey to show you, with code, how to turn advantages into assets and work around the performance issues you might encounter in Ring.

An antic Persian proverb says, "Taking the first step with the good thought, the second with the good word, and the third with the good deed, I enter paradise." Think of the first introductive chapter of the book as the first step with good thought, the current one as the second step with good word, and the remaining pages as the third step with plenty of achievements and good deeds.

CHAPTER 3

Inputs to Ring

A programming language is a factory for transforming input to output. Ring is no exception. In the following two chapters, your objective is to learn how the language intercepts data as input, how it transforms input internally by applying algorithmic logic, and how it exposes input as output to be consumed by the users of the program. Together, these chapters form the second part of the book called "Practical Ring."

By "practical," I mean that what you are learning here will be not superficial instructions for taking a user's input, applying some `ifs` and `elses` to it, and sending it to the screen, as you will find in many beginner books. No, things are serious here, because in the real world, even if you know the language by heart, many problems related to algorithmic data acquisition, storage, and transformation will arise, both at the code level and at the program architecture level. In this chapter, we will face these problems, understand them, come with up elegant solutions to them, and challenge the Ring language to help us reign over them.

Ring, because of its inherent flexibility and expressiveness, will help us conquer these input/output problems by allowing us to write quick lines of working code and then rewrite our program, as if we were telling a story, not writing code.

After mastering these extensive learnings distilled from hand-on experience in real-world projects, you can confidently take charge of any complex requirement related to managing data inside a computer program. Hence, you will gain the expert-level techniques to write efficient Ring algorithms. So, bear with me, be patient, and follow along with this step-by-step tutorial, which is dense but instructive and intentionally augmented by dozens of visualizations and yet practical code examples.

In particular, this chapter teaches you how to capture data in Ring programs, as well as, more interestingly, how to deal with complexity in code by preventing it from happening at the data input level, by adopting expressive variable naming conventions, by helping you find your way in the jungle of user interface events, and by pragmatically embracing the golden software architecture principle of all time: separation of concerns.

© Mansour Ayouni 2020
M. Ayouni, *Beginning Ring Programming*, https://doi.org/10.1007/978-1-4842-5833-0_3

The first thing a programming language does is intercept data entries. Without data, what a computer program can do? Nothing really. A programmer entering code (hard-coding) is a common practice to get started but is prone to many risks and hidden problems (section "Inputs in the Code"). Also, the user can be asked to enter data in the console or at the command line (section "Inputs in the Console") or in a graphical user interface, where the MVC design pattern[1] becomes a mandatory tool to understand and work with. Ring makes it easy to use by visually designing the windows of your application in the Form Designer and by generating all the complex staff for you (section "Inputs from the GUI"). Or maybe the data comes from a text file (section "Inputs from Text Files") or a database (section "Inputs from the Database"), and therefore you need to establish a data acquisition framework enabling your application to connect to diverse data formats and deal with them in a unified way. We end the chapter with a final enhancement of the design of the NorthAfrica app we worked on (section "Final Refinement") and a listing of other data input options, required by modern software (section "Other Inputs").

Whether it's hard-coded data, command-line data, text data, GUI data, or database data, you can pick this chapter and learn how Ring can rule them all.

Nine Things You Will Learn

Specifically, you'll do the following in this chapter:

- Get data input into your Ring program from many sources

- Mitigate code complexity with good naming and code organization

- Design graphical user interface (GUI) applications using the Form Designer

- Master events in GUI programming

- Work with the MVC pattern and design clean software architectures

- Refactor, reuse, and extend code

- Develop a universal data connector in Ring

---

[1]A *design pattern* describes a conceptual solution of a programming problem and is made to be reusable. Model-View-Controller (MVC) is one of the most commonly used patterns in the domain of GUI development. We will see in the section "Inputs from the GUI" that an internal tool of Ring Notepad, called the Form Designer, makes use of MVC, in the background, while you are visually designing the windows of your application.

- Transform data using lists

- Develop multiplatform applications

Inputs in the Code

The easiest way to feed data into your program is to write it directly in your code. Listing 3-1 shows an example of a program that does this.[2]

Listing 3-1. family.ring

```
// Computing the average age of my family
aAges = [ :Haneen=5, :Teeba=8, :Cherihen=36, :Mansour=43 ]
nAverage = 0
nSum = 0

// Iterating over the data in aAges list
for aPerson in aAges
    nSum += aPerson[2]     # Accumulating data items
next

// Calculating the average and displaying the result
nAverage = nSum / len(aAges)
? nAverage      # Gives 23
```

Here, the data about the ages of my family members is hard-coded in the program in plain text. This is done, like in all programming languages, by hosting the data in variables.

Using Variables to Host Data in Code

It's worth mentioning, from the start, that there is no such a strict type called CONSTANT in Ring. We just have variables that we can change any time.[3] In my case, when I use a variable as if it were a constant, I write it in uppercase so I can visually identify it.

---

[2]Name it family.ring and save it.

[3]This is a pragmatic choice since, in some other languages, what is called a constant can be changed, which is absurd.

Then I assume my own responsibility, as a programmer, is to treat it as a value that I will never change at runtime.[4]

It's language abuse then if we talk of constants in the scope of Ring programming, but we will do it anyway. Consciously.

To show the use of constants in hosting your data inside the code, let's make a program that does a dummy[5] calculation of months, weeks, and days in a period of three years. See Listing 3-2.

Listing 3-2. hardcoded1.ring

```
// Computing months, weeks and days in 3 years - Version 1
NB_MONTHS_YEAR = 12        # Number of months per year[6]
NB_WEEKS_MONTH = 4         # Number of weeks per month
NB_DAYS_WEEK = 7           # Number of days per week
NB_DAYS_YEAR = 365         # Number of days per year


// Number of months in 3 years
numMonths_3Y = NB_MONTHS_YEAR * 3          # Gives 36 months

? "In " + 3 + "years you get:"
? " " + numMonths_3Y + " months"
```

---

[4]If your application requires such a strict type, then it is easy to implement it as a *user-defined* data type. Go back to Chapter 2 to revise how you can use a Ring object to do this. Hence, in our current case, Constant can be defined as a class with two attributes, the name of the variable and its value. The new command takes this form: oConstant = new Constant(name,value). Then, in the init() method, which is the *constructor* of the class (more on this in Chapter 7), you fill in the attributes with the name and value sent by the new instruction. But, there is a constraint you need to implement inside the class: *only one* copy of the oConstant object can be created, and once created, it never changes! This is easy to do, though, by embracing the *singleton* design pattern. Google it and find a pseudocode around from the Internet, paste it in Ring Notepad, and try to adjust it in the Ring language. If you don't find something satisfying, try with this: https://refactoring.guru/design-patterns/singleton.

[5]What you should consider here is the overall logic of the calculation and not the exact results. In fact, a year contains 52 weeks as you know, and three years contains approximately 156.429 (= 3 * 52.143) weeks and not 144 as it is performed by our program.

[6]As an organization tip, I propose we make use of // and #, the two symbols of comments in Ring, as much as we can, in respect to this rule: // is used for commenting a block of code, and # is used for commenting a line of code. This is a matter of personal taste, though, so feel free to break it if you want.

```
// Number if weeks in 3 years
numWeeks_3Y = NB_WEEKS_MONTH * numMonths_3Y
? " " + numWeeks_3Y + " weeks"              # Gives 144 weeks

// Number of days in 3 years
numDays_3Y = numWeeks_3Y * NB_DAYS_WEEK
? " " + numDays_3Y + " days"                # Gives 1008 days
```

Write it down in a new file called hardcoded1.ring and save it to the current folder c:\ringbooks\chap3. When you execute it, then you get the following:

```
In 3 years you get:
  36 months
  144 weeks
  1008 days
```

This seems great, but wait.

Avoiding Magical Numbers

3 is a magical number in this code sample, meaning it's a value that is hard-coded without any meaning other than what the code writer knows. In fact, I know it is the number of years, because I am the one who wrote it, but how this can be conveyed to other readers without ambiguity, especially when we are programming "on the large"?[7]

To solve this problem, create a second copy of the program and name it hardcoded2. ring. Put 3 inside a variable called numYears. And use it wherever 3 is evoked in your code. So, at the beginning of the program, write the following:

```
numYears= 3     # 3 is no longuer a "magical number"
```

---

[7]The Ring language has been designed to be useful while "programming in the small" (small codebase and small team, usually when you are training other people in programming or showing them a pedagogical and simplistic solution to an algorithmic problem) as well as while "programming in the large" (millions of lines of code and dozens of programmers). This book contains small code samples but also some bigger ones. In the real world, you will be always evolving in the context of large programs, so in this section and the entire book, I take it seriously to train you on how to deal with the common real-world, sometimes difficult parts of Ring.

Then replace all the 3{s} with numYears, like the following, for example:

```
numMonths_3Y = NB_MONTHS * numYears     # Gives 36 months
```

What we get is a better program that makes use of a variable to avoid the dark magic of hard-coded numbers inside our code; see Listing 3-3.

Listing 3-3. hardcoded2.ring

```
// Computing months, weeks and days in 3 years - Version 2
numYears = 3

NB_MONTHS_YEAR = 12      # Number of months per year
NB_WEEKS_MONTH = 4       # Number of weeks per month
NB_DAYS_WEEK = 7         # Number of days per week
NB_DAY_YEAR = 365        # Number of days per year

// Number of months in 3 years
? "In " + numYears + " years you get:"
numMonths_3Y = NB_MONTHS_YEAR * numYears     # Gives 36 months
? " "+ numMonths_3Y + " months"

// Number of weeks in 3 years
numWeeks_3Y = NB_WEEKS_MONTH * numMonths_3Y # Gives 144 weeks
? " "+ numWeeks_3Y + " weeks"

// Number of days in NUMYEARS years
numDays_3Y = numWeeks_3Y * NB_DAYS_WEEK      # Gives 1008 days
? " " + numDays_3Y + " days"
```

Run it and be sure nothing has been broken.

```
In 3 years you get:
   36 months
   144 weeks
   1008 days
```

Now, think for a moment about the names of these variables: numMonths_3Y, numWeeks_3Y, and numDays_3Y. What is wrong about them?

There is no consistency in our naming strategy. Having the **_3Y** postfix in numMoths**_3Y** no longer makes sense, since the number of years, now hosted in numYears, can be changed to any value other then 3. This is the showcase where 3 is not only a magical number but a magical and hidden defect in the same time!

In my experience, this is one of the most common reasons for code complexity created by beginners when they name a variable (something that can change) after the name of a constant (something that should stay unchanged). To fix it, adjust the current hardcoded2.ring file to say it the clean way, as shown in Listing 3-4.

Listing 3-4. hardcoded2.ring

```
// Computing months, weeks and days in some years – Version 2
numYears = 3

NB_MONTHS_YEAR = 12       # Number of months per year
NB_WEEKS_MONTH = 4        # Number of weeks per month
NB_DAYS_WEEK = 7          # Number of days per week
NB_DAYS_YEAR = 365        # Number of days per year

// Number of months in a given number of years (numYears)
? "In " + numYears + " years you get:"
numMonths = NB_MONTHS_YEAR * numYears        # Gives 36 months
? " "+ numMonths + " months"

// Number of weeks in a given number of years (numYears)
numWeeks = NB_WEEKS_MONTH * numMonths        # Gives 144 weeks
? " "+ numWeeks + " weeks"

// Number of days in a given number of years (numYears)
numDays= numWeeks * NB_DAYS_WEEK             # Gives 1008 days
? " " + numDays + " days"
```

So, never rely on a name like numMonths_**3Y** for your variables. Also, note the changes I made to the text of the comments (in bold in Listing 3-4): we are no longer referring to 3 but to a given number of years!

Now, save it (as the same file, hardcoded2.ring) and execute it:

```
In 3 years you get:
   36 months
   144 weeks
   1095 days
```

This has the same result but with an interesting additional feature: the possibility of changing numYears as you want and getting all the calculations updated. For numYears = 300 years, for example, you have the following:

```
In 300 years you get:
  3600 months
  14400 weeks
  100800 days
```

This nice feature solved part of the complexity that is still there,[8] inside your code.

Mitigating Code Complexity

Currently, our program structure exposes a serious threat regarding the order of execution of the variables hosting our data. Let's analyze it by looking closely at Figure 3-1.

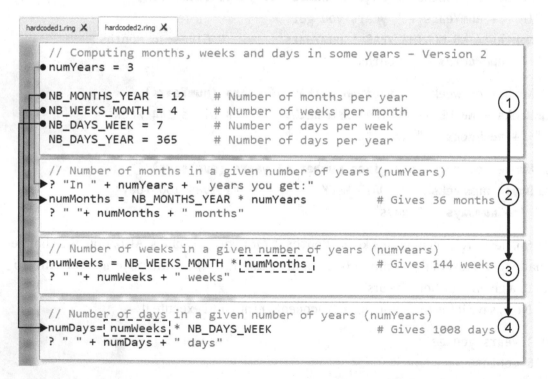

Figure 3-1. *Four blocks of code, clean naming of variables, but...*

---

[8]Besides data dependency between variables as we will see in a minute, there are several animals in nature that sleep this way, like dolphins and crocodiles.

Here, even if the code flows seamlessly across four well-defined parts (1 to 4, as you can see on the right side of the figure) and the variables declared in the first part are used cleanly in every other part[9] (follow the arrows in the left side), there is a critical point happening in two places that we should be aware of.

- In part 4, the `numWeeks` variable is dependent on its calculation in part 3.

- In part 3, the `numMonths` variable is dependent on its calculation in part 2.

This kind of dependency, owing to the use of global variables, is a bad thing, especially in large programs, because it makes your code hard to understand and fragile at the same time. Why hard to understand? Because you can't find where it changed and how the chain of changes has impacted the ultimate value of the variable in the current place of your code. Why fragile? Try to move part 4 before part 3, for example, or part 3 before part 2, and then execute: it will break!

The morale of the story is that global mutable state can be evil.

There is a hot discussion in the programming community on whether mutability, the change of global variable values, is a good or bad thing.[10] Some say it is a bad design, while others claim it gives them freedom. You should make your own decision based on your particular programming style and real-world context.[11]

Personally, I start by thinking about the algorithmic problem in hand, without limiting myself by this immutability paranoia. My data is defined in front of my eyes, right in the code, using constants, global variables, and local variables alike. Once I'm done logically with the solution, I take out my perfectionist sword and start iterating on localizing the state of the program as much as possible by transforming globals to local variables.

---

[9]Note that the last constant in part 1, `NB_DAYS_YEAR`, is not used in any place in the program. It's simple then: either use it or drop it! Next, we will make a decision about it.

[10]Read the interesting answer at `https://tinyurl.com/rvg4fyg` by Sai Komanduri, on the Hashnode web site, to the question, If global state is evil, then why do industry frameworks specializing in program state management, such as Redux and MobX, make use of it by promoting we maintain the global state if the program is inside a global object?

[11]You'll learn more about the practical use of global variables in "Using Global Variables."

Usually, this means my code parts are redesigned in functions (or classes) while separating between concerns, as much as I can, so every function gets one and only one clear mission. That's why I expressed my concern about the program structure and its flow of execution, as shown in Figure 3-1. This is what refactoring means after all: good naming conventions, minimal dependency between variables, careful separation between concerns, and the design of independent but complementary parts of the overall program.

Did I say refactoring? Let's refactor then.

Refactoring the Data Side

In practice, refactoring our current program means implementing the following two guidelines:

- The constants are defined together inside one container: a hashed list.

- All the functional parts of the code (2 to 4 in Figure 3-1) are redesigned in functions, and even in a class if this makes sense.

In particular, those functions should be independent and self-contained so they always return the same result if they are fed with the same input data and can be called in any order.[12]

The first guideline can be immediately translated to this Ring code:

```
data =
[
    :NB_MONTHS_YEAR = 12,
    :NB_WEEKS_MONTH = 4,
    :NB_DAYS_WEEK = 7,
    :NB_DAYS_YEAR = 365
]
```

Our data is no longer dispersed. It is hosted in the same container, the data[] list. As we learned in the previous chapters, this indexed list (or hash list) can be accessed directly by specifying the name of the index between two [] prefixed by a colon (:). Here's an example:

---

[12]We will be learning a lot about the art of using functions in Chapter 7.

- data**[** **:NB_DAYS_MONTHS** **]** returns **12**.
- data**[** **:NB_DAYS_WEEK** **]** returns **7**.
- And so on.

At this level, it's sufficient to know that : can be used inside a hashed list as a decorator of the index used to access the corresponding value. But in reality, the : is a general replacement in Ring of "" in delimiting the value of a string. Hence, for example, instead of saying s = "sun", you can say s = :sun; it's the same.

You may be asking, why do we use these colons to access a hashed list? Well, what happens behind the scene is worth explaining.

To be in line with what we said before, the use of a colon with indexes inside a list means that those indexes are strings themselves. Thus, if we have the following list:

```
a = [ :name = "Nestor" , :age = 48 ]
```

then, internally, the :name = "Nestor" part is represented by Ring in a first inner list like this:

```
[ "name" , "Nestor" ]
```

The :age = 48 part is represented by a second inner list like this:

```
[ "age" , 48 ]
```

The complete representation is the assembly of two inner lists inside the main a[] list like this:

```
a = [    [ "name" = "Nestor"], [ "age" = 48 ]    ]
```

Then we can write the following, by just replacing 🔲 with 🔳, and replacing 🔲 with 🔳, like this:

```
a = [    [ :name = "Nestor"], [ :age = 48 ]    ]
```

If you were to cope with the internal representation and if you want to access the name value, for example, then you should access the first item of the a[] list (which is itself an inner list) and then access the second item of that inner list to find the required value, "Nestor". In Ring code, this is equivalent to saying a[1][2], which is exactly what Ring kindly does, for us, when we say a[**:name**].

Now tell me what is the equivalent of a[**:age**]? Yes, a[2][**2**].

As a general rule, Ring takes the `string` you put as an index between the [ ], performs a quick search of the inner list containing that string in its first item, and then returns the second item corresponding to the required value.

We can say "Thank you, Ring!" because such a feature enhances our programming experience and enables us to write code while thinking in it naturally and hiding its complex implementation.[13]

Now, after implementing the first guideline by refactoring the data side, let's move to the second one and refactor the code side[14] of our program.

Refactoring the Code Side

The second guideline mentioned in the previous section can be implemented by transforming every one of the three parts of the program (from 2 to 4 in Figure 3-1) into a function. For example, to successfully refactor this code snippet from part 3 into a clean function, do this:

```
// Number of weeks in numYears years
numWeeks = NB_WEEKS_MONTH * numMonths    # Gives 144 weeks
? " " + numWeeks + " weeks"
```

Then two dependencies must be eliminated.

- numYears, which is visible here as a global variable and hence can affect the code whenever it changes in any corner of the program, must be transformed to a parameter of the function, pNumYears,[15] for example. When the function is designed to depend exclusively on its parameters and never on any global variable, then the returned number of weeks for a given pNumYears will be always the same, whatever happened.

---

[13]Any time you find the word *implementation* in this book, then understand it as the Ring code of the thing we are implementing: implementing a function is writing its Ring code, and implementing an architecture is designing the files, packages, classes, and functions in Ring and making them work together in a functional program.

[14]Data side and code side are used here to refer, respectively, to data structures (variables) from one side, and functions and classes from the other side.

[15]Note that I usually prefix the name of *parameters* of a function with the letter **p** to easily identify them in code. In larger programs, I always add a letter to identify the parameter type, so it becomes **np**NumYears here, because it is of type number. In the Ring code base, you will find that **c** is used for strings (character in C jargon), **a** for lists (array in C jargon), and **o** for objects. Personally, I add **b** for Booleans (true or false) even though they don't exist, as such, in Ring. In large programs, I also use **$** for global variables and **@** for object attributes.

- The formula used here contains a dependency with the numMonths variable that is calculated elsewhere. Every time its implementation changes then, our code snippet is impacted. Instead, the same calculus can be made using constants, which are not supposed to change.

The result is more resilient[16] and predictable code. It's even more expressive, as shown here:

```
// Number of weeks in a given number of years
func numWeeks(pNumYears)
    numWeeks = data[:NB_WEEKS_MONTH] *
               data[:NB_MONTHS_YEAR] *
               pNumYears

    result =
    "In " + pNumYears + " years you get " + numWeeks +
    " months"

    return result
```

A similar reflection can be made about this formula we have in part 4.

```
// Number of days in a given number of years
numDays = numWeeks * NB_DAYS_WEEK            # Gives 1008 days
```

To do this easily, we only need to invite our unused constant so far, NB_DAYS_YEAR, multiply it by whatever number is hosted in NUMYEARS, and we are done. Here is the new formula:

```
numDays = NB_DAYS_YEAR * NUMYEARS // Gives 1095 days
```

We are not only more elegant conceptually, but also more precise arithmetically, since the first formula completely misled us. Frankly speaking, the number of days in three years has never been 1008 but **1095** (= 365 * 3).

By generalizing the guideline to the entire codebase, we get the new program in Listing 3-5. Write this code into a new file called hardcoded3.ring.

---

[16]Resilience is a value of software quality obtained by minimizing the changes you need to make to your current code region when other regions of the program change.

111

Listing 3-5. hardcoded3.ring

```
// Computing months, weeks and days in 3 years - Version 3
// Our constants are organized in a list
data =
[
        :NB_MONTHS_YEAR = 12,
        :NB_WEEKS_MONTH = 4,
        :NB_DAYS_WEEK = 7,
        :NB_DAYS_YEAR = 365
]

// Feel free to ask any question with any value in any order:
? numDays(3)          # number of days in 3 years
? numWeeks(3)         # number of weeks in 3 years
? numMonths(3)        # number of months in 3 years

### OUR FUNCTIONS GO HERE ###


// Number of months in a given number of years
func numMonths(pNumYears)
      numMonths = data[:NB_MONTHS_YEAR] * pNumYears
        result =
              "In " + pNumYears + " years you get " + numMonths +
              " months"
        return result

// Number of weeks in a given number of years
func numWeeks(pNumYears)
      numWeeks = data[:NB_WEEKS_MONTH] *
                    data[:NB_MONTHS_YEAR] *
                    pNumYears
        result =
              "In " + pNumYears + " years you get " + numWeeks +
              " weeks"
        return result

// Number of days in a given number of years
```

```
func numDays(pNumYears)
    numDays = data[:NB_DAYS_YEAR] * pNumYears
    result =
    "In " + pNumYears + " years you get " + numDays +
    " days"
    return result
```

Execute the program. The same results are generated, as shown here:

```
In 3 years you get 1095 days
In 3 years you get 144 weeks
In 3 years you get 36 months
```

Of course, the three instructions responsible for that are as follows:

```
? numDays(3)
? numWeeks(3)
? numMonths(3)
```

These can calculate the results for any number of years and in any order. Our code side of the program is now composed of well-defined functions and deservers applause. But...[17]

Even those functions are open to an additional[18] and useful refactoring.

Separating Between Concerns

As a golden rule for the design of your functions, let them do one thing and do it well, instead of stuffing them with various features and operations. This is another source of software complexity that you should avoid from the beginning. In our case, the functions we just designed perform two different operations: making the calculation and generating the output. These are two different concerns, and they must be separated.

---

[17]Are you going to hate me for my unterminated "Buts?" Maybe, *but* this is my way of progressively showing you the complexities of programming without listing them all from the start in a way that could hurt beginning learners and demotivate them. Progressive discovery is a first-class citizen in the writing style of the entire book, so please be prepared.

[18]One *additional* refactoring could be the transformation of the code on a class: the constants will be its attributes, and the functions will be its methods. This is easy to do, but is there any added value to it? I'm not sure. Instead, the next section comes with an additional but *useful* idea of refactoring...

To do so, an output() function could be added and called from inside all the other functions to prepare the output in a string, without printing it yet in the screen (using ?). Once returned to the calling code, we let the caller decide what to do with it: printing it to the screen, using it in any other computation, or blowing it on the wind! Why should we care?

Save the current file (hardcoded3.ring) as hardcoded4.ring so we can work on our fourth version of the program. Then, at the end of the file, add the code of the output() function as shown in Listing 3-6.

Listing 3-6. Part of hardcoded4.ring

```
// Generating the output
func output(pNumYears,nResult,cUnit)
     cResult =      # Note this is different from nResult
          "In " + pNumYears + " years you get " + nResult +
          " " + cUnit
     return cResult
```

This function is made to be autonomous. Therefore, all the required information to independently do its job is provided: the number of years in pNumYears, the result of the computation already done by the calling function in nResult, and the label of the cUnit we are making the calculation in (:days, :weeks, or :months). Of course, all the existing formulas must also be redesigned so they are dependent only from the pNumYears parameter and the constant read in the data[] list. For example, the first one, numMonths(), looks like Listing 3-7.

Listing 3-7. Part of hardcoded4.ring

```
// Number of months in pNumYears
func numMonths(pNumYears)
     numMonths = data[:NB_MONTHS_YEAR] * pNumYears
     cResult = output(pNumYears,numMonths,"months")
     return cResult      # Read this side remark in the footnote¹⁹
```

---

[19]We will be able to replace the two last lines in only one and say return output(pNumYears,num Months,"months") directly without using the intermediary cResult variable. It's true, but using it informs the reader of the type returned (the **c** in **c**Result), which is important to enhance the overall readability of the code.

If done right, Listing 3-8 shows what you should have as a complete listing of the program.

Listing 3-8. hardcoded4.ring

```
// Computing months, weeks and days in 3 years - Version 4
// Our constants are organized in a list
data =
[
    :NB_MONTHS_YEAR = 12,
    :NB_WEEKS_MONTH = 4,
    :NB_DAYS_WEEK = 7,
    :NB_DAYS_YEAR = 365
]
// Feel free to ask any question, in any order:
? numDays(3)
? numWeeks(3)
? numMonths(3)

### OUR FUNCTIONS GO HERE ###

// Number of months in pNumYears
func numMonths(pNumYears)
    numMonths = data[:NB_MONTHS_YEAR] * pNumYears
    cResult = output(pNumYears,numMonths,"months")
    return cResult

// Number of weeks in pNumYears
func numWeeks(pNumYears)
    numWeeks = data[:NB_WEEKS_MONTH] *
               data[:NB_MONTHS_YEAR] *
               pNumYears
    cResult = output(pNumYears,numWeeks,"weeks")
    return cResult
```

```
// Number of days in pNumYears
func numDays(pNumYears)
      numDays = data[:NB_DAYS_YEAR] * pNumYears
      cResult = output(pNumYears,numDays,"days")
      return cResult

// Generating the output
func output(pNumYears,nResult,cUnit)
      cResult =
      "In " + pNumYears + " years you get " + nResult +
      " " + cUnit

      return cResult
```

Execute it and compare the result with the previous versions. They are all quiet in terms of output, but the last version exceeds them all in terms of the quality of software code.

There's one little thing I want to add to this subject of mastering data in your code: the use of global variables.

Using Global Variables

What about using global variables inside your programs?

As I said earlier when I first talked about mutability, some programmers will say they hate globals because they alter the state of the program, and others will say they do need them because they make their lives easier. Some programming languages don't support them at all, such as Java and Haskell. Others limit their visibility at the program file level, like Python, and still others can extend their visibility to external files, like C. Some languages define them exclusively at the top level of the program, like C++, while others can have them defined anywhere even inside functions, like PHP. A number of older languages, such as BASIC, had only global variables, no more.

In particular, the programming language Closure features a kind of immutable and persistent data structure that always preserves the previous version of variables when they are modified. Technically, when the programmer changes a new value to an existing variable x, then its old value is preserved untouched, in memory, and a new version of x is created to hold the new value. Such a conservative approach, inspired from the functional programming paradigm,[20] provides a radical protection of the state of the program and is good for developing heavy data transactional systems and multithreaded applications.

---

[20]Ring supports the functional paradigm. You'll learn more about this in Chapter 7.

Is that mutable or not mutable? In such religious wars,[21] the voice of wisdom is always in between, and to wisdom the Ring language obeys.

Any variable you define outside of functions is considered to be global by Ring. This means that it will be visible in any place of your program, including functions. On the contrary, any variable you define inside a function is considered to be local to that function, visible inside it, and invisible to the rest of the program. If you want to define your variables outside of functions and you don't want them to be globals, Ring provides the main function that you can use in the main region of your program, like this:

```
Func main {
    myVar1 = 10
    myVar2 = 20
    // Your code of the main region continues here
}
### Your functions go here ###
Func myFunc1 { ... }
Func myFunc2 { ... }

### Your classes go here ###
Class myClass { ... }
```

Thus, the two variables myVar1 and myVar2 are visible to all the code written in the main region of your program without being globals anymore. You'll learn more about the visibility of variables at different scopes[22] (global, local, and object scope) in Chapter 6.

For now, I'll show how a global variable, when used wisely, can pragmatically add value to our program. The use case we want to implement is simple: providing us with the possibility to run the same hardcoded4.ring program but in two different modes.

---

[21]Read "Global Variables Are OK, and In Fact Necessary," an article written by Norm Matloff, at https://tinyurl.com/uf6bo8g. Then read "Why Global Variables Are Evil?" on the Learn C++ web site at https://tinyurl.com/rlkyze9.

[22]Remember, Ring is a lexically scoped language that defines the scope of variables depending on their place in the code. Review it in Chapter 2.

- **Verbose mode**: The output function generates a whole sentence like it is currently implemented (? numDays(3) returns "In 3 years you get 1095 days").

- **Nonverbose mode**: The output function returns just the number related to the calculation (? numDays(3) returns just 1095).

To do that, save the current file as hardcoded5.ring. Then use a global Boolean,[23] name it bVerboseMode, and set it to false by default. At the beginning of the program, write the code in Listing 3-9.

Listing 3-9. Part of hardcoded5.ring

```
bVerboseMode = false
```

Now, the output function should be changed to include the required conditional logic,[24] as shown in Listing 3-10.

Listing 3-10. Part of hardcoded5.ring

```
// Generating the output
func output(pNumYears,nResult,unit)
    if bVerboseMode = false
        cResult = nResult      # Only number is computed
    else
        cResult =
        "In " + pNumYears + " years you get " + nResult +
        " " + unit    # A whole sentence is computed
    ok
    return cResult      # The output is returned to the caller
```

Execute this code and you get the following:

```
1095
144
36
```

---

[23]Reminder, there is no such a strict type called Boolean in Ring. You can use true and false variables, which correspond, respectively, to the numeric values 1 and 0. This has been covered in Chapter 2. Don't hesitate to go back and review it, if necessary.

[24]Note that, in Ring, if you have a variable bFine = true, then if bFine = true {doSomething()} can be replaced by if bFine { doSomething }, while if bFine = false { doSomething } can be written if **not** bFine { doSomething }. So nice indeed.

Change bVorboseMode = false to **bVerboseMode = true**, and you get the following:

```
In 3 years you get 1095 days
In 3 years you get 144 weeks
In 3 years you get 36 months
```

A lovely global, isn't it?

Inputs in the Console

Suppose we are asked to enhance our previous program by allowing the user to define, by herself, the output mode. If our user is a programmer or someone who can comfortably deal with computer code, then all what we have to do is to give her a copy of the code and ask her to install Ring, or better yet, Ring Notepad, and then play with the bVerboseMode variable right there in the editor!

That's impractical, I agree. That's why Ring comes with a standard keyword for intercepting the user's output as she is typing something on the keyboard. It allows her to give her data input to Ring via the Give keyword. Also, Ring makes it possible to have our program intercept data coming from the command line by typing, for example, ring. exe hardcoded5.ring –true to run the hardcoded5 program in verbose mode. In the following two sections, I give you quick hints on how you can do it.

Using the Give Command

I am going to be brief in this section, so let's look at a short example from the Ring documentation (see Listing 3-11).

Listing 3-11. tempo.ring

```
See "Enter the first number: " Give nNum1
See "Enter the second number: " Give nNum2
See "Sum: " + ( 0 + nNum1 + nNum2 )    # Tell me: why 0 + ?25
```

---

[25]As covered in Chapter 2, Ring performs an implicit conversion of types depending on the first value identified after the = operator. So, if you say x = 2, then x contains the number 2, and when you say x = "" + 2, then x contains the string "2" because "" tells Ring to convert the type of the variable to string. Similarly, when x = "2" and you say x = 0 + "2", then 0 + tells to Ring to convert the x string back to a number.

119

Executing this code in the tempo.ring file in Ring Notepad (Ctrl+F5) shows the first string as "Enter the first number: " in the Output window and waits for data entry. The data entry is what you type in the Input field at the bottom left of the Output window, as shown in Figure 3-2.

Figure 3-2. *In the Output window, type your first number in the Input field*

Try with 3 and then 4 and expect the complete output to be as follows:

```
Enter the first number: 3
Enter the second number: 4
Sum: 7
```

The same thing can be done on the console. Let's try it (Ctrl+R); see Figure 3-3.

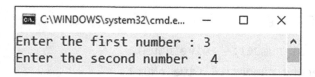

Figure 3-3. *Type your numbers in the console*

Any problem?

The console was in a hurry and didn't show you the answer.

In fact, it was so quick that "Sum: 7" has disappeared. We need to stabilize it by simply adding the code in Listing 3-12 at the end of the code.

Listing 3-12. Part of tempo.ring

```
Give Anything
```

Anything is a variable that we used to force Ring to wait until a key is pressed, and then the program ends.

Getting Arguments from the Command Line

Because we are talking about input from the console, one could ask if it is possible to obtain data inputs from the command line when executing a Ring executable like this:

```
c:\ringbook\myprogram.exe -arg1 -arg2
```

or when calling a Ring script like this:

```
c:\ringbook\myprogram.ring -arg1 -arg2
```

where arg1 and arg2 are the two arguments that the Ring executable (in the first case) or the Ring script (in the second case) will receive and work with internally.

We are not going to show how it is done here, but yes, this is possible due to a standard global variable of type list, available for every Ring program, called sysargv. Ideally, you can learn how to use it in the Ring documentation,[26] along with other useful system functions I advise you to look at, listed here:

- System("tempo.exe -arg1 arg2"), which enables you to execute system commands in the runtime

- SysGet("PATH"), which enables you to get the content of one of the environment variables of your operating system (PATH in this example)

- And many other functions that enable you to identify, at runtime, the operating system on which your application is running and, thus, target it with a specific code, such as isWindows(), isWindows64(), isUnix(), isMacOS(), isLinux(), isFreeBSD(), and isAndroid()

---

[26]http://ring-lang.sourceforge.net/doc1.11/systemfunc.html#get-command-line-arguments

Dealing with data coming from outside your program, from the operating system in particular, is not something a modern programmer can escape, since the software domain is moving toward mobile phones, embedded devices, self-driven cars, and autopiloted drones. However, GUI applications remain by far the major interface for capturing data inputs in our software world.

Inputs from the GUI

Now, what if your user needs to enter her data in a graphical window like in Figure 3-4?

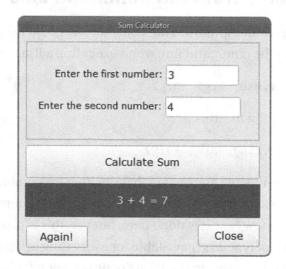

Figure 3-4. Data input in a graphical window

As you see, this is a calculator app specializing in addition. First things first, let's build the window graphically using an included tool in Ring Notepad called the Form Designer.

Creating Windows in the Form Designer

The Form Designer can be activated by selecting View ➤ Form Designer window from the Ring Notepad main menu or by pressing the Ctrl+Shift+F keys. Figure 3-5 shows a general overview of the Notepad user interface with focus on the region related to Form Designer.

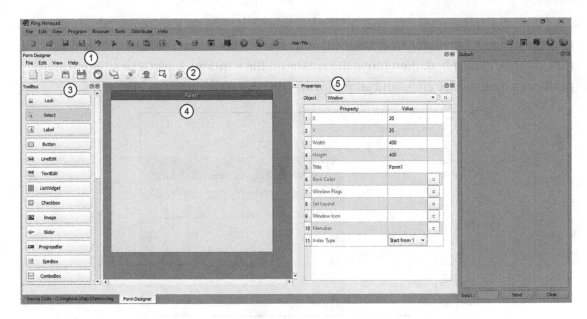

Figure 3-5. *User interface of the Ring Form Designer*

You can switch between the Form Designer and the Code Editor (currently I have `tempo.ring` open, as you can see in Figure 3-5) by activating the related tab on the bottom-left side of the user interface. The Form Designer application has a main menu (1), an icon bar (2), a toolbox (3), a workspace (4) containing an empty form (or window if you want), and a Properties panel (5).

The Toolbox and the Properties panel can be turned on/off by selecting View ➤ Toolbox or View ➤ Properties from the main window (of the Form Designer and not Ring Notepad[27]).

Actually, the Properties panel shows the attributes of the window. Try to change a couple of them by typing a width of 320 and a height of 350, for example, and observe the impact of that change on the window in the workspace.

---

[27]Having two main menus and two icon bars in the same user interface, one for the Ring Notepad application and the other for the Forms Designer application, is somehow misleading. It is better to have them in the same main place, even if this is not trivial to do. Maybe the Ring team, when reading this, can think of a creative solution for this ergonomic issue.

Scroll down the Toolbox panel on the left side of the screen to discover plenty of graphic widgets[28] available by default. To add one to the window, a LineEdit[29] widget, for example, click it first, then move the cursor on the window, select a position to start, perform a long mouse click, and start moving the cursor, as shown in Figure 3-6.

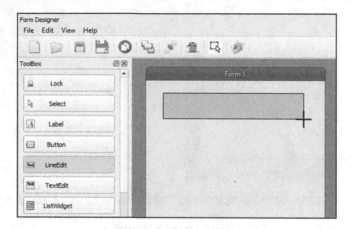

Figure 3-6. *Using the mouse to define the region of the selected graphic widget*

Note that the active widget selected in the toolbox is highlighted (so you know what you are working on). Now release the cursor so you have the LineEdit widget painted on the screen, as shown in Figure 3-7.

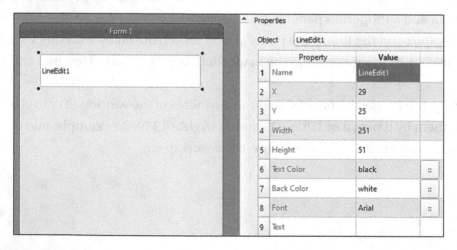

Figure 3-7. *A widget painted on the form, with its attributes displayed in the Properties panel*

---

[28]They are also called graphic controls, graphic objects, or UI elements (where UI stands for user interface).

As you see, the LineEdit widget is still selected, and its properties are displayed in the panel on the right. You can play with them if you'd like. Change the Text Color and Back Color properties if you want by clicking ▦ to the right and choosing your preferred colors from the displayed color selector.[30]

To deselect the current graphic widget, click anywhere in[31] the window but outside the widget itself. To select it again, click it. Now, you can move[32] it on the window by making a long click inside the field and dragging it around (without releasing the mouse). Or you can scroll the mouse over one of its borders and stretch it in one direction or another, as shown in Figure 3-8.

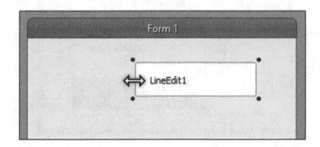

Figure 3-8. *Using the mouse to change the dimensions of a graphic widget*

You can even drop it completely by pressing the Delete button in your keyboard while the widget is selected. But I doubt you may need it, since what I want you to do now is to duplicate it by selecting Edit ➤ Duplicate from the main menu (or by pressing Ctrl+Shift+V). Adjust the duplicated widget position to be under the first one. By the way, note that the Edit menu contains other interesting options (but it is not required to go with them now). Also, set the names of the two LineEdits to, respectively, `edtNumber1` and `edtNumber2`. These names will be used later when writing code for our application logic.

---

[29]A field where the user can enter text and edit it in one line. The widget allowing the user to edit multiline text is TextEdit.

[30]The standard color selector of your operating system is displayed. This feature is made possible because the Forms Designer itself is written in Ring and because Ring relies on the cross-platform Qt framework in its windowing system. You'll learn more about the happy but mutually respectful marriage between Ring and Qt later in the chapter.

[31]If you click outside the window in the dark gray zone of the workspace, then the widget is not deselected, which is not that natural. Maybe the Ring team will consider this and enhance it.

[32]Here I will describe how to move a selected widget with the mouse, but you can also move it using the arrow keys in your keyboard.

Add a button and place it anywhere[33] under the two LineEdits and then set its Text property to `Calculate Sum`. Finally, add a Label widget and put it under all his friends. Name it `lblResult` so this name can be used later in programming. Set its `Back Color` to dark gray and its `Text Color` to white, for example. Figure 3-9 shows my window right now.

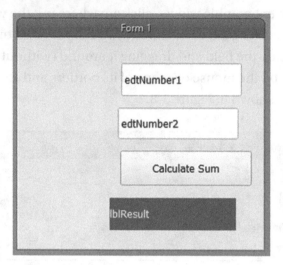

Figure 3-9. *Four widgets not correctly aligned on the form*

Make a multiple selection of the widgets by selecting Edit ➤ Select Objects from the main menu of Form Designer. When the popup window is displayed, use it to select the widgets by clicking their names successively in the list, as shown in Figure 3-10 (clicking a selected item will deselect it).

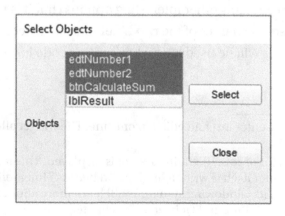

Figure 3-10. *Selecting multiple widgets*

---

[33]Don't worry if they are not aligned; we will be fixing this in a moment.

I left the last one for you (lblResult); click it and then click the Select button. Your widgets are all selected. Click anywhere in the window to deselect them.

Now try to do it the natural way by drawing a virtual region around all the widgets using the mouse (by pressing the left button, drawing a region around them, and then unleashing the button). Interestingly, you get the screen shown in Figure 3-11.

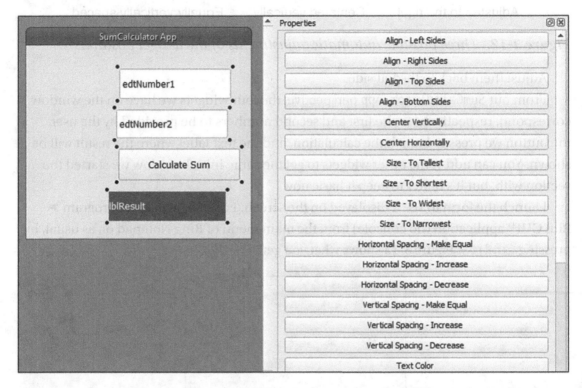

Figure 3-11. *Smart actions when many widgets are selected using the mouse*

As you can see, you can take a bunch of smart actions to provide values for common attributes in one operation and organize your widgets on the screen. Apply, for example, Align - Left Sides and then Size - To Widest by clicking their relative buttons in the Properties panel. Our widgets are kindly aligned now and have all the same width. Play with the other actions; they are super powerful and can help you achieve any adjustment you need in practice. In particular, I want you to achieve what's shown in Figure 3-12.

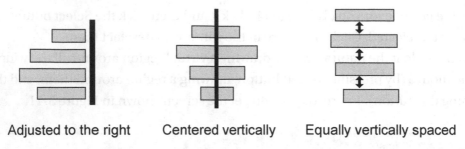

Adjusted to the right   Centered vertically   Equally vertically spaced

Figure 3-12. *Three possible automatic adjustments of the widget positions*

Adjust them back to the left side.

From our `SumCalculator App` perspective, the four widgets we have on the window correspond, respectively, to the first and second numbers to be provided by the user, the button we press to launch the calculation, and the text label where the result will be shown. You can add some other widgets to get the same initial window we started the section with, but it's better to keep it basic now.

Launch the form to see it displayed on the screen. For that, just select Program ➤ Run GUI[34] application (no console) from the main menu of Ring Notepad or, as usual, by pressing Ctrl+F5. Figure 3-13 shows what you get.

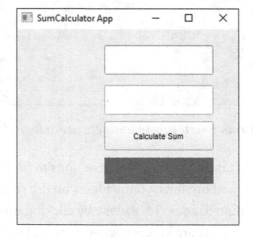

Figure 3-13. *Automatic alignment of four widgets on the form*

This is a toy window, though, and some useful functionality needs to be implemented. I'll be more than happy to help you do it, but before that, you really need to understand what is going under the hood.

---

[34]GUI stands for graphical user interface. Thus, UI stands for user interface.

Understanding the Generated Files from the Form Designer

As we said before, the Form Designer is written completely in Ring. Its source code is available and can be found in the `c:\ring\applications\formdesigner` folder. You can even include it seamlessly in any of your applications like it was included in Ring Notepad (read the introductive comments in the `formdesigner.ring` file). Also, everything Ring does, from parsing your program code to transforming it to bytecode to providing you with a complete WYSIWYG system to designing your interactive forms, is totally transparent, and nothing is left, like with other technologies, inside a dark hole.[35]

So, what happens exactly when our widgets are visually designed?

Save the form by selecting File ➤ Save as from the main window of the Form Designer, select a new folder called SumCalc under `c:\ringbook\chap3`, and save the form file there under this name: `sumCalculator.rform` (note that you won't need to type the `.rform` extension because it will be added automatically).

When the form is saved, some files were generated, behind the scenes, all written in the Ring language. Verify them by exploring the SumCalc folder, as shown in Figure 3-14.

Figure 3-14. *Three files generated by the Form Designer*

---

[35]Ring is unique in terms of transparency. To show you this in practice, consider any one of the programs we wrote in the previous chapters, `helloring.ring` for example. You can see what is happening in each compiler stage and what is going on at runtime in the Ring Virtual Machine by executing this in the command line:

```
ring helloring.ring -tokens -rules -ic
```

As an output, you will get all the tokens generated by the scanner and the grammar rules used by the parser, and even the bytcode prepared by Ring for your code before it is executed by the virtual machine! Think of your students if you are teaching them how compilers work.

As you can see, the three files are as follows:

- SumCalculator.**rform**: This is where the graphic interface of the window is described (as is, without any information about how it is implemented). It corresponds to what the user sees, a window of that type, a button in this position, etc. That's why I'll call it the *description* file.

- SumCalculator**View**.ring: This is where the user interface is actually fabricated. It says how the UI elements described earlier are implemented, using this particular function or that particular graphic library (Qt in our case[36]). That's why I'll call it the *presentation* file.

- SumCalculator**Controller**.ring: This is where the Ring functions necessary to respond to the various events invoked by the user while using the window (clicking on a button, for example) are written. That's why I'll call it the *interaction* file.

Save the form right now by pressing ⊟ in the icon bar of the Form Designer. Then close it by selecting File ➤ Close from the main menu. Now, let's open the first file, SumCalculator.**rform**, in an external text editor, and try to figure out how the form has been automatically described. In my case, I used Notepad++ and hide some lines to get this compact general overview of the file, as shown in Figure 3-15.

---

[36]As we said before in Chapter 1, Ring is strategically aligned with the Qt framework (a full reference of the supported Qt classes in Ring can be found at https://tinyurl.com/qmzw462). The Ring programmer who plans for a level of mastery in Ring will benefit a lot from learning how Qt works, but this is not an obligation. You should also note that Qt is not the only GUI library available in Ring (Allegro and LibSDL are just two other options), and we can even bind any C or C++ other library in a quasi-automated way (it is an advanced topic, but, for the sake of curiosity, you can explore it at https://tinyurl.com/rxbhr3p).

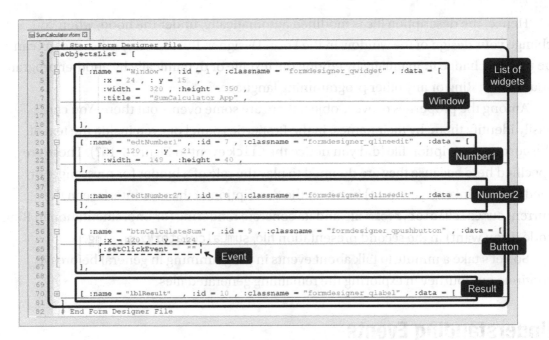

Figure 3-15. *Structure of sumCalculator.rform file in Notepad++*

It's all about a simple Ring `list` called `aObjectsList`. Every item is a hash list itself corresponding to one of the five widgets forming the application (`Window` being the fifth one along with the four widgets we added manually to the form). The hash list contains the widget attributes as they were defined in the Properties panel of the Form Designer.

Try to change the `title` of the form by editing line 6 in the current text file, like this:

`:title = "`**SumCalculator App**`"`

Save it, close it, and go back to Ring Notepad. From the main menu of the Form Designer, select File ➤ Open, and find `SumCalculator.`**rform** in the `c:\ringbook\` `chap3\ringcalc` folder. Open it and observe the new title of the form: it has changed.

Now add a text Label to the form, for example, or change any attribute of the current widgets in the Properties panel. Save the form, switch back to your external text editor, and open the same `sumCalculator.`**form** file again: it has changed.

131

Hence, the description file is modified automatically, under the hood, when you change your design of the window in the Form Designer. But also, any other means can be used to change it: manually by editing the text file or dynamically by another program you write in Ring or any other programming language.[37]

Among the properties of every object there are some events out there. You can easily identify them, by their names, in the Properties panel or even inside the text of the current description file (did you notice the `Click` event in Figure 3-15?). These are specified here because they are doomed to play the role of a binder (or messenger or mediator or linker if you want) between the description of the user interface in the current `sumCalculator.rform` file and its concrete rendering (or implementation in Ring code if you want) in the second presentation file, `sumCalculatorView.ring`.

So, let's take a minute to talk about events in programming in general before we continue our journey in exploring the remaining generated files.

Understanding Events

Events are the most known source of software complexity. They are both difficult to introduce[38] and hard to implement in code. Yet, they are largely misunderstood by beginners and experienced programmers alike, while being prone to divergent doctrines in defining them and rigorously classifying them, even by the gurus of the software industry.[39]

---

[37]Actually, the last option hides a powerful feature that gives you full control over dynamically adapting the user interface to the execution context of the app, independently from the development environment and the programming language, simply by changing data in a text file. In the next section, we will discuss how you can benefit from this window of flexibility in adapting your user interface to different platforms, by telling Ring to change the content of the presentation file at runtime. Also, we will learn how to modify text files, dynamically in Ring, in Chapter 4.

[38]View this 10-minute video for a gentle introduction to events and event-driven programming in making GUI applications: `https://tinyurl.com/wfnhgv8`.

[39]Martin Fowler wrote a famous article to discuss this problem while talking about four types of events we can find in modern software systems: notification events, state-transfer events, log events, and sourcing events. Please note that I've simplified the original names adopted by Martin for better expressivity. Read his article here: `https://tinyurl.com/z6jp99y`. Then if you have time, attend to his Goto conference about the same subject here: `https://www.youtube.com/watch?v=STKCRSUsyP0`.

One of the nice courses I found on the Internet that provides an instructive yet simple introduction to events and event-driven programming is the one by Code.org, found here:

https://curriculum.code.org/csp-18/unit5/1/

Besides explaining how events work in a GUI application like the one we are currently developing, its true value resides in the clarity of definitions provided, which you should embrace and understand from the start of your programming journey with events.[40] During your learning experience, inside this book and elsewhere in the future, you will be most likely confronted with many variations of the jargon used, which is actually one of the additional causes of complexity of the discipline of computer science in general and this subject of events in particular.[41]

In fact, a GUI application is a real-time software system[42] composed of a main window, a main events loop, and a number of graphic widgets. The term *real-time* means that the main events loop is listening all the time to what is happening inside the window. Its role is to intercept any event fired by the user on a widget (click, mouse-over, etc.) and route the execution flow to the part of code specified by the programmer to handle this specific event. A quiet complex system indeed![43]

---

[40]In particular, this lesson, entitled "Introduction to Event-Driven Programming," promotes the adoption of the following set of vocabulary:

- **Callback function**: A function specified as part of an event listener; it is written by the programmer but called by the system as the result of an event trigger.
- **Event**: An action that causes something to happen.
- **Event-driven program**: A program designed to run blocks of code or functions in response to specified events (e.g., a mouse click).
- **Event handling**: An overarching term for the coding tasks involved in making a program respond to events by triggering functions.
- **Event listener**: A command that can be set up to trigger a function when a particular type of event occurs on a particular UI element.
- **UI Elements**: On-screen objects, like buttons, images, text boxes, pull-down menus, screens, and so on.
- **User Interface**: The visual elements of a program through which a user controls or communicates with the application. Often abbreviated UI.

[41]In Chapter 9, I lay out my critiques of the *definitional fuzziness* of the software domain and analyze the root causes of software complexity as I've been experiencing it during three decades of programming practice.

[42]Games are also real-time software systems based on a main game loop and number of game objects events. We will be learning this in detail in Chapter 8.

[43]In Chapter 8, you'll discover yet another interesting real-time software system, where the main loop plays a fundamental role: games.

The Ring Form Designer makes it really easy to work with events. Although they are omnipresent across the three files being generated, you will always need just to specify them in the Properties panel and then program them in the third interaction file (`sumCalculator`**`Controller`**`.ring`) as a normal Ring function. At this level, it is sufficient to enforce the idea that events, in any GUI application, have three roles.

- From the user perspective, they allow the user to interact with the user interface.

- From the programmer perspective, they provide you with a place to write the reactions of the application to the triggered[44] events (we say that you are handling them or controlling[45] them) in Ring functions.

- They form the application architecture perspective, and they form a bridge to let the user interface (presentation layer) communicate indirectly with the description layer, without being coupled together but, instead, by delegating the control of this communication to the third interaction layer.[46]

Figure 3-16 is a visualization that says it all in pictures. Just follow the numbered arrows from left to right.

---

[44]Events are triggered by the underlining library used by Ring for GUI programming, Qt by default. Thus, a main loop is iterating over time inside the window and listening to any event that could happen. And once it happens, the loop adds the necessary information about it (especially the object happening on and its type) in an event list. Another loop maintained by the `Controller` of the application (in the interaction layer) iterates over the event list and performs them one by one. To every event, it finds the required `Callback` function the programmer has defined as a reaction for the event and executes it.

[45]Hence the name `Controller` used in MVC. You'll learn more about this in the "Three Values of MVC in GUI Design" section.

[46]In the "Three Values of MVC in GUI Design" section, you will discover the huge advantages of this separation of concerns of your GUI application to three specialized layers.

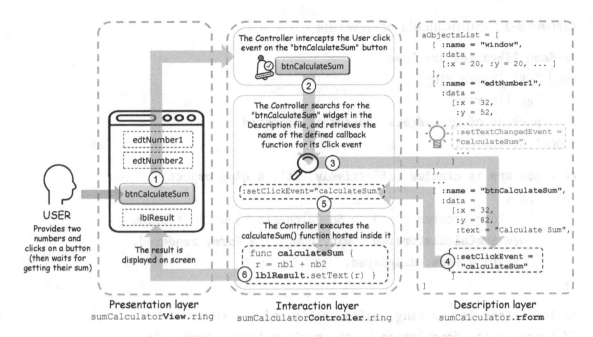

Figure 3-16. *What is happening under the hood of the files generated by the Form Designer*

Figure 3-16 draws the mental model you should adopt while thinking of the big picture of the event-driven system established by Form Designer inside your code base to accelerate the development of the GUI of your application. In fact, among the several actions implicated in the click process visualized in the figure, only actions 4 and 5 are required to be done by you, the programmer. All the others are done automatically for you!

After watching how the UI has been described automatically inside the description file, sumCalculator.**rform**, let's see how its presentation aspect has been fabricated in the sumCalculator**View**.ring.

Fabricating the User Interface

Let's open the description file, SumCalculator**View**.ring, directly in Ring Notepad. Read it and try to understand its structure. To help you, I've simplified it in Listing 3-13 and commented it a bit for the sake of explanation.

Listing 3-13. SumCalculatorView.ring

```
// Some libraries are loaded
Load "stdlibcore.ring"
Load "guilib.ring"
// A package of Qt widgets classes is imported⁴⁷
import System.GUI

// A new app is created (effectively, it's a qApp object)
 new App {
        // Form created based on SumCalculatorView class below
        new SumCalculatorView { win.show() } # Form, rendered.
        exec() # Form, displayed.
 }

// This class is the Ring implementation of the form
// based on its description in the sumCalculator.rform file
class SumCalculatorView
        // The window is fabricated
        win = new MainWindow() {
                // Window attributes
                move(24,15) resize(320,350)
                setWindowTitle("SumCalculator App")

                // The first widget is fabricated
                edtNumber1 = new LineEdit(win) {
                        // widget attributes
                        move(120,21) resize(149,40)
                        setText("")

                        // Triggering Events supported by the widget
                        // if ("") is empty then nothing happens
                        setTextChangedEvent("")
                        setcursorPositionChangedEvent("")
                        seteditingFinishedEvent("")
```

---

⁴⁷To get an idea about the richness of Qt widgets supported, browse to this file: C:\Ring\
  extensions\ringqt\guilib\modernlib.ring

```
        setreturnPressedEvent("")
        setselectionChangedEvent("")
        settextEditedEvent("")
}

// The second widget is fabricated
edtNumber2 = new LineEdit(win) {
        // Idem
}

// The button is fabricated
btnCalculateSum = new PushButton(win) {
        move(120,124) resize(149,39)
        setText("Calculate Sum")
        setBtnImage(btnCalculateSum,"")

        // Clikc Event, triggered on the button
        setClickEvent("")
}

//...
}
```

The file contains a class of the same name, SumCalculator**View**, which reproduces thoroughly the content of the first description file, sumCalculator.**rform**, while augmenting it with some implementation staff: a Ring class and a bunch of Ring libraries (StdLibCore[48] and GuiLib[49]) along with a package[50] of specialized classes in GUI programming, System.GUI.

---

[48]StdLibCore contains only the functions of the StdLib library, while this one contains both functions and classes. The StdLib folder can be explored at c:\ring\ringlibs\stdlib. You'll learn more about this in the section "Adapting the Connector to the Database."

[49]GuiLib is the Ring library for developing GUI applications. While being independent, by design, from any low-level graphic windowing system, the current implementation is relying on a complete binding written in Ring for the Qt framework so it can be used directly in your programs (available through the RingQt extension). Compared to other available bindings from other programming languages, like PyQt and Qt for Python, for example, the Ring binding offers the advantage of being more complete and totally free and open source.

[50]Packages are used as containers of many classes of the same domain, so your application is kept organized. Read about them at http://ring-lang.sourceforge.net/doc1.11/oop.html#packages.

At the beginning of the main region[51] of the file, an App is initiated (which is actually a Qt app[52]) with an instance of the previous class. Then, the window is rendered (using win.show()) and then displayed on the screen (using exe(), and both refer to the functions of the same name we discovered in Chapter 1 when we first met with the Qt framework).

In other words, both the description and the presentation are done; what is missing is the user interaction staff.

Responding to User Events

A substantial part of the code in the SumCalculator**View** file we worked on in the previous section is dedicated to events. They are listening for any manipulations being fired by the user when interacting with the form, such as the following:

- Clicking a button: setClickEvent("")

- Changing the text in a LineEdit: setTextChangedEvent("")

- Selecting text inside a LineEdit: setSelectionChangedEvent("")

- And so on[53]

What you need to do now is to define an action to respond to every event you should trigger (those left empty, "", won't be managed by the event system and are therefore totally idle). All that is required is providing the name of a function (or more precisely a method, although they are the same in Ring[54]), because the code itself will be written

---

[51]The main region of a Ring file starts from the beginning of the file and ends at the limit of the first function or class available. Sometimes, if the programmer wants, it can be wrapped in a main { } function to prevent the use of global variables.

[52]You were introduced to the use of this qApp object in Chapter 1.

[53]To get the complete list of the user interface events supported by Ring, in the RingQt library, for every graphic widget, take a look to the files you can find in the following folder: c:\ring\extensions\ringqt\events

[54]For the sake of semantic elegance and code expressiveness, let's use the name *method* for the functions we define inside classes (and let's use the def keyword for defining them) and use the *function* name when we write them outside classes (and use the func keyword to define them). Func and Def are the same.

later in the third interaction file. That method will be evoked by Ring (and, behind the scenes, by the main loop maintained internally by the Qt event management framework famously called Signals and Slots[55]) at runtime as a response to the user event.

To do that, switch back to the Form Designer, select the only button you have on the form, and then set the set**Click**Event property to calculateSum as a name for your method, as shown in Figure 3-17.

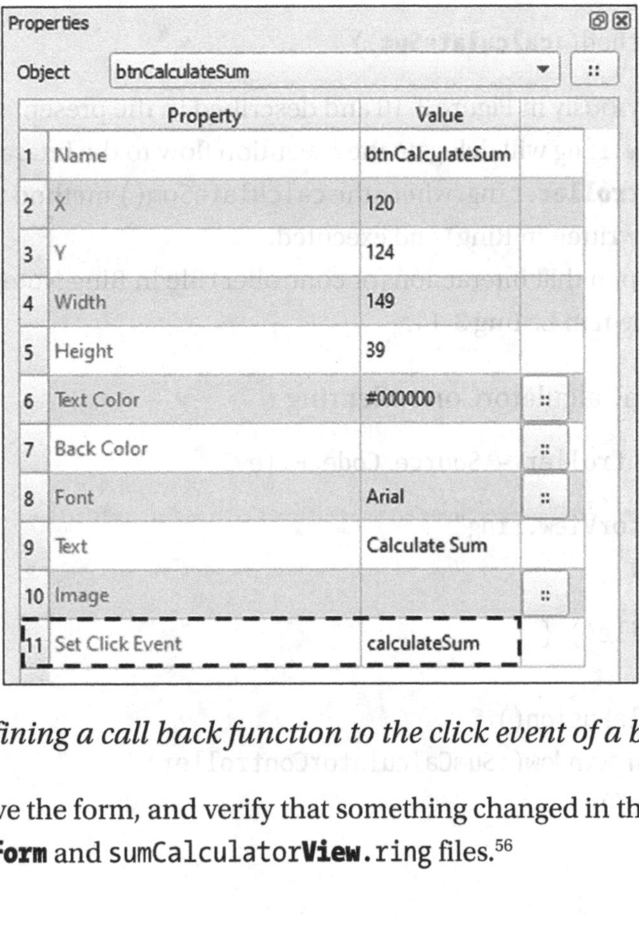

Figure 3-17. Defining a call back function to the click event of a button widget

Once done, save the form, and verify that something changed in the sumCalculator.**rform** and sumCalculator**View**.ring files.[56]

---

[55]For your general culture, take this 10-minute or so video on Slot and Signals. What you will discover is actually the same thing happening when you define actions for your GUI events, here in Ring.

[56]For that, close them if they are still open without saving and then open them again.

Hence, in the inner list starting with :name = "btnCalculateSum" in the sumCaculator.**rform** file, the line related to setting the Click event became the following:

```
:setClickEvent = "calculateSum"
```

While in the btnCalculateSum {} block in the sumCalculatorView class in the sumCalculator**View**.ring file, the line related to setting the Click event became the following:

```
setClickEvent(Method(:calculateSum))
```

As exposed previously in Figure 3-16 and described in the presentation file, sumCalculator**View**.ring will delegate the execution flow to the interaction file, sumCaculator**Controller**.ring, where the calculateSum() method will be implemented (i.e., written in Ring) and executed.

Hurry up and open that interaction (or controller) file in Ring Notepad. Indeed, the code is clear, as shown in Listing 3-14.

Listing 3-14. SumCalculatorController.ring

```
# Form/Window Controller - Source Code File

load "SumCalculatorView.ring"
import System.GUI

if IsMainSourceFile() {
        new App {
                StyleFusion()
                open_window(:SumCalculatorController)
                exec()
        }
}

class SumCalculatorController from windowsControllerParent

        oView = new SumCalculatorView
```

Inside the SumCalculatorController class, an instance of the presentation class, SumCalculatorView, is invited from the sumCalcularor**View**.ring file[57] and hosted inside an object variable, oView. This particular object composition technique[58] will help us access all the graphic objects (which was defined in the user interface layer) and manipulate them right from the interaction layer of the app. For example, we can set the default numbers to 12 and 8 by adding the lines in **bold** hereafter, as shown in Listing 3-15.

Listing 3-15. Part of SumCalculatorController.ring

```
class SumCalculatorController from windowsControllerParent
    oView = new SumCalculatorView

    // Set default numbers
    oView.edtNumber1.setText("12")
    oView.edtNumber2.setText("8")
```

Launch the application (Ctrl+F5) and watch the result, as shown in Figure 3-18.

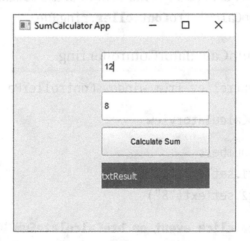

Figure 3-18. *Providing default values in the controller file*

You made it, but a better solution for displaying default values is to define them in the description file (in the Properties panel, by entering them in the Text property) and let the Form Designer generate them automatically in the presentation file. As general

---

[57]Note that this file has been loaded from the start using load "sumCalculatorView.ring".
[58]You'll learn more about object composition when you learn about object-oriented programming (OOP) in Ring in Chapter 7.

advice, let the controller (the interaction file) contain what is dynamic by nature. By "dynamic," I mean the computations you need to make after something happened in the life of the program (a user or system event). The default values are rather static and can be provided before the program starts. Therefore, their best place is the model of our application (the description file).

Delete theses lines from sumCalculatro**Controller**.ring:

```
// Set default numbers
oView.edtNumber1.setText("12")
oView.edtNumber2.setText("8")
```

In the Form Designer, select the two LineEdits, one by one, and enter 12 and then 8, respectively, in their Text attribute in the Properties panel. Save and run. It's the same result as in Figure 3-18 but with a cleaner implementation.

What's next? Writing the sumCalculate() method, in the same interaction file, to respond to the click event of the btnCalculateSum button.

Add what is in **bold** in Listing 3-16 at the bottom of the SumCalculatorController class from the current sumCalculatro**Controller**.ring file.

Listing 3-16. Part of SumCalculatorController.ring

```
class SumCalculatorController from windowsControllerParent

    oView = new SumCalculatorView

    // Set default numbers
    oView.edtNumber1.setText("12")
    oView.edtNumber2.setText("8")

    // Responding to click event on btnCalculateSum button
    func calculateSum
        oView {
            nNumber1 = 0+ edtNumber1.text()
            nNumber2 = 0+ edtNumber2.text()
            nSum = n1+n2
            cResult = "" + n1 + " + " + n2 + " = " + n
            lblResult.setText(cResult)
        }
```

Save the file (Ctrl+S) and then launch the form again. Click the Calculate Sum button. The result is computed and displayed in the lblResult text zone, as shown in Figure 3-19.

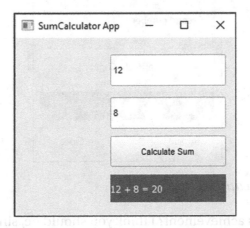

Figure 3-19. *A fully functional calculator that make sums*

It's working perfectly. Still the user interface design is far from being satisfactory. Let's try a little enhancement.

Enhancing the User Experience

If you ask me for ergonomic advice, I will tell you to add the missing descriptive texts in front of every LineEdit, embellish your user interface by choosing a larger font size, and complete the user experience by adding two buttons at the bottom of the window.

- An Again! button to re-initiate the form by setting the numbers to zeros (i.e., to empty "" strings).

- A Close button, well, to close the window. If the button is called btnClose, then the command you need is oView.win.close().

As a final result, Figure 3-20 shows your first GUI application in Ring.

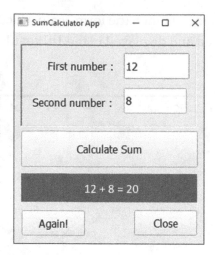

Figure 3-20. *A more beautiful app*[59]

Are you happy of this achievement? I think you should be, since what you learned so far gave you the foundation for developing nearly any professional user interface. Still, the domain of GUI programming needs a lot of practice and a deep understanding of the user experience (UX) in interacting with the graphic widgets. Don't move forward before doing these three homework tasks:

1. Allow the user to get the sum as she is entering the numbers in the corresponding fields. Think of setting the `textChangedEvent` property of the two widgets to the same `calculateSum` function we used before for the button.[60]

2. Prevent the user from entering other than numbers in the LineEdit fields. You can control the numbers when the user leaves the field by relying on a new method you name `onlyNumbers()`[61] that you

---

[59]Note that the text of the result has been centered. Tell me how you can make it in the Form Designer?

[60]If you are feeling lazy, we will be doing this together in the next section. But if you want to be a rigorous learner, do it now and correct yourself by discovering the solution later.

[61]Note that although it is not required in Ring, I always put () after the name of a function so that I know that it is a function! I also always add _f at the end of the name of a function that *returns a function*, getfunc_f() for example, just to know that the returned thing is a function. In Chapter 7, you will learn that functions are first-class citizens in Ring and that you can save a variable with myfunc = func {...}, execute it from a variable with call(myfunc), send it as a parameter to another function (f for example) with f(myfunc), and return it from functions with return myfunc.

specify in the **editingFinished**Event in the Properties panel. In the sumCalculator**Controller**.ring file, you would implement its behavior by coloring the text of the related number in red, for example.

This would be enough to notify the user of possible mistakes, but if she doesn't care, an additional control needs to be implemented inside the calculateSum() method by displaying an error message in a message box, for example.[62]

3. Carefully read the "User Interface Principles" article[63] from Microsoft about the rules you should follow in designing intuitive desktop user interfaces. In particular, the 20 tips proposed there are all realizable without much effort thanks to the visual development experience allowed by the Form Designer.

What you learned so far is largely sufficient, from a beginner perspective, but as you are evolving in designing GUI applications, for desktop and mobile devices, take your time to study those resources in the documentation center.

- Using the Ring designer:

  http://ring-lang.sourceforge.net/doc1.11/formdesigner.html

- Desktop and mobile development using RingQt:

  http://ring-lang.sourceforge.net/doc1.11/qt.html

- Building RingQt applications for mobile:

  http://ring-lang.sourceforge.net/doc1.11/qtmobile.html

---

[62]How do you show a MessageBox in Ring? Find the instructions in the Ring documentation. In the next section, I provide you with some helpful links.

[63]https://tinyurl.com/so3qc89

Three Values of MVC in GUI Design

This separation of the three aspects of the GUI application (which I called description-presentation-interaction, for a good reason,[64] while they are better known in the software industry as the Model-View-Controller pattern) is essential to crafting a clean and agile software architecture. In particular, this helps achieve three strategic values of any modern piece of software: code reusability, code testability, and targeting of multiple platforms. Let's discuss them, briefly, one by one.

Code Reusability

A beautiful illustration of how MVC empowers code reusability is when the same function we write in the controller layer (the interaction layer in our terms), `calculateSum` for example, can be used by many other widgets in our form. Want to practice?

If you were attentive enough while visualizing Figure 3-15, there was a bulb near the `TextChanged` event of the `edtNumber1` LineEdit. This was planned for the practical example we will do now to show how the `calculateSum` method can be executed when the user changes any of the same two numbers on the screen, as shown in Figure 3-21.

---

[64]MVC has been democratized as a software architecture pattern by the effervescence of web frameworks. Unfortunately, this movement has somehow "polluted" the purity of the SoC principle behind MVC (SoC stands for separation of concerns). Read this article from Matt Burgess to get my point (`https://tinyurl.com/ucoqwwz`). Such purity has been demonstrated in how the Ring Form Designer works for us under the hood and generates three separate files, one for each aspect: the user interface design (description), the management of user events (interaction), and the generation of the display on-screen (presentation). If you are totally new to MVC, then this is fine; the section will put you on a good footing. But if you belong to the generation of programmers who have been "educated" with the mentioned MVC web frameworks, then I kindly ask you to unlearn them. To do that, I propose you carefully read a tutorial from the Qt documentation (`https://tinyurl.com/qvhmkqx`) that explains how MVC is embraced by the Qt framework. This is fundamental about deeply understanding how GUI programming works in Ring because the language is, by design, influenced by the Qt vision of enabling data-driven applications.

```
[ :name = "edtNumber1",
    :data =
      [:x = 32,
        :y = 52,
```
```
        :setTextChangedEvent =
          "calculateSum",
```

Figure 3-21. *Did you notice the bulb in Figure 3-15?*

To do this, go to the Form Designer and open the sumCalculator.**rform** file if it isn't already there. Select the two widgets corresponding to the numbers, edtNumber1 and edtNumber2, one by one, and set their **textChanged**Event properties to calculateSum, as shown in Figure 3-22.

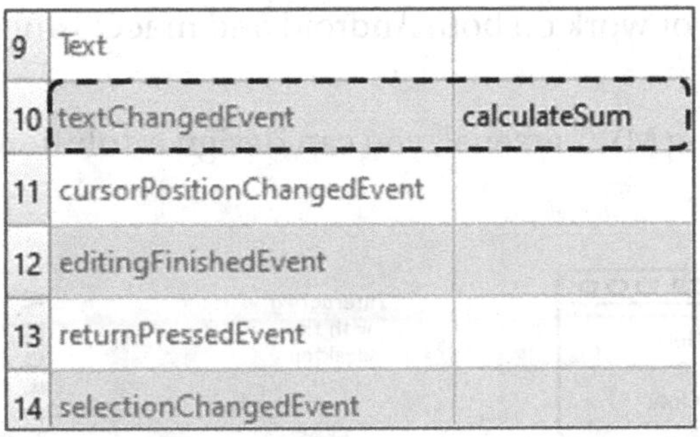

9	Text	
10	textChangedEvent	calculateSum
11	cursorPositionChangedEvent	
12	editingFinishedEvent	
13	returnPressedEvent	
14	selectionChangedEvent	

Figure 3-22. *Properties panel: reutilizing the calculateSum function*

Save and run and then test the form. While you are entering a number, the sum is live-calculated, and the lblResult label is updated! Congratulations, you've been reutilizing many times the same calculateSum function code you wrote only once!

Code Testability

Usually when you are using the Form Designer to make your GUI applications, the eventual bugs come essentially from the code you are writing inside the callback functions hosted in controller layer (interaction file). Because they are functions, and if you design them to be self-contained as we learned in "Refactoring the Code Side," then your testing activity is enhanced because it covers small blocks of code with no dependencies at all with the user interface itself.

Under the umbrella of MVC or without it, always think of writing testable code. This can be as easy as designing small functions and classes and narrowing their dependency on the rest of the world. Also, and without disturbing your programming flow with the so-called Test-Driven Development (TDD) practice, you can adopt the Ring way of testing itself using little scripts providing values for your code and replaying them any time you make a change so that the consistency of your application is not broken.

To see how this is done, explore the following folder: `c:\ring\tests`. Usually, this is my preferred angle of attack when I want to understand how a given standard function works.

Targeting of Multiple Platforms

Sorry, it is unavoidable! Whatever customer you are making a computer program for, or whatever software company you are working for as a programmer, you will need to make it runnable at least on desktop, mobile, and maybe web platforms. And if you don't mind, let the mobile flavor work on both Android and macOS and on both small and large screens.

Armed with your Ring MVC arsenal, you can design a solution like Figure 3-23.

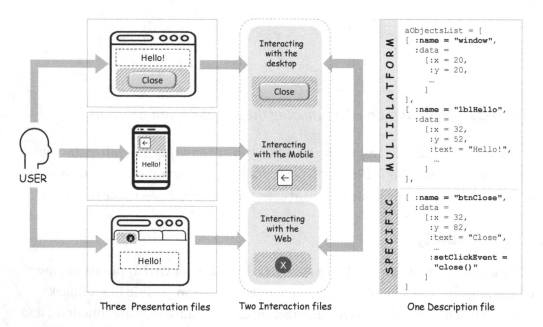

Figure 3-23. *A solution architecture for a cross-platform GUI application*

It's always interesting when you have to deliver the "same" user interface to three different platforms: desktop, web, and mobile. They are completely different in regard to their underlined technologies. Still, portions of our code can remain the same and can remain multiplatform (shown in Figure 3-23). Hence, instantiating a text label `"Hello!"` at the position `(32,52)` of the screen can be interpreted in the same way[65] by a desktop window, a web browser, and a mobile screen.

On the other hand, there are some specificities of each platform in dealing with some graphic objects. Take the example of the Close button shown in Figure 3-23. While the desktop understands it and provokes the current window to be closed, there is no such a "closing" thing in a browser or on a mobile device. In fact, closing happens at the tab level in the browser, and this is not managed in principle by the web application context (it is a sovereign decision of the user who is free to close any tab independently from the application logic running inside the tab). While in a mobile device and if we cope with the Android application model, what you are allowed to do is to go back to the previous screen; that's it.

Those differences represent hard problems well known by experienced developers. Based on the Ring user interface model generated for us, it is possible to manage them by making three different implementations of the view of our system (three versions of the `sumCalculatorView.ring` file) where we specify whether the close button should be rendered on each platform or not. All we need to do after that is call the correct version of the file depending on the user execution platform, using the system function we discovered earlier such as `isAndroid()`, `isMacOS`, `isLinux()`, and so on.

Ultimately, the true fruit of the SoC of three layers is that it allows us to change our technological choices, now or in the future, without breaking the whole application. If you find Ring tightly coupled to `Qt` as a GUI library while you are not comfortable with everything `Qt`, make another implementation of the `sumCalculatorWinView.ring` file with the graphic library of your choice. And if you are targeting the Web, then instead of using `GuiLib`, use the `WebLib` library and develop your user interface using the language of the Web.[66] Plug it in the system, and the system will work.

---

[65]To ensure your coordinates work as expected on various platforms, it is advisable to not specify them with concrete values. Instead, try to describe them relatively (the x is in the center of the frame, the button is in the bottom left of the same frame, etc.). This can be done by computing coordinates at runtime or, better yet, by using graphic layouts, visually in the Form Designer (`https://tinyurl.com/shcv868`) or by code using RingQt (`https://tinyurl.com/wcr4l2c`).

[66]You got a basic introduction to web development in Ring in Chapter 1. Unfortunately, we won't cover it in detail in this book. If you are interested, there is a good help page with a lot of examples in the Ring documentation center at `https://tinyurl.com/wl44lyr`.

On the controller side, as shown in the figure, we could refactor our sumCalculator**Controller**.ring file into two controllers: one for managing the events occurring in the desktop and mobile and one specialized in managing the web events. It is one possible solution, motivated by the similarities between desktop and mobile on one hand and the particularity of web interactions, managed in part on the front end using JavaScript, on the other hand.

Finally, on the model side, I decided to leave the same unique description file since the difference related to describing the Click event of the Close button can be dealt with, dynamically, in the Controller by doing the following:

- First, verifying the current platform (using the same isAndroid()-like instruction)

- Second, routing the execution to a dedicated flavor of the close() function written specifically for Android phones (android_goback(), for example)

I won't show it in code this time, because we don't have enough space. In the next section, however, you'll learn how to get data from text files, while designing a clean data acquisition architecture in code since there is no tool similar to the Form Designer that does it for us.

Inputs from Text Files

Many software applications use text as a plain old data source. Generally, the text file hosts brute-structured data or a bunch of configuration properties you want to edit independently from the executable program. In Ring, you can simply read a file by importing its content to a string using the read() function.

Reading Data from a Text File

Create a text file named data.txt and save it to a folder called NorthAfricaApp. Inside the file, write the code in Listing 3-17 about these six North-African countries[67]: Mauritania (MAU), Morocco (MOR), Algeria (ALG), Tunisia (TUN), Libya (LIB), and Egypt (EGY).

---

[67]Use the beauty of whitespace, without moderation, to craft clear and readable text.

Listing 3-17. data.txt

```
"CNTRY",   "POP",   "GRO",    "MED",    "DEN"
  "MAU",    4.42,    2.73,    19.70,     4.29
  "MOR",   35.70,    1.30,    27.90,    80.10
  "ALG",   41.30,    1.74,    27.50,    17.30
  "TUN",   11.50,    1.12,    31.10,    74.20
  "LIB",    6.37,    1.28,    27.20,     3.62
  "EGY",   97.60,    1.93,    24.70,    98.00
```

Population (POP) is measured in million people, population growth (GRO) is measured in percent per year, median age (MED) is measured in years, and population density (DEN) is measured in people per km.2 The data is taken from Wolfram|Alfa, which compiled it from The World Factbook of the United States Central Intelligence Agency.[68]

Specifying the NorthAfrica App

Our objective is to generate a string from data like this:

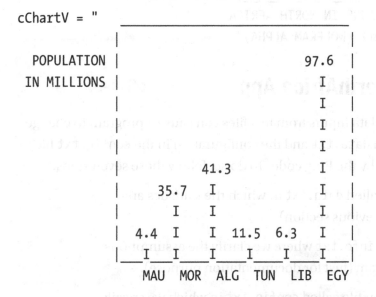

```
cChartV = "   _____
               |                                |
 POPULATION    |                        97.6    |
 IN MILLIONS   |                         I      |
               |                         I      |
               |                         I      |
               |                         I      |
               |                         I      |
               |           41.3          I      |
               |    35.7    I            I      |
               |     I      I            I      |
               |  4.4 I     I  11.5  6.3  I      |
               |__I___I___I___I___I____I___I__|
                   MAU  MOR  ALG  TUN  LIB  EGY

           COMPARING POPULATIONS IN NORTH AFRICA
            DATA OF 2015-2017 (WOLFRAM|ALPHA)"
```

---

[68]Take a look at the example from Wolfram|Alpha here: https://www.wolframalpha.com/input/?i=tunisia.

Awesome bar chart, isn't it?

Also, we are going to generate from the same file, if we have time, a horizontal version of the same chart in a string like this:

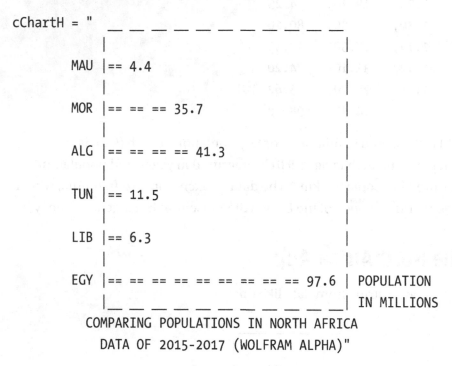

```
cChartH = "  _ _ _ _ _ _ _ _ _ _ _
              |                       |
        MAU  |== 4.4                 |
              |                       |
        MOR  |== == == 35.7          |
              |                       |
        ALG  |== == == == 41.3       |
              |                       |
        TUN  |== 11.5                |
              |                       |
        LIB  |== 6.3                 |
              |                       |
        EGY  |== == == == == == == == == 97.6 | POPULATION
              |_ _ _ _ _ _ _ _ _ _ _| IN MILLIONS
           COMPARING POPULATIONS IN NORTH AFRICA
             DATA OF 2015-2017 (WOLFRAM ALPHA)"
```

Seven Steps to the NorthAfrica App

In this section, I will show how data inputs from text files can cause a program to change. In practice, changing the data in data.txt and the configuration in the config.txt files will change the chart generated by the Ring code. To do so, follow these seven steps:

1. Provide the data file called data.txt in which the statistics are hosted (done in the previous section).

2. Write a text file called info.txt where we clarify the assumptions and rules of our program (just for documentation purpose).

3. Provide a configuration file called config.txt in which we specify the variable of comparison (population, population growth, median age, or population density) and the chart orientation (horizontal or vertical).

4. Write a Ring file called `transformer.ring` responsible for reading the data in `data.txt` and transforming it into a manageable format by Ring: `List[]`.

5. Write a Ring file called `datagraph.ring` where we prepare the data in a format allowing us to directly construct a particular type of chart without a hassle.

6. Write a Ring file called `chartRenderer.ring` containing the code that renders the data contained in a `datagraph` in a particular visual chart hosted in a `string`.

7. Change data and configuration in the text files and see how the charts instantly change.

Creating Conventions and Configuration Files

Now we will start step 2 listed in the "Seven Steps to the NorthAfrica App" section.

Listing 3-18 shows a first draft of the `info.txt` file.

Listing 3-18. info.txt

```
==========================================
    NorthAfricaApp : List of conventions
==========================================
- The program is designed in conformity with the principle
  of separation concerns: data, presentation,
  and interaction, and may be more.

- Number of variables (columns) in the data file
  is 5, any value out of this range is simply ignored

- Number of records of data (or lines) is 6 corresponding
  to the number of north African countries, any record
  out of this range is simply ignored

- The first 6 records are assumed to be correct and
  reflecting the exact six north African countries

- "" are used inside the data file to simplify the
  identification of strings by Ring code
```

- Possible values of variables are: "POP" for population,
  "GRO" for population growth, "AGE" for median age, and
  "DEN" for population density

- Possible value of countries are: "MAU" for Mauritania,
  "MOR" for Morroco, "ALG" for Algeria, "TUN" for Tunisia,
  "LIB" for Libya, and "EGY" for Egypt

- Possible values of chart orientations are: "V" for
  vertical, and "H" for horizontal

- Default value for variables is "POP", and default value
  for orientation is "V"

Now for step 3 of the steps listed in the "Seven Steps to the NorthAfrica App" section.

With the data file being in place (step 1), we created the configuration text file (step 2), so now we furnish it with the information in Listing 3-19.

Listing 3-19. config.txt

```
COMPARE-ON = "POP"
ORIENTATION = "H"
```

Name it `config.txt` and save it in the same `NorthAfricaApp` folder we are working in.

Transforming Text Data into a Ring List

Now for step 4 of the steps listed in the "Seven Steps to the NorthAfrica App" section.

In Ring Notepad, create a new file called `transformer.ring`. This transformer will read the data in `data.txt` and transform it into the following Ring code:[69]

```
aData =
[      [ "CNTRY",   "POP",   "GRO",    "MED",    "DEN" ],
       [  "MAU",    4.42,    2.73,    19.70,     4.29 ],
       [  "MOR",   35.70,    1.30,    27.90,    80.10 ],
```

---

[69]Why this format in particular? Well, because it is visually appealing and corresponds to normal tables of data everyone can understand. It's also how Excel and similar software represent tabular data.

```
    [    "ALG",    41.30,    1.74,    27.50,    17.30 ],
    [    "TUN",    11.50,    1.12,    31.10,    74.20 ],
    [    "LIB",     6.37,    1.28,    27.20,     3.62 ],
    [    "EGY",    97.60,    1.93,    24.70,    98.00 ]
]
```

The generated code will be hosted inside a string variable. Then the content of this string is executed dynamically using the eval() function to produce the same effect as if it were introduced by hand. So, how are we going to code it? It's not that difficult, as shown here:

- We read the text file. Text data is put in a native Ring string.

- We add [and] before and after every line respecting the syntax of a Ring list.

- We constitute the Ring code describing the aData[ ] list and run it dynamically.

- We show the result of our work by printing the list.

Listing 3-20 shows the implementation of this thinking in Ring inside the file transformer.ring.

Listing 3-20. tranformer.ring

```
// Preparations
d = read("data.txt") // reading text file
a = str2list(d) // transforming the text to a list

// Transformation - step 1: adding [ and ]
for i = 1 to len(a) //= 7; number of lines in the text file
      a[i] = "["+a[i]+"]"
next i

// Transformation - step 2: hosting the data in a list
cData = "aData = [ " + NL
for i = 1 to len(a) // =7
      cData += TAB + a[i]
      if i < len(a) { cData += ", " + NL }
next i
cData += NL + " ]"
```

```
// Dynamic creation of aData list
cCode = ""
cCode += "// Data transformed in Ring lists" + NL
cCode += cData
// Show the code
? cCode
eval(cCode)

// Data is now ready to be managed as a Ring list. Examples:
? NL + "// Example 1: reading the list of variables"
? variables()

? "// Example 2: reading the data of Marocco (? aData[3])"
? aData[3]

? "// Example 3: reading the list of countries"
? countries()

func variables()
        return aData[1]

func values()
     aVal = []
     for i=2 to len aData
          aVal + aData[i]
     next i
     return aVal

func countries()
     aCtr = []
     for i=2 to len(aData)
          aCtr + aData[i][1]
     next i
     return aCtr
```

Save it and execute it. Now compare the result we expected at the beginning of the section with the result shown in the Output window of Notepad.

```
// Data transformed in Ring lists
aData = [
        ["CNTRY", "POP", "GRO", "MED", "DEN"],
        [  "MAU",  4.42,  2.73, 19.70,  4.29],
        [  "MOR", 35.70,  1.30, 27.90, 80.10],
        [  "ALG", 41.30,  1.74, 27.50, 17.30],
        [  "TUN", 11.50,  1.12, 31.10, 74.20],
        [  "LIB",  6.37,  1.28, 27.20,  3.62],
        [  "EGY", 97.60,  1.93, 24.70, 98.00]
]
```

We're doing good.

Preparing Data for Showing a Graph

Now for step 5 of the steps listed in the "Seven Steps to the NorthAfrica App" section.

What we need now is to prepare the datagraphs for our charts. Wondering what these "datagraphs" are? How do they differ from the dataset we have in our aData list? And why do we need them? All good questions.

To explain the point, let's consider the Excel sheet shown in Figure 3-24 containing the same dataset and a bar chart based on the horizontal chart we want to make.

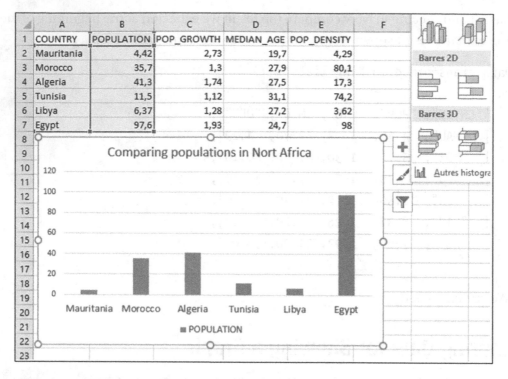

Figure 3-24. *A dataset and a bar chart in Excel*

In Excel, it's live and happens like magic. But under the hood it takes a long way to get from the data sheet to the visual graph. Indeed, Excel thinks of the x and y axes, the scope of values they will represent (from min to max), how many steps they contain, and what the length is of each step. Then Excel calculates the height of every bar depending on the ratio between the value of the variable and the total length of the axis. Finally, it organizes all this data in a matrix directly consumed by the graph: the matrix is the datagraph. I told you it was a lot of work!

If the datagraph matrix is done, then the graph is easy to render. The matrix is somehow an invisible layer on top of the graph itself. In its simplest form, every cell is either 0 or 1. Visually speaking, Figure 3-25 shows what I mean.

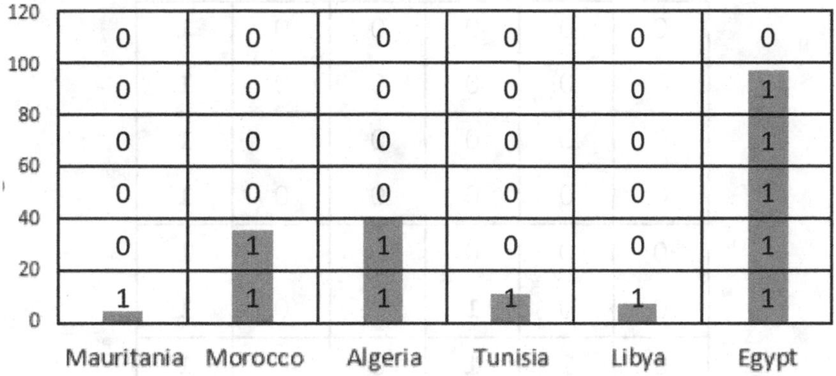

Figure 3-25. *A matrix (or datagraph) is a numerical description of the graph*

In our case, the y axis will span from 0 to 100, subdivided into 10 steps. Therefore, yi, the y coordinate of the variable i, is obtained by applying this simple formula:

$$y_i = upper \left(\frac{P_i}{P_{max}} * 10 \right)$$

where $i \in$ {MAU, MOR, ALG, TUN, EGY}.

Then, after we round the results to one decimal and elevate them to the upper integer, our values will look like Table 3-1.

Table 3-1. *Ratios and Approximated Values*

i	p_i	y_i
Mauritania	4,42	0,5 → **1**
Morocco	37,7	3,7 → **4**
Algeria	41,3	4,2 → **5**
Tunisia	11,5	1,2 → **2**
Libya	6,37	0,7 → **1**
Egypt	97,6	10,0 → **10**

Thus, the matrix of the horizontal graph can be easily concluded, as shown in Figure 3-26.

0	0	0	0	0	**1**
0	0	0	0	0	**1**
0	0	0	0	0	**1**
0	0	0	0	0	**1**
0	0	0	0	0	**1**
0	0	**1**	0	0	**1**
0	**1**	**1**	0	0	**1**
0	**1**	**1**	0	0	**1**
0	**1**	**1**	**1**	0	**1**
1	**1**	**1**	**1**	**1**	**1**
MAU	MOR	ALG	TUN	LIB	EGY

Figure 3-26. *This is the matrix; this is the datagraph!*

The datagraph of the horizontal chart can be obtained by simply turning the previous matrix to the right, so we get Figure 3-27.

MAU	**1**	0	0	0	0	0	0	0	0	0
MOR	**1**	**1**	**1**	**1**	0	0	0	0	0	0
ALG	**1**	**1**	**1**	**1**	**1**	0	0	0	0	0
TUN	**1**	**1**	0	0	0	0	0	0	0	0
LIB	**1**	0	0	0	0	0	0	0	0	0
EGY	**1**	**1**	**1**	**1**	**1**	**1**	**1**	**1**	**1**	**1**

Figure 3-27. *Datagraph of the horizontal chart*

Let's write an algorithm to reproduce this case in Ring. We start from the `lists` instantiated dynamically by the transformer. We consider only the first variable (Population), and we end up with only one of the two datagraphs, the horizontal one.[70]

First, open the `transformer.ring` file we wrote in the previous section and comment out the lines for printing to the screen using the ? keyword, because we no longer need them. Save the file. Then create a new file called `datagraph.ring` and furnish it with the lines of code[71] shown in Listing 3-21.

Listing 3-21. datagraph.ring

```
// Loading data from Ring lists
load "transformer.ring"

// Reminder: Just to have the dataset under our eyies:
# aData =
# [
#                 [ :CNTRY,  :POP, :GRO,  :MED,  :DEN ],
#                 [  :MAU,  4.42, 2.73, 19.70,  4.29 ],
#                 [  :MOR, 35.70, 1.30, 27.90, 80.10 ],
#                 [  :ALG, 41.30, 1.74, 27.50, 17.30 ],
#                 [  :TUN, 11.50, 1.12, 31.10, 74.20 ],
#                 [  :LIB,  6.37, 1.28, 27.20,  3.62 ],
#                 [  :EGY, 97.60, 1.93, 24.70, 98.00 ]
# ]

// Generating the Datagraph of Population variable
# Will be generated in the following list of lists:
aDatagraph = []
# Final result should be:
```

---

[70]It is always a good idea to simplify the problem at hand by focusing on one case and try to solve it. In algorithmic thinking, this is called a *divide-and-conquer* strategy that we rely on a lot in this book.

[71]I intentionally provided detailed comments of the code so you can get an idea of how I'm thinking of the steps necessary to solve the whole problem. In the real world, I don't encourage you to comment as much, because if your code is not self-explanatory, then maybe you have a weakness in your thinking.

```
# aDatagraph = [
#             [ 0, 0, 0, 0, 0, 1 ],
#             [ 0, 0, 0, 0, 0, 1 ],
#             [ 0, 0, 0, 0, 0, 1 ],
#             [ 0, 0, 0, 0, 0, 1 ],
#             [ 0, 0, 0, 0, 0, 1 ],
#             [ 0, 0, 1, 0, 0, 1 ],
#             [ 0, 1, 1, 0, 0, 1 ],
#             [ 0, 1, 1, 0, 0, 1 ],
#             [ 0, 1, 1, 1, 0, 1 ],
#             [ 1, 1, 1, 1, 1, 1 ]
# ]
```

```
# The number of "1"s (cells containing 1 in the matrix) for
# each country (record) is defined by this formula:
#     y(i)= upper( POP(i)/POP(max) *10 )
#             -> upper is the ceil() function in Ring
#             Example: y(ALG) = ceil((41.3 / 97.6) * 10) = 5
#     Result must be contained in this indexed list:
aPOP = []
# aPOP Shoud be:
#     [:MAU=1, :MOR=4, :ALG=5, :TUN=2, :LIB=1, :EGY=10]
#     And you read it like this:
#     Given that a single vertical bar is formed of 10 cells
#     The vertical bar of MAU -> 1 cell containing "1" each
#     ""      ""      "" of MOR -> 4 cells     ""          ""
#     ""      ""      "" of ALG -> 5 cells     ""          ""
#     ""      ""      "" of TUN -> 2 cells     ""          ""
#     ""      ""      "" of LIB -> 1 cell      ""          ""
#     ""      ""      "" of EGY -> 10 cells    ""          ""
#     All the others are containing "0"s.
```

// Calculating the maximum value of Population, ymax

```
ymax = aData[2][2] // setting default value at the 1st one
for y=2 to 7 // 7 is len(aData), line 1 is excluded because 55
// it corresponds to names of countries
```

```
        if aData[y][2] > ymax
               ymax = aData[y][2]
        end
next y
```

// Definining number of cells containing "1"s in every bar

```
for y=2 to 7
        nPop = aData[y][2]
        yi = ceil( (nPop/ymax) * 10)
        aPOP + [ aData[y][1], yi ]
next y
#->Gives aPOP=[:MAU=1,:MOR=4,:ALG=5,:TUN=2,:LIB=1,:EGY=10]
```

// Generating the datagraph of the population variable

```
# Remember: aPOP tells us about the "1"s in the matrix
# What we need to do, is to inject these "1"s in an empty
# matrix (full of "0"s)
# Let's start with an empty matrix
aDatagraph = []
for i=1 to 10
        aDatagraph + [ "0", "0", "0", "0", "0", "0" ]
next i
# Now we have aDatagraph containing:
#       [ 0, 0, 0, 0, 0, 0 ],
#       [ 0, 0, 0, 0, 0, 0 ],
#       [ 0, 0, 0, 0, 0, 0 ],
#       [ 0, 0, 0, 0, 0, 0 ],
#       [ 0, 0, 0, 0, 0, 0 ],
#       [ 0, 0, 0, 0, 0, 0 ],
#       [ 0, 0, 0, 0, 0, 0 ],
#       [ 0, 0, 0, 0, 0, 0 ],
#       [ 0, 0, 0, 0, 0, 0 ],
#       [ 0, 0, 0, 0, 0, 0 ]
```

```
// Next we inject the "1"s of aPOP in the aDatagraph matrix
# Remember aPOP=[:MAU=1,:MOR=4,:ALG=5,:TUN=2,:LIB=1,:EGY=10]
for x=1 to 6 // Number of countries
      n = 10 - (aPOP[x][2]) + 1
      for y = n to 10
            aDatagraph[y][x] = "1"
      next y
next x

# Now we have our final aDatagraph containing:
#      [ 0, 0, 0, 0, 0, 1 ],
#      [ 0, 0, 0, 0, 0, 1 ],
#      [ 0, 0, 0, 0, 0, 1 ],
#      [ 0, 0, 0, 0, 0, 1 ],
#      [ 0, 0, 0, 0, 0, 1 ],
#      [ 0, 0, 1, 0, 0, 1 ],
#      [ 0, 1, 1, 0, 0, 1 ],
#      [ 0, 1, 1, 0, 0, 1 ],
#      [ 0, 1, 1, 1, 0, 1 ],
#      [ 1, 1, 1, 1, 1, 1 ]

// To test it you show every horizontal line and see
// if you are right:
? aDatagraph[5]
#      should give a list of "0"s except the
#      last cell which is "1", while
? aDatagraph[10]
#      should give a list of 10 "1"s
```

After testing the result, comment out the lines containing the output to the screen using the ? keyword; we no longer need them. We can use the same logic for the remaining variables (population growth, median age, and population density). I will learn it for you as homework. For the moment, we can congratulate ourselves for accomplishing step 6 of our script. What remains is to show the bar chart. For that, we program the chart-rendering feature in a new chartRenderer.ring file.

Rendering the Graph Inside a Text String

Now for step 6 of the seven steps we're working on.

As requested at the end of the previous section, create a new file called chartRenderer.ring in the same working folder of NorthAfricaApp.

The chart renderer will simply parse the datagraph hosted in the Datagraph matrix and print it in a string that we can show on the screen. We start by loading the datagraph we created in the previous step. Then we parse it to form the resulting string of the chart line by line. For that, you can add a legend and a title, as shown in Listing 3-22.

Listing 3-22. chartRenderer.ring

```
// Loading the datagraph matrix
load "datagraph.ring"
# Reminder: our aDatagraph contains:
# [ 0, 0, 0, 0, 0, 1 ],
# [ 0, 0, 0, 0, 0, 1 ],
# [ 0, 0, 0, 0, 0, 1 ],
# [ 0, 0, 0, 0, 0, 1 ],
# [ 0, 0, 0, 0, 0, 1 ],
# [ 0, 0, 1, 0, 0, 1 ],
# [ 0, 1, 1, 0, 0, 1 ],
# [ 0, 1, 1, 0, 0, 1 ],
# [ 0, 1, 1, 1, 0, 1 ],
# [ 1, 1, 1, 1, 1, 1 ]

cGraph = ""

// Constituting the graph string cGraph
for y = 1 to len(aDatagraph) // =10
     cGraph += spc(1) + graphline(y) + NL
next y

cGraph += graphlabels()

// Showing the graph on the screen
? cGraph
```

```
// Functions (Take your time to study them by yourself)
     func graphline( n )
            aLine = aDatagraph[n]
            cLine = ""
            for i=1 to len(aLine) // =6
                 if aLine[i] = 0
                       cline += "."
                 but aLine[i] = 1
                       cLine += ."I"
                 ok
                 cLine += spc(3)
            next i
            return trim(cLine)

     func graphlabels()
            cLabels = ""
            aLabels = countries()
            for i=1 to len(aLabels)
                 cLabels += aLabels[i] + spc(1)
            next i
            return trim(cLabels)

     func spc(n)
            str = ""
            for i=1 to n
                 str += " "
            next i
            return str
```

If everything is done right, then what you see in the output window when you run the chartRenderer.ring program will look like Figure 3-28.

```
  .    .    .    .    .    I
  .    .    .    .    .    I
  .    .    .    .    .    I
  .    .    .    .    .    I
  .    .    .    .    .    I
  .    .    I    .    .    I
  .    I    I    .    .    I
  .    I    I    .    .    I
  .    I    I    I    .    I
  I    I    I    I    I    I
 MAU  MOR  ALG  TUN  LIB  EGY
```

Figure 3-28. *Our bar chart in the Output panel, a little bit simpler than what we dreamed of but still beautifully scribbled in the Output window*[72]

What about the second chart, the horizontal one? Well, it requires another version of chartRenderer.ring and may be another version of datagraph.ring. It depends on the strategy you adopt and the level of SoC[73] you adhere to. But, in all cases, the initial data in data.txt remains the same. The transformer.ring file also remains the same whatever graph you want to design. And if you need a version of a given bar chart for a specific platform, a smartphone for example, then only one file must be changed: chartRenderer.ring. Things are crystal clear; you are just rendering the same chart to a different platform. Other programmers who are fond of the Tunisian shakshuka[74] may change everything they did and start from scratch. But you, no, because you've done it, you've "committed" your first clean design in Ring!

What if you make this second horizontal chart by yourself? You will gain a lot of knowledge while trying even when (and mainly when) you don't succeed.

Now we move to another strategic type of input you should have in your skillset of programming in Ring: inputs from a database.

---

[72]In a real-world application, I would rather use a QChart widget from the Qt framework (which is not supported yet in the current version we are working on in the book) or simply use QProgressbar like this example in the Ring documentation: https://tinyurl.com/up8axhk.

[73]Do you remember what SoC stands for? Yes, separation of concerns.

[74]We talked of shakshuka in the first chapter. It's the Tunisian flavor of the Italian "spaghetti code."

Inputs from the Database

A database is a physical store of data. Your programing language can only open a connection to it, read some data from it, record some data in it, and finally close the connection with it. Outside these windows of possibilities, when you need advanced actions such as searching and filtering, then you must talk in the language of the database plus of your programming language. The Structured Query Language (SQL), being the ultimate standard language of databases, should be learned. But this is not our focus in this book.

In this section, you'll learn how to connect to a SQLite database in Ring (after creating it and storing our data in it, of course) while using that data to show the same bar chart we crafted in the previous section.

The main thing to consider when working with databases is that they are structured in tables. A table is a datasheet, like those we have in Excel, with a number of well-defined columns and a set of data records with a vector of data related to every column. Designing a database means creating tables and, for every table, specifying its structure by specifying its columns. All that remains is to fill the tables with data and read it back when needed.

Connecting to a SQLite Database

We start by creating a new file called database.ring and save it to the NorthAfricaApp folder. The steps to go through in our program are simple:

1. Loading the sqlitelib.ring library containing the necessary functions to deal with a SQLite database in Ring

2. Initializing the database using sqlite_init() and opening a connection to it using sqlite_open()

3. Writing the SQL queries[75] for designing the database structure, inserting data in the database, and executing these queries against the database using sqlite_execute()

4. Writing a SQL query that selects data from the database and showing it on the screen

---

[75]A SQL query is a single command written in SQL, the ultimate "programming language" for interacting with data stored in databases. Contrary to imperative programming languages like Python, Java, and C#, SQL is declarative, in that it allows us to describe the result we want to have. Ring is both imperative and declarative (more on this later).

Listing 3-23 shows the complete code you should write in the database.ring file.

Listing 3-23. database.ring

```
load "stdlib.ring"    # Contains code to manage databases
// Importing the Ring libraray
load "sqlitelib.ring"
// Creating an object containing an instance
// of a SQLite database
oSQLite = sqlite_init()
// Creating the database pysically in the current folder
sqlite_open( oSQLite, "northafrica.db" )
    # => the database is created but still empty
// Desining the structure of the database
sql = "
        CREATE TABLE COUNTRY (
                CNTRY TEXT NOT NULL,
                POP REAL NOT NULL,
                GRO REAL NOT NULL,
                MED REAL NOT NULL,
                DEN REAL NOT NULL );
        "
sqlite_execute(oSQLite,sql)
    # => the database contains a COUNTRY table
    # but is still empty
// Filling the database with data
sql = "
    INSERT INTO COUNTRY
    ( CNTRY, POP, GRO, MED, DEN )
    VALUES
    ( 'MAU', 4.42, 2.73, 19.70, 4.29),
    ( 'MAR', 35.70, 1.30, 27.90, 80.10),
    ( 'ALG', 41.30, 1.74, 27.50, 17.30),
    ( 'TUN', 11.50, 1.12, 31.10, 74.20),
    ( 'LIB', 6.37, 1.28, 27.20, 3.62),
    ( 'EGY', 97.60, 1.93, 24.70, 98.00);
    "
```

```
sqlite_execute( oSQLite, sql )
    # => the data is there in the database
// Reading the data back from the database
sql = "SELECT * FROM COUNTRY"
aResult = sqlite_execute( oSQLite, sql )
// Showing the result on screen
? aResult
```

Excellent. It is sufficient now to verify that it works. We will come back to aResult in "Adapting the Connector to the Database" to understand its structure and see whether it needs some help to cope with the format we agreed on for the datagraph. Now, using both text and a database to feed the graph invites us to reflect on the architecture of the NorthAfricaApp.

Designing a Clean Data Acquisition Architecture

Before we go further, there is a design reflection we need to make about the overall architecture of our NorthAfricaApp. To show the point, let's craft a visual representation reflecting what we have done until now, as shown in Figure 3-29.

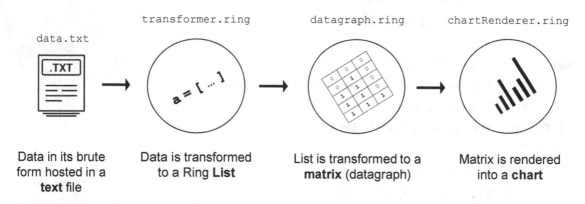

Figure 3-29. *A visual design of the actual data acquisition and tranformation solution*

Our system begins with a data hosted in a structured text file, which is transformed to a native Ring List to make it programmable. Then we compute that data into a matrix (datagraph) to prepare it for rendering without hassle. Finally, the matrix is parsed and rendered in a bar chart contained in a native Ring String. The string is shown on the screen.

Despite its clarity, Figure 3-29 shows the most important value of our architecture: reusability and ease of extension. Indeed, with the system we designed, as I said before, making new graphs (a pie chart or a comparative bar chart, for example) won't require[76] more than providing a new datagraph with a new renderer (while reusing the same data source and the same transformer). At the same time, adapting a given graph to different platforms can be done by providing a specific renderer for each platform (while reusing the same datagraph, transformer, and data source). Such gains are better represented if the visual is modified to look like Figure 3-30.

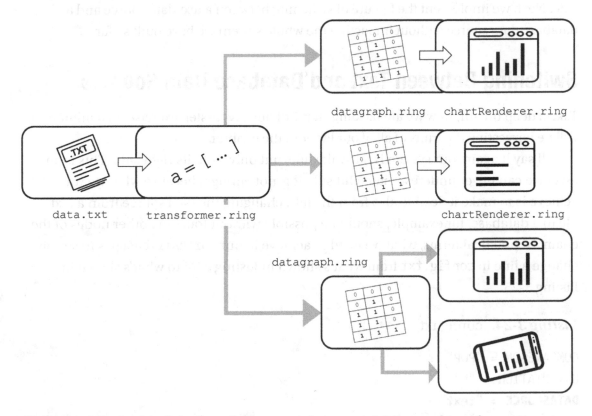

Figure 3-30. *A visual design of the target data acquisition and tranformation solution*

---

[76]On the GUI side, this will require more than a text string to render the graph as we did in this basic tutorial. As mentioned earlier, the QChart widget, when added to the Form Designer's Toolbox, will offer a nice solution to this requirement. Maybe the Ring team will add it for us when they learn we are in need.

At the bottom in the figure, in particular, the same `datagraph.ring` file has been used to render a bar chart in two different platforms, a web browser and a mobile phone. In real-world projects, this decision can be motivated by the fact that the rendering technology used on both platforms is the same: a cross-platform web engine, like WebKit,[77] for example (on which Qt WebView and by consequence the Ring Form Designer `WebView` widget are based) running on a desktop and also on mobile devices.[78]

What we are concerned with in this chapter, however, is data input, so let's stay focused on achieving extensibility on the left side of the architecture and not on its right side. Next, we implement the feature of switching between a text data source and a database data source without impacting the whole system we have built so far.

Switching Between Text and Database Data Sources

Take a deep breath; now we are tackling step 7 of our seven-step exercise. In a minute we will be harvesting the fruits of all of our labor in the chapter.

I'll say it again: our system is fairly flexible, but only from its right side. This is an asset we can never underestimate. But still, it is not enough, because what we want to achieve is to make it flexible also from the left: changing the data source from a text file to a database, for example, should be possible without touching other nodes of the chain. In practical terms, what we need to achieve in our `NorthAfricaApp` is to simply change a line in `config.txt` from what's shown in Listing 3-24 to what's shown in Listing 3-25.

Listing 3-24. config.txt

```
COMPARE-ON = "POP"
ORIENTATION = "H"
DATASOURCE = "text"
```

---

[77]WebKit is a browser engine developed by Apple to be used by web browsers but also included in desktop and mobile applications to render web pages: `https://webkit.org`.

[78]This can be achieved in the Form Designer using the `WebView` widget or by code using the `QWebView` class of the `GuiLib` library. Here you find an example of how it is used: `http://ring-lang.sourceforge.net/doc1.11/qt.html?#using-qwebview`.

Listing 3-25. config.txt

```
COMPARE-ON = "POP"
ORIENTATION = "H"
DATASOURCE = "database"
```

Our bar chart should be there with the same data displayed on the screen, but coming this time from a database and not a text file and without being impacted by the fundamental change of data source we've just made. Think about it for a while: how exactly can we make it happen?

Well, many answers are possible. The one that first comes to my mind is to adapt the first three lines of transformer.ring by removing the code responsible for connecting a text file and replacing it with code connecting to a database. This means that a transformer must be written to every data source. You can go for it, but one can argue that there will be a cost. Think of the situation where your system contains 30 transformers for 10 different data sources and the logic of transformation itself needs to be changed. Your cost can be devided by 10^{79} if you had only one place that does transformation independently from the data source. Right?

An intermediate node between the data source and the transformer would then be necessary. I'll call it the universal data connector; it's the code that effectively connects to a data source, whatever this data source is, and delivers an abstract data format to the transformer whose job is transformation. Visually speaking, the whole system architecture would look like Figure 3-31.

---

[79]Theoretically, but in reality, you gain more or less depending on the situation.

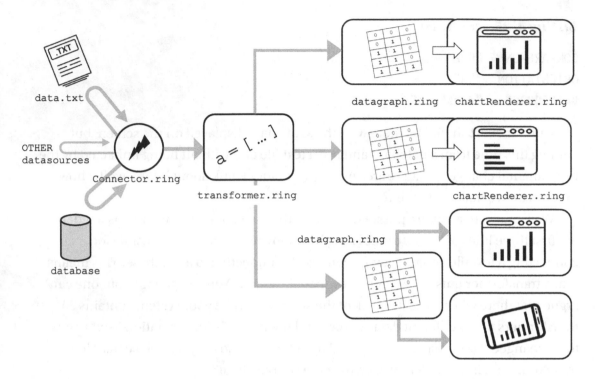

Figure 3-31. *The solution design, made flexible from the right side (multiple data format input)*

Without delay, let's experiment with this design option by implementing a universal data connector in Ring.

Implementing a Universal Data Connector

The first thing we should do is to go back to `transformer.ring` and see how we can refactor it so the specific part of connecting to a text data source, indicated as (1) in Figure 3-32, is separated from the part of transformation itself (2).

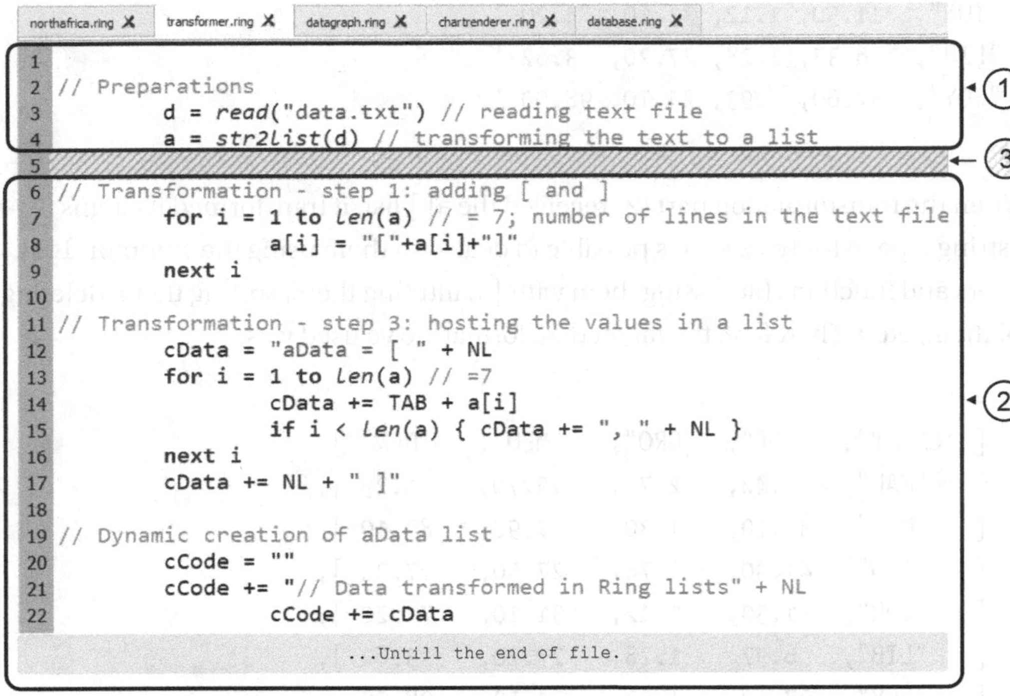

Figure 3-32. *Refactoring the transformer by separating two concerns: connection and tranformation*

For the separation to be effective, a particular focus should be put on the zone in between (3). In fact, this zone stimulates us to ask an important question: what is the intermediary data that format zone (2) needs to be fed so it does its job without caring about how zone (1) is working?

If we are to maintain the same data format we opted to use for the text files (in the section "Transforming Text Data into a Ring List"), then the transformation zone (2) would need a List of seven lines of strings, where the first line corresponds to the names of variables, and the remaining six lines of strings contain the data records, one country per line, like this:

```
a =
[
    ' "CNTRY","POP", "GRO","MED", "DEN" ' ,
    ' "MAU",    4.42, 2.73, 19.70,  4.29 ' ,
    ' "MOR",   35.70, 1.30, 27.90, 80.10 ' ,
    ' "ALG",   41.30, 1.74, 27.50, 17.30 ' ,
```

```
'  "TUN",   11.50, 1.12, 31.10, 74.20 '  ,
'  "LIB",    6.37, 1.28, 27.20,  3.62 '  ,
'  "EGY",   97.60, 1.93, 24.70, 98.00 '
]
```

When the transformation part (2) received the a[ ] list, it transformed its items from string type to list type, so it is possible to deal with them using the common list operators and functions (accessing them with [ ], filtering them, sorting them, deleting one of them, etc.). Therefore, the target data format we've used was:

```
aData =
[     [ "CNTRY",  "POP",  "GRO",   "MED",   "DEN" ],
      [  "MAU",   4.42,  2.73,  19.70,   4.29 ],
      [  "MOR",  35.70,  1.30,  27.90,  80.10 ],
      [  "ALG",  41.30,  1.74,  27.50,  17.30 ],
      [  "TUN",  11.50,  1.12,  31.10,  74.20 ],
      [  "LIB",   6.37,  1.28,  27.20,   3.62 ],
      [  "EGY",  97.60,  1.93,  24.70,  98.00 ]
]
```

We went back to these details because it is always useful to develop a memorable mental model of the system in hand before you undertake any refactoring that impacts its structure. In particular, the first criteria of a successful separation of concerns, like the one we are planning to make here, is to get the same result as before while enhancing the organization of the program parts.

Another thing you should always remember is the goal of the refactoring project itself, expressed in terms of the value you will gain. This is easy to lose, like a needle in a haystack, owing to the throng of technical details and sometimes because of feelings of anxiety and puzzling frustration. In our case, the refactoring is made to allow us to diversify our data sources while keeping untouched the same chain of operations coming after the connection staff: transformation and rendering of the final chart.

Figure 3-33 summarizes where we are and what we should do.

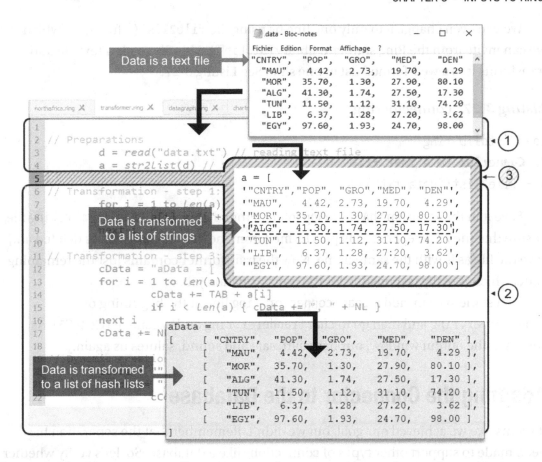

Figure 3-33. *Necessary work to separate the connection and transformation concerns*

Therefore, let's "disconnect" the connection part from the transformation part in this `transformer.ring` file by creating a new file called `connector.ring` (see Listing 3-26) that is responsible solely for connecting to the `data.txt` data source and returning the same `a[]` list.

Listing 3-26. connector.ring

```
// Connecting to a text file
d = read("data.txt") // reading text file
a = str2list(d) // transforming the text to a list
```

We can even change it to only one line by using the `file2list()` function, which we can invite from the Ring standard library (StdLib[80]). This file reads a text file and transforms it to a well-formed list in one shot. See Listing 3-27.

Listing 3-27. connector.ring

```
Load "stdlib.ring"
// Connector to a text file
a = file2list("data.txt")
```

Save it in the same `NorthAfricaApp` folder. From the original `transformer.ring` file, ensure that the `// Preparations` part formed from the first three lines was deleted and save the file as is with the same name. Now the transformer contains just the remaining code, which is really responsible for the transformation job.

To test the system, add a `load connector.ring` line at the beginning of `transformer.ring` and then go to `chartrenderer.ring` and execute it (Ctrl+F5). As shown in the output window, our bar chart, safe and sound, salutes us again.

Adapting the Connector to the Database

It seems like we achieved our goal, but we didn't. Remember that the separation has been made to support other types of connections like a database. So, let's verify whether the data structure returned by the database connection obeys the same format returned by the connection to the text file.

From the previous code we wrote in the `database.ring` file against the `northafrica.db` SQLite database, the lines shown in Figure 3-33 create the `aResult[]` list. See Listing 3-28.

---

[80]It is important to understand what this standard library contains. To do so, open the file `stdlib.ring` in the `c:\ring\ringlibs\stdlib` folder or consult it online in GitHub at this address: `https://tinyurl.com/vqv5nqx`. There you'll find that it is formed of two sublibraries, `StdClasses` and `StdLibCore`, and a bunch of classes for supporting various database systems and Internet protocols (ODBC, SQL, SqlLite, PostgresLib, InternetLib, and OpenSSL). In particular, `StdClasses` is used to load common classes required by Ring (discover them here: `https://tinyurl.com/sj7yrk8`), and `StdLibCore` is used for loading common functions (discover them here: `https://tinyurl.com/tetj2b6`). Always do this exercise and benefit from Ring being open source to understand how it is designed.

Listing 3-28. Part of database.ring

```
// Reading the data
sql = "SELECT * FROM COUNTRY"
aResult = sqlite_execute( oSQLite, sql )

// Showing the result
? aResult
```

Go back to the file (`database.ring`), execute it again, and contemplate the content of aResult in the Output window to try to figure out what is the exact structure of that list. Because the way the list is "vertically" visualized does not help in understanding its deep structure, try to craft a mental representation[81] of it by playing like this:

- Run aResult[1] to show the first element of the list.

- For the first element, show its first and second elements by trying aResult[1][1] and aResult[1][2], respectively.

- Do the same with other numbers from 1 to 6.

There is a particular function in the standard library called list2code() that could also help, because it translates a list at runtime to its corresponding Ring representation. But unfortunately, the way it is rendering the result, vertically, one element per line, doesn't help either to visually infer the structure of the list. Try it if you want:

- In database.ring, replace the last line of ? aResult with ? list2code(aResult).

- Execute the file to show the result in the Output window.

Anyway, after many trials, you should be able to discover that aResult[], the list returned from the connection to the SQLite database, is in fact a list of lists of lists. In simpler terms, it is a list with a depth of level 3. Such a structure can be expressively written with a taste of hash list sugar, like this:

---

[81]I think the visual display of a deep list should be enhanced in Ring. I hope that the Ring team will take this into consideration.

```
aResut = [
 [ :CNTRY='MAU', :POP=4.42, :GRO=2.73, :MED=19.7, :DEN=4.29 ],
 [ :CNTRY='MAR', :POP=4.42, :GRO=2.73, :MED=19.7, :DEN=4.29 ],
 [ :CNTRY='ALG', :POP=4.42, :GRO=2.73, :MED=19.7, :DEN=4.29 ],
 [ :CNTRY='TUN', :POP=4.42, :GRO=2.73, :MED=19.7, :DEN=4.29 ],
 [ :CNTRY='LIB', :POP=4.42, :GRO=2.73, :MED=19.7, :DEN=4.29 ],
 [ :CNTRY='EGY', :POP=4.42, :GRO=2.73, :MED=19.7, :DEN=4.29 ]
]
```

Clearly, this is a different structure than the one we must provide to our transformation factory in transformer.ring, which is, again, like this:

```
aData =
[       [ "CNTRY",  "POP",  "GRO",  "MED",  "DEN" ],
        [  "MAU",   4.42,   2.73,  19.70,   4.29 ],
        [  "MOR",  35.70,   1.30,  27.90,  80.10 ],
        [  "ALG",  41.30,   1.74,  27.50,  17.30 ],
        [  "TUN",  11.50,   1.12,  31.10,  74.20 ],
        [  "LIB",   6.37,   1.28,  27.20,   3.62 ],
        [  "EGY",  97.60,   1.93,  24.70,  98.00 ]
]
```

Some data format unification work is then necessary!

Unifying the Data Format Delivered by the Connector

If we look to the structure of aResult[ ] as listed in the previous section, compared to the target structure we opted for in the case of the text data source, then two adaptations must be made.

- Variables must be extracted from the first line of the source aResult[ ] and stored as a list in the first line of the target a[ ].

- Data must be extracted from the source aResult[ ], one country per line, and stored sequentially in the target a[ ].

Visually speaking, Figure 3-34 shows what we need to do.

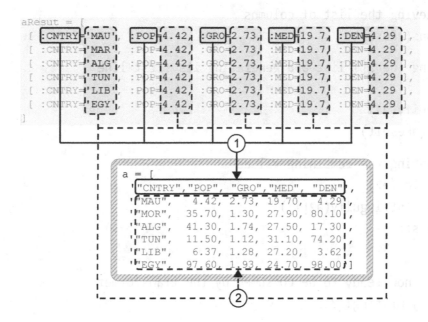

Figure 3-34. *Transforming data into a universal format*

Because our aim in this chapter isn't learning how to make advanced transformation algorithms but acquiring the necessary skills to manage data input into your real-world Ring programs, I will just show you the code I wrote to implement the logic behind Figure 3-34. It is well commented, though, so try to get a sense of it. But before that, create a new file called dbconnector.ring and then start Ringling (see Listing 3-29).

Listing 3-29. dbconnector.ring

```
load "stdlib.ring"
// Connecting to SQLite database
load "sqlitelib.ring"

oSQLite = sqlite_init()
sqlite_open( oSQLite, "northafrica.db" )

// Returning the dataset in the aResult[] list
sql = "SELECT * FROM COUNTRY"
aResult = sqlite_execute( oSQLite, sql )

// Adapting the aResult list to the target format
// compatible with the transformer
```

```
# 1. Retrieving the list of columns
a1 = columns(aResult)

# 2. Setting the a[] list and generating its first line
a = []
a + stringuify(a1)
a2 = lines(aResult)

# 3. Generating the remaining values
for i=1 to len(a2)
        str = stringuify(a2[i])
        a + str
next i

# -> a[] is now ready to be consumed by the transformer
# test it by writing: ? a

// Functions

        # This function transforms a list of strings into
        # a string enclosed inside two commas
        func stringuify(a)
                str = ""
                // Adding "" to every string
                for s in a
                    s = '"' + s + '"'
                next s
                // Adding ","
                for i=1 to len(a)-1
                        if i<len(a)
                                str += a[i] + ", "
                        ok
                next i
                str += a[i]
                return str
```

```
# This function retrieves the names of variables
# in a string with every variable enclosed inside
# two commas : (1) in the figure 3.34
func columns(a)
        aTemp = []
        for i=1 to len(a[1])
                aTemp + a[1][i][1]
        next i
        return aTemp

# This function makes the same job as Columns() but
# with all the values of the dataset : (2) in the figure
func lines(a)
        aLines = []
        aTemp = []
        for i=1 to len(a)
                for v=1 to len(a[v])
                        aTemp + a[i][v][2]
                next v
                aLines + aTemp
                aTemp = []
        next i
        return aLines
```

Save this **db**connector.ring file in the NorthAfricaApp folder. At the same time, go back to the connector.ring file and rename it as **txt**connector.ring. In the NorthAfricaApp folder, physically delete the connector.ring file since we no longer need it. Also, in the same folder, delete the binary file of the SqlLite database, northafrica.db, so we can restart the chain on a clean base.

Tired? I understand. Now we can test everything and see whether the work done about the seventh and last point in the solution script we agreed on at the beginning of the section will be rewarding.

Testing Our Data Acquisition Architecture

You know what? We have reached step 7 in our plan for our refactoring project! Do the following:

1. In `transformer.ring`, change the first line `load "connector.ring"` to `load "`**`txt`**`connector.ring"`.

2. Activate the tab of the `chartRenderer.ring` file (open it again if you closed it) and execute it (Ctrl+F5). Let's look together at the Output window in Ring Notepad and say: "Hello dear chart!"

3. Back in `transformer.ring`, change the first line with **`db`**`connector.ring`.

4. Go to `chartrenderer.ring` again, execute it, and look at the Output window. It says: "Hello dear same chart!"

The bar chart is displayed without structurally changing any file in our pipeline other than specifying the good connection file in `transformer.ring`. We didn't even touch the `datagraph.ring` and `chartRenderer.ring` files. That is awesome, except there's one little detail: the final refinement.

Final Refinement

For our `NorthAfricaApp` to be really clean, a main file should be created and serve as a single point of control to the whole program. The idea is to wisely decide where to call a file from another so the logic flow is correct. Currently, the flow of our program parts (or files) looks like Figure 3-35.

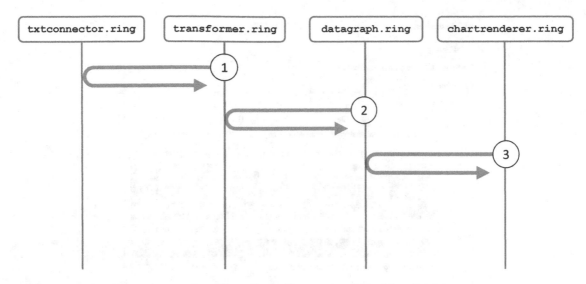

Figure 3-35. *The current loading flow diagram of the NorthAfrica app*

It is not a bad choice right now, but if the system gains in complexity and more calls become necessary, then you, or any reader of your code, might get confused. To avoid this situation, we will relay all the load calls in our program to a single new file. For that, create a new file in the NorthAfricaApp folder and name it, simply, northafrica.ring.

Before you write anything in that file, delete all the load statements you have in all the *.ring files. A nice way to find them is to use the "Find in file" feature in Ring Notepad that you can access by selecting Menu ➤ Edit ➤ Find in files. Enter **load** in the search field, browse to the NorthAfricaApp folder, and hit Search or hit Enter on the keyboard to display the window in Figure 3-36.

Figure 3-36. *Finding files in Ring folders*

Note that I have highlighted some files (`connector.ring`, `database.ring`, and `tempo.ring`). They are not needed, so it is better to delete them from the NorthAfricaApp folder (clean is clean, isn't it?).

After all the `loads` are deleted (except those that are specific to loading `StdLib` and `SqlLiteLib` libraries), open "Find in files" and perform the same search to ensure you have no unwanted results and something was not left behind.

Inside `northafrica.ring`, write the code in Listing 3-30.

Listing 3-30. northAfrica.ring

```
load "txtconnector.ring"
load "transformer.ring"
load "datagraph.ring"
load "chartrenderer.ring"
```

Execute it (`northAfrica.ring`). It's functional.

Personally, I would go a little further to establish a semantic meaning for this piece of code. In fact, calling the datagraph and the transformer are two specific functions I can delegate to the chart renderer. So, I cut the load "transformer.ring" and load "datagraph.ring" lines from the current northafrica.ring file and paste them at the beginning of chartRenderer.ring. I test the app, and I find that everything is OK.

Also, I would encapsulate the chart display feature in a function inside chartRenderer.ring and name it showchart(). See Listing 3-31 (the lines in bold are the added lines to the file).

Listing 3-31. Part of chartRenderer.ring

```
load "transformer.ring"
load "datagraph.ring"

func showgraph()
        cGraph = ""
        // Constituting the graph string cGraph
        for y = 1 to len(aDatagraph) // =10
                cGraph += spc(1) + graphline(y) + NL
        next y
        cGraph += graphlabels()
        // Showing the graph on the screen
        ? cGraph
```

Then I call it from the main file after the chartRenderer.ring file is loaded. My final content of the northafrica.ring file looks like Listing 3-32.

Listing 3-32. northAfrica.ring

```
load "txtconnector.ring"
load "chartrenderer.ring"

showgraph()
```

Tell me that it wasn't that beautiful, and I'll feel disappointed. If so, this is your penalty: create a new file called `chartPrepare.ring` that does the following:

1. Read the default data source from the `config.txt` file.

2. Call the **txt**`connector.ring` file if `DATASOURCE="`**text**`"` and call **db**`connector.ring` if `DATASOURCE="`**database**`"`.

3. In the main `northafrica.ring` file, replace the first line `load` `"`**txt**`connector.ring"` (or `"`**db**`connector.ring"` if you changed it) with `load "`**chartprepare**`.ring"`.

Frankly, your final `northafrica.ring` file is more expressive than mine; see Listing 3-33.

Listing 3-33. northAfrica.ring

```
load "chartPrepare.ring"
load "chartRenderer.ring"

showGraph()
```

Other Inputs

Today's software deals with emerging forms of inputs you should be concerned with. In this section, I won't really help you because I'll just cite them, with an indication or a little example. It's up to you to make an effort and learn more.

- Inputs from the Web (HTML pages) and the Internet APIs (HTTP requests)

- Inputs from binary files (images, voice, etc.)

- Inputs from XML files

- Inputs from Office software (Microsoft Word and Excel)

- Inputs from legacy business software suites (SAP BAPI or Salesforce API)

- Inputs from gestures on the screen of a mobile phone and from body gestures in front of the Xbox gaming console

Summary

Even if you decide not to go deeper with this connectivity forest (after all, you are learning how to program and not how to make a gigantic data acquisition and analytics engine[82]), rest assured: this chapter gave you the skills you need to deal with the most common input scenarios you may encounter in your real software projects. So please, don't move on if this chapter is not 100 percent mastered.[83] Read it again, write your own version of the code, and if you can, design a whole new clean architecture, with a different number of layers, other data formats, and more connections.

It is Sunday, July 28, 2019: Tunisia and Cameroon are to vie for the men's African Nations title in volleyball. Guaranteed, it will be a hot competition between the Falcons of Carthage and the Lions of Africa! Can I leave, please?

---

[82]Despite that, and in all modesty, what we made together during the chapter is the foundation of any system of the sort meant to manage data in enterprise systems. As a Ring programmer, this will give you a substantial advantage in understanding such challenges and be prepared to tackle them in the real world.

[83]Or, at least, 99 percent.

SUMMARY

CHAPTER 4

Outputs of Ring

When you speak, you are emitting a voice in the air that is understandable by the audience. When you move, you are performing an animation of your body in the space that is observable by the attendees. When you code, you are exposing the data resulting from your computer thinking through a medium that is perceivable by the user of your program.

In this chapter, I will show you how Ring can display data on a screen and save it to a file, in a database, on a web page, and even in a printable document.

To do so, we will build on the `NorthAfricaApp` project we created in Chapter 3 and augment it with new capabilities other than simply "rendering" data in a `string` variable.

Nine Things You Will Learn

In this chapter, you'll do the following:

- Perform data outputs in Ring in many formats

- Analyze an existing codebase

- Design a clean layered software architecture in Ring

- Change the core keywords and operators of the language

- Use BASIC syntax in Ring programs

- Write HTML pages in Ring

- Use a Qt widget to render PDF files in Ring

- Write text files and copy binary files

- Handle errors and exceptions

191

© Mansour Ayouni 2020
M. Ayouni, *Beginning Ring Programming*, https://doi.org/10.1007/978-1-4842-5833-0_4

Before We Start

To start with a clean base, download the zipped file of the NorthAfricaApp project available online[1] or on the book's page on the Apress web site, extract the folder under c:\ringbook\chap4, rename the folder to northAfricaAppV2, and then open the Project Files explorer in Ring Notepad using the menu View ➤ Project Files (Ctrl+J) if it is not open yet. Browse the tree view until you reach the folder you just downloaded, as shown in Figure 4-1. Then select the northafrica.ring file to open it in the Code Editor.

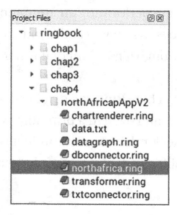

Figure 4-1. *Project Files explorer in Ring Notepad*

Every time you have a programming project (an application with many files), create a folder for it (usually with the name of the app itself), and then use the Project Files explorer to get the following advantages:

- All your files are visible in one place while you are programming.

- You can go back and forth between your files instantaneously.

- When you want to add a new file to your project, the current folder is selected by default so you just need to enter the name and click the Save button.

Let's create a tempo.ring file and add it to the project. To do so, be sure that one of the files in the northAfricaV2 folder (or the folder itself) is selected in the Project Files explorer. Then select File ➤ New (Ctrl+N) in the main menu of Ring Notepad. When the

---

[1]https://tinyurl.com/u55gajp

window shown in Figure 4-2 is displayed, type **tempo** (without .ring because it will be added automatically) and click Save.

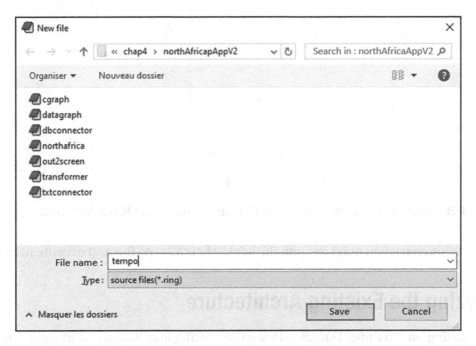

Figure 4-2. *Adding a new file to the northAfricaAppV2 project*

The file tempo.ring is then added to the folder in the Project Files tree view and opened in the Code Editor.

Refactoring the Right Side

Sam and Dan are two programmers on the NorthAfricaApp team. Sam was the original designer of the app, but he is going on vacation.[2] Dan is selected to implement a future enhancement. He will power-charge the app so it can expose the generated graph on several platforms: the screen, a text file, a database, a web page, and a printable file.

---

[2]Dan travels to Tunisia, the land of one of the most influential towns in human history: Carthage. Also, this nation gave to the world Hannibal, the general and statesman who is widely considered as one of the greatest military commanders in history. Here is a 10-minute video (in French) that reconstructs the town in 3D: https://tinyurl.com/tm6pokg.

As a reminder from what we've done in Chapter 3, Figure 4-3 shows the graph as displayed in the Output window of Ring Notepad.

Figure 4-3. *The chart displayed in the Output window in Ring Notepad*

To get this chart, you need to open the northafrica.ring file and execute it, that's it.

Analyzing the Existing Architecture

Before starting on anything, Dan asks to see the existing architecture of the app. Sam answers him by showing him the diagram in Figure 4-4.

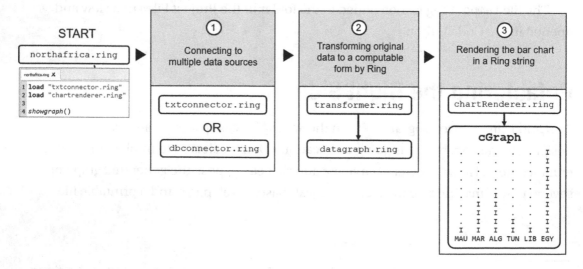

Figure 4-4. *Original architecture of the NorthAfricaApp*

This is the conversation Sam and Dan have:

- **Sam**: As you see, everything starts with the `NorthAfrica.ring` file where the call flow is defined. Then, the three layers of the app architecture are executed chronologically.

  In the first layer (1), a connection with the data source, being a text file or a database, is created.

  Then, the returned data is transformed in layer (2) to a data structure (a Ring `list` called `aDatagraph`) that describes the graph content and simplifies its future rendering in layer (3).

  Finally, layer (3) receives the datagraph, parses it, and renders it in a Ring `string` called `cGraph`. The string is used to show the graph on the screen (in the Output window in Ring Notepad).

  Is the app architecture understood? And your mission clear enough?

- **Dan**: Yeah. I've been called on to take the same agility you made on the left side regarding multiple data input (in the previous chapter) and implement it on the right side by allowing multiple data output.

- **Sam**: Exactly! I'm thrilled to know how you are going to approach that architecturally.

- **Dan**: Thank you, Sam, that seems great. But, before that, I need to look closely to how your architecture design (shown in Figure 4-4) has been implemented in terms of Ring files and `load` statements. This is fundamental to assessing whether the diagram accurately reflects the reality of what you've done in the code.

- **Sam**: OK. Let's browse the codebase together. See Figure 4-5.

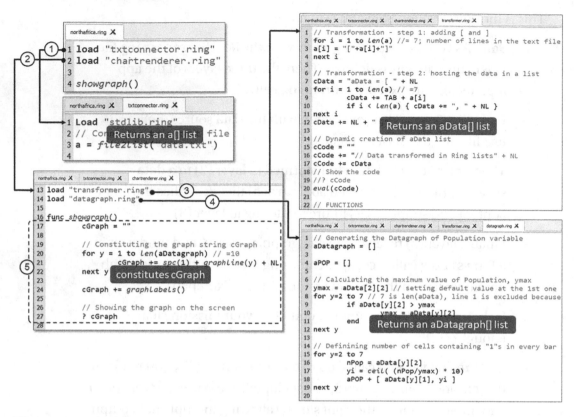

Figure 4-5. *Implementation in Ring of the program architecture shown in Figure 4-4*

- **Sam**: As you can see, the program execution starts in the file northafrica.ring by loading the connector, which is the txtconnector.ring file (1). But you can call the dbconnector. ring file instead, if you want. Whatever data source you specify, the connection returns a data structure hosted in an a[] list.

  Then the chartRenderer.ring file is loaded (2). At the beginning of this file, transformer.ring is loaded (3). The transformer works on the a[] dataset and transforms it to a better format, aData[], ready to be transformed to a datagraph.

Then the execution flow comes back to the `chartRenderer.ring` again, carrying the `aData[]` list in its hands. At this level, the `datagraph.ring` file is loaded (4), and a `Datagraph[]` list is returned.[3]

Finally, rendering of the graph inside a Ring string called `cGraph` is performed in file `chartRenderer.ring` (5), more specifically, using the `showgraph()` function.

Is this clear enough, Dan?

- **Dan**: Absolutely, you've done a great job.

  Still, the call flow you implemented using `load` commands breaks the logical order defined in the architecture diagram. This can be confusing! Rather, I'll reorganize the sequence of calls to explicitly reflect the design of the architecture.

For that, Dan opens the `northafrica.ring` file and modifies it to look like Listing 4-1.[4]

Listing 4-1. `northafrica.ring`

```
// Layer 1
load "txtconnector.ring"
// Layer 2
load "transformer.ring"
load "datagraph.ring"
// Layer 3
load "chartrenderer.ring"

showgraph()
```

Of course, in `chartRenderer.ring`, the first two lines are no longer need. Dan deletes them.

```
load "transformer.ring"
load "datagraph.ring"
```

---

[3]As you saw in Chapter 3, the datagraph is a better format of the `aData[]` list that simplifies the job of the graph renderer.

[4]Follow along with Dan; you are in good hands.

Then, he saves the file.

Next, he goes back to the main file `northafrica.ring` and executes it. In the Notepad Output window, the chart is displayed. Good move!

Designing a Target Architecture

Let's take a look at the target architecture as drawn by Dan on the board of the room (Figure 4-6) and then compare it with the existing one in Figure 4-5.

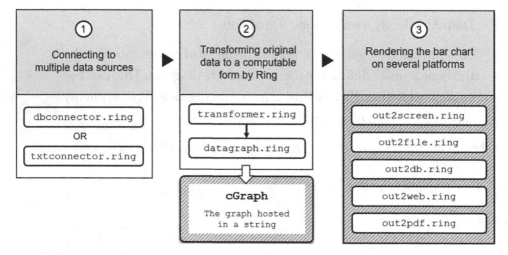

Figure 4-6. *Target architecture to be implemented by Dan*

Figure 4-6 demonstrates the wise decision taken by Dan of leaving the (1) and (2) layers untouched (same files), while moving the fabrication of the `cGraph` string from layer (3) back to layer (2). This means that `cGraph` is no longer considered as a rendering thing by Dan, but as an intermediary format provided by layer (2) and used by layer (3) to render the graph in many different formats.

- On the screen, using a file called `ou2screen.ring`: cGraph is simply printed using the `?` keyword.

- In a text file, using a file called `out2file.ring`: cGraph is printed to the file using the `write()` standard function.

- In an HTML web page, using a file called out2web.ring: He's not sure how to do it, but, for sure, Dan will be looking toward the Ring WebLib library.

- Finally, in a PDF document, using a file called out2pdf.ring: cGraph will be printed using a specific widget from the RingQt library that automates the use of PDF files.

Hence, by reviewing the code in the chartRenderer.ring file, we find that the showchart() function is doing two operations.

- Fabricating the cGraph string from the datagraph matrix

- Showing the graph by printing it on the screen using ? cGraph

A separation of concern (SoC) is required here. So, follow these steps:

- Let's save the current file (chartRenderer.ring) as cgraph.ring.

- In cgraph.ring, delete the first line, func showgraph().

- Also, inside the same cgraph.ring file, delete the two lines responsible for displaying the cGraph on the screen.

  ```
  // Showing the graph on the screen
  ? cGraph
  ```

- Save the file (cgraph.ring).

- In the main northafrica.ring file, delete the last line, showgraph().

In the new design, chartRenderer.ring doesn't exist. As shown in Figure 4-6, it will be replaced with a file for every target platform. Therefore, follow these steps:

- In the main file, northafrica.ring, delete the line Load "chartRenderer.ring" (note that layer 3 became empty).

- Open the current northAfricaAppV2 folder (in your operating system's File Explorer).

- Delete the chartRenderer.ring file.

Let's get back to the main file called northafrica.ring. Listing 4-2 shows its updated content (Dan just added some useful comments).

Listing 4-2. northafrica.ring

```
// Layer 1
load "txtconnector.ring"        # can be also "dbconnector.ring"
                                # text data returned in an a[] list
// Layer 2
load "transformer.ring"         # a[] transformed to aData[] list
load "datagraph.ring"           # aData[] mapped in an aDatagraph[]
load "cgraph.ring"              # cGraph made from aDatagraph[]
// Layer 3
                                # cGraph will be used here
```

As you can understand from the flow of ideas conveyed by the code itself and by the comments added by Dan just now, you can test the program by simply adding ? cGraph at the end of the file. Do this and execute the file. The graph is shown in the Output window of Ring Notepad as expected.

However, this is a dirty maneuver to just be sure we didn't corrupt the system with the changes we made. In respect to the new architecture design (see Figure 4-6), Dan will start implementing the rendering layer of the program (layer 3) by providing a file for the first target platform (the screen). To follow along, do these steps:

- Create a new file in the current directory and call it out2screen.ring.

- Inside the file, just write ? cGraph and save it.

- Go back to the main northafrica.ring file.

- Add Load "out2screen.ring" at the end of the file and save it.

The complete listing of the main northafrica.ring file looks like Listing 4-3.

Listing 4-3. northafrica.ring

```
// Layer 1
load "txtconnector.ring"        # can be also "dbconnector.ring"
                                # text data returned in an a[] list
// Layer 2
load "transformer.ring"         # a[] transformed to aData[] list
```

```
load "datagraph.ring"              # aData[] mapped in an aDatagraph[]
load "cgraph.ring"                 # cGraph made from aDatagraph[]
// Layer 3
load "out2screen.ring"             # renders the graph on the screen
```

Execute it. Everything should be OK: the final result but also the underlining clean (or at least, willing to be clean) architecture!

Before he goes forward in implementing the other output formats, Dan will share with us some useful tips from the jar of his Ring expertise.

Using See Instead of ?

As you can see, "outputting" data to the screen is made possible with the use of the ? keyword. Ring brings another command you can use: the See command.[5]

Open the `tempo.ring` file in the current `northafricaAppV2` folder. Then try Listing 4-4 (Ctrl+F5).

Listing 4-4. `tempo.ring`

```
? "Apress"
SEE "Editions"
```

They give the following clean output:

```
Apress
Editions
```

But what if you inverse the order of the two lines by saying SEE before ?? You get EditionsApress. Why?

This is because while the two keywords are equivalent in showing a string in the screen, one leaves a new line at the end (?) while the doesn't (SEE).

This seems to be a minor difference, but in practice it isn't. In fact, one can argue that ? can be replaced by SEE + NL, which is true, but adding a new line every time with code can be a waste of time. Anyway, Ring is made for freedom, and you are free to use one or another of the two keywords depending on your taste.

---

[5]Do you remember when we first discovered this keyword in Chapter 1?

Inviting BASIC into Ring

What if you prefer the classic BASIC print command instead of SEE? It's simple to do.

In fact, Ring offers the ability to change its keywords to new ones defined by the programmer, using the ChangeRingKeyword command.

At the beginning of your current tempo.ring file, add the following:

```
ChangeRingKeyword see print    # print is substituted to see
```

And then change ? and see to print in the remaining code. The tempo.ring file looks like Listing 4-5.

Listing 4-5. tempo.ring

```
ChangeRingKeyword see print
print "Apress" + NL
print "Editions"
```

Changing Ring keywords and even Ring operators (like +, -, <, and >) is a critical feature with a lot of power, since you are able to adjust the internal syntax of Ring dynamically without limit. This empowers you to start up your own programming language in minutes, not months. But this is also a dangerous feature that a programmer should use with a sense of responsibility.

In our case, the change we made will impact every future line of code. So, it is advisable to reset everything to its initial state at the end of the program, as shown in Listing 4-6.

Listing 4-6. tempo.ring

```
// Changing a keyword
ChangeRingKeyword see print
print "Apress" + NL
print "Editions" + NL
// Back to the initial syntax
ChangeRingkeyword print see
SEE "Beginning Ring Programming"
```

This syntax flexibility can be implemented on a wider scale by creating a syntax file to every programming language flavor you, or your team, prefer to use while writing Ring programs. Let's experiment with it to use Ring like it was plain old BASIC.

To do so, create a new file called BasicOn.ring and put the code shown in Listing 4-7 inside it.

Listing 4-7. basicon.ring

```
ChangeRingKeyword   see    print
ChangeRingKeyword   ok     endif
ChangeRingKeyword   next   endfor
ChangeRingKeyword   end    endwhile
```

Save it in the current folder.

You may think now that we are going to use the Load command to import this file, but we don't. In fact, Load is actionable by the compiler in the parsing phase, but ChangeKeyword is actionable before that, in the scanning phase.[6] That's why Ring provides a specific keyword for importing the syntax files: LoadSyntax.

Now, in tempo.ring, write the code shown in Listing 4-8, reread it, and then run it.

Listing 4-8. tempo.ring

```
// Let's talk in basic
LoadSyntax "basicon.ring"

x = 10
while x > 0
        print "x = " + x + nl
        for t = 1 to 10
```

---

[6]Ring is based on its own compiler and virtual machine, both designed in ANSI C (in approximately 20,000 lines of code), which gives them a lot of power and a small footprint. Mahmoud Fayed developed them using the PWCT visual programming tool (http://pwct.org), which we will talk about briefly in Chapter 9 as a killer application of Ring, being downloaded +21 million times! Now, this visual tool is being rewritten from scratch using Ring. I told you this story because, while you are using Ring, it is useful to understand the motivations behind it. And one of them was the creation of a flexible, powerful, and small language that helps in making a visual programming tool like PWCT. Many features of Ring, like the substitution of standard keywords with the user-defined ones we saw earlier, along with the support of declarative and natural paradigms, were invented in Ring for a practical reason and to solve a real-world problem the language inventor confronted in his project. As far as I am concerned, as a Ring programmer, the overall impact on Ring itself was phenomenal with many interesting features, and we will cover the most important of them in this book.

```
                        if t = 3
                                print "number three" + nl
                        endif
            endfor
            x--
endwhile
```

 # Back to Ring dialect
```
ChangeRingKeyword print    see
ChangeRingKeyword endif    ok
ChangeRingKeyword endfor   next
ChangeRingKeyword endwhile end

see "done" + nl
```

Isn't that wonderful? Every time you need it, you say it in BASIC while you are Ringling. The same can be made with any syntax of any programming language.

Do you know any champion other than Ring with such a flexibility?

Using the Standard print( ) Function

The Ring language comes with a standard print() function that you can use by loading the StdLib library.

In tempo.ring, erase everything and start typing load.

You will notice that an IntelliSense helper is displayed so you can select an option in a menu instead of typing it by hand. In our case, we select load "stdlib.ring" by clicking it using the mouse or directly by using the arrows and Enter keys on your keyboard, as shown in Figure 4-7.

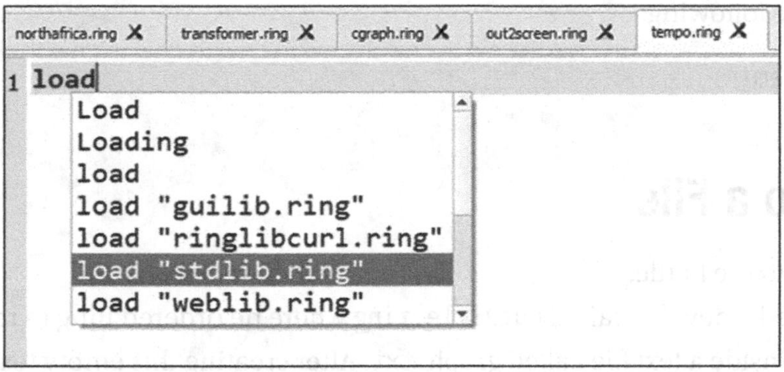

Figure 4-7. *IntelliSense in Ring's Code Editor*

Simply write the code in Listing 4-9 to print the Hello! text in the Output window.

Listing 4-9. tempo.ring

```
load "stdlib.ring"
print("Hello!")
```

Then, you can use \n or \t, for example, in the text to generate respectively a new line and a tabulation, as shown in Listing 4-10.

Listing 4-10. tempo.ring

```
load "stdlib.ring"
print("Hello!\nDear friend")
```

This will print the following:

```
Hello!
Dear friend
```

Also, you can insert the value of a variable in the text by using #{variable_name}, as shown in Listing 4-11.

Listing 4-11. tempo.ring

```
load "stdlib.ring"
cName = "Arem"
print("Long live #{cName}!")
```

You get the following:

Long live Arem![7]

Output to a File

Let's get back to the battle.

Dan created a new file called out2file.ring where he ordered Ring to render the cGraph string inside a text file called graph.txt. After creating this empty text file in the current folder (using the operating system's File Explorer), he wrote the code shown in Listing 4-12 in the out2file.ring.

Listing 4-12. out2file.ring

```
write("graph.txt",cGraph) # saving the cGraph in the file
cFile = read("graph.txt") # Reading the file content
? cFile  # Showing the file on screen
```

Then, he went back to the main northafrica.ring file and said load "out2file.ring" instead of load "out2screen.ring". See Listing 4-13.

Listing 4-13. northafrica.ring

```
// Layer 1
load "txtconnector.ring"          # text data returned in an a[] list
// Layer 2
load "transformer.ring"           # a[] transformed to aData[] list
load "datagraph.ring"             # aData[] mapped in an aDatagraph[]
load "cgraph.ring"                # cGraph made from aDatagraph[]
// Layer 3
load "out2file.ring"              # can also be "out2screen.ring"
```

---

[7]This is the name of my beautiful mom, Dèda, as I call her. In Arabic, the word a*rem* means "abundant." It's about abundance in health, emotional wealth, and ethics of care.

Do the same as Dan and execute the `northafrica.ring` file. In the Notepad Output window, you get the chart, but most importantly, you'll get the physical text file, in the application folder, filled with the same chart as it is shown in my Windows File Explorer, as shown in Figure 4-8.

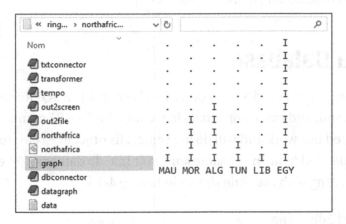

Figure 4-8. *The chart rendered in a text file (graph.txt) using the write() function*

`write()` is a powerful function not limited to writing to text files but also to binary files such as EXEs. To make a copy from the `ring.exe` executable, for example, it is enough to write the lines in Listing 4-14, in an empty `tempo.ring` file.

Listing 4-14. `tempo.ring`

```
try
        cFile = read("c:\ring\bin\ring.exe")
        write("ring2.exe",cFile)
        SEE "Copying the binary file done successfully."
catch
        SEE "An error happened: " + NL
        SEE cCatchError
done
```

Test this. Assuming that your Ring installation was made in the `c:\ring` folder, then `ring.exe` is copied, and a new EXE file with the same content but with a different name (`ring2.exe`) is created in the current `northafricaApp.ring` folder.

Note that we used `try/catch` statements to capture any error that could happen (in the first block under `try`) and manage it by ourselves (in the second block under `catch`) without breaking the program execution. Usually, you would need this when the operation is not managed by Ring but by the system (connecting to a database, reading and writing files to disk, talking to the network, etc.).[8]

Output to a Database

In the previous chapter, we used SQL to design a `TABLE` inside a SQLite database, using the `CREATE` command, and saved some data in it using the `INSERT` command.

Dan appreciated our work and will do the same. His objective is to store the `cGraph` string inside a dedicated table in the same `northafrica.db` database. Then he created a file called `out2db.ring` with the code shown in Listing 4-15.

Listing 4-15. `out2db.ring`

```
// Opening a connection with the db
load "sqlitelib.ring"
oSQLite = sqlite_init()
sqlite_open( oSQLite, "northafrica.db" )

sql = "SELECT * FROM COUNTRY"
aResult = sqlite_execute( oSQLite, sql )

? aResult
```

In this code, Dan was just testing whether the database exists and contains data. Run the code and observe the result.

---

[8]The error and exception management system, in any programming language, is worth studying to get a profound understanding of how the language works. In Ring, there are three types of messages you will encounter: compiler errors (`https://tinyurl.com/todjekn`), runtime errors (`https://tinyurl.com/r6z2p4s`), and environment errors (`https://tinyurl.com/qnsrhh4`). We don't have enough space to cover them in this book, but I invite you to read them, imagine what they do, and keep them in filigree during your programming journey with Ring. In a nutshell, when you master them all, you've mastered the language!

The database exists, and the data is stored there. Now, delete these lines because they have widely played their role:

```
sql = "SELECT * FROM COUNTRY"
aResult = sqlite_execute( oSQLite, sql )

? aResult
```

To store the cGraph inside the northafrica.db database, the steps are as follows:

1. Design a new TABLE and name it GRAPH.

2. Inside the table, create a field called content. This is where the cGraph is hosted.

3. If you want, you can add some additional information about each graph by adding other fields: a source field to specify the data source, and a comment field to say something about the graph.

The complete content of the out2db.ring file becomes Listing 4-16.

Listing 4-16. out2db.ring

```
// Opening a connection with the db
load "sqlitelib.ring"
oSQLite = sqlite_init()
sqlite_open( oSQLite, "northafrica.db" )

// Creating the GRAPH table
sql = "
CREATE TABLE GRAPH (
            CONTENT TEXT NOT NULL,
            DATASOURCE TEXT NOT NULL,
            COMMENT TEXT NOT NULL ) ;
);
"

sqlite_execute( oSQLite, sql )
```

```
// Storing the cGraph in the table
sql = "
            INSERT INTO GRAPH
            ( CONTENT,
              DATASOURCE,
              COMMENT)
            VALUES
            ( '" + cGraph + "',
            'Wolfram|Alpha',
            'Your comment...');
"
sqlite_execute( oSQLite, sql )
```

```
// Reading the graph from the db
sql = "SELECT * FROM GRAPH"
aResult = sqlite_execute( oSQLite, sql )
? aResult[] // Try aResult[1][1][2] to show just the Graph
```

To test it, you need to activate the main northafrica.ring file and replace load "out2file.ring" with load "out2db.ring", as shown in Listing 4-17.

Listing 4-17. northafrica.ring

```
// Layer 1
load "txtconnector.ring"          # text data returned in an a[] list
// Layer 2
load "transformer.ring"           # a[] transformed to aData[] list
load "datagraph.ring"             # aData[] mapped in an aDatagraph[]
load "cgraph.ring"                # cGraph made from aDatagraph[]
// Layer 3
load "out2db.ring"                # or "out2screen" or "out2file"
```

Run the northafrica.ring file. Again, you should be able to see the graph in the Output window of Ring Notepad. In this case, we were successful to help Dan achieve the database option of his design.[9]

To summarize, three options for rendering the chart are now implemented: screen, text file, and database. Dan's clean design enables us to navigate from one platform to another simply by specifying the corresponding file in the load command in the main northafrica.ring file: out2screen.ring to show the chart on the screen, out2file.ring to save it in a text file, and out2db.ring to store it in a database.

So nice! Let's continue.

Output to a Web Page

If you remember, we dealt with printing in a web page in Chapter 1. Remember that when we write the code in Listing 4-18 in an empty tempo.ring file, "Hello, World!" must be replaced by cGrapgh.

Listing 4-18. tempo.ring

```
load "weblib.ring"
import System.Web

new page { text("Hello, World!") }
```

If you were Dan, then you would create a new file called out2web.ring and paste the code in Listing 4-19 inside it.

Listing 4-19. out2web.ring

```
load "weblib.ring"
import System.Web

new Page { text(cGraph) }
```

---

[9]In practice, we never use a database just to save one record like we've done now. A database is made to hold large volumes of data with the promise of using them in our programs to achieve a business value. In our case, it would be interesting if we stored the same statistics about the north African countries over a period of 100 years, for example, with thousands of records. The business value would be the development of an interactive dashboard helping decision-makers in those countries to understand the patterns of evolution of their population, in time, and how they have been impacted by some events in their history (war, a policy reform of the health sector, and so on).

This shows the generated HTML code of the page in the Output window. But what we need is a concrete HTML file that hosts the graph, say graph.html. To do so, we need to avoid new Page and replace it with new htmlPage, as shown in Listing 4-20.

Listing 4-20. out2web.ring

```
load "weblib.ring"
import System.Web

p = new htmlpage { text(cGraph) }
write( "graph.html",p.output() )
```

Then in the main northafrica.ring file, you will change load "out2db.ring" with load "out2web.ring". Run it. Browse the current NorthAfricaApp folder and find graph.html. Double-click it and see the result in your browser. It works, but it is visually unsatisfying, as shown in Figure 4-9.

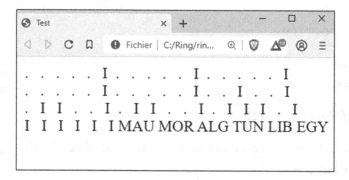

Figure 4-9. The chart rendered in an HTML page, unorganized!

Maybe we are in trouble!

Don't panic, this will always happen in the real world every time you use a technology that is new or you try to apply a general solution to a new terrain. In such cases, a kind of technical feasibility study needs to be performed.[10]

---

[10]Many programmers, and programming teams, underestimate the cost of jumping to code without analyzing the fuzzy regions of the requirements. Hence, they don't adopt the habit of understanding the feasibility of what is required by the customer technologically before delivering production code. In practice, besides the learning value behind this approach, the time you spend challenging your thoughts and assumptions by writing small code experiments will be rewarding.

Studying the Feasibility of Printing cGraph in a Web Page

The goal of this study is to identify the source of the problem encountered in the rendering of the cGraph string inside a web page, as observed in Figure 4-9. After understanding what happened, it is required that we assess its impact on the solution we designed.

In fact, in our case, the problem comes from the ignorance by HTML of the new lines (NL) contained in the cGraph string. If we try an example, you can better understand it: in the out2web.ring file (Listing 4-20), replace text(cGraph) with text(c). Before this line, insert c = "Line1". What you get then is Listing 4-21.

Listing 4-21. out2web.ring

```
load "weblib.ring"
import System.Web

c = "Line1"
p = new htmlpage { text(c) }
write( "graph.html",p.output() )
```

Run it and refresh (F5) the same web page currently in your browser. Right now it shows "Line1" at the top of the page. What if we change c string to the following:

```
c = "
Line1
Line2
"
```

Refresh the page. You see? The new line is completely ignored, as shown in Figure 4-10.

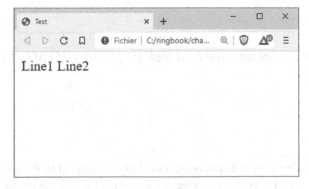

Figure 4-10. *The new line ignored by the HTML page*

Let's try another option and replace the value of c in out2web.ring with Listing 4-22.

Listing 4-22. Part of out2web.ring

```
c = "Line1" + NL + "Line2"
```

It's the same result.

A possible solution for that is to tell Ring to embrace the HTML standard and use the <div> tag, which helps structure the page in zones or divisions. The default behavior of <div> on all browsers is that it leaves an automatic new line at the end of its content.[11] In our case, the tags will just contain one line of text each, as shown in Listing 4-23.

Listing 4-23. out2web.ring

```
load "weblib.ring"
import System.Web

p = new htmlpage {
         div { text("Line1") }
         div { text("Line2") }
}
write("graph.html",p.output())
```

Execute it and refresh the browser. Finally, it's resolved, as shown in Figure 4-11.

Figure 4-11. *A new line generated in a web page using HTML divs*

---

[11]This can be changed using CSS style sheets. CSS is fully supported in Ring WebLib. Take a full tour of the features of the library, from configuring an Apache web server to writing dynamic web sites in Ring, here: https://tinyurl.com/we5m4kd.

If you look to the source code of the `graph.html` file (just click it in the Project Files tree view in Ring Notepad), you will find that the generated HTML code by Ring looks like Listing 4-24.

Listing 4-24. `graph.html`

```html
<!DOCTYPE html>
<html lang="en">
<head>
    <title>Test</title>
    <meta charset='UTF-8'>
    <script
    src="https://ajax.googleapis.com/ajax/libs/jquery/1.11.3/jquery.min.js">
    </script>
</head>
<body>
        <div style="">
                    Line1
        </div>
        <div style="">
                    Line2
        </div>
</body>
</html>
```

The limitation of interpreting a new line (NL) inside a string for one of our target platforms (namely, the web target) means that we can no longer rely on `cGraph` as a reliable intermediate format. A substantial change in the architecture of the app is then necessary!

Yet Another Architecture Refactoring

How are you going to make it, Dan?

Well, like Figure 4-12.

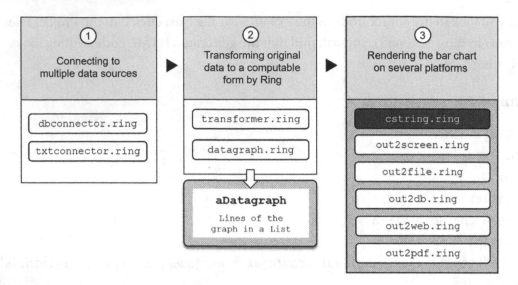

Figure 4-12. *cGraph is substituted by aDatagraph as an intermediary format*

While looking at this new update of the architecture, it's always good to take a look at its last version; see Figure 4-6. This is useful to capture the rationale of Dan's thinking. Instead of building, in layer (2), on cGraph string as an intermediate format, we use the aDatagraph list instead so we are free to parse it line by line, in layer (3), and fabricate whatever output format we want: screen, text, database, web, or PDF.

Remember, in the chartRenderer.ring file, that aDatagraph list contains the code in Listing 4-25.

Listing 4-25. Part of chartRenderer.ring

```
# Reminder: our aDatagraph contains:
          # [ 0, 0, 0, 0, 0, 1 ],
          # [ 0, 0, 0, 0, 0, 1 ],
          # [ 0, 0, 0, 0, 0, 1 ],
          # [ 0, 0, 0, 0, 0, 1 ],
          # [ 0, 0, 0, 0, 0, 1 ],
          # [ 0, 0, 1, 0, 0, 1 ],
          # [ 0, 1, 1, 0, 0, 1 ],
          # [ 0, 1, 1, 0, 0, 1 ],
          # [ 0, 1, 1, 1, 0, 1 ],
          # [ 1, 1, 1, 1, 1, 1 ]
```

Keeping this matrix in mind, you can easily imagine how every module of the rendering layer (3) can take its own way by parsing the aDatagraph and formatting the output.

Now, create a third copy of the app folder and name it northafricaAppV3. Close all the opened files in Ring Notepad to start with a new and clean base.[12]

The first thing we should do is purely organizational and will be applied to the main northafrica.ring file. Look at its current structure in Listing 4-26 and tell me what load line should be moved from one layer to another.

Listing 4-26. northafrica.ring

```
// Layer 1
load "dbconnector.ring"
// Layer 2
load "transformer.ring"
load "datagraph.ring"
load "cgraph.ring"    # Do you suspect this line?
// Layer 3
load "out2db.ring"    # or "out2screen.ring" or "out2file.ring"
```

Bravo! It's the line load "cgraph.ring" that should be cut from the // Layer 2 part and pasted at the beginning of the // Layer 3 part. Never underestimate the insistence of Dan to implement these details; trust me, these details are a result of the reflexes of the great software architects. Now, our main file is totally conformant to the logical software architecture designed in Figure 4-12; see Listing 4-27.

Listing 4-27. northafrica.ring

```
// Layer 1
load "dbconnector.ring"
// Layer 2
load "transformer.ring"
```

---

[12]In your professional projects and even on a day-by-day basis, you should use a Version Control System like Git to keep track of your code base lifecycle and stay organized. You can find a short and instructive video introducing Git here: https://tinyurl.com/t7eseuk. Then, look at this visual tutorial written by Vincent Tunru: https://tinyurl.com/yx6ru7x7. Finally, I advise you to consider getting a beginner book on the subject, like Apress' *Beginning Git and GitHub* written by Mariot Tsitoara, for example (https://tinyurl.com/txclndc), and start using Git in all your projects.

```
load "datagraph.ring"
// Layer 3
load "cgraph.ring"        # the file in the good logical place
load "out2screen.ring"  # or "out2file.ring" or "out2db.ring"
```

Once the form is OK, let's tackle the substance of the problem by implementing the web target correctly.

Correctly Implementing the Web Target

After a hot coffee, on a rainy morning, Dan tells us the following.

All the rendering modules in layer (3) are based on the aDatagraph produced by the transformer in layer (2), right? At the same time, all the rendering modules but out2web. ring[13] use the cGraph string generated by the cstring.ring file. Visually speaking, if we put a spotlight on part of the app architecture (go back to Figure 4-12), Figure 4-13 shows what I mean.

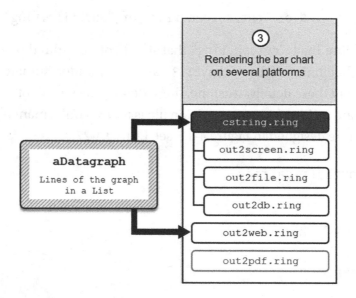

Figure 4-13. *Three modules in layer (3) making use of cstring.ring*

---

[13]Remember, this was a matter of interpreting new lines (NLs) inside the cGraph string with HTML.

Concerning `out2pdf.ring`, we cannot decide on it now because we didn't experience it yet. So, we will leave it for later consideration. Let's concentrate on the web side of our multiplatform rendering service.

Create a new file in the current folder `northaAfricaAppV4` and name it `out2web.ring`.

Logically, the code of `out2web.ring` is similar to `cstring.ring`. In fact, we are parsing the `aDatagraph` line by line and then printing it either in a `string` variable or in an HTML page. Let's recall the portion of code of `cstring.ring` that is responsible for this parsing and printing operation; see Listing 4-28.

Listing 4-28. Part of `cstring.ring`

```
// Constituting the graph string cGraph
for y = 1 to len(aDatagraph) // =10
            cGraph += spc(1) + graphline(y) + NL
next y

cGraph += graphlabels()
```

Then comes the code of the functions used: `graphline()`, `graphlabels()`, and `spc()`.

From a web page perspective, the same logic is used, but the printing occurs inside div tags in the `htmlPage`. In `out2web.ring`, write the code in Listing 4-29.

Listing 4-29. Part of `out2web.ring`

```
load "weblib.ring"
import System.Web

p = new htmlpage {
            for y = 1 to len(aDatagraph) // = 10
                        div { text( spc(1) + graphline(y) + NL ) }
            next y

            div { text( graphlabels() ) }
}
write( "graph.html",p.output() )
```

Save the file.

219

Of course, we need to add the code of the graphline(), graphlabels(), and spc() functions from cstring.ring to the current out2web.ring file so it works. But Dan won't accept having it duplicated in two files, and he is right: duplication is always a good indication that your system requires a refactoring.

Don't ask him, I'm sure he will be thinking of it this way: those functions are logically related to the datagraph, and all future modules that call the datagraph.ring file should be able to parse it line by line (using the graphline() function) and read its labels (using the graphlabels() function). Therefore, these must be moved to the bottom of the datagraph.ring file!

What do you think? If you have another strategy, try it. For me, I've moved them the Dan way, saved all the files, and tried to switch to the web output by doing these steps:

- Going to northafrica.ring file

- Changing load "out2db.ring" (or whatever platform is currently active) to load "out2web.ring"

- Saving and executing the file (Ctrl+F5)

Doing so, the graph.html file is physically updated in the application folder. There we reach it and open it in the web browser to get the screen shown in Figure 4-14.

Figure 4-14. *Our graph, timidly displayed in a web page*

Intellectually, I may be satisfied, but artistically nope. Let's change it by using HTML tables, one of the complete set of features supported in Ring by the WebLib library and that enable you to write Ring code as if you are writing a pure HTML file!

Writing HTML in Ring

As you may know, HTML is a declarative language where you compose things to show them in a browser. To make a table, you specify its start and end tags (`<table>` and `</table>`), as well as its header (`<th>` and `</th>`), rows (`<tr>` and `</tr>`), and cells (`<td>` and `</td>`).

Ring frees your mind from learning another language while providing you with the same declarative style[14] to compose your HTML table. Type Listing 4-30 in an empty `tempo.ring` file.[15]

Listing 4-30. `tempo.ring`

```
Load "weblib.ring"
Import System.Web

New Page
{
        divstart([ :style = styledivcenter("400px","500px") ] )
            style(styletable() + styletablerows("t01"))
        tablestart([ :id = :t01, :style= stylewidth("100%") ])
                rowstart([])
                            headerstart([]) text("Number")
                            headerend()
                            headerstart([]) text("square")
                            headerend()
                rowend()
                for x = 1 to 10
                            rowstart([])
                                cellstart([]) text(x)
                                cellend()
                                cellstart([]) text(x*x)
                                cellend()
                            rowend()
```

---

[14]In Chapter 7, you will learn how you can design your domain-specific language, like the one provided here in the WebLib library, using the declarative paradigm of the Ring language.

[15]I've taken this example from the Ring documentation at http://ring-lang.sourceforge.net/doc1.10/web.html.

```
                next
        tableend()
    divend()
}
```

Execute it and observe the HTML output generated by this Ring code in the Notepad Output window. Compare every Ring command to its equivalent HTML tag. Think of it as if Ring were an HTML expert writing a web page for you, while you are describing it in Ring.[16]

With a minimal effort, you can put the generated code in a text file named `test.html` and then show it in the browser. Figure 4-15 shows what you get.

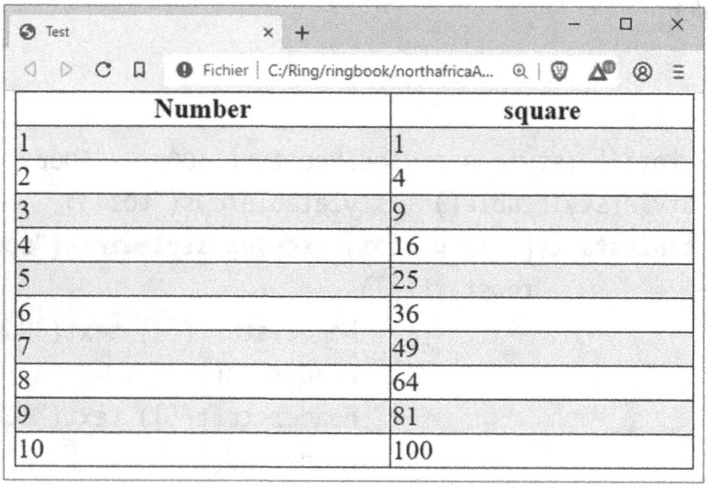

Figure 4-15. A sample HTML table

This being said, I will leave it to you to do as a personal exercise where the `out2web.ring` module generates a beautiful HTML table containing the graph that you can display in the browser, centered on the page, similar to Figure 4-16.

---

[16]Of course, this is not the only way you can make web programs in Ring. Several other options are available, including writing HTML files and incrusting Ring scripts inside them, as you would do with Python or PHP. Web programming is a nice and vast domain, beautifully supported by Ring, but, unfortunately, we won't go further with it in this book.

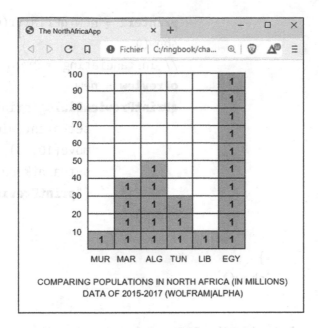

Figure 4-16. Our graph, faithfully displayed in an HTML table

Waiting for Dan to help you? Don't bother him please, he has been switched to another task: generating the graph in a printed file (next section).

Output to a Printed File

Today's printings happen mainly in PDF files. In this section, Dan shows us how to do it in Ring using the RingQt library. Qt was introduced to you in the first and third chapters, so please go back to them if you don't remember how it works with Ring.

As you see, Dan has created a new file and named it out2pdf.ring. He saved it in ring current folder. Inside the file, he tried the code in Listing 4-31.

Listing 4-31. out2pdf.ring

```
load "guilib.ring"

// Creating a Qt application to host the PDF preview window
        new qApp {
                win1 = new qwidget() {
                        setwindowtitle("Printer Preview Dialog")
                        setgeometry(100,100,675,480)
```

```
                                printer1 = new qPrinter(0)
                                show()
                                // instanciating a Printer (PDF) Preview
                                oPreview = new
                                qPrintPreviewDialog(printer1) {
                                        setParent(win1)
                                        move(10,10)
                                        setPaintRequestEdevent
                                        ("printPreview()")
                                exec()
                                }
                        }
                        show()
}

// Printing the graph inside the PDF preview
func printPreview()
        printer1 {
                painter = new qpainter() {
                        begin(printer1)
                        myfont = new qfont("Times",18,-1,0)
                        setfont(myfont)
                        yy=10
                        for y = 1 to len(aDatagraph) // =10
                                yy += 40
                                drawtext(10,yy, spc(1) +
                                graphline(y) )
                        next y
                drawtext(10,yy+40, graphlabels() )

                printer1.newpage()
                endpaint()
                }
        }
```

Executing the code, you will see the screen in Figure 4-17 where you can print the file right to your printer.

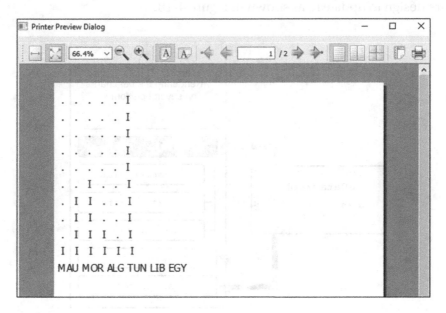

Figure 4-17. *Printing the chart in a PDF file*

When RingQt adds support for QChart widgets in the future,[17] then come back to this exercise and do a better job of visualizing the generated chart as a native widget. For now, this is an explanation (a short one) of the code in Listing 4-31.

First, a new qApp object is created. This object is made with a window called win1. A virtual printer called printer1 is also created (based on the qPrinter class). The window will contain a widget (qWidget) hosting a printer preview dialog (qPrintPreviewDialog). The preview is stored in an object called oPreview. Its job is to show the content of the printer as constructed in the printPreview() function. exe() and show() are responsible for constructing the window and showing it on the screen.

---

[17]If you remember, we talked about the support of charts in the RingQt extension in Chapter 3 when we dealt with GUI programming using the Form Designer. These particular widgets (QChart and QChartView) make it easy to make visually rich graphic charts in Ring. When I asked about them in the Ring Google Group, Mahmoud told me that they are on his to-do list. Read our discussion here: https://tinyurl.com/u72j9qh. To get an idea of what would be possible to do right in your Ring applications, once this feature is added, look to the several samples provided here in the Qt documentation page: https://tinyurl.com/rx7aqkk.

By the way, the code inside the printPreview() function shows that we have used aDatagraph directly to fabricate the chart in the PDF. That brings us back to Dan's architecture design to update it, as shown in Figure 4-18.

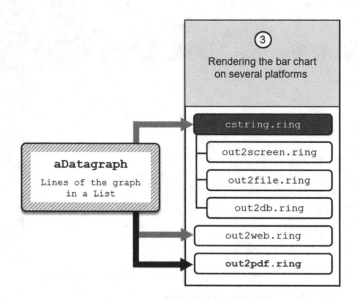

Figure 4-18. *The PDF output relies also on the aDatagraph list*

There is an additional enhancement you can do, which I'll leave as an exercise for you.

Look back closely at the code that implements the storage of the cGraph chart inside the database (go back to the file out2db.ring in Listing 4-14), specifically to the lines in Listing 4-32.

Listing 4-32. Part of out2db.ring

```
// Storing the cGraph in the table
sql = "
          INSERT INTO GRAPH
          ( CONTENT,
            DATASOURCE,
            COMMENT)
          VALUES
```

```
    ( '" + cGraph + "',
    'Wolfram|Alpha',
    'Your comment...');
"

sqlite_execute( oSQLite, sql )
```

You could say the following to Dan:

- I see that we are storing the cString as is in the database.

- A database is tabular by design and was meant essentially to store data records and not portions of text.

- Why don't we do the same as for out2web.ring and out2pdf.ring and free ourselves from the blindness of a compact string and get the data directly from the official intermediary: aDatagraph?

While you talk, Dan seems convinced. This encourages you to provide your first contribution to the architecture design of the NorthAfricaApp in the form of this change in the application diagram, as shown in Figure 4-19.

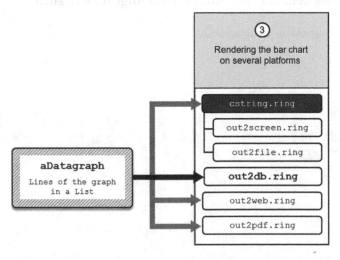

Figure 4-19. *Your contribution to the enhancement of the app architecture design*

What remains is implementing this in Ring by adjusting the necessary code (in the portion listed in Listing 4-32) and adopting the good Loading call flow.

What's Next

Congratulations. The first two chapters in the "Practical Ring" part (Chapters 3 and 4) are now done.

You are now aware of the inputs and outputs of Ring; you've understood them and practiced them. You know how to capture data, store it in the program, and expose it in various forms and on several platforms. You know that architecture is a strategic asset when it comes to coding for flexibility. At the same time, a lot of refactoring has been done to continuously enhance your program. You worked with practical examples, built around a real-world data acquisition and transformation application, called NorthAfricaApp, to see these dynamics in action.

It's time, then, to look inside the box and discover how Ring applies algorithmic thinking on input data to transform it into outputs. An exciting fifth chapter is waiting for you!

Oh, yes, Tunisia won, for the 10th time, the men's African Nations title in volleyball for 2019 against Cameroon. You can congratulate me for that, and for another thing also: my cousin Abdessalem Ayouni[18] won the gold medal in the 800m at the African champion of athletics held in Rabat, Morocco on August 28th, 2019.

---

[18]https://en.wikipedia.org/wiki/Abdessalem_Ayouni

CHAPTER 5

Crafting Ring Algorithms

In its most basic form, designing an algorithm, whatever programming language you are using, is all about transforming inputs to outputs. Hence, at its heart, programming is the process of crafting a logic flow from the data received and delivering data to the user as a solution to a problem.

In this chapter, you will learn the language constructs in Ring to turn your data into an algorithmic flow for making computations and for making decisions. The result of such a transformation process is commonly called the *data flow*. Three basic ways of creating a data flow with your algorithms, also called *control structures*, are sequence, selection, and iteration. Selection is commonly known as *branching*, and iteration is also known as *looping*.

From a beginner's perspective, this chapter forms the heart of the book. That's why I have adopted a purely visual approach to explaining every piece of knowledge in this chapter.

I invite you to embrace the visual approach to programming described in this chapter. First, you'll design a diagram of your logic flow before you turn it into computer code in Ring. Then, I will explain the three basic forms of logic flow mentioned earlier. Meanwhile, I will guide you through my own strategy of designing clean code via a visual thinking paradigm. Next, I will go deeper into the features and control structures provided by Ring, so you will use the `for`, `for in`, `while`, `switch`, `do/again`, `step`, `exit`, `loop`, and `try/catch` statements in this chapter. Then, I will take you from the basic details related to logic flows in a given algorithm to a higher level of organizing the logical parts of a whole program. Then I will give you three rules of the logic craftsperson: "clean order," "one start, one end," and "clean logical parts." Finally, I will leave you with some homework to encourage you to apply the knowledge acquired in a practical challenge.

© Mansour Ayouni 2020
M. Ayouni, *Beginning Ring Programming*, https://doi.org/10.1007/978-1-4842-5833-0_5

Nine Things You Will Learn

In this chapter, you'll do the following:

- Use a visual method of learning programming

- Think visually in code and solve algorithmic problems

- Write expressive and learnable code by embracing the visual thinking paradigm

- Use the three forms of logic flows: sequence, selection, and iteration

- Combine those forms to shape complex logic flows

- Identify the happy path of an algorithm

- Understand the three algorithmic levels: human-oriented, logic-oriented, and computer-oriented

- Practice the advanced forms of control structure you would find in real-world programs

- Learn the three golden rules of programming craftsmanship

Before We Start: Long Live Visuality!

Bret Victor[1] said, "Programming is a way of thinking not a rote skill. People understand what they can see. If a programmer cannot see what a program is doing, she can't understand it. Thus, the goal of a programming system should be to support and encourage powerful ways of thinking and to enable programmers to see and understand the execution of their programs."

---

[1]Bret Victor is an interface designer, computer scientist, and electrical engineer known for his talks on the future of technology. Victor received attention for his talks "Inventing on Principle" (2012) and "The Future of Programming" (2013). Now he is working on his Dynamicland vision where "programming" occurs in a visible space: a room. A "programmer" uses her sight and her body to "touch" the program she is creating and live inside it. This vision, if achieved, will free us from being slaves of our screens and IDEs, and will transform programming into a humanized activity open to everyone. You can find more on Dynamicland.org.

Unfortunately, today's programming environments are not well suited to visualizing the programming process, from design to execution. Programmers should exercise their mental skills to imagine how the code should behave and how the final program will execute.

A few visual helpers are embedded into our IDEs.[2] They usually have a syntax spelling checker, a static error and exception notifier, and, sometimes, colored circles in the debugger to attract our attention to disruptions. In reality, these can be distractions more than useful helpers.

The whole experience of today's programming is hindered by the lack of visuality of both the logic flow (how the code is written) and the execution flow (what's happening when the program runs).[3] Regarding the logic flow that we are interested in during this chapter, we adopt a pure visual approach to teach you the basic constructs of making an algorithm in Ring. To do this, we can get valuable support from the Drakon project, a visual computer programming language, that I have found useful not only in learning how to program but in solving problems algorithmically and by stimulating the visual thinking muscles of our minds.

A Snapshot of Drakon: What and Why?

Drakon is a visual language from the aerospace industry for representing algorithms, processes, and procedures. Its goal is to make code easy to comprehend. It was created to capture software requirements for spacecraft control systems. Gradually, the language has gained recognition outside of aerospace. Developers and business analysts use it to document software of different types.[4]

Compared to other visual and flow-oriented languages, Drakon has the power of transforming a messy flowchart into a concise and learnable diagram, as shown in Figure 5-1.

---

[2]Examples are Visual Studio from Microsoft, Eclipse IDE from IBM, and Ring Notepad.

[3]This particular facet of visualizing computer programs when they execute will be covered in Chapter 6 so you, as a Ring programmer, can "watch" your variables living in runtime and "moving" between the local, object, and global scopes. In the current chapter, we will focus on the visibility of the design facet of the computer code and not on its runtime facet.

[4]The content of this section is widely based on the explanations given by https://drakonhub.com, an online tool providing the Drakon language in a web browser. The open source Drakon project itself, with a free desktop version of the software, can be found at http://drakon-editor.sourceforge.net/.

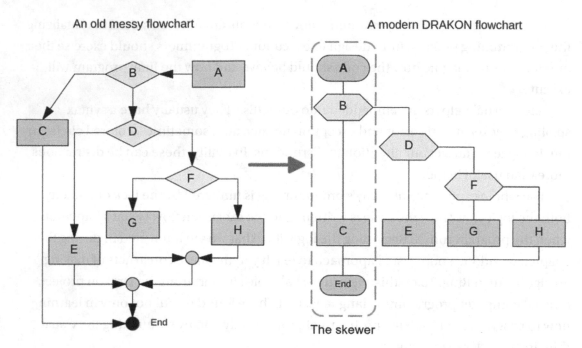

Figure 5-1. *Conventional flowchart compared to a Drakon flowchart*

To make it consistent and simple, a Drakon diagram is based on these golden principles:

- Line intersections are forbidden.

- Only straight lines and right angles are allowed.

- Arrows are replaced with plain lines.

- Time in the diagram flows downward; branching goes to the right.

Additionally, the language has two useful features unavailable in other visual languages.

- The skewer[5], like the one previously in Figure 5-1, highlights the happy path through the diagram.

---

[5]The skewer is a long piece of wood or metal used for holding pieces of food, typically meat, together during cooking. The Drakon Project uses it as a metaphor for the side line that maintains all the other components of the flowchart.

- The silhouette, which is a particular version of a Drakon diagram better suited for larger algorithms, will be described later in the chapter; it breaks up the algorithm into its logical parts and helps manage complexity.

Figure 5-2 shows a minimal Drakon diagram. It shows a simple algorithm named "Good day" with only three steps: Eat breakfast, Eat lunch, and Eat dinner.

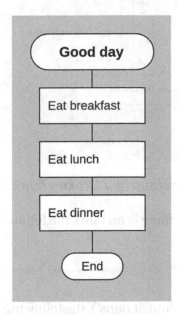

Figure 5-2. *A basic sequential Drakon flowchart*

The name of the diagram is in the start icon ("Good day"). It is located at the top of the diagram. Each rectangular box contains an action, which is an order to be executed by the computer. The end is at the bottom. There is no need for arrows because the next icon is always below.

The more elaborate example in Figure 5-3 implements the "Go out" algorithm in Drakon. The boxes show the order of actions. The truncated diamond contains a question. The diagram includes two use cases depending on the state of the weather outside: whether it rains or not.

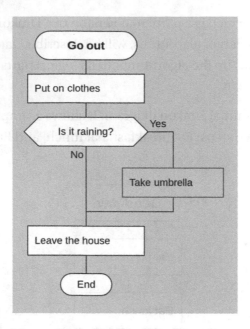

Figure 5-3. *Conditional branching in a Drakon flowchart*

In the first use case (go out, there is no rain), the following actions are executed:

- Put on clothes

- Leave the house

While in the second one (go out, it rains!), the following actions are executed:

- Put on clothes

- Take umbrella

- Leave the house

In Drakon, answers to a question are not equal. The good answer goes down. The bad answer goes to the right. The second use case is slightly less pleasant than the first use case. Therefore, the path related to the second use case goes through the right part of the diagram. The farther to the right, the worse it is.[6]

The main vertical is nothing other than the skewer we presented in the previous section. The skewer shows the happy path.

Enough introductions. Let's practice.

Three Forms of Logic Flows

When data is input into your program, there are three basic constructs you will find in all programming languages to craft logic with that data: sequence, selection, and iteration. Specifically, these are three different ways of controlling the order of your lines of code and, thus, the order of their execution by the computer.

Sequence

A program like the one in Listing 5-1 uses only a sequence of lines.[7]

Listing 5-1. diskaria.ring

```
// Computing the area of a disc
pi = 3.14
r = 5                  # This is the radius
area = r * r * pi      # This is the disc area
SEE area               # Gives 78.50
```

Visually speaking, Figure 5-4 shows the same sequence described in Drakon.

---

[6]You could say that good and bad and pleasant and unpleasant are relative judgments that cannot be consistent across people and even across different statuses of the same person. How this can be used in a structured discipline like programming? My short answer is that programming is structured by design, but in reality isn't, because those who write it are human beings. There is a lot of fussiness on what we say in code. In small programs, good and bad relate to the programmer assessment of the situation, but we need to stay consistent with that across the entire program. In large codebases, the customer perspective needs to be adopted: the happy path is what makes the customer happier, and the less pleasant path is what she tries to avoid happening in the first place.

[7]Test it in a `diskaria.ring` file you create inside the folder for this chapter: `c:\ringbook\chap5`.

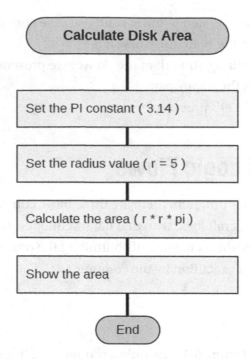

Figure 5-4. *Area calculation algorithm "written" in Drakon*

Four steps are organized in a sequence to solve this basic mathematical problem. The first two steps are rather computer-oriented, since the machine needs to get the values of pi and the radius of the disk. The third step is logic-oriented, since the area can be obtained only when we apply the provided mathematic formula. The fourth and last step is a human requirement since the result should be exposed to the user; otherwise, her problem is not considered to be solved.

This separation between these three types of logic is the cornerstone of building strong programming skills. In fact, when they are facing a problem to solve, many programmers (they are millions today) start by focusing on the computer-oriented requirements, which is wrong! These are implementation details, so please don't let them clutter your thoughts. Instead, think of what your users need as a result first and then restrict your thinking to the logic-oriented part of your algorithm.

Computer language constraints come at the end of the story and must be considered as a supporting layer of a technical feature so your program avoids technical problems, is secure, and has acceptable performance.[8]

What if we take a second basic example requiring a sequence of logic flow but in the other way? For example, we can expose a problem, think of a logical solution for it, describe the solution in a Drakon diagram, and only then transcribe it in Ring.

- **The problem**: Calculate the number of weeks in 222 days.

- **The solution**: Given that a week contains 7 days, then 222 days would contain 222/7 weeks, which means 31.71 weeks. Thus, the answer is really 32 weeks.

Here is the algorithmic sequence:

1. Set 222 in a constant.

2. Divide it by 7.

3. Take the result and round it to the upper integer.

4. Show that result. This is the number of weeks!

Figure 5-5 shows the Drakon visualization.

---

[8]Performance optimization is one of the main requirements of software quality. *Performance* can be defined as the amount of work performed by a computer to accomplish a programming task. Many factors influence program performance: time spent by the program execution (including the time program itself, the operating system time, and the network time), speed of the CPU, and, especially, complexity of the program code. In Chapter 9, I will give you a hint about how this is approached by professional programmers in term of planning for the time and space complexity of computer programs.

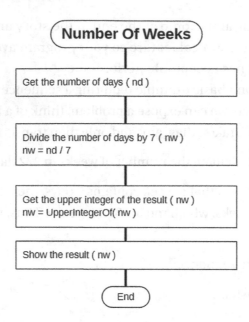

Figure 5-5. *"Number Of Weeks" algorithm "written" in Drakon*

Let's translate Figure 5-5 to Ring in a new numweeks.ring file, as shown in Listing 5-2.

Listing 5-2. numweeks.ring

```
// Defining the number of weeks
// contained in a number of days
nd = 222          # step 1: get the number of days
nw = nd / 7       # step 2: divide it by 7
nw = ceil( nw )   # step 3: round it to upper integer
see nw            # step 4: show the result
```

This parallelism between what you design visually in Drakon and what you write as code in Ring is the most important lesson you should distill from this section. You will see its true value in the upcoming sections of the chapter.

An Arabic proverb says, "Patience is the key to relief."

Selection (or Branching)

When a sequence of actions is flowing in a computer program, the actions are executed in the order of their appearance, one by one. As is the case in real life, and at a given step of the sequence, we often must make a selection between two or more secondary paths. Therefore, the flow of data depends on a logical condition or on the answer to a question, for example. Every secondary path is itself a sequence inside the sequence.

Look at Figure 5-6.

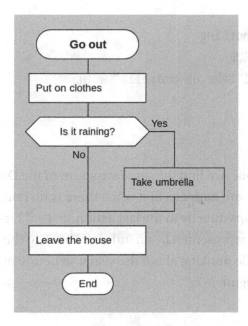

Figure 5-6. *"Go out" algorithm "written" in Drakon*

Before you go out and leave the house, there is a sequence of actions you do: you put on your clothes, and then you leave. But what if it is raining outside? In this case, you should also take an umbrella.

You have made a selection for the next step depending on the answer given to the question "Is it raining?" If the answer is "no," then the next action is "Leave the house," but if it is "yes," the next one is "Take an umbrella" and then "Leave the house."

Programmatically, in almost any language, selection is expressed by the use of an `if` statement. Let's see it in action while Ringifying the same algorithm as before inside a new file called `goout.ring`, as shown in Listing 5-3.

Listing 5-3. goout.ring

```
// Go out
isRaining = FALSE # Can be also set to TRUE
c = "I put on my clothes" + NL
if isRaining = FALSE
            // do nothing
else  # isRaining = TRUE
            c += "I take an umbrella" + NL
ok
c += "I go out"
? c
```

When we scan this code, we find the same structure of the Drakon diagram we saw in Figure 5-6. The happy path happens first when there is no rain, and thus `isRaining = FALSE`. The execution jumps directly to the last action: `c += "I go out"`.[9] The unhappy path, when it's raining, is represented by an indented bock to the right. Train your eyes to read the Ring code while thinking about the visual structure of the Drakon diagram in your head, as shown in Figure 5-7.

---

[9]Do you know what += used for? For example, n += 1 is an abbreviation of n = n + 1, yet it is more elegant and generally comes with better speed. You can also use n -= 3, n *= 5, and so on.

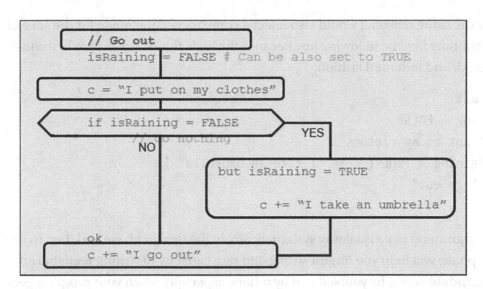

Figure 5-7. Visual analogy between Drakon diagram and a Ring algorithm[10]

This is not a visual dogma, though, but a tangible, visual way of thinking in code that results in learnability and nice organization. In fact, I would reject an equivalent version of the same algorithm that goes like this just because the golden happy path rule is broken:

```
// Go out
isRaining = FALSE
c = "I put on my clothes" + NL
if isRaining = TRUE
            c += "I take an umbrella"
            else
                    // do nothing
ok
c += "I go out"
? c
```

---

[10]Note the change I made for better readability: but instead of else. Read about the syntax flexibility of the Ring language in the documentation center: http://ring-lang.sourceforge. net/doc1.11/syntaxflexibility.html.

For the same reason, I would also reject a compact version made for the sake of code economy like the following just because the logic flow is not visible in a consistent, structured, and indented fashion:

```
// Go out
isRaining = FALSE
c = "I put on my clothes"
if isRaining = TRUE { c += "I take an umbrella" }[11]
c += "I go out"
? c
```

Programming in a visual way systematically in the design phase and then in the coding phase will help you forge a strong and rare capacity of writing readable and understandable code by yourself and by others, especially when your program gets larger.

Iteration (or Looping)

The power of a computer as a "thinking machine" resides in iteration. It has the ability to repeat tasks many, many times, without any sweat from the programmer. This is what distinguishes it from a human mind.

Visually speaking, Figure 5-8 shows how an iteration is drawn (called a *cycle* in Drakon).

---

[11]I will explain the use of brackets ({ }) later in the chapter.

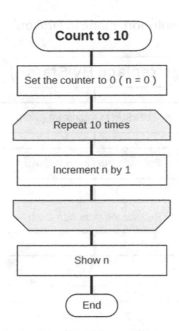

Figure 5-8. *"Count to 10" algorithm "written" in Drakon*

As you can see, we are counting to 10. The algorithm iterates over an integer variable 10 times, adding 1 to it every time. In programming, this is better known as a `for` loop statement. In Ring, this translates to Listing 5-4.[12]

Listing 5-4. count10.ring

```
// Count to 10
n = 0
for i = 1 to 10
      n++
next i
? n
```

Sometimes, the repetition can iterate over a list of things so that it is possible to modify them. To illustrate the case, let's solve this: replace every letter of the word TUNISIA with an asterisk (*).

The solution is to iterate sequentially over the letters available in the word TUNISIA and, for each letter, replace it with a *.

---

[12]Please note that I'm aware this is not the cleanest approach to a counting algorithm, but it is helpful for the sake of pedagogy. By the way, test it in a new count10.ring file.

Figure 5-9 shows the visual solution, made in Drakon.

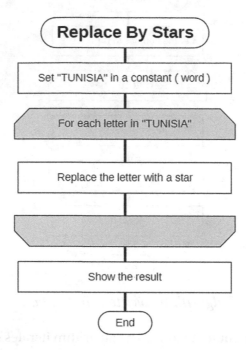

Figure 5-9. *"Replace By Stars" algorithm "written" in Drakon*

Obviously, this can be implemented using the for loop. Written in Ring, the Drakon diagram becomes Listing 5-5 (test it in a new `stars.ring` file).

Listing 5-5. stars.ring

```
// Replace by stars (using "for" loop)
word = "TUNISIA"
for i in word                  # Iterating over the word
         word[i] = "*"          # Changing the current letter with *
next
? word                         # Result should be "*******"
```

This can be implemented also using a for in loop (called the foreach loop in other languages). To do so, we would write something like Listing 5-6 (in a new file called `stars2.ring`).

Listing 5-6. stars2.ring

```
// Replace by stars (using "for in" loop)
word = "TUNISIA"
i = 0
for letter in word          # Iterating over the word
          i++
          word[i] = "*"   # Changing the current letter with *
next
? word
```

Although this does the job, it doesn't make sense, since for in should be used in Ring primarily to modify lists and not strings.[13] Listing 5-7 shows an example of this and shows that you can test it inside an empty stars3.ring.

Listing 5-7. stars3.ring

```
// Modify a list using for in
aList = "A":"D"             # Same as aList = [ "A","B","C","D" ]

for letter in aList      # Iterating over the list
       letter += "*"     # Changing the current item in the list
next
? aList     # Gives aList = [ "A*","B*","C*","D*" ]
```

You might ask then, when do you use for and when do you use for in?

Difference Between for and for in

Well, technically speaking, everything that you can do with a for loop can be done with for in. Still, the following list may help you see differences between them while using them in Ring:

---

[13]You'll learn more about this in the next section.

- for is suitable for iterating over strings or any list for which the number of items (to iterate on) can be known in advance. For example, to loop over the letters of cString = "TUNISIA", we say the following:

```
for i = 1 to 7        // Because we know it contains 7 letters
```

or we can say the following:

```
for i = 1 to len(cString) // Because it is possible to
                          // compute the number of
                          // iterations using len()
```

To access the current item, you need to use a counter i (or any name you choose for this number variable) like this:

```
for i = 1 to len(cString) { ? cString[ i ] }
```

- for in is designed for looking through lists when you don't know how many items they contain. When an aList is used to store data coming from user input or a connected web service, then you can say the following:

```
for item in aList
```

without being concerned with how many items are there (you know they can vary from one user to another or from a web service request to another).

For every item accessed by the loop, you can write code without worrying about its range in the aList since there is no counter provided but the item in person is at your disposal. Hence, you can say the following:

```
for item in aList {? item} # Print the current item14
```

---

[14]You can use any variable name you choose instead of item. Usually this needs to reflect the nature of the list items. So, if we are iterating over a list of people called aPersons[ ], we say for person in aPerson[ ].

The difference can be better identified when the option for one of the two loop formats becomes a matter of life and death (I mean, when only one makes the job correctly, either for or for in). Here are two use cases to help explain this point:

- What if you want to iterate over a list in steps of 3 or in descending order? Only for can do it. To jump a number of steps in your loop, you say the following:

```
for i=1 to 6 step 2 { ? i }      # Goes over 1, 3, and 5
```

When you want to loop over cString = "TUNISIA" in descending order, you say the following:

```
# Displays the letters upside down
for i=7 to 1 step -1 { ? cString[i] }
```

- What if you want to delete an item while you are iterating over a list (the third item in ["1","2","3","4","5"] list, for example)? When you make it using for in, you are done.

```
a = "1":"5"
i = 0
for letter in a
        i++
        if letter = "3" { del(a,i) }
next
? a      # Gives ["1","2","4","5"]
```

And when you use for, you are also done.

```
a = "1":"5"
i = 0
for i = 1 to len(a)
        if a[i] = "3" { del(a,i) }
next
? a           # Also gives [ "1","2","4","5" ]
```

Now, let's make a change in the current item (by adding a * at its right), just after the deleting operation happens. With for in, we get in trouble (item 4 is not managed by the loop).

```
a = "1":"5"
i = 0
for letter in a
        i++
        if letter = "3" { del(a,i) }
        letter += "*"
next
? a     # Gives ["1*","2*","4","5*"]
```

But with for, we have done it correctly.

```
a = "1":"5"
i = 0
for i = 1 to len(a)
            if a[i] = "3" { del(a,i) }
            a[i] += "*"
next
? a             # Also gives [ "1*","2*","4*","5*" ]
```

Always experiment before you decide, and if you are not sure, it's always safer to opt for...for.

Infinite Loops

What if you want to perform a jump to infinity? It's easy to do with a for loop that increments its upper limit continuously. Try Listing 5-8 in the infinity.ring file.

Listing 5-8. infinity.ring

```
infinity = 1

for i=1 to infinity
      ? i
      infinity++
next i
```

In the Output window, the program starts counting and never stops. In real-world applications, called *real-time applications*, such as GUIs and games, you will need such infinite loops (called *main loops*) to be a main observers of your program to trigger events and define actions to handle the events.

Sadly, the problem with the solution we came up with here is that infinity is a mere illusion. The execution will lead to a place where the number `infinity` can't afford to receive more ++s and Ring Notepad will show a `Stack Overflow` error.[15]

In the next section, you will learn that the `while` loop is what we should use, among other interesting techniques, for crafting the logic flow of your Ring algorithms.

To close this section, and for the love of sharing, let me say that the first program I ever wrote with a `for` loop dates back to 1989, on an MSX-Basic computer. It looked like Figure 5-10.

```
10    OPEN "GRP:" AS #1
20    SCREEN 2 : COLOR 15,4,4 : CLS
30    A$ ="MESSAGE"
40    FOR I = 0 TO LEN(A$)
50    Z=0
60    FOR X=50 TO 51.8
70    PRESET ( X + Z×a₁+I+a₂, y + Z× a₃).4
80    PRINT#1, MID$(A$,I+1,1)
90    Z=Z+1
95    NEXT X
100   NEXT I
```

Figure 5-10.   Three decades ago, there was a handwriting programmer...

In Chapter 9, you will learn why this program was written by hand. Meanwhile, don't fly away. The serious staff on crafting logic flows has just begun!

---

[15]It's not a stack overflow really, but a numeric overflow, even if the first error is correctly reported by Ring Notepad. I will explain the root error and how you can "unleash" it in the next section when I introduce `while` loops. For now, you can reflect on the difference between the two kinds of error by reading those definitions online.

- Overflow: `https://tinyurl.com/utbkceq`
- Numeric (or arithmetic) overflow: `https://tinyurl.com/tzubzem`
- Stack overflow: `https://tinyurl.com/yx85h2rz`
- Call stack: `https://tinyurl.com/crmdrwr`

More on Logic Flows

In real-world programs, the three basic constructs of logic flows we saw in the previous section are always combined to represent complex logic constructs. In this section, I will show relevant samples of such combinations.

Vertical Selections

Sometimes the flow of logic is addressed by a successive number of questions (or selections, if you prefer).

For example, to buy a puppy, you first need to ask if you have enough money, and then, if the answer is yes, whether puppies are on sale that day. After you take a puppy among those that are available in the shop, you would ask yourself if you liked it or not. And only then would you move to the action of buying it. Figure 5-11 shows the underlining logic of the "Buy a puppy" algorithm written in Drakon.

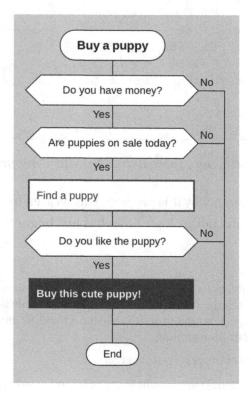

Figure 5-11. *"Buy a Puppy" algorithm "written" in Drakon*

To tell the story in Ring, some implementation details are required, as listed here:

- Some Boolean[16] variables need to be declared so we can use them to make the logical decisions required (iHaveMoney or not, puppies are onSale or not, and when I select one, do iLikeIt or not).

- Two lists are required, one for the available puppies for sale in the shop (aPuppies[]) and the other for the list of my preferred puppies (aMyPref[]).

- Some functions are necessary to complete the actions required by the algorithm: getAPuppyFrom() to pick a puppy randomly from the aPuppies[] list, doILikeThis() to see whether the picked puppy belongs also to aMyPref[] list, and, finally, buy() to move to the action and effectively buy one.

Outside of this implementation staff, which I don't want you to focus on,[17] the Drakon diagram is described in the IF block in bold hereafter (write it inside a new puppy.ring file), as shown in Listing 5-9.

Listing 5-9. puppy.ring

```
// Bye a puppy

iHaveMoney = TRUE
onSale = TRUE
iLikeIt = FALSE

aPuppies = [ "Beagle" , "Terrier" , "Pug" , "Maltese" ]
aMyPref = [ "Poms" , "Beagle" , "Pug" , "Shih Tzu" ]
```

---

[16]As mentioned in previous chapters, Ring doesn't provide a native form of Boolean variable. These can be expressed by the two variables TRUE and FALSE, which correspond to the numbers 1 and 0, respectively. In Ring, everything is TRUE except the number zero, which is FALSE.

[17]In fact, you shouldn't care about the // Functions part of the program because what we are learning here is what is related to the "thinking" stuff designed in the Drakon diagram. Structurally, this corresponds to the main region of a Ring program, as presented in previous chapters. Remember that functions and classes in Ring go always to the end of file, and this is really useful to stay focused on the problem at hand.

251

```
if iHaveMoney and onSale
        cPuppy = getAPuppyFrom(aPuppies)
        iLikeIt = doILikeThis(cPuppy)
        if iLikeIt
                buy(cPuppy)
        ok
ok

// FUNCTIONS

func getAPuppyFrom( a )
            n = random( len(a) ) + 1
            if n > len(a) { n = len(a) }
            c = a[n]
            return c

func doILikeThis( c )
            if find( aMyPref , c ) != 0
                            bFound = TRUE
            else
                            bFound = FALSE
            ok
            return bFound

func buy( p )
    ? "I bought a wonderful " + p + " :)"
```

Save it and execute it several times[18] to see how the program reacts randomly.

Now, let's compare the core of our code with the correspondent Drakon diagram, as shown in Figure 5-12.

---

[18]Don't be disappointed if the result is "nothing" in the Output window. Try again many times (Ctrl+F5) so that the randomness engine generates a number corresponding to an existing puppy in the aMyPref[ ] list. We will fix this soon in the section.

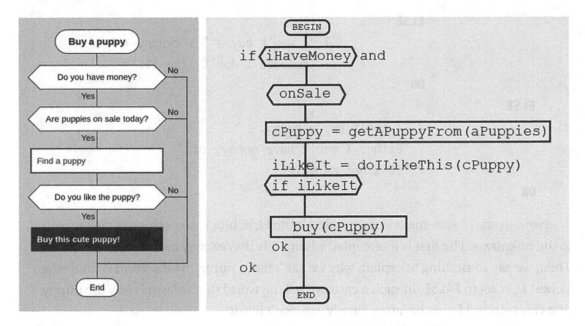

Figure 5-12. *Comparative view of "Buy a puppy" algorithm between Drakon and Ring*

The two representations are identical, which is really a good sign, but wait...

Logically we are done, but programmatically nope. In fact, there is a "nothing" gap that we should leverage. You would agree that executing the program many times before we get a concrete result in the Output window isn't something we can be proud of. That's why our thinking should be adjusted to intercept all the cases where "nothing" is generated so we can show "something" informative to our users.

To make it happen, an ELSE block should be written for every IF statement. See Listing 5-10.

Listing 5-10. Part of puppy.ring

```
IF iHaveMoney AND
onSale
        cPuppy = getAPuppyFrom(aPuppies)
        iLikeIt = doILikeThis(cPuppy)
        IF iLikeIt
                buy(cPuppy)
```

253

```
                    ELSE

                            ? "I won't buy a " + cPuppy + " !"
                            ? "Because I don't like it."

                    OK

            ELSE

                    ? "I can't buy a puppy."
                    ? "Either I don't have money, or,"
                    ? "it's not on sale"

        OK
```

Now, every IF statement is augmented by an ELSE block, so nothing is delivered to the unknown. The first is intercepted when both iHaveMoney and onSale are FALSE. Then, we say something to explain why we can't buy a puppy. The second is fired when iLiketIt is set to FALSE. In such a case, we tell the world that we won't buy the puppy that was selected for us because, simply, we don't like it!

Insert these new lines in the initial program file, test it, and verify how the program reacts to every execution with a clear and informative message, as shown here:

```
I won't bye a Terrier !
Because I don't like it.

I bought a wonderful Beagle :)

I bought a wonderful Pug :)

I won't bye a Maltese !
Because I don't like it.
```

Deep Selections

When we added ELSE blocks in the previous section to every IF statement, we resorted to the use of indentation, which is a way to show the hierarchies in the code. We added some complexity and started to construct deeper levels (or deeper selections, to embrace the title of this section) by using more indented code blocks. There is a breakpoint we need to make here.

Indentation is helpful because it helps express that a portion of code "belongs" to another one. The problem is that every programmer can have a different intent behind that "belongs" thing. Usually, and especially in long code, a huge mental effort is necessary to get it right and understand the logical structure right from the indentation template.

Hello to the thorny problem of learnability of today's computer code!

To be precise, I define the problem of learnability as the inability of a programmer to distill the logical flow of an algorithm straightforwardly from the structure of the code, based on its indentation.

Believe me, if you are aware of this, then you're on your way to programming craftsmanship. Even better, follow me in thinking visually in code using the Drakon semantics, and you will see that this will develop your reflexes for writing well-structured and learnable text code.

My advice to you, as a visual thinker and programmer, is to stay away from using indentation in a free-form, nonrigorous, and complexity-prone manner. Embrace the Drakon paradigm, and think of indentation in these ways:

- Drakon creates a visual separation between the happy and less happy scenarios by posing the first strictly vertically and progressively indenting the second to the right.

- The result is a reading experience that immediately shows what the programmer meant for the internal logical workings of the algorithm.

- The traditional paradigm of writing code has no knowledge of such a "happy scenario," so programmers are free to think of what comes to their mind first, depending on their very own intuition and psychological status.

- Conventional code writing uses indentation only to clarify the "technical" hierarchy of the code blocks, not for communicating the intrinsic logical meaning.

- The result, when it comes to writing large code, even if it is well indented, is that a huge mental effort is necessary to understand the logic meant by the programmer who wrote that code.

Practice? Yes, nothing is better than practice.

Here I will show you a sample algorithm with a deep selection, first in Drakon and then in Ring code. After that, we will do the same as in the previous section and compare the two representations; then I will propose some enhancements to the visual structure of our Ring code.

The problem narrative is as follows: you take a train every morning to get to your office.[19] Before that, you need to drive about 10 km from your house to the train station. There you need to park the car, preferably without paying any money, and then enter the platform and wait for the train. If you are in Moscow, a train passes exactly every seven minutes, and if you are in Giza, Egypt, this will take probably two to three hours! But these are just understandable cultural differences (my hugs to my Egyptian friends, who will accept this joke, because joking, itself, is also a distinguished and shining Egyptian cultural difference). When the train comes, you board it, right? Great. Figure 5-13 shows how we think of it visually in Drakon.

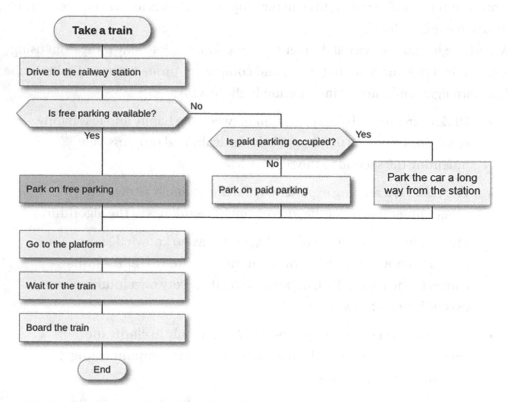

Figure 5-13. *"Take a train" algorithm "written" in Drakon*

In Ring, and after taking 30 seconds[20] to understand Figure 5-13, I begin by writing the structure of the happy path as shown in Listing 5-11 (write it in a new `takerain.ring` file).

---

[19]I dedicate this to one of my friends on the Apress team who will recognize himself in the story.

[20]Don't take this as gospel. I pretend I'm fast, but in reality I'm notably slow in thinking before writing any code. So, take your time!

Listing 5-11. taketrain.ring

```
// Take a Train Program

begin()
            drive()
            if isFreeParking = :AVAILABLE
                            parkOnFree()
            ok

            goToPlatform()
            waitForTrain()
            boardInTrain()
theend()
```

Here, I really need your attention, because I'm unveiling my own way of thinking visually in code, by translating a Drakon diagram to Ring code, progressively, and by securing a small logical achievement in every incremental step. The first one is the writing of the happy scenario without any ELSE branch at all!

The readability advantage of what we've done is obvious. Hence, we can immediately learn that the algorithm happy scenario is about the following:

- **drive():** Driving from my house to the train station

- **parkOnFree():** Parking my car in a free space

- **goToPlatform():** Entering the train platform

- **waitForTrain():** Waiting for the train (singing and looking around because I'm stranger in Moscow)

- **boardInTrain():** Boarding the train

So, let's concentrate on making this code workable. To do so, we will add a function to every *something* with a () in our code, and we will declare an isFreeParking variable to use it as a conditional router for the IF statement. Then we get Listing 5-12.

Listing 5-12. taketrain.ring

```
// Take a Train Program
isFreeParking = :AVAILABLE

takeTrain()
drive()

            if isFreeParking = :AVAILABLE
                        parkOnFree()
            ok

            goToPlatform()
            waitForTrain()
            boardInTrain()
theEnd()

// FUNCTIONS
func begin()
            ? "BEGIN" + NL

func theEnd()
            ? NL + "END"

func drive()
            ? "I'm driving from house to train station." + NL

func parkOnFree()
            ? "I've found a free place in the parking." + NL

func goToPlatform()
            ? "I've parked now. I enter to the platform." + NL

func waitForTrain()
            ? "I'm waiting for train, and looking around :)" + NL

func boardInTrain()
    ? "I'm in Giza, the train took only 7 minutes to come :)" +
    "It's boarding, bye!"
```

Save it in a `taketrain.ring` file and execute it; the happy path is beautifully crystallized in the output window like this:

```
BEGIN

I'm driving from house to train station.

I've found a free place in the parking.

I've parked now. I enter to the platform.

I'm waiting for train, and looking around :)

I'm in Giza, the train took only 7 minutes to come :)
It's boarding, bye!

END
```

In other terms, all this ⸢ happy part ⸥ of our main Drakon diagram is now covered and correctly implemented in Ring, as shown in Figure 5-14.

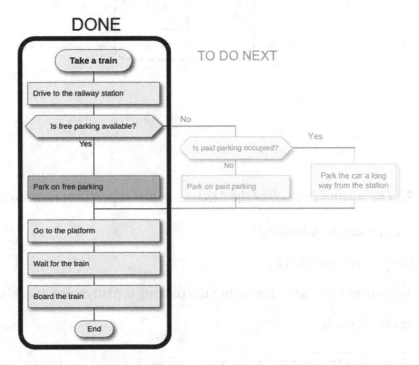

Figure 5-14. *Happy path of the "Take a train" algorithm written in Drakon*

Now we can turn to the ¦middle part¦ of the diagram: the deeper selection, the less happy path of the logic flow.

Here is the narrative: If there is no free parking available, then I turn to paid parking and try to find a nonoccupied place for my car. Ideally, this place is found, and my car is parked in it. Again, I won't retain my desire of Ringifying it.

So, the first thing to do is to set the isFreeParcking condition to :UNAVAILABLE[21] as it is required by the diagram logic (the first NO hereafter), as shown in Figure 5-15.

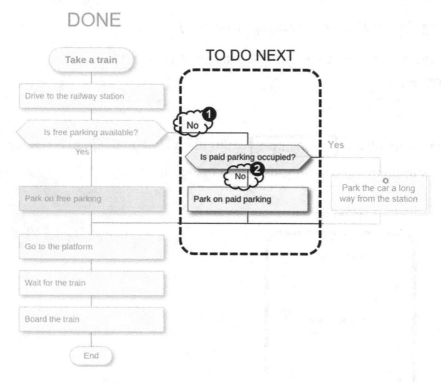

Figure 5-15. *The second branch of the "Take a train" algorithm written in Drakon*

Hence, you can say the following:

```
isFreeParcking = :UNAVAILABLE
```

Second, we can add a condition whether the parking is paid or not like this:

```
isPaidOccupied = FALSE
```

---

[21]It is always better to use TRUE and FALSE variables to represent logical conditions. Despite this, the use of a string like :AVAILABLE and :UNAVAILABLE in the current case can provide us with more clarity and expressiveness.

And we set it to FALSE as it is required by the logic that was designed in the second part of our diagram (the second NO in Figure 5-15).

Then, these lines:

```
if isFreeParking = :AVAILABLE
            parkOnFree()
ok
```

become the following:

```
if isFreeParking = :AVAILABLE
              parkOnFree()
else        # its :UNAVAILABLE => first NO in the figure above
    if isPaidOccupied = FALSE    # => the second NO
                    parkOnPaid()
    ok
ok
```

Finally, we add the corresponding function to the "Park on paid parking" rectangle we have in Figure 5-15, and we name it parkOnPaid().

```
func parkOnPaid()
        ? "I found a place in a paid parking so I take it!" + NL
```

If you save the file (taketrain.ring) and execute, you get the following:

```
BEGIN

I'm driving from house to train station.

I found a place in a paid parking so I take it!

I've parked now. I enter to the platform.

I'm waiting for train, and looking around :)

I'm in Giza, the train took only 7 minutes to come :)
It's boarding, bye!

END
```

Excellent. But what if there was no place in the paid parking? This leads us to the third and last part of the diagram, as shown in Figure 5-16.

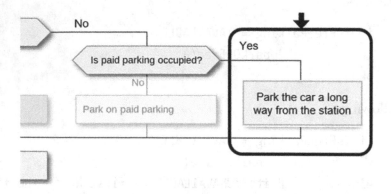

Figure 5-16. *The less happier path of the "Take a train" algorithm written in Drakon*

To activate it in our code, we change isPaidOccupied to TRUE, which is the translation to the Ring code of the "Yes" line in Figure 5-16.

isPaidOccupied = **TRUE**

The lines that currently say the following:

```
        if isPaidOccupied
              parkOnPaid()
    ok
```

become these:

```
        if isPaidOccupied
              parkOnPaid()
        else
              parkOutside()
    ok
```

For sure, we create a new function called parkOutside() that says the following:

```
func parkOutside()
    ? "Unfortunately, I must park away from the station." + NL
```

Save and execute. Here is the result:

```
BEGIN

I'm driving from house to train station.
```

Unfortunately, I must park away from the station.

```
I've parked now. I enter to the platform.

I'm waiting for train, and looking around :)

I'm in Giza, the train took only 7 minutes to come :)
It's boarding, bye!

END
```

You see? Thinking visually, with Drakon representation in mind, helped us to write correct and consistent code, without any mental hassle. Now, look to the whole text of the Ring program and analyze it visually, again and again (Listing 5-13).

Listing 5-13. taketrain.ring

```
// The Take a Train Program
isFreeParking = :UNAVAILABLE
isPaidOccupied = TRUE
```

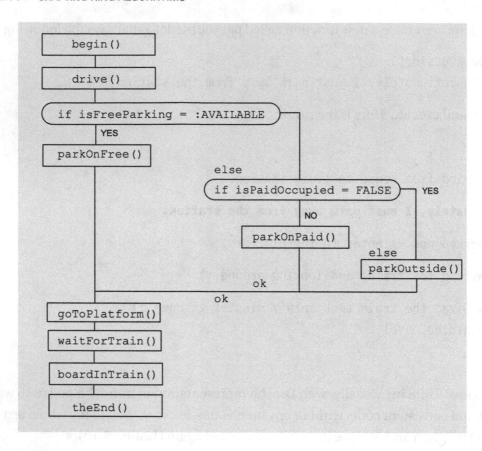

// FUNCTIONS

```
func begin()
        ? "BEGIN" + NL

func theEnd()
        ? NL + "END"

func drive()
        ? "I'm driving from house to train station." + NL

func parkOnFree()
        ? "I've found a free place in the parking." + NL

func parkOnPaid()
        ? "I found a place in a paid parking so I take it!" + NL
```

```
func parkOutside()
            ? "Unfortunately, I must park away from the station." + NL

func goToPlatform()
            ? "I've parked now. I enter to the platform." + NL

func waitForTrain()
            ? "I'm waiting for train, and looking around :)" + NL

func boardInTrain()
  ? "I'm in Giza, the train took only 7 minutes to come :)" +
    NL + "It's boarding, bye!"
```

Condition-First Iteration: while

You have discovered that iteration is one of the most important forms of logic flow. In particular, it is what represents the power of a machine to repeat billions or trillions of tasks in a fraction of a second. You also saw how selection helps us route the logic flow conditionally. Now, what if we discover how can we merge the two: iterations and selections?

Let's start, in the current section, with the first form of combination we call *condition-first* iteration and leave the second one, *condition-last iteration*, to the next one.

Condition-first iterations correspond to the well-known while loop, which is a continuous iteration of the logic flow until a specified condition is satisfied. Such a condition is specified at the beginning of the loop. Let's see a visual example; see Figure 5-17.

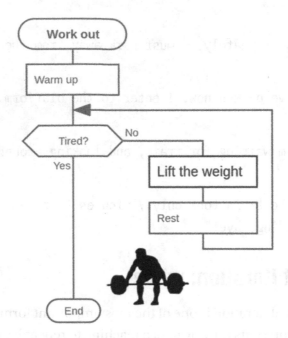

Figure 5-17. *The "Work out" algorithm written in Drakon*

You've got it, and I didn't help you by any visual indication, right?

Here is the narrative: you are a champion, so you work out. Then you do it continuously:

- You lift the weight.

- You take a rest.

- You iterate the two first actions.

But if you get tired, you simply end it. This condition is forced to be verified at the beginning of the iteration.

Ringifying it, while internalizing the visual representation of the algorithm, requires these tactics:

1. Implement the first vertical happy scenario without any branching or indented selections.

2. Move to the right of the diagram and implement one level a time by adding the necessary ELSE block.

3. Analyze your text code, read it, and communicate it, while thinking about the visual representation in your head.

Before you delve into coding, think of the conversion between your Drakon diagram and the necessary Ring stuff you need to write. When you start writing, it's simple: don't consider more than the first happy path. All the details and other deeper selections will come later. Visually speaking, Figure 5-18 shows the happy path.

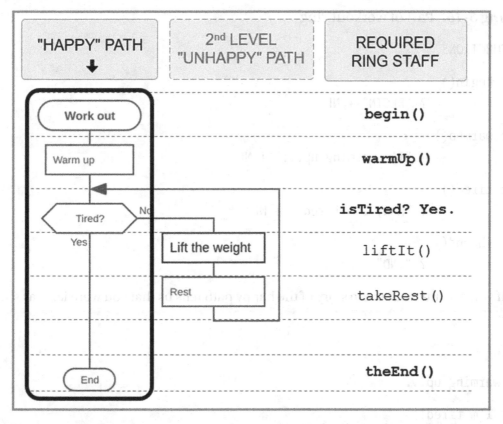

Figure 5-18. *Analysis of the required implementation in Ring of the Drakon algorithm*

Make a new Ring file, call it `workout.ring`, and start by using the bold functions in the "Required Ring Staff" column, as shown in Listing 5-14.

Listing 5-14. workout.ring

```
begin()
warmup()
if isTired = TRUE
          tired()
Ok
theend()
```

Of course, you need to add a line at the start of the file, as shown here:

```
isTired = TRUE
```

and add all the necessary functions at the end, as shown in Listing 5-15.

Listing 5-15. Part of workout.ring

```
// FUNCTIONS

func begin()
            ? "BEGIN" + NL

func warmup()
            ? "I'm warming up..." + NL

func tired()
             ? "Now, I'm tired!" + NL

func theend()
               ? "END"
```

If you execute it, then the story of the happy path tells us that you were lazy, as shown here:

```
BEGIN

I'm warming up...

Now, I'm tired!

END
```

Then we move to the right portion of the diagram. Visibly, when you read it, you can identify that the branching happens in the ⟨Tired?⟩ node, when the answer to the question is NO. By analogy, to activate this part of the diagram, isTired needs to change from TRUE to FALSE (the NO in the previous diagram).

```
isTired = FALSE
```

At this level, if you save the file and execute it, you get the following:

```
BEGIN

I'm warming up...

END
```

Well, by combining this result with the fact of not being tired (isTired = FALSE), one could implicitly conclude that I'm going to lift the weight one more time, take a rest, and then decide again to repeat the same two actions, depending on whether I get tired or not. It seems straightforward, but be careful: you are not writing a letter to your mom to let here implicitly infer the feelings between the lines. You are writing a letter to the Ring compiler who won't be comfortable with your writing style unless you are totally explicit about what you want to say!

That's why the isTired = FALSE case should be managed and never left to the unknown. Hence, add an ELSE block to the IF statement in the main region of the program, as shown in Listing 5-16.

Listing 5-16. Part of workout.ring

```
begin()
        warmup()
        if isTired = TRUE
            tired()
        else
            lift()
            rest()
        Ok
theend()
```

As usual, two new functions are added at the end of the file, as shown in Listing 5-17.

Listing 5-17. Part of workout.ring

```
func lift()
            ? "I lift the weight."

func rest()
            ? "I take a rest."
```

Now, execute it so you get the following:

```
 BEGIN

I'm warming up...
```

I lift the weight.
I take a rest.

```
END
```

In Tunisian dialect, we have this nice proverb that says, "Getting a red face is better than having a broken heart." It's more or less equivalent to saying frank reactions are better than fake smiles. We use it to encourage people to be explicit about what they want, even if it sometimes hurts. Clarity always saves misunderstandings and social conflicts. This applies perfectly to the programming domain: many hard bugs and unexplainable anomalies are driven by adopting this kind of implicitness (leaving some ELSE branches unspecified) when they can be avoided, at the root level, by embracing explicitness all the time!

Now, the actions of the right portion are executed, but only once. Nevertheless, what we want is a continuous iteration as long as the champion is still not tired (isTired = FALSE).

In terms of the Drakon diagram, it turns back to Ringify this callback arrow, as shown in Figure 5-19.

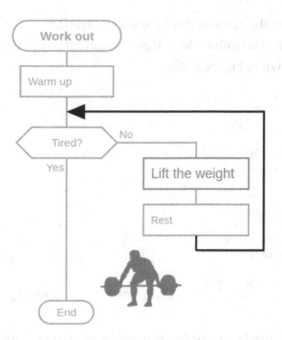

Figure 5-19. *Symbol of continuous iteration in Drakon*

Unfortunately, continuous iteration can't be implemented with an IF statement. That's why Ring, like other programming languages, gives us the programmatic construct to make it happen: the while statement.

Let's replace the IF block in the Listing 5-17 with Listing 5-18.

Listing 5-18. Part of workout.ring

```
while isTired = FALSE  // While I'm not tired…
           lift()   // repeat this,
           rest()   // and this.
end // note the use of "end" and not "ok"
```

Yes, but…

You aren't going to execute it, right? Anyone who reads it, even without a programming background, would doubt that the program will run continually until the computer is completely out of memory!

If you insist, do it in the console this time using Ctrl+R.[22]

What happened? It is an infinite loop that you can interrupt by pressing Ctrl+C on your keyboard, as shown in Figure 5-20.

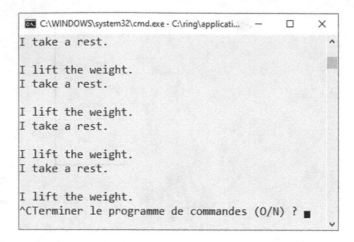

Figure 5-20. *An infinite loop can be stopped in the console using Ctrl+C*

Why has this happened? Simply because there is nothing inside the while block that forces the isTired condition to become TRUE and thus helps the poor loop find a window for recovering from the infinity dark hole and taking a deep sigh of breath.

So, never forget that when you use a while statement, you need to find a place inside it to change the loop condition to the inverse of its value defined in the head[23] of the block; otherwise, you've experimented with the cost you are willing to pay.

---

[22]Always use the console to test your programs that deal with infinite loops and a large amount of data. There you can interrupt the execution, anytime you want, by simply pressing Ctrl+D on the keyboard. In the Output window of Notepad, you are obliged to wait until an error message is displayed or close the IDE and open it again, which is impractical. You will prefer the console, in this situation, for another reason related to the nature of the error generated by Ring. To explain it, let's take the case where the iteration loops over a number and increments it indefinitely (we will have an example like this in the next section). When you run the loop on the console, the error you get is Numeric Overflow, which corresponds to the root of the problem you are facing. When you use the Notepad Output window, which uses internally a QTextEdit widget using a QProcess object from the Qt framework, the error you will get is Stack Overflow, which is not wrong but camouflages the root error (Numeric Overflow) and prevents it from happening and being communicated to you. This is risky and misleading, especially when you are developing critical applications.

[23]You will see in the next section that this condition can be also at the bottom of the while block.

To fix it, we need to agree on the exit condition of the loop. Suppose we want to stop it when it reaches a maximum of 3 iterations; in that case, we write the code in Listing 5-19.

Listing 5-19. Part of workout.ring

```
n = 0                        # A counter used for the exit condition
while isTired = FALSE
            lift()
            rest()
            ? ""
            n++
            if n = 3 { isTired = TRUE } // Forces the loop to stop
end
```

Save it and test it. I observe you, right now, repeating the `lift()` and `rest()` actions three times before you feel tired and leave the training room. It won't be sufficient to develop strong muscles, but let's say it's better than nothing.

Before we move to the next section, let me explain something related to the syntax that uses **{** and **}** in this line:

```
if n = 3 { isTired = TRUE }
```

In fact, this is equivalent to writing the following:

```
if n = 3
{
isTired = TRUE
}
```

Or:

```
if n = 3
    isTired = TRUE
end
```

And it is relevant to the following:

if n = 3 isTired = TRUE **end**

This is freedom of speech, my friends, which is one of the cultural[24] cornerstones of Ring.

Condition-Last Iteration: do again

What if the same "continuous" iteration is conserved, but the condition is verified at the end of the loop and not at its beginning?

The corresponding visual thinking can be represented as shown in Figure 5-21.

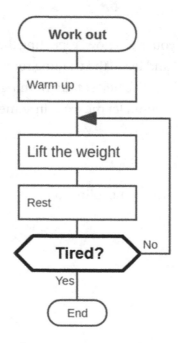

Figure 5-21. *A condition-last iteration in a Drakon algorithm*

---

[24]To learn a language, you need to understand its culture. This includes the motivations of the language designer and the challenges he wants to solve, along with the design options he implemented to distinguish his language from other programming languages. In many places in the book, I try to show you the cultural aspects of the Ring language, so please pay attention to them. Also, the discussion I had with Mahmoud Fayed, the Ring inventor, as presented in the appendix of the book can be enlightening and really useful.

In Ring, this is done using a do again statement, as shown in Listing 5-20.

Listing 5-20. Part of workout2.ring

```
n = 1
do
    lift()
    rest()
    ? ""
    if n = 3 { isTired = TRUE }
    n++
again isTired = FALSE
```

Save a copy of the current program as workout2.ring and include the lines from Listing 5-20 in the file. Execute it, and observe the results, as shown here:

```
BEGIN

I'm warming up...

I lift the weight.
I take a rest.

I lift the weight.
I take a rest.

I lift the weight.
I take a rest.

END
```

The results are identical to what we had in the first version of the program with the while command. This is how they are different:

- do again makes sure that the contained block of actions is executed at least once.

- while can possibly never execute, in the case of an unverified condition in the first place (in our case, when the first line of the workout.ring program is modified to isTired = TRUE).

Depending on what you want, use the right loop.

- If you want the loop to run at least once, use do again.

- Otherwise, use while.

It's as simple as that.

Multiple Selections

What if you need to select one option from several cases that are available to you? Here, and for the sake of brevity, I won't show the visual model in a Drakon diagram, leaving you the chance to make it by yourself.[25]

So, in Ring, switching can be made using a switch command, as shown in Listing 5-21[26] (test it in a new menu.ring file).

Listing 5-21. menu.ring

```
See "

            Main Menu
            ---------
            (1) Say Hello
            (2) About
            (3) Exit
"

Give nOption      # Recieves a value from the keyboard

Switch nOption
            On 1      See "Enter your name : "
                      Give name See "Hello " + 12 name + NL
            On 2 See "Sample : using switch statement" + NL
            On 3 See "Bye!"
            Other See "Bad option..." + NL
Off

Give Anything      # In case you run it int the console
```

---

[25]Here is some sincere advice: use this visual paradigm until it becomes unnecessary to you and is a natural reflex, in other words, a spontaneous way of thinking in code!

[26]This example is taken as is from the Ring documentation.

It's difficult to find another programming language as flexible as Ring. You will always find alternative ways to say anything. Personally, I sometimes prefer using an if/but statement to specify a switching rather than using switch itself, just because I am nostalgic about the old BASIC days. Therefore, I will write the switching part of the previous code like this:

```
if nOption = 1
            See        "Enter your name : "
                       Give name See "Hello " + name + NL
            but 2 See "Sample : using switch statement" + NL
            but 3 See "Bye!"
            else See "Bad option..." + NL
ok
```

Not convinced? No problem, because other alternatives are open to you. You can change to the more classical elseif as an IF alternative, or you can change on a case-by-case to the switch alternative to make it look like this:

```
switch nOption
            case 1 See "Enter your name : "
                       Give name See "Hello " + name + NL
            case 2 See "Sample : using switch statement" + NL
            case 3 See "Bye!"
            else See "Bad option..." + NL
end
```

Other Ring Control Structure Techniques

In this section, you will discover some useful constructs you can use in Ring to achieve fine control over your logic flow. They are all presented directly in the code, based on the content available in the Ring documentation.

Using for in to Modify Lists

We have already seen this previously in the chapter: when we used for in to traverse the items of a list, those items can also be modified inside the loop. In Listing 5-22, 1 to 5 are traversed and modified by their string counterparts: one to five.

Listing 5-22. tempo.ring

```
aList = 1:5      # => aList = [ 1, 2, 3, 4, 5 ]
// replace list numbers with strings
for x in aList
            switch x
            on 1  x = "one"
            on 2  x = "two"
            on 3  x = "three"
            on 4  x = "four"
            on 5  x = "five"
            off
next
see aList       # print the list items
```

At this level, there are some important aspects of controlling logic flows you need to consider:

- The logic flow is constructed by the flow of data between the different parts of your code.

- Data is hosted in variables, and the value of these variables is constrained by the scope they are used in.

- Data can be sent from one place to another in your code, as a function call or an object parameter. Also in this case, the values can differ depending on the variable type and the overall structure of the code.

- In particular, variables can be sent while disconnecting them from their initial value. In this case, we say that they are sent *by copy* (or *by value*). Any modification in the new context would have no effect on the initial value.

- Also, in other cases and configurations, variables can be sent without cutting their link with their original value. We say that they are sent *by reference*. Any modification of the value is a modification of the initial variable in its original context.

Then we understand that the x variable used in the previous code by the `for in` statement is traversing the list by reference. Then, modifying its value inside the scope of the IF statement (lines 5 to 9) means that the original values of the `aList` variable are modified.

This was just a small introduction to the important subject of scoping, one of the reasons a programmer makes logical mistakes and code contains hart-to-find errors. In Chapter 6, I give all that you need to master it and transform it into a decisive advantage.

Stepping with the for Statement

We can use the `step` option with the `for` statement to skip a number of items in each iteration. Listing 5-23 shows an example (write it in a new file called `step-forward.ring`).

Listing 5-23. step-forward.ring

```
aList = 1:10  # Creates a list containong numbers from 1 to 10
// Printing odd items inside the list
for x in aList step 2
    see x + nl
next
```

Note that the step can also be negative, so you can run the loop backward. For example, counting from 10 to 1 in Ring looks like Listing 5-24 (write it in a new file called `step-backword.ring`).

Listing 5-24. step-backward.ring

```
for x = 10 to 1 step -1
    ? x
next x
```

That's it for this section 😶.

Exiting from One or Two Loops

We discovered `exit` in the early introductory chapters, and you can use it to go outside one or more loop levels. Listing 5-25 shows an example (write it in a new file called `exit1.ring`).

Listing 5-25. exit1.ring

```
for x = 1 to 10 # The only loop level we have
        see x + NL
        if x = 5 exit┐ok   # Exits the loop
next             │
O←───────────────┘
```

Or it can be used to exit from two loop levels in one jump, as shown in Listing 5-26 (write this code inside a file called `exit2.ring`).

Listing 5-26. exit2.ring

```
for x = 1 to 10 # First loop level
        for y = 1 to 10 # second loop level
                see "x=" + x + " y=" + y + nl
                if x = 3 and y = 5
                        exit 2┐  # Exits from the 2 loops,
                              │  # not only the current one
                ok            │
        next                  │
        O←────────────────────┘
next    │
O←──────┘
```

Of course, many people in the programming landscape would say to go against this practice of exiting a loop. I understand their position since such a command interrupts the logic flow in an inconsistent way. This can be a source of complexity and generates errors that are hard to identify and solve.

This reminds us of the same problem regarding the use of the GOTO[27] command. This is wise, but Ring is a pragmatic, realistic, and free language, and it leaves you with the whole responsibility of using `exit` only when necessary, at your own cost, dear friend!

---

[27]Do you know that Linux, one of most secure and efficient software applications in the world, makes use of GOTO extensively? OK, but these are coding gurus, and you'll do better not to imitate them.

Using the loop Keyword

Unlike the `exit` keyword that interrupts the execution flow, the `loop` keyword serves to increment it smoothly by leaving, immediately, the current iteration and going to the next one.

Listing 5-27 shows an example (write it in a new file called `loop.ring`).

Listing 5-27. loop.ring

```
for x = 1 to 10 # The loop will stop when x reaches 3
     if x = 3
              see "Number Three" + nl
                  loop ─┐
     ok ────────────────┘
  ─►see x + NL
next
```

The same discussion about the `exit` subject applies here, so use the `loop` command responsibly.

Short-Circuit Evaluation

Short-circuit evaluation, minimal evaluation, or McCarthy evaluation (after John McCarthy) is the semantics of some Boolean operators in some programming languages in which the second argument is executed or evaluated only if the first argument does not suffice to determine the value of the expression.[28]

Ring embraces this law. If the first argument of the `AND` operator is `FALSE`, then there is no need to evaluate the second argument. The result will be `FALSE`.

To show it in code, let's consider two variables, `x` and `y`, and set up them, respectively, to `0` (which is equivalent to `FALSE`) and `10`, and then try to see how the code in Listing 5-28 executes (test it in the `short-circuit.ring` file if you want).

---

[28]This is a beautiful definition from Wikipedia.

Listing 5-28. short-circuit.ring

```
x=0 y=10
if x and y # Won't pass because "if x" ⇔ "if x = TRUE"
           # while x is currently FALSE (=0)
    ? "Hi!"
ok
```

If you run this, you'll get nothing, because Ring evaluates if x and finds it FALSE (because, again, 0 equals FALSE), so the iteration is interrupted, and the program ends.

To make it more explicit, the same thing happens if we write the code (in a new file called short-circuit2.ring) shown in Listing 5-29.

Listing 5-29. short-circuit2.ring

```
x = 2 y = 10
if x=3 and y=10    # Won't pass because x=2 is different from 3
    ? "Hi!"        # and "y = 10" will be considered by Ring
ok
```

Now, make the necessary edits to show "Hi!" in the output window.

By analogy, if the first argument of the OR operator is TRUE, then there is no need to evaluate the second argument, and the result will be TRUE. Listing 5-30 shows an example (write it in a new file called short-circuit3.ring).

Listing 5-30. short-circuit3.ring

```
x = 1   y = 0   # Equivalent to x = TRUE   y = FALSE
if x or y       # will pass although y is FALSE because x is TRUE
    ? "Hi!"
ok
```

To resume it, keep in mind the following two rules when you are making a logical evaluation with AND and OR:

- **In case of AND**: Look at the first operator, and if it evaluates to FALSE, then Ring ignores all the rest.

- **In case of OR**: Look at the first operator, and if it evaluates to TRUE, then Ring ignores all the rest.

Spirit gymnastics?

Yes, it is, and it will become a reflex with a lot of practice.

Exceptions (try/catch)

We've touched on exceptions in the previous chapter; errors and exceptions occur when your algorithm has caught a fever. In programming, they are unavoidable.

Still, when the logic carried out by your algorithm is broken, for any reason, then it is possible to capture it and force it to die peacefully without destroying your program. In Ring, this is implemented with a try/catch statement.

To test this, let's execute the bad code in Listing 5-31 (write it to a new file called badcode.ring).

Listing 5-31. badcode.ring

```
X= 10 y = 0
? x / y
```

The program is broken, and Ring tells you why, as shown here:

```
Line 2 Error (R1) : Can't divide by zero !
```

Now, to intercept the execution flow and direct it the way you want, use the code in Listing 5-32 (in a new catched.ring file).

Listing 5-32. catched.ring

```
X= 10 y = 0
try
        ? x / y
catch
        ? "ERROR"
end
```

Then the program does not end, and the programmer has control of what to do next. The programmer can end it gently without disruption or choose to carry on the logic flow in another direction.

In the following section, I will add some useful details about how Ring manages logical evaluation.

Useful Details About Evaluation

This section contains some reminders because we have talked about this subject in the previous chapters.

When you are programming in Ring, and, more specifically, when you are designing the logic flow of your algorithm and are confronted with a situation where you want to make a logic evaluation with AND or OR, keep in mind that True and False are variables defined by the language where

- True = 1

- False = 0

Here, everything evaluates to TRUE except 0, which is the only thing in Ring that evaluates to FALSE! So, if we write the code in Listing 5-33 (test it in a new file called true.ring), then if 5 evaluates to TRUE because it's different from zero.

Listing 5-33. true.ring

```
if 5
    see "Hi!" + NL
ok
```

It's as simple as that!

In the next section, I bring you a broader view of how your logic structure should be organized by applying my three craftsman commandments. Follow me, yalla.[29]

Three Commandments of the Logic Craftperson

When you are writing an algorithm, think of yourself as a craftsman who is shaping the clay by applying different movements and pressures with his hands, with his fingers, and even with his breathing system, to finally get a beautiful artifact.

The clay is the data, the movements are the computer logic constructs (mainly sequence, selection, and iteration), the artifact is the program, while the pressure and breathings are your personal style of programming, something you will never learn inside a book but only after many years of trial-and-error correction practice. See Figure 5-22.

---

[29]An Arabic term that means let's go!

Figure 5-22. *Crafting is touching, shaping, and feeling the clay of code between your hands[30]*

Throughout this section, I will share with you my personal techniques of crafting clean logic flows inside a Ring algorithm. They should complement the basic knowledge you gained in the previous sections and open your eyes to some practical recipes you will rarely find documented in other beginner books.

The following are my three commandments to you.

The First Commandment: Clean Order

The golden rules learned from Drakon at the beginning of the chapter apply here. Always design your algorithm so it flows visually in two directions: vertically and down first and then horizontally to the right.

The vertical-down always direction represents the happy path, and the horizontal-right direction gives the space where you indent the less pleasant stuff. If you adopt this technique and stick to it as a cultural asset, then your writing experience is enhanced, and by consequence, reading the code you've already written, whatever length it has, becomes straightforward. Look at the structure of this code, as shown in Figure 5-23.

---

[30]This is a free photo from this public domain: `https://tinyurl.com/yxq4kosv`.

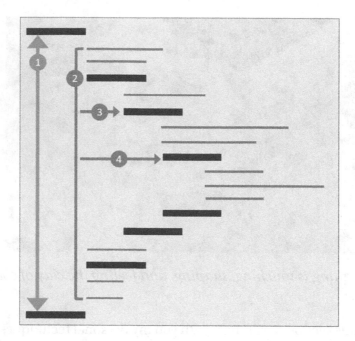

Figure 5-23. *Your code when it is clean and meaningful!*

This is how I can immediately make a mental representation of it:

- The vertical visual line (1) helps me, while being purely virtual, immediately recognize the limits of the algorithm: where it starts and where it ends. At this level, I need to collect any information I can on the inputs and outputs of the algorithms. Before reading any line of code, I will think about the possible logical processing that could transform the input data to produce the output.

- The happy path of the resolution of the problem at hand is immediately recognizable due to the virtual line (2). At this level, I just care about that happy path, with no exceptions, no special cases, and no other indentations. Understanding the essentials before the extensions is rewarding for anyone who wants to understand and master the general problem addressed by the algorithm.

- The indentation of code to the right is key to help me identify the next less pleasant path (3) and then the next less pleasant one (4), and so on.

As my final advice for this first technique, try to never exceed three indentations however complex your case is. You will always find a way to refactor your problem and describe the solution in a clean and wise way![31]

The Second Commandment: One Start, One End

In your algorithmic land, it's totally fenced, except two exits: one for entering, as shown by (1) in Figure 5-24, and one for quitting (2).

Any external or internal call, from a place to another in your program, if not rigorously controlled, becomes the root cause of unwanted turbulence in your logic flow.

If your current algorithm needs to be called from outside (I mean from another algorithm in your program), then the call must be directed to the very start point (3). To make this happen, you can encapsulate the main code in a function or a class, and the start point will be the signature of that function or class, with the necessary parameters required by the call.

You protect your territory from any invasive access (4). You never permit an internal piece of your algorithm to be called directly from outside the algorithm.[32] And if you don't, your code can be transformed easily to an unreadable spaghetti, or Tunisian shakshuka (see Figure 5-24).

[31]A practical example of that will be presented in Chapter 8 when we will refactor one of the games delivered with Ring.

[32]Those who have practiced object-oriented programming know that these principles are actuated by the object paradigm itself (privacy and method call). Nevertheless, many OOP programmers can deviate from these principles and come with unorganized classes of code. Take it then as a general-purpose rule you should follow, whatever programming paradigm you opt for. By the way, in Chapter 7 you will discover the fluency of the Ring language in supporting many programming paradigms (structured, OOP, functional, declarative, natural and dynamic programming) and make a meaningful connection between them.

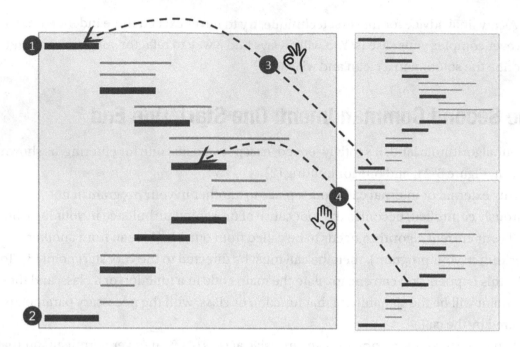

Figure 5-24. *Avoid invasions, and respect the law "one start, one end"*

Also, inside the same algorithm, never leave the house from the window, as shown in (1) in Figure 5-25, and let the flow of your data go downstairs to the endpoint before quitting the scope of the land; see (2) and then (3).

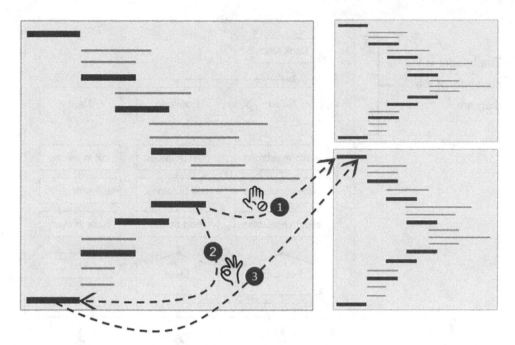

Figure 5-25. *Let your data flow go downstairs (2+3); never go out from the window (1)!*

The Third Commandment: Clean Logical Parts

Your program will always grow in time and become more complex as you are adding new features and writing new code. Controlling the logic flow becomes a matter of keeping the whole program organized.

This important subject of modularity and program architecture has been dealt with in practice in Chapters 3 and 4. Therefore, I will just raise your awareness of the fact that the way you organize the parts of your program is a determinant factor of the overall fluency of your logic flow.

In Drakon, the answer to this "clean logical parts" concern is a visual diagram type called Silhouette. In what we have seen so far, the Drakon diagrams are of primitive type. One can use them to solve and represent basic algorithms and relatively simple logic. For all the other cases, Silhouette is a better option. Figure 5-26 shows an example program for cooking lunch.

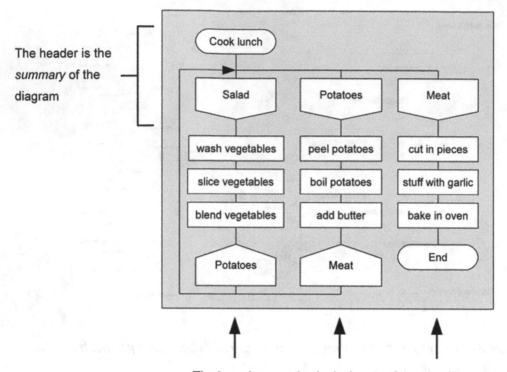

The header is the *summary* of the diagram

The branches are the *logical parts* of the algorithm

Figure 5-26. *Clean logical parts in a Drakon program*

To get it really clean while implementing this program in Ring, you should keep in mind that the flow of logic must follow the directions defined by the Drakon diagram. In practice, to do it right, you can control rigorously the calls from one part to another, so:

- The Salad part calls only the Potatoes part.

- The Potatoes part calls only the Meat part.

- The Meat part do its job and ends the program.

Any disruption you put on this clean design, by calling the Meat part from the Salad part, or, more specifically, the Slice vegetable portion from the boil potatoes portion, will generate for you (once again!) a plate of shakshuka, and you'll never understand how it was cooked!

Finally, if you are still wondering what parts and portions can be in a concrete Ring program, then for your convenience, parts are modules or packages, and portions are functions or objects in Ring.

Before You Leave: Homework!

In this chapter, you learned a lot!

These are the foundational techniques for any programmer. And what is programming if it is not a matter of crafting logic? Therefore, you need to make an effort and revise everything you've seen; especially practice thinking visually in your algorithmic problem, painting it in a Drakon diagram, and then writing it in Ring.

As homework, look at Figure 5-27, infer its narrative (no more than one paragraph), understand its structure and its logic flow, and write it and test it in Ring.

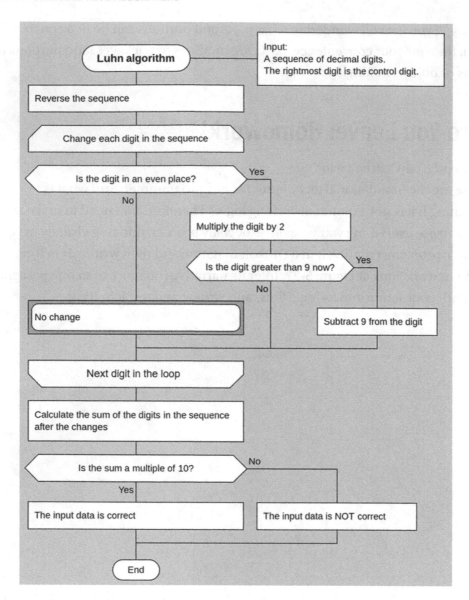

Figure 5-27. *Turning it from a Drakon flowchart to a Ring program*

Summary

There are other advanced forms of logic flows that I didn't cover in this chapter, like recursion, parallelization, and synchronization. But what we have done is largely sufficient for a nice start in tackling any common problem in Ring.

That's the end of the chapter. Thank you, craftspeople!

## CHAPTER 6

Juggling with Scopes

When data flows inside your algorithm, it is hosted in variables. Those variables travel from one corner of your program to another depending on several factors: the program structure, the design of your logic flow, the calling and sending strategy, and so on. In other words, they depend on the *scope* they are living in, or moving in, if you prefer.

Scope defines the *visibility* of your variables in the eyes of the Ring runtime. Depending on their location in the code, they are considered to be global or local variables.

Sometimes you'll have a conflict between two variables. A conflict occurs when you use the same name for two variables in two different scopes: a global name variable with the value "you", for example, and a local name variable with the value "me" inside a function. In such a situation, what value does Ring use: you or me?

Being a different programming language built for flexibility and learnability, Ring allows you to compose a hierarchy of objects using opening and closing braces ({ and }). In such a case, Ring shifts the current scope from an object to another, which is revolutionary but also uncommon and somehow risky!

This chapter will cover how to deal with all this and master the sport of juggling with scopes.

Nine Things You Will Learn

In this chapter, you will do the following:

- Understand how Ring sees variables depending on their lexical scope

- Prevent conflicts between global, local, and object scopes

- See how Ring switches object scopes using braces

- See how this object scope switching enables the design of a hierarchy of objects

© Mansour Ayouni 2020
M. Ayouni, *Beginning Ring Programming*, https://doi.org/10.1007/978-1-4842-5833-0_6

- Experiment with the techniques of preventing scope complexity in large programs

- Avoid global scope altogether in your program using the `main()` function

- See how Ring manages the scope inside a `for` loop

- Understand the role of the `self` and `this` keywords in object scopes

- Debug variables and trace the call stack using the TraceLib library

Scopes: Why Should You Care?

In Ring, we have access to three types of scopes: global, local, and object scopes.

In programming, if we have access to more than one scope, then problems may occur if we don't manage things correctly. It's always more secure to reduce the number of visible scopes in a given portion of your code, but sometimes, it's not up to you such as when you are using existing code or importing external libraries.

Some programming languages force you to manage the scope in a certain way, while others do not. As mentioned in Chapter 2, Ring uses lexical scoping to define the visibility of variables depending on their position in code. Every language has a specific philosophy of how to manage such visibility.

In the course of this chapter, you will discover that Ring obeys special and simple scope rules that are designed for flexibility first and then security.

Ring is designed to support programming in the small and programming in the large. When you are writing small programs, managing scopes is usually natural and easy. Things get harder when your program becomes larger. In this case, many functions, classes, and variables are used simultaneously. Scopes can rapidly be tedious to deal with and a source of many errors.

Don't be afraid. You'll end up with a clear vision of the scope functioning model by following me carefully. Once again, I'll visualize everything to help make my point without complications.

It's important to note that a Ring program is organized conventionally in respect to the following order: the *load* region, then the *code* region, then the *functions* region, and, finally, the *classes* region.

The code region (marked by the two arrows in Figure 6-1) is where scopes "happen." In fact, this is the part that forms your program logic. All the others are just descriptions of your organizational coding assets, such as libraries, functions, and classes.

That said, we are ready to start!

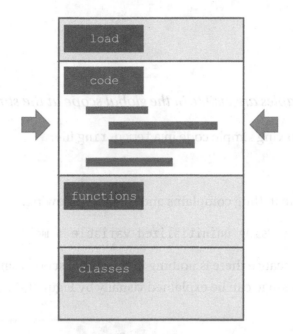

Figure 6-1. *Structure of a Ring program: scope happens in the region between the arrows*

Three Variable Scopes: Global, Local, and Object

In Ring, we have three possible variable scopes: global, local, and object. Simply put, globals are accessible everywhere, locals are seen only inside a function, and object variables (or attributes) are restricted to the scope of their object.

In the following three sections, you will learn the details of each type of scope.

Global Scope

When Ring starts a program and before executing any statement, there is a global scope that is active by default and ready to receive any variable you can define in your code. See Figure 6-2.

Figure 6-2. *No variables are visible in the global scope at the start of the program*

Let's write the following simple code in a `tempo.ring` file:

```
1 me
```

Yes, just me! Execute it. Ring complains and says the following:

```
Line 1 Error (R24) : Using uninitialized variable : me
```

We got this error because there is nothing in the global scope that is defined as a me variable. This error message can be explained visually by Figure 6-3.

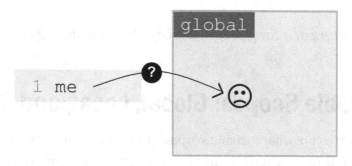

Figure 6-3. *The me variable is invisible in the global scope*

To solve this problem, we need to move the me variable to the global scope so Ring can find it. A simple way of doing this is to *define* it before it is first used, as shown in Listing 6-1.

Listing 6-1. tempo.ring

```
1 me = "Mansour"
2 me
```

Execute this code again, and you'll see the error message has disappeared. Figure 6-4 shows a visual explanation of what happened.

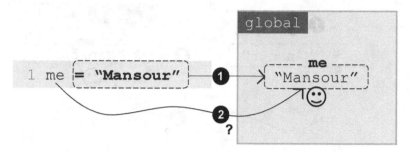

Figure 6-4. *The me variable is visible in the global scope*

Let's solve the same problem differently. First, get back to the initial code, as shown in Listing 6-2.

Listing 6-2. tempo.ring

```
1 me
```

Execute it to enforce the error in the Output window again. Now, create a new file called fed-lobal.ring and use the code in Listing 6-3.

Listing 6-3. fed-global.ring

```
1 me = "Mansour"
```

Save the file. Then go back to the initial tempo.ring file and add the code in Listing 6-4 (the first line in bold).

Listing 6-4. tempo.ring

```
1 load "globals.ring"
2 me
```

Execute. The problem is solved. In fact, loading the file "fed" the global scope of our program with a defined value of the me variable so Ring was able to find it. See Figure 6-5.

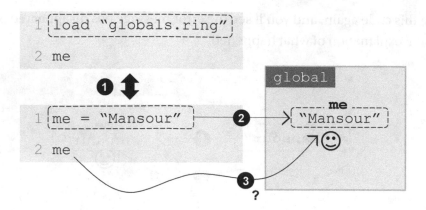

Figure 6-5. *The me variable is visible in the global scope.*

When your variables are global, they are accessed from anywhere. In a new file called globals.ring, try the code in Listing 6-5.

Listing 6-5. globals.ring

```
1 me = "Mansour"
2 you = "Friend"
3 ? me
4 ? you
```

Unsurprisingly, you get this in the Output window:

```
Mansour
Friend
```

But if you delete line 2, causing the you variable to be undefined, then Ring raises an error when this variable is used in line 4:

```
Line 4 Error (R24) : Using uninitialized variable : you
```

You've got it. From what we have done so far, we can deduce the following: at its start, a program is provided with a global scope. Every global variable used inside this scope must be defined before it is used. Otherwise, an Uninitialized variable error is raised, causing your program to be aborted.

Now, let's move to the second type of program scope: the local scope.

Local Scope

In Ring, locality is related to functions. Local scope is then activated when a function is defined.

In a file called `locals.ring`, let's declare ourselves (me and you) in two global variables and add a small `show()` function to display our values on the screen, as shown in Listing 6-6.

Listing 6-6. locals.ring

```
1 me = "Mansour"
2 you = "Friend"
3 show()
4
5 func show()
6         ? me
7         ? you
```

Execute. Nothing has changed in the behavior of this program compared to the previous one, since we have the following:

```
Mansour
Friend
```

But in reality, a lot of internal staff was taken on by the Ring engine, specifically, in dealing with scopes. Let me explain.

Global Is Visible Inside Local

When Ring starts on the first line and reads the me variable, it immediately tries to find it anywhere in the global scope. But it almost didn't find it. Ideally, and just before raising any error, the me variable is defined by = "Mansour". Ring takes it as a de facto value for the variable. The same thing happens for the you variable. This means that the global scope is populated with two friends, accessible from anywhere in the program, me and you, as shown in Figure 6-6.

Figure 6-6. *The me and you variables are visible globally (in the global scope)*

In line 3, there is a call for a function, show(). Ring obeys and knocks at that function's door in line 5. Immediately, a local scope is activated to host any variable (or parameter) declared inside the function. In our case, there are no variables declared, and therefore the local scope remains empty. Nevertheless, inside the show() room, we are still visible, me and you, because we are super globals! See Figure 6-7.

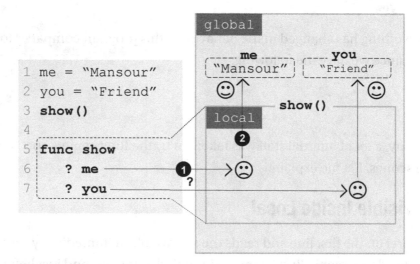

Figure 6-7. *Both the me and you variables are invisible locally but visible globally*

Localizing Variables

To make a variable local, define it inside a function. Let's try this by declaring a them variable inside the show() function and printing it on the screen. To do so, take a copy of the current locals.ring file and name it function-scope.ring, as shown in Listing 6-7. Then add to it the bold part of the listing.

Listing 6-7. function-scope.ring

```
1 me = "Mansour"
2 you = "Friend"
3 show()
4
5 func show
6          ? me                  # A global variable visible everywhere
7          ? you                 # Idem
8          them = "Others"       # A local variable, visible here inside
9          ? them                # the show() fuction only
```

Execute it, and you will get the following:

```
Mansour
Friend
Others
```

Visually speaking, Figure 6-8 shows what happened in the head of Ring.

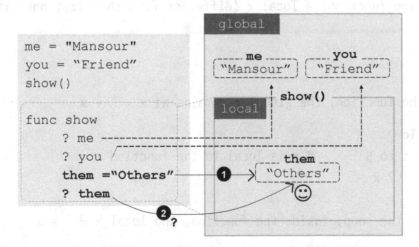

Figure 6-8. *The me and you variables are visible globally, and the them variable is visible locally*

When you are inside a function, you can see all the variables declared there because they are local, but you can also see all the global variables, because they are global.

Of course, the them variable won't be accessible outside of the function. For proof, try to say ? them before line 3's show( ).

```
Line 3 Error (R24) : Using uninitialized variable : them
```

You see?

The Special Case of Loops

Let's talk about one more thing before the section ends. When for loops are used, Ring activates a local scope for them. In other words, all the variables are declared inside the loop *except the counter itself,* which is local and can't be seen outside the loop. The counter deserves an explanation. Type the code in Listing 6-8 into a new file called loop-scope.ring.

Listing 6-8. loop-scope.ring

```
x = 10
? "x starts global at x = " + x + NL

? "Inside the function, a local x (different from the first one) iterates
5 times:"
countTo()
? ""

? "After the function, the global x remains at x = " + x

func countTo
    for x = 1 to 5        # x is local to the function
            ? x
    next x
    ? "After the loop, inside the function, the local x = " + x
```

Run the code and observe the result, as shown here:

```
x starts global at x = 10
```

```
Inside the function, a local x (different from the first one) iterates 5
times :
1
2
```

```
3
4
5
After the loop, inside the function, the local x = 6

After the function, the global x remains at x = 10.
```

I think the output is pretty expressive.

It's time, then, to tackle the third type of scope: object scope.

Object Scope

Before we talk about object scopes, select the `local-scope.ring` file we worked on at the beginning of the chapter, and execute it again, as shown in Figure 6-9.

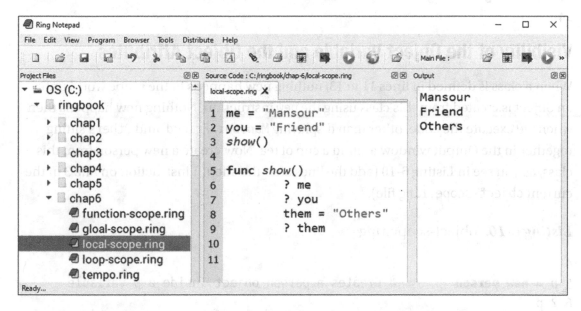

Figure 6-9. *local-scope.ring file selected and executed in Ring Notepad*

Then, make a copy of it (`local-scope.ring`) and name it `object-scope.ring`. Then, add the code lines shown in bold in Listing 6-9 at the end of the file.

Listing 6-9. object-scope.ring

```
01 me = "Mansour"
02 you = "Friend"
03 show()
04
05 func show()
06          ? me
07          ? you
08          them = "Others"
09          ? them
10
11 class Person
12          name # Those two attributes will be local to the
13          age  # object scope created from this class
14
```

Visibility of the Object Variable and the Object Attributes

When a class is defined in lines 11 to 13, nothing new happens in the scope world until an object is created from this class using the new instruction. Nothing new happens then when we execute the code, other than displaying Mansour, Friend, and Others sitting together in the Output window around a cup of tea. Now create a new person from this class, as you see in Listing 6-10 (add the lines after the show() instruction on line 3 in the current object-scope.ring file).

Listing 6-10. object-scope.ring

```
4
5 p = new person        # Creates a person object inside a p variable
6 ? p
7
```

When we execute the program, we get this:

```
Mansour
Friend
Others
name: NULL
age: NULL
```

304

Visibly, the ? keyword in line 6, acting in the global scope, was able to reach the newly created p object and display its (still empty) attributes.

Under the hood, while the p variable is occupying a royal chair in the global scope, an object scope is activated for the object it refers to. Inside that object, and, more precisely, inside its object scope, the name and age variables are sitting calmly in the local scope.

Therefore, Ring does two things behind the scenes:

1. A global p variable (of type object) is added to the global scope of the program.

2. Two local variables, name and age, are added to the object scope of the p object.

Visually speaking, Figure 6-10 shows what happens.

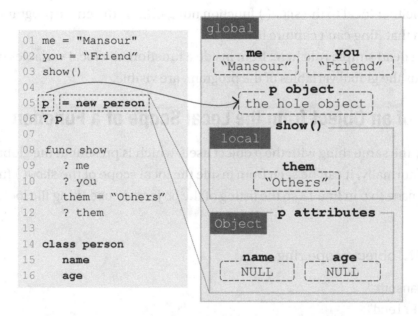

Figure 6-10. *The p object is visible in the global scope, and the name and age attributes are visible in the object scope*

What is visible in the global scope is the object as a whole,[1] not its elementary attributes. Perhaps, if you try to say ? name in line 7, for example (in the global region of the program), then Ring won't recognize it, because it is not visible outside the p object scope. In fact, this is what you will get:

```
Line 7 Error (R24) : Using uninitialized variable : name
```

Visibility of an Object Attribute from the Local Scope of a Function

Now, what if we try to evoke the name variable (or *attribute* if you prefer) from the show() function? Do you think Ring will be able to see it? At the end of the show() block, on line 13, add ? name, and then execute it. Ring answers with the same message, as shown here:

```
Line 13 Error (R24) : Using uninitialized variable : name
```

name is neither local to the show() function nor global to the entire program. It's normal then that Ring can't capture it.

There's a dead simple rule here: from inside a function, the local variables of the function, plus the global variables of the program, are visible.

Visibility of an Object from the Local Scope of a Function

Now let's try the same thing with the p object itself, which is present in the global scope in line 5, so normally, it can be seen from inside the local scope of the show() function.

Change name to p in line 13 so the listing of the object-scope.ring file looks like Listing 6-11.

Listing 6-11. object-scope.ring

```
01 me = "Mansour"
02 you = "Friend"
03 show()
04
```

---

[1]In reality, this is not the object with its entire content but only a reference to it, in memory, that is held in the variable representing the name of the object. But this stuff has no added value for you, since this is managed in the background as a C pointer by the Ring compiler and the virtual machine.

```
05 p = new Person
06 ? p
07
08 func show()
09          ? me
10          ? you
11          them = "Others"
12          ? them
13          ? p          # Evoking an object from a function
14
15 class person
16          name
17          age
18
```

Execute it. An error occurs, as shown here:

```
Line 13 Error (R24) : Using uninitialized variable : p
```

The reason for the error is that when the show() function is called on line 3, Ring executes every line in its block, including ? p on line 13. At this level, the p object *has not been created yet*, and the global scope doesn't contain a copy of it (with a little patience, it will be created later on line 5).

To fix the problem we have, just move p = new person in line 5 *before* the call of the show() function in line 3. Then, save it as object-scope-solved.ring. The updated listing looks like Listing 6-12.

Listing 6-12. object-scope-solved.ring

```
01 me = "Mansour"
02 you = "Friend"
03 p = new Person # p object created before show() is called
04 show()
05
06 ? p
07
08 func show()
09          ? me
```

```
10          ? you
11          them = "Others"
12          ? them
13          ? p          # Evoking an object from a function
14
15 class person
16          name
17          age
```

Execute the file, and you get the following:

```
Mansour
Friend
Others
name: NULL
age: NULL

name: NULL
age: NULL
```

You are done, but there is no need to print the object two times, once from the show() function (called on line 3) and once from the ? p instruction on line 7. Old wisdom calls to neglect the first one.

Visibility of an Object Created Inside a Function

In the previous section, we created an object at the global level, and we verified its visibility inside the local scope of a function. Now we will take on the reverse scenario by creating an object inside a function and then verifying its visibility outside.

Make a copy of the current object-scope.ring file, call it object-confusion.ring, and adapt it to look like Listing 6-13.

Listing 6-13. object-confusion.ring

```
01 me = "Mansour"
02 you = "Friend"
03
04 show()       # p Object is created "locally" in the function
05 ? p.name # let's access the object from the global scope!
```

308

```
06
07 func show
08         ? me
09         ? you
10         them = "Others"
11         ? them + NL
12
13     p = new person          # p Object is created inside the
14                             # function local scope
15 class person
16                  name
17                  age
18
```

As you can see, we created the p object inside the local scope of the show( ) function on line 13, and then we tried to see its name attribute outside it, in the global scope, by calling it on line 5 via ? p.name.

Execute this to see how Ring reacts, as shown here:

```
Mansour
Friend
Others

Line 5 Error (R24) : Using uninitialized variable : p
```

As you can see, there are two parts in this output.

- The first part contains the values of the three variables: me, you, and them. Ring finds them because they are all visible in the global scope.

- The second part, in which we are interested here, is an error you became familiar with: neither the p object evoked on line 5 nor its name attribute is visible in the global scope!

Local Scope of Object Methods

Here's another tip to end the section: the methods defined inside a class will have their own local scopes when an object is created from that class. All the locality rules you have learned about so far are applicable. An example will clarify this.

Let's make another copy of the object-scope.ring file, name it method-scope.ring, and adjust it to look like Listing 6-14.

Listing 6-14. object-method-scope.ring

```
01 me = "Mansour"
02 you = "Friend"
03
04 show()
05
06 p = new person
07 ? p.info()
08
09 func show
10              ? me
11              ? you
12              them = "Others"
13              ? them + NL
14              y = 20        # y : defined locally in the function.
15                            # If used here it's ok, but not outside.
16
17 class person
18              name = "Mansour"
19              age = "43"
20
21              def info
22                      x = 10    # x : defined locally in the method
23                      ? x       # therefore, Ring can see it.
24
25                      ? name    # name and age are both globals
26                      ? age     # therefore, Ring can see them.
```

```
27
28                            ? y          # y : wasn't defined anywhere in
29                                         # the method. Therefore, Ring will
30                                         # not see it.
```

Once executed, this is what we get:

```
Mansour
Friend
Others

10
Me
43
Line 28 Error (R24) : Using uninitialized variable : y
called from line 7
```

There are three portions in the output we can describe, as follows:

1. The first one was generated because of the execution of the show() function called on line 4 and starting on line 9. It contains the values of the two *global* variables, me and you (lines 10 and 11), plus the value of the *local* variable them defined on line 12 and used on line 13.

    me and you were visible because they are globals, while them was visible because it is local to the function and has been used inside that function.

2. The second portion is called by p.info() on line 7, with the p object being created just before that on line 6. The info() method starts on line 21, where a *local* variable called x is defined and given the value of 10 on line 22. The value is printed successfully on line 23.

On lines 25 and 26, two variables (or attributes) belonging to the current object scope are used: name and age. They are both visible to Ring and are printed successfully.

3. The third portion contains an error. Ring complains because it doesn't find any y variable (evoked on line 28) in the local scope of the current method.

    You could argue that y was defined on line 14 inside the show() function. You are right, but these are two different and *intangible* local scopes: what is defined in one of them cannot be accessed from the other!

Object Scope Switching Using Braces

Here's another important fact about object scopes: these can be activated *immediately* when you use braces ({ and }) just after the new keyword. This is a critical feature and key differentiator of Ring! Let's see it in action.

For example, say you have the new file called braces-access.ring shown in Listing 6-15.

Listing 6-15. braces-access.ring

```
// Currently the scope is global
// Let's create a first person object using braces
p = new Person {
          // the socpe moves from global to object scope
          name = "Said" age = 44  # Object attributes are visible
          ? info()                # The object method is visible
}
// The scope turns back to global again
// Let's create a second one
p = new Person {
          // the socpe moves from global to object scope again
          name = "Khaled" age = 45
          ? info()
}
// An so on.
```

```
// An so on...

Class Person
          Name age
          def info()
                    ? "Name : " + name
                    ? "Age  : " + age
```

Then the Ring runtime moves immediately from the global scope to the object scope. Thus, all the object attributes and methods become visible. Execute it and observe the results, as shown here:

```
Name : Said
Age  : 44

Name : Khaled
Age  : 45
```

Creating objects becomes a game for kids, a seamless thinking process. But the magic arises when it comes to playing with *hierarchies*. And this deserves a dedicated example, so create a new file called wapp.ring.

As you should know, a GUI application is made up of windows. A window is a group of zones. A zone contains one or more graphic widgets. A graphic widget can be a text label, a text edit, a button, an image, etc.

Our mission is to model that kind of application.

To do this, let's imagine the hierarchic composition of the application (see Figure 6-11).

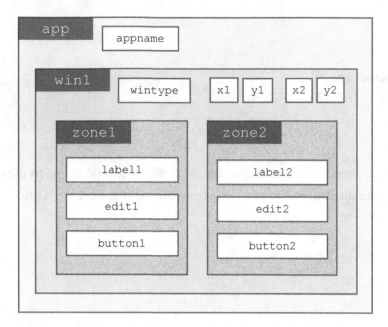

Figure 6-11. *A hierarchical model of a GUI application*

How many classes do we need to model all the components of the app application? Did you say six? No, four classes are all what we need: App, Win, Zone, and Widget. Write the code in Listing 6-16 inside the wapp.ring file (Listing 6-16).

Listing 6-16. wapp.ring

class app

```
        name
```

class win

```
        wintype        # Can be "modal" or "non-modal"
```

class zone

```
        # Has no attributes
        # Will serve as a container
```

class widget

```
        type           # Can be "Label", "Edit", "Button", or "image"
```

At this point, this code is not intended to be executed; I just want to show you the principle of using hierarchies in object scope and how they are designed using braces. So, let's shape the skeleton of the app *using braces*. At the beginning of the program, use the code in Listing 6-17.

Listing 6-17. Part of wapp.ring

```
app1 = new app {
        win1 = new win {
                zone1 = new zone {
                        // Graphic widgets go here
                }
                zone2 = new zone {
                        // Graphic widgets go here
                }
        }
}
```

Without a hassle, we were able to implement an object hierarchy as if we were using a WYSIWYG forms editor. And because braces provoke a change of the current scope to the object scope, then all the object attributes and methods can be used freely inside the { } region. In our case, graphic widgets can be "added" to each zone, as shown in Listing 6-18.

Listing 6-18. Part of wapp.ring

```
zone1 = new zone {
        lable1 = new widget { type = "label" }
        edit1 = new widget { type = "edit" }
        button1 = new widget { type = "button" }
}
```

It's as simple as that. Do the same with zone2 and look at the code as a whole. Observe how things are described in a comprehensive way because of this killer feature of the language that allows you to change object scopes using braces. In the previous section of the chapter, I provided you with an extended version of this program that is fully functional.

Other general-purpose programming languages don't allow this level of freedom because of their fear of *breaking the norms* of program security. But Ring allows us to do it because the first concern in its design, as a programming language, is flexibility *and then* security. This doesn't mean security isn't considered but that programmers should benefit responsibly from the flexibility of the language while assuming responsibility for any possible impacts that flexibility could have on security.

In fact, using braces in Ring by crafting object hierarchies is made possible by the establishment of two world-class innovative paradigms in Ring: declarative and natural language programming. These were presented in previous chapters and will be dealt with in more detail in Chapter 7.

Case of self and this Keywords

I want to talk about an important detail here about the braces use case with the self keyword: a differentiation needs to be made for when they are used to reference an object *in* the class region versus *inside* a class method.

In a nutshell, self is generally used inside a class method to reference the current object defined by the class. This is probably crystal clear, but the ambiguity we want to clarify here arises when we use braces to change the scope to another object. This will be better understood when we look at Listing 6-19 (save it in a new file called self-scope-class.ring).

Listing 6-19. self-scope-class.ring

```
01 p = new person        # an object scope is activated for p
02 ? p.info()            # the info() method is invoked
03
04 class person
05     name = "Mansour"      # the class region is run
06     j = new job {         # before the info() method is
07         ? self.name       # executed. Self references
08     }                     # p and not j object!
09
10     def info
11         age = 43
12         ? age
13
14 class job
15     name = "programmer"
```

Run this and you get the following result:

```
mansour
43
```

You may be a little bit surprised! Did you expect to see `programmer`, not `mansour`? Despite `self` being used *inside* the braces defining the scope of the j object from the `job` class, the `name` attribute that is considered by Ring is the one on line 5 belonging to the p object (created from the current `person` class).

The rule here is that `self`, when used inside braces that creates an object in the class region, references the object created by the main class and not the one created by the braces.

By contrast, if we use `self` between braces in a class method, things become more obvious, and `self` references the object created by the braces. This can be easily verified when we move the three lines from 6 to 8 right inside the `info` method. To do so, make a copy of `self-scope.ring` and name it `self-scope-method.ring` and then adjust it to look like Listing 6-20.

Listing 6-20. self-scope-method.ring

```
01  p = new person
02  ? p.info()
03
04  class person
05          name = "Mansour"
06
07          def info                    # braces are used inside a
08                  j = new job {       # class method not a class
09                      ? self.name     # region. Therefore, self
10                  }                   # references the j object,
11                                      # hence the value
12                  age = 43            # "programmer"
13                  ? age
14
15  class job
16          name = "programmer"
```

Execute it, and meet your (and my) favorite job worldwide: `programmer`!

You should ask the following here: if `self` is not useful to reference the p object (created from the `person` class) inside the `info` method, what do you do then? Ring gives you the answer: use `this` instead of `self`. Try this by changing line 9 in Listing 6-20 to look like Listing 6-21 (in the same `self-scope2.ring` file).

Listing 6-21. self-scope2.ring

```
07                      def info
08                          j = new job {
09                              ? this.name # this instead of self
10                          }
```

See the result. It's `Masour`. Do you know who he is?[2]

Object Scope Access Using Dot Operator

To end this topic, I will add this tip: when you use the `dot` operator to access an object variable, only the attributes of that object are searched by Ring and not the internal blocks of its methods. So, say we have Listing 6-22 (in a new file called `dot-scope.ring`).

Listing 6-22. dot-scope.ring

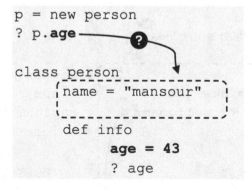

---

[2]I was named after one of the most famous ancient sophists in Tunisia, Sidi Mansour, whose shrine is in the region of Sfax and who has followers, even today, from around all Africa. The legend says that he was able to establish recognition and respect due to high spirituality, social compassion, and dedication to divine knowledge.

The age variable is *not found*, although it is defined inside the info() method. Yes, you can test it by yourself, and if you do, you'll get an error.

```
Line 2 Error (R12) : error in property name, property not found! : age
```

In the next section, you will learn how to commit some *scope conflicts*. Interested? You can't say no.

Managing Conflictual Scopes

What you learned in the previous section is instrumental to working with scopes. But what about *juggling* with them, as promised in the title of the chapter?

Juggling with scopes requires you to learn how to commit conflicts between scopes and how to avoid them. This is what we will be doing, but let's start with a clarification of what we mean by the word *conflict*.

Put succinctly, there is a conflict between two scopes when they both contain variables with the same name. Many example scenarios will be used to explain this.

Conflict Between the Global and Object Scopes

Look at the code in Listing 6-23 after saving it to a new conflict1.ring file, as shown in Listing 6-23.

Listing 6-23. conflict1.ring

```
01 age = 21          # defines name as a global variable
02 p = new person    # creates p object from person class
03 ? p               # prints the infos of the object
04
05 class person
06             name              # defines a name attribute for person
07             age               # conflictual: what Ring will do?
08
09             def info
10                     ? name
11                     ? age
```

319

There are two variables with the same name, age, one in the global scope on line 1 and the other in the object scope on line 6. As a first impression, you may think that name on line 6 is an attribute for the person class, but it isn't!

The proof is to execute the code and see the result, as shown here:

age: NULL

This means that the object p contains only one attribute called age with the value NULL.

You might ask, why is Ring ignoring the name attribute on line 6? Well, because it isn't an attribute but a global variable. Don't forget: when you type the name of variable, Ring looks first in the local scope, then in the object scope (in our situation they are the same because we are in the class region), and finally in the global scope where it finds the name variable defined so it takes it.

To solve the problem so that you can see the two attributes, name and age, printed in the Output window, you have an elegant tool: the main function!

Make a copy of the current conflict1.ring file and name it conflict1-solved1.ring. At the start of the new file, insert what is in bold, as shown in Listing 6-24.

Listing 6-24. conflict1-solved1.ring

```
01 func main     # the main code is hosted in a main() function
02          name = "mansour"
03          p = new person
04          ? p
05
06 class person
07                    self.name
08                    self.age
09
10                    def info
11                              ? name
12                              ? age
```

Everything that has been written in the global "area" before is now *local* because it is enclosed in a main() function. This is a special kind of function that is called by Ring automatically at the start of the program, unlike the other user-defined functions. There will not be a collision between the two variables named name. In fact, when Ring encounters name in the class region, it doesn't even need to search further because there's no global scope anymore! name is then considered as an attribute of the person class like age. You'll execute the code and see they are printed together, as shown here:

```
name: NULL
age: NULL
```

Another way to solve the problem is to use self with every class attribute, which is tedious but more secure. No collision with the other scopes is left to the unknown. Make a copy of the conflict1.ring file and name it conflict1-solved2.ring. Then adjust its content to look like Listing 6-25 (additions are in bold hereafter).

Listing 6-25. conflict1-solved2.ring

```
01 age = 21
02 p = new person
03 ? p
04
05 class person
06                 self.name               # self is added to name
07                 self.age                # self is added to age
08
09                 def info
10                           ? name
11                           ? age
```

Run it to ensure you have the same correct result.

```
name: NULL
age: NULL
```

A third way is to decorate all your class attributes with an @ prefix, or any other convention you define for yourself. To test this, make a copy of the original conflict1.ring file and name it conflict1-solved3.ring. Then change it to match the bold parts of Listing 6-26.

Listing 6-26. conflict1-solved3.ring

```
01 age = 21
02 p = new person
03 ? p
04
05 class person
06                    @name          # name has been changed to @name
07                    @age           # age has been changed to @age
08
09              def info
10                          ? name
11                          ? age
```

Run this, and you get the following:

```
@name: NULL
@age: NULL
```

If you want, you can decorate your global variable with a $ prefix, for example. To do so, make a copy from the original conflict1.ring file and call it conflict1-solved4. ring. Then, change just the first line, as shown in Listing 6-27.

Listing 6-27. conflict1-solved4.ring

```
01 $age = 21              # age is changed to $age
02 p = new person
03 ? p
04
05 class person
06                    name
07                    age
08
09              def info
10                          ? name
11                          ? age
```

Execute it and you get the following result, since **$age** and age are totally two different things:

```
name: NULL
age: NULL
```

Of course, nothing prevents you from using the four solutions together, or separately, for better control of your scopes. It just depends on your own preference and own style. To summarize, if you have a conflict between a global scope and an object scope, you can rely on these four solutions:

- Enforcing object scope by using self with the object attributes

- Avoiding global scope by using a main function

- Decorating your global variables with a $ prefix

- Decorating your class attributes with an @ prefix

This is the rule you should take away from this section: when you write an attribute in a class region, Ring starts searching for it, first, in the object scope itself (the same class region). If it's found, then it uses it. If not, it continues searching for it in the global scope; if found, it uses it. But, if the variable doesn't exist anywhere, Ring defines it as a new attribute for the class.

Conflict Between the Object and Local Scopes

To be able to identify a conflict between an object scope and a local scope, let's look carefully at Listing 6-28 after saving it to a new file called conflict2.ring.

Listing 6-28. conflict2.ring

```
01 func main
02    name = "Nice"
03    p = new person {
04          name="Mahmoud"
05          address="Egypt"      #➜ object scope
06          phone = "000"                              #➜ local scope
07    }
08    // Displaying the object attributes
09    see p
10    ? ""
11    // Displaying the name variable
12    ? name
13
14 class Person
15          name
16          address
17          phone
```

Execute this, and observe the result, as shown here:

name: NULL
address: Egypt
phone: 000

Mahmoud

What happened? It looks like name = "Mahmoud" on line 4 didn't have any effect.

The code activates an object scope (for the p object from the Person class) *inside* the local scope of the main function. When the braces are opened on line 3, the scope shifts from local to object.

And when name is used on line 4, inside the object scope, Ring does not realize that this name variable exists in the same scope, as an attribute of the p object. In fact, Ring starts looking first at the "higher level" (i.e., in the local scope of the main function). There it finds it on line 2. Thus, the statement name="Mahmoud" on line 4 is interpreted as a *change of value* of the name variable from Nice to Mahmoud. Therefore, the name attribute of the object p itself remains as defined in the class person on line 13: a beautiful NULL.

To avoid such a complicated conflict, apply one of the solutions we summarized at the end of the previous section. Personally, I would just use @ before the name attribute when I declare it in the person class (on line 15) and do so with the name attribute when I enter the object scope inside the braces (on line 4). More systematically, I would change the whole code by copying the current conflict2.ring file to a new conflict2-solved. ring file and decorating it as shown in Listing 6-29.

Listing 6-29. conflict2-solved.ring

```
01 func main
02         name = "nice"
03         p = new person {
04                         @name ="mahmoud"        # It's clear I'm dealing with
05                         @address="Egypt"         # object attributes
06                         @phone = "000"
07         }
08         see p
09         ? ""
10         ? name                    # It's clear I'm dealing with a local variable
11
12 class person
13                         @name
14                         @address
15                         @phone
```

Write it to a new file called conflict2-solved.ring and execute it. The output looks like this:

@name: Mahmoud
@address: Egypt
@phone: 000

Nice

What do you think?

Conflict Between the Global and Local Scopes

I'll leave this kind of conflict to you as an exercise. Make it happen and then solve it. As an indication, use a variable in the global area of the code (i.e., before functions and classes) and then write a function that uses a variable with the same name internally. Play with the value, run it, and adjust.

This is *juggling* after all.

Tracing Variables Using TraceLib

During this chapter, we relied on a visual representation to understand how Ring manages scopes based on a given structure of code. This is good for learning complex stuff for the first time but is less practical to be used in everyday programming.

At any level of your code, you need to get a list of your variables and their relative values so the conflicts are detected. To do so, you have a strong tool that is your best friend: the debugger!

The debugger is a dynamic follower of your coding journey—your spy's eye on the internal functioning of the Ring runtime. Execute your code and, instead of using the final result without any questioning, ask questions of what happened, how, and in which order!

You can even slow down the time machine to execute your program step-by-step and see what changes in every step.

Learning how to debug a program is a large issue, and we don't have enough space to cover it in this book. In the meantime, you can focus on listing your variables depending on their scope type, along with their values. This is, on its own, a great advantage.

Like everything else in the language, the debugger is written in Ring. And you can invite it into your program world through a simple load "tracelib.ring" command and then launch it, in its interactive mode, by using the breakpoint() function.

To experience it, let's create a new file called debugme.ring in which you write the code shown in Listing 6-30.

Listing 6-30. debugme.ring

```
01 load "tracelib.ring"
02
03 test1()
04
05 func test1
06         x = 10
07         see :test1 + NL     # Remember :test1 <=> "test1"
08         t = 12
09         BreakPoint()        # launches the interactive debugger
10         see "After breakpoint!" + NL
11         see "t = " + t + nl
12         see "End of program!" + NL
```

Save the code and execute it in the console (Ctrl+R) so you see the Interactive Debugger menu, as shown in Figure 6-12.

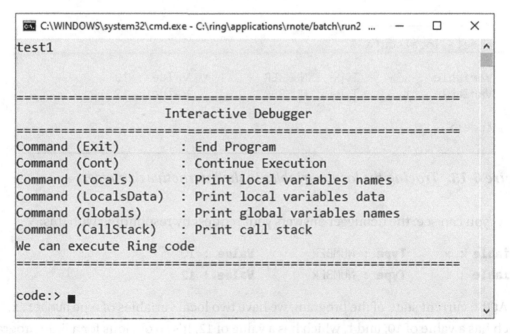

Figure 6-12. *The Inteructive Debugger menu displayed in the console*

At the top, you have the normal output of the code executed before the `breakpoint()` function. Then, you have the main menu of the Interactive Debugger showing the six different commands you can choose from by writing them in the input field at the bottom and hitting Enter.

- Leaving the interactive debugger: `exit`

- Continuing the execution of the program until a new `breakpoint()` is detected or to the end of the program: `cont`

- Listing the local variables: `locals`

- Listing the local variables and their actual values: `localsdata`

- Listing the global variables: `globals`

- Printing the call stack, which consists of the chain of calls made in the program: `callstack`

Try to debug the local data of the program by entering `localsdata` at the command line, as shown in Figure 6-13.

```
code:> localsdata

Variable : x        Type : NUMBER        Value : 10
Variable : t        Type : NUMBER        Value : 12

code:>
```

Figure 6-13. *Tracing the local variables in the interactive debugger*

As you can see, the debugger answers your request by responding with this:

Variable : x   **Type** : NUMBER   **Value** : 10
Variable : t   **Type** : NUMBER   **Value** : 12

At the current state of the program, we have two local variables of type number: x, which has a value of 10, and t, which has a value of 12. It's so obvious for a little program, but all the benefits of such a debugging feature will be more appreciated when you are programming *in the large*, with dozens of global and local variables and a relatively deep chain of function calls.

This particular feature of tracing the call stack is important in debugging large programs. In fact, one of the main sources of code complexity is the density of the calling map between functions and methods. To show you how you to use the `CallStack` instruction in practice, take a look at this code example (write it down to a new file called `chain.ring`):

```
load "tracelib.ring"
node1()

### FUNCTIONS
func node1
        ? "Node 1"
        node2()

func node2
        ? "Node 2"
        node3()

func node3
        ? "Node 3"
        breakpoint()
```

As you can see, we defined a chain of three nodes in the form of three functions: node1, node2, and node3. In the main region of the program, we call the first node by saying node1(). Then, this node calls the next one (node2()), and the next calls the next one (node3()).

To visualize this chain in the *call stack* of the program runtime, we use the `TraceLib` library and set a breakpoint at the end of the node3 function. Setting the breakpoint there will force the execution to stop so we can ask the Interactive Debugger to inform us about the path of the chain. Execute the program using Ctrl+R. In the console, write `callstack` and then press Enter. Take a look at the result, as shown in Figure 6-14.

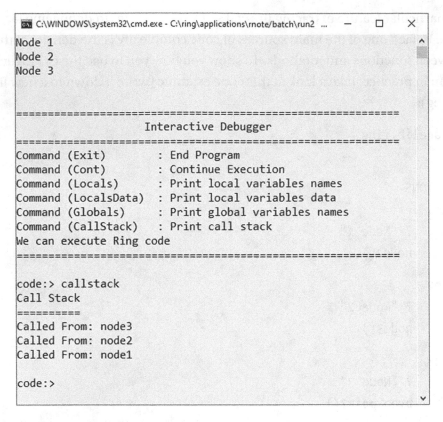

Figure 6-14. *Tracing the call stack of the chain.ring program*

The debugger reacts by displaying the call stack in the inverse order like this:

```
Call Stack
==========
Called From: node3
Called From: node2
Called From: node1
```

You should read this like this:

- The program was interrupted at the end of function node3(), and we can see that the function was called from function node2() and that function node2() was called from function node1().

- Node1() was then the first call in the chain, and node3() is the last one.

- In between, node2() relays the execution from node1() to node3().

This is a simple call stack, though. In real life, especially in large projects, it will be certainly more complex. It's up to you, then, to take your time (all your time!) when interrogating the debugger and reconstructing the call chain. Doing this systematically and with patience and accuracy when you have a hard piece of code to deal with will always reward you in your fight against complexity. Otherwise, I'm sorry to say that your battle has already been lost.[3]

Before we end the chapter, let's take a look at the code samples we have achieved so far (Figure 6-15).

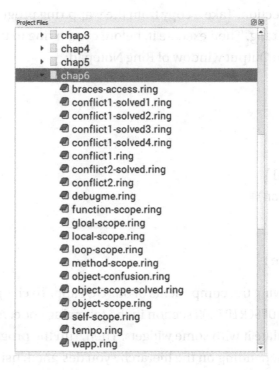

Figure 6-15. *A set of of code examples for juggling with scopes*

These carefully designed examples will save you hours of perplexity if you practice them many times and go back to them, from time to time, to revise them. Good advice is priceless as they say. And this is one of the best pieces of advice I can give you: if you are

---

[3]Personally, I believe that Ring Notepad not having a visual debugging tool is an advantage. Using the TraceLib library, inside the code, helps you embrace the true meaning of debugging, which is understanding not only fixing bugs but what is happening at runtime. Read this article written by John Sonmez entitled "A Programmer's Guide to Effective Debugging" to understand my point: `https://tinyurl.com/wjwjrsh`.

beginning a programming career, whatever language you use, misunderstanding scope will be your number-one obstacle to becoming a welcomed member on real-world programming teams!

A Gift: Extended wapp.ring Program

In this final section, I would like to give this gift to you: an extended and working version of the wapp.ring program we worked on in the "Visibility of an Object from the Local Scope of a Function" section. Take a copy from the wapp.ring program in a new file and call it wapp-extended.ring. Then execute it, before even trying to understand it. This is what you will see in the Output window of Ring Notepad:

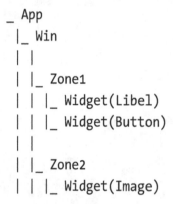

```
_ App
 |_ Win
 | |
 | |_ Zone1
 | | |_ Widget(Libel)
 | | |_ Widget(Button)
 | |
 | |_ Zone2
 | | |_ Widget(Image)
```

It's a treeview showing the components of our GUI app. To change its structure, play with the ### APP DESCRIPTION section in the following code. Add a third zone, for example, and populate it with some widgets. Then, run the program again. The app hierarchy is changed depending on the hierarchy you designed, using object braces, right inside the Ring code.

Read the code now along with the comments several times. Use a pen and paper to dissect the program structure, reconstitute the scopes and how they work, and look at the variables and how they move, inside and between the scopes, and at how the call stack is chained in the runtime. Finally, once the code is well understood, do the following exercise:

1. Go back to the original wapp.ring program and work on upgrading it to the same code as the new extended version we have here.

2. Try to design the code with the same app structure as shown in Figure 6-11.

Now, I leave you to a meticulous reading of the program, shown here:

PROVIDING A LIST TO SERVE
AS A CONTAINER FOR THE APP

```
        aTree = []
        /* This list will be used in two places:
                        1. the add() method in every class uses
                           it to add an objet to the App world
                        2. the show() function uses it to display
                           The treeview of the App on the screen
        */
```

APP DESCRIPTION

```
        // Using braces and object scopes to
        // describe the hierarchy of the App
        App = new app {
                // The App includes only one window
                Win = new win {
                        // first zone in the window
                        z1 = new Zone {
                                name = "Zone1"
                                // Graphic widgets go here
                                        w1 = new Widget {
                                            type = "Libel"
                                        }
                                        w2 = new Widget {
                                          type = "Button"
                                        }
                        }
                        // Second zone in the window
                        z2 = new Zone {
                            name = "Zone2"
                            // Graphic widgets go here
                            w3 = new Widget { type = "Image" }
```

```
                              }
                    }
            }
```

DYNAMIC CONSTRUCTION AND DISPLAY
OF THE PROGRAM OBJECTS

```
        // The list of objects created by the
        // code above is dynamically constructed
        aObj = globals()

        // Then, the tree of the App is displayed
        show()
```

THE DISPLAY FUNCTION

```
        func show()

                // Dynamically constructing the Ring code
                // that calles the show() method on every object
                for i=3 to len( aObj ) - 1
                        eval(aObj[i]+".add()")
                next
                /* For the code written in the APP DESCRIPTION
                   section above, this function generates the
                   following Ring code:
                             => App.add()
                                Win.add()
                                z1.add()
                                w1.add()
                                w2.add()
                                z2.add()
                                w3.add()
                */

                // The aTree is then constructed (see the code
                // of add() method in every class here after
                // All what remains is to display it
                ? aTree
```

THE APP WORLD CLASSES

```
class App
        name
        def add()
                aTree + "_ App"

class Win
        wintype # can be "modal" or "non-modal"
        def add()
                aTree + " |_ Win"

class Zone
        # will serve as a container
        name
        def add()
                aTree + ( " | |" + NL +
                         " | |_ " + name )

class Widget
        name
        type # can be "label", "edit", or "button"
        def add()
                cStr = " | | |_ Widget(" + type + ")"
                aTree + cStr
```

Summary

That's it for this sixth chapter of the book and the last one in the second part, "Practical Ring." You now have the practical foundation necessary for digging into the more advanced, magical stuff. Turn to the final part of the book, "Magical Ring," starting with Chapter 7. I'll be waiting for you there.

CHAPTER 7

Functions, Objects, and Beyond

On Stackoverflow.com,[1] one programmer wondered how people learn object-oriented programming after programming using functions for so long. The programmer asks, "Especially, how did you succeed in unlearning to code using functions and start seeing your code as objects?"

You are not alone, my friend. Many programmers come to Ring from the peaceful land of plain old procedural languages like Visual Basic, Delphi, and the like. They struggle with the complexity behind objects and object orientation and can't understand why doing simple things they could do in seconds, by such putting a button on a form and calling a simple function, requires many lines of code, two or three libraries to import, and several objects to instantiate and methods to invoke. All that just to get the same result as showing a `Hello, world!` on the screen when a button is clicked!

Nevertheless, this is just one facet of the model. Those who are object-native are confronted with the inverse difficulty: they can't change their minds easily to capture the functional way of designing algorithms. Today, everyone is invited to embrace the comeback of functions, ported by the ubiquitous JavaScript[2] and the boom of the serverless computing model enabled by the combination of cloud, mobility, big data, microservices, and the distributed Internet of Things (IoT). They are struggling with functions, not only as a coding construct but also as a design approach and a vision for modern software architectures.

---

[1]https://stackoverflow.com/questions/2688910/learning-to-think-in-the-object-oriented-way

[2]To understand how functional programming came back due to the rise and maturity of JavaScript, read this interesting Medium article written by Eric Eliott called "The Rise and Fall and Rise of Functional Programming": https://tinyurl.com/rk7r9oc. If you find it a bit long, go directly to the section "The Rise of Functional Programming."

© Mansour Ayouni 2020
M. Ayouni, *Beginning Ring Programming*, https://doi.org/10.1007/978-1-4842-5833-0_7

The problem is neither functions nor objects but the mental model, the ability of representing the programming activity as abstractions and relationships and not as lines of code. Functional programming is not about functions but about mixing functions and combining them in collaborative pipes of logic flow. Object orientation is not about objects but composing software using communicating objects. Finally, objects can't do anything without functions, and functions lose a lot when they completely ignore objects.

Therefore, you, as a modern programmer, should understand them both and use them both, right in the same programming environment. Ring happens to be one of these programming environments. Its multiparadigm nature offers you the flexibility of functions as well as the versatility of objects in the same bucket. Not only are all the industry-scale requirements of object-oriented programming (OOP) and functional programming (FP) supported, but additional paradigms are built on top of them, such as declarative and natural programming. This chapter is your one-stop guide for going beyond technical knowledge to mastering the gymnastics of algorithmic thinking in Ring.

Welcome to one of the most instructive chapters of the entire book.[3]

Nine Things You Will Learn

You'll do the following in this chapter:

- Master the techniques related to using functions and objects in Ring

- Embrace the spirit of functional programming and object orientation with Ring

- Develop a self-consciousness of when to go functional and when to go object-oriented

- Practice the art of logic composition using both functions and objects

- Master the key differentiators of Ring in term of functions and objects features

- Fabricate functions and secure the object world in Ring

- Discover the four object composition techniques in Ring

---

[3]As usual, create a chap7 folder in the c:\ringbook folder along with a tempo.ring file.

- Play with object braces and understanding the class event mechanism

- Implement and use declarative and natural layers in your Ring programs

Functions and Functional Style

Our thinking system as humans is function-oriented: you want to achieve something, so your brain designs the necessary steps to make it happen. That's why functions reflect the pragmatic side of our reality: everything consists of actions, operations, and processes. In linguistics, functions are the verbs, while objects are the names.

In programming, though, a function is not just an action but a piece of meaning that you should compose to create a solution design for your algorithmic problem. Mastering the techniques of functions is something, and thinking in functions is another thing. Literally, you should learn the functions and go beyond them to train your mind to embrace the functional programming paradigm. This first part of the chapter helps you to do them both while discovering the richness and power of using functions in Ring.

Defining and Calling Functions

A function is a block of code that receives input, transforms it, and returns output to the place from where it was called.

In Ring, a function is defined using the func keyword like this:

```
func hello
      put "Hello!"
end
```

You can write this alternatively using the def keyword like this:

```
def hello
      put "Hello!"
end
```

In all cases, end is optional, because the end of a function in a Ring program is always delimited by the beginning of another function, by another class, or just by the end of file (or by the return keyword, but this will be introduced in a second). As a convention, and for better code readbility, I usually use "func" with functions and "def" with methods (functions inside classes).

To call a function, then, from any place of your program, you just need to use its name and say `hello()`, for example. In Ring, you can call the function before you define it, as shown in Listing 7-1.

Listing 7-1. hello.ring

```
hello()    # the function is called here, defined below
def hello
      put "Hello!"
end
```

Test this in a new file called `hello.ring`. Ring responds with this:

```
Hello!
```

As a collateral remark, note the use of the PUT keyword as an alternative to SEE and ?. If you remember, we used it in Chapter 1, when we said "hello" to the console.

Usually, a function should return a value using the `return` keyword. For example, one can call the function in Listing 7-2 by saying `sum(2,3)`, and the function will return `2 + 3` and then return `5`.

Listing 7-2. sum.ring

```
? sum(2,3)
func sum(n1,n2)
    return n1 + n2
```

Write this code in a new file called `sum.ring` and test it yourself.

Another feature to stress here is that functions in Ring are used first and then defined later at the end of the file. As mentioned in the previous chapter, when we exposed the structure of a Ring program (in Figure 6-1), this was not simply a stylish differentiator but a cultural asset of the language: when you write code, Ring wants you to focus on the thinking facet of the algorithm (the problem to solve) and after that on the implementation part of that thinking (in terms of functions and classes).

In practice, a function is usually equipped with some parameters that form its inputs. So if we want our `hello()` function to become conscious of the name of the person it is supposed to welcome, then we adapt the `hello.ring` file to look like Listing 7-3.

Listing 7-3. hello.ring

```
hello()

func hello(friend)
        put "Hello dear " + friend + " !"
```

Our function now contains one parameter, and it will expect the caller to provide it at the start. So, if we try to run the code, we get an error, as shown here:

```
Calling function with less number of parameters!
```

To solve this problem, you need to say "hello" to your friend `Kalidia` as shown in Listing 7-4 (always in the `hello.ring` file).

Listing 7-4. hello.ring

```
hello("Kalidia")

func hello(friend)
        put "Hello, dear " + friend + "!"
```

When you execute this, the function will kindly say the following:

```
Hello, dear Kalidia!
```

You must send the exact number of parameters required by the function. In our case, add a descriptor of your feelings while welcoming a friend and adapt the `hello()` function to look like Listing 7-5 (again in the `hello.ring` file).

Listing 7-5. hello.ring

```
hello("Kalidia")

func hello(friend, feeling)
    put "Hello, dear " + friend + "!" + NL
    put "I'm really " + feeling + " to meet you."
```

Execute the code, and then you get the same error again, as shown here:

```
Calling function with less number of parameters!
```

In fact, hello() is waiting for two values, a friend and a feeling, while the call in the first line of the program contains just one. Let's fix it by saying hello("Kalidia","happy"), hello("Kalidia","surprised"), or any other feeling you want. Run it to see the result. In my case, it shows the following:

```
Hello, dear Kalidia!
I'm very happy to meet you.
```

There is another way to call a function in Ring using the call() standard function, but I'll leave that for later.

Sending Parameters and Returning Values

There are two key considerations you need to keep in mind while sending parameters. First, a function parameter is a variable that plays the role of a container for the value you want to send to your function. Therefore, a parameter must be of a certain type: a number, a string, an object, or a list. Second, sending a value from one place to another can be done by reference (we also say *by variable*) or by copy (and we also say *by value*).

Let's take this piece by piece and understand it by looking at an example. Imagine we need a function to which we send a number, and then it calculates the next number to it (number + 1). Thus, when we use the code in Listing 7-6 in nextnum.ring and execute it, we get 10.

Listing 7-6. nextnum.ring

```
1 a = 9
2 nextof(a)
3
4 func nextof(n)
5     ? n+1
```

The first thing to note here is that a has been defined, from the beginning on line 1, as a number. Therefore, when we call the function on line 2 by sending the same a variable, Ring understands that the parameter n in the called function on line 4 must be a number too! On line 5, adding the number 9 to the number 1 gives naturally the result 10, which is of type number, of course. The proof is to change the code of the previous example to look like Listing 7-7 (in the same file, nextnum.ring).

Listing 7-7. nextnum.ring

```
1 a = 9
2
3 r = nextof(a)
4 ? r
5 ? type(r)
6
7 func nextof n
8    return n+1
```

Now, the function nextof() doesn't do any printing but returns n+1 as output, using the return keyword. Once returned, the value is stored in the variable r on line 3. And because Ring gives a type to any variable depending on the value it first receives, then r is set to the same type as its value, n+1, which is actually number.

Line 5, ? type(r), will tell us if our thinking was good. Execute the code and look at the result, as shown here:

```
10
NUMBER
```

By analogy, if we change line 1 to a = "9", which means that a is no longer number but string, then the addition on line 8 will be interpreted by Ring as a concatenation of two strings, "9" and "1". The returned type is then a STRING, and its value is "91". Test it to see the result yourself.

Now we move to the second consideration we announced at the start of the section: parameters can be sent either by reference or by value.

If a parameter is sent by reference, then it maintains a "live" relationship with its source variable.[4] So, when its value changes inside the called function, so does its value in the source variable. In Ring, lists and objects are always sent by reference. Type the code in Listing 7-8 in a new byref.ring file.

---

[4]Under the hood, this relationship is maintained by the address of the variable in memory, also known as a Pointer. But, you don't need to care about this because this is managed internally by the language.

Listing 7-8. byref.ring

```
1 a = [1,2]
2 ? "Before : " ? a
3 ? "Inside : " ? f(a)
4 ? "After  : " ? a
5
6 func f(a)
7     return a + 3
```

Execute it so you get the following:

```
Before :
1
3
Inside :
1
2
3
After  :
1
2
3
```

As you see, the list has been changed inside the function (3 is added); therefore, the original list has also been impacted.

The other types, numbers and strings, are sent by copy. Therefore, when a value is changed inside the function, the source variable isn't affected, because what you are managing is a whole new copy of the value, not the original one Try this in a new file called bycopy.ring, as shown in Listing 7-9.

Listing 7-9. bycopy.ring

```
1 a = 2
2 SEE "Before : " SEE a + NL
3 SEE "Inside : " SEE f(a) + NL
4 SEE "After : " ? a + NL
5
```

```
6 func f(a)
7     a++
8     return a
```

a is set to 2 on line 1 and then changed on line 7 (incremented by 1). Nevertheless, its original value is not impacted. Run the code to see the proof.

```
Before : 2
Inside : 3
After  : 2
```

At this level, two legitimate questions can be asked.

- Why did Ring make this choice (sending lists and objects by reference and sending numbers and strings by copy)?

- What if we want to do the inverse of what Ring wants to do, meaning sending a list or an object by copy, for example?

As a short answer, Ring has adopted a pragmatic approach by considering that lists and objects can carry large data, and, hence, they are sent by reference for better performance. But if we need to work on a list or an object locally inside a function independently from its source value, then Ring gives you the = operator to make a deep copy of it. Try this in a new file called deepcopy.ring, as shown in Listing 7-10.

Listing 7-10. deepcopy.ring

```
1 a = [1,2]
2 ? "Before : " ? a
3 ? "Inside : " ? f(a)
4 ? "After  : " ? a
5
6 func f(a)
7     aa = a    # aa is a deep copy of a
8     aa + 3
7     return aa
```

Execute it so you get this:

```
Before :
1
2
Inside :
1
2
3
After  :
1
2
```

With this deep copy feature, Ring gives you the freedom to embrace a pure functional style where functions are not allowed to change values in the global scope. For every same input, they will provide the same output. But this comes, sometimes, with a performance cost.

An alternative to deeply copying the sent object or list is provided by the value() function from the StdLib library. We can test it with the same code we wrote earlier containing a list sent by reference and adapt it to be sent by copy, but just using value(), as shown in Listing 7-11 (write it in a new file called byvalue.ring).

Listing 7-11. byvalue.ring

```
1 Load "stdlib.ring"
2
3 a = [1,2]
4 ? "Before : " ? a
5 ? "Inside : " ? f(value(a))
6 ? "After : " ? a
7
8 func f(a)
9     return a + 3
```

Run it and you get the following:

```
Before :
1
2
```

```
Inside :
1
2
3
After :
1
2
```

As you see, what has been changed inside the function is a copy of the a list, not the original list itself. This is an illustration of how easy you can break the standard way of doing things in Ring and send a list or an object by copy and not by reference.

Next we will jump to another interesting subject: how can we make our function's parameters optional in Ring?

Using a List for Optional Parameters

At a first glance, when we look at an error message like Calling function with less number of parameters, we might think that Ring is a rather conservative language that lacks flexibility, which isn't true. In fact, sending your parameters inside a list solves the problem, provided you learn how to use it.

Before looking at an example, you should understand why optional parameters are sometimes needed. The case arises when the user of your program or another developer wants to use your code and finds it unnecessary to send one of the parameters defined in the signature of your function.

Let's suppose your program contains a form asking the user to provide her name, job, and age, but only name is required, as shown in Figure 7-1.

Figure 7-1. *Only one piece of information is required from the user: her name*

347

There are many possible combinations of parameters that the user could send before calling the info() function (which will be defined later) by clicking the OK button.

- All three values (name, job, and age) are sent.

- Only the value name is sent.

- name is sent along with job only.

- name is sent along with age only.

How can we respond to all these cases in only one function by resorting to a beautiful list? Save the code in Listing 7-12 in a new file called params.ring.

Listing 7-12. params.ring

```
1 info("Ahmed", "Programmer", 36)
2
3 func info(name, job, age)
4     ? "Name : " + name
5     ? "Job : " + job
6     ? "Age : " + age
```

Save it and run it. The three values are sent from line 1 to the required three parameters defined on line 3. So, there's no problem at all, as shown here:

```
name : Ahmed
job : Programmer
age : 36
```

If you don't send any of the three parameters or if you send more than three of them, then an error is raised, right? But what if you send a NULL value for the parameter you don't want to provide, like this?

```
1 info("Ahmed", "Programmer", NULL)
```

Your code will work, and this is what you will get:

```
name : Ahmed
job  : Programmer
age  :
```

Remember, NULL is processed by Ring as a normal empty `string`. But this is not what we really want. Our objective is to make it possible to call the function like this:

```
info("Ahmed", "Programmer")
```

or like this:

```
info("Ahmed")
```

or even like this:

```
info()
```

And still the code of our same function works!

`List` is a dynamic thing, containing nothing or many variables of any type: `numbers`, `strings`, `objects`, and even other `lists` inside the main `list`. The idea is to use it as a container for our parameters and parse its content inside the function according to the several cases we want to manage.

Take the code in Listing 7-13 and save it in a new file called `optional.ring`.

Listing 7-13. optional.ring

```
1 info([])
2
3 func info(aParam)     # aParam is a list of parameters
4     ? "name : " + aParam[:name]
5     ? "job  : " + aParam[:job]
6     ? "age  : " + aParam[:age]
```

Do you remember hashed `lists`? Go back to Chapter 2 to refresh your memory if you want. It is sufficient to remember here that a hashed list is a list of lists, where every list element is formed with two members: a key of string type and a value of any type. Here's an example:

[["name","Ahmed"] , ["job","Programmer"] , ["age",36]]

"name", "job", and "age" are the keys, and "Ahmed", "Programmer", and 36 are their respective values. The hash list, aHash, can be written like this:

```
aHash = [ :name = "Ahmed" , :job = "Programmer" , :age = 36 ]
```

The main operations of a hash list are getting the value of a particular element by its key (aHash[:age] would give 36 in our case) and accessing a key-value pair with its range in the list (aHash[3] would give the list ["age",36]).

Let's get back to our code (in optional.ring). Execute it and you'll get this in the Output window:

```
Name :
Job  :
Age  :
```

Play with other scenarios, like this one, for example:

```
1 info([ :name = "Ahmed" ])
```

and you get this:

```
Name : Ahmed
Job  :
Age  :
```

and you get this:

```
1 info([ :name = "Ahmed" , :age = 36 ])
```

and you get this:

```
Name : Ahmed
Job  :
Age  : 36
```

Of course, the strict order of your parameters is not required, so if you say this:

```
1 info([ :age = 36, :name = "Ahmed" ])
```

you get the same result.

Recursion: When a Function Calls Itself

If you make a call to a function f() from inside that function, then it will execute infinitely...until all the available memory for your program is completely consumed. Let's make that happen! Write this in a new recursion.ring file, as shown in Listing 7-14.

Listing 7-14. recursion.ring

```
1 f()
2 func f
3     ? "Hi!"
4     f()
```

Run it. Wait for a while, and read the error message you get, as shown here:

```
Error (E2) : Out of Memory!
```

This function is recursive because it calls itself. Recursion generates an iteration over the function code and can continue infinitely, unless we define a condition that stops it. So if we want our recursion to happen 10 times, then we must use the code in Listing 7-15, for example (in the same `recursion.ring` file).

Listing 7-15. recursion.ring

```
1 n=0
2 f()
3 func f
4     ? "Hi!"
5     n++
6     if n<10 { f() }    # Necessary to avoid infinity!
```

If you run this, then you get Hi! exactly 10 times, with is equivalent to saying this:

```
for n = 1 to 10
     ? "Hi!"
next n
```

But, in practice, recursion over a list of things is used when an iteration of the same action is necessary until the end of the list. The most commonly used sample of code to illustrate this is the calculation of the factorial of a number n. As an example, Figure 7-2 shows the calculation visually for the factorial of 3.

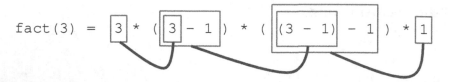

Figure 7-2. *A visual illustration of how a factorial of 3 is computed*

Visibly, 3 is first multiplied by the factorial of 2, and then the result is multiplied by the factorial of 1. Let's do the same visual exercise for factorials of 4 and 5. You can probably sense it: there is a logical pattern that is repeating itself here. Hence, a factorial of n is obtained by multiplying this, every time, with a factorial of n-1 until reaching 1. This is a recursion we can express programmatically, as shown in Listing 7-16 (write it in a new `factorial.ring` file).

Listing 7-16. factorial.ring

```
1 ? fact(3)
2
3 def fact n
4    if n = 0
5        return 1
6    else
7        return n * fact(n-1)
8    ok
```

Recursion can theoretically be used to model any case where an iteration is needed, forming a strong alternative to loops. This explains why recursion is considered a cornerstone of the functional programming paradigm, as we are going to discover now.

Beyond Functions, the Functional Programming Paradigm

Functional programming is a style of building software programs based solely on functions and without changing the values of variables outside the scope of these functions.

Such functions are autonomous (or deterministic) and never reach beyond the window to change the global state of the program, or the states of other functions and objects (no side effects!). They are pure functions because the same inputs always provide the same output. They are first-class functions because they can be stored in a variable, sent as a parameter to another high-order function, or returned as the output of a function. A function can be anonymous and have no name at all (also called a *lambda*), can be nested in a hierarchy of functions, and can be compared logically to another function to check them for equality.

Some programming languages are more or less strictly functional, like Erlang, Closure, F#, Elm, and Elixir. In the case of Ring, all the functional features stated in the first paragraph of this section are available, while other programming styles are possible (procedural, object-oriented, declarative, meta-programming, and natural). As a Ring programmer, you go functional only when it is required. So, before delving into the technicalities, let's explain briefly what the main pros and cons are of the so-called functional programming paradigm and when it is really needed.

Three Pros

First, and because autonomous functions never share the state of your program, testing a complex codebase means testing every function one at a time. No cross-module thinking is needed, and more interestingly, there are no surprises because one of your variables has changed in an unknown place of your program.

Second, functions provide a level of expressiveness because they are oriented to describe the objective of the code, not how it is implemented. When you call a function, its signature (formed with its name and the list of parameters) is everything that you need to know. In the future, when the internal implementation of the function changes, it doesn't impact the rest of the program where your function has been called.

Third, because your functions can be first-class, anonymous, and nested, then you can combine them, organize them declaratively, and mash them up in a way that transforms programming to a creative experience similar to talking to your computer in a natural language. You'll learn more about this later when we talk about the important subject of software composition using functions in the section "Composing Functions."[5]

Three Cons

You can constrain your function to never change the value of a variable coming in as input by copying it locally and creating whatever processing you need in that particular copy of the original data. Obviously, this can generate performance problems, especially when the variable hosts a large quantity of data.

---

[5]Software composition will also be approached from the object perspective in the section "Inheritance and Composition."

Sticking to the immutability principle (variables don't change; a new copy is made and changed) means that even loops aren't welcome. Recursion is then used, as you learned in the previous section, as a de facto tool for designing iterations. But this is not that natural, yet it's less expressive than simply using a plain old for/next loop.

Finally, there are some computer domains that can never be modeled purely in functions, like input/output (I/O) when connecting to a database or printing text on the screen, or like GUI programming, which is, by definition, made to depend on data from outside the scope of the whole program (the mouse events or the user's finger touching the mobile screen).

Areas of Application

In the beginning, functional programming was used to solve specific problems, but nowadays, many large software companies use it as a first-class choice to deal with large parallelized, distributed, and big data–enabled systems. A pragmatic programmer who is willing to embrace the functional culture can build a core system in a functional way, while covering it with an imperative layer for all the stuff that cannot be implemented in pure functions. But, usually, everything that can be programmed in functions can also be done in objects. The choice of one paradigm or another is a matter of programming style and benefits from being driven by the problem to solve and not personal feelings.

In the remainder of the section, you will learn how Ring embraces the various features of the functional programming paradigm.

Pure Functions

In Listing 7-17 (write it in a new unpure.ring file), f(n) increments pragmatic programmer any number n it receives by x. Let x = 1. Then, f(5) will naturally lead to returning 5 + 1, which equals 6.

Listing 7-17. unpure.ring

```
x = 1

? f(5)

func f(n)
     return n + x
```

f() isn't pure, because it depends on the value of the x variable that is located outside its scope. To purify it, we need to include the value to be incremented in the function signature, as shown in Listing 7-18 (try it in a new file called pure.ring).

Listing 7-18. pure.ring

```
? f(5,1)

func f(n, x)
    return n + x
```

There is no global variable in the picture anymore! f(n,x) is now pure and never depends on the rest of the world.

Immutable State

In Listing 7-19 (write it in a new mutable.ring file), the function makes an adjustment to the value of the global variable x by multiplying it by the number it receives as an input.

Listing 7-19. mutable.ring

```
x = 10
? f(5)
func f(p)
    x = x * p
    return x
```

The state of the program, in particular its global state, has been altered by the function. To fix that, we make a copy of x locally in the function, work on it, and leave the global variable untouched. To do so, make a copy of mutable.ring file, name it immutable.ring, and then change it, as shown in Listing 7-20.

Listing 7-20. immutable.ring

```
x = 10
? f(5)

func f(p)
    x1 = x
    x1 = x1 * p
    return x1
```

As mentioned in many places in the book, the = operator makes a deep copy of the value of x inside x1, whatever its type is. This is particularly useful when the variable sent to the function is of type list or object, which is sent by reference by default.

First-Class Functions

Functions are first-class citizens in Ring. One can store them in a variable and then call them from that variable, pass them as parameters to other functions, and return them as output. We will just see an example of the first feature and leave the two others for your own consideration (you can learn about them from the Ring documentation).[6]

In Listing 7-21, f is a variable of type string containing the name of one of the two functions we want to call, f1 or f2. Calling a function stored in a variable can be done using the call keyword to which we add the required parameters of the called function. Try it in a new file called calledfunc.ring.

Listing 7-21. calledfunc.ring

```
f = "f1"
call f("Sara")

func f1(name)
      ? "Hello to " + name + " from f1"

func f2(name)
      ? "Hello to " + name + " from f2"
```

If you run this code, then you get Hello to Sara from f1. If you want the message to be called from the f2 function, then change the first line to f = "f2". And if you want to say "hello" to Dora instead of Sara, then change the second line to call f("Dora"). An interesting technique is to postpone your decision of what function to execute, and with what input values, until your program is running and you have more context.

---

[6]http://ring-lang.sourceforge.net/doc1.11/fp.html?highlight=functional#first-class-functions

Higher-Order Functions

Higher-order functions can take other functions as parameters. To see it in action, let's write an algorithm that composes an arbitrary binary number formed of eight digits, 11100100, for example.

The smallest component of the number, the 1 or 0 digit, is generated using the Ring random() function that we encapsulate in a function of our own called f(). Then this f() function is called eight times to generate the final number. Therefore, a times(8,:f) function is used to call the f() function eight times.

Create a new highfunc.ring file and use it as shown in Listing 7-22.

Listing 7-22. highfunc.ring

```
func main()
    times(8,:f)      # The function f() is sent as an input
                     # to the times() function
func f()
    see random(1)    # generates a random digit (0 or 1)

func times(pn, pf)   # pf parameter contains the f() function
    for i = 1 to pn
            call pf() # f() is called using the value of pf
    next i
```

Run it and you get, for example, 00111110. Run it again, and you get 10101001. Run it again and you get 01011100. And so on and so on![7]

Anonymous Functions

Ring allows you to write functions without specifying a name for them. These are called *anonymous functions*, or, more simply, *lambdas*. You can store them in a variable and then call them, as shown in Listing 7-23 (test this in a new anonymous.ring file).

---

[7]Note that the same function we implemented here exists in the StdLib library. You'll learn more about this in this entry in the Ring documentation: http://ring-lang.sourceforge.net/doc1.11/stdlib.html?times-function#times-function.

Listing 7-23. anonymous.ring

```
f1 = func x,y { ? x+y }      # A function without a name!
call f1(2,3)                 # gives 5
```

Or, more interestingly, you can pass it as a parameter to another function. To see it in action, let's consider a list of words for which you want to generate a list of numbers corresponding to the length of every word. So if we have the following list, aWords = ["Ring", "Ruby", "Python"], then we should get aLen = [4, 4, 6].

To do this in Ring, we can rely on an anonymous function that counts the length of a given word, and then we apply this to every element of the aWords list. To do so, write the code in Listing 7-24 in a new file called fmap.ring.[8]

Listing 7-24. fmap.ring

```
aWords = [ "Ring", "Ruby", "Python" ]
f = func w { return len(w) }     # Our lambda

aLen = map( aWords, f)        # Iterate over the word list and
                              # apply f() to every word

? aLen

func map( paList, pf )        # p => remind us they're parameters
         aResult = []
         for i = 1 to len(paList)
             n = call pf( paList[i] )
             aResult + n
         next i
         return aResult
```

Run the code and you get the list [4,4,6] displayed in the Output window like this:

```
4
4
6
```

---

[8]The term *map* is commonly used in programming for algorithms like the one presented here. Practically, a map is a list of items and a function that is mapped to the items, i.e., applied to every one of them.

Nested Functions

Anonymous functions can also be used to design nested functions in Ring. A nested function is a function called inside another function. We can use a nested function to organize our code as shown in Listing 7-25 (save the code to a new fnested.ring file).

Listing 7-25. fnested.ring

```
? sayHiBye("Bert","Mariani")

func sayHiBye(firstName, lastName)
    f = func(p1,p2) {              # function inside a function!
        return p1 + " " + p2
    }
    ? "Hi " + call f(firstName,lastName)
    ? "Bye " + call f(firstName,lastName)
```

Run it and you get the following:

```
Hi Bert Mariani
Bye Bert Mariani
```

Composing Functions

Writing programs with function composition is a lot of fun! To do it in code, suppose we have a bunch of functions for returning parts of a string hosted in a **pStr** variable[9]: first(pStr,n) to retrieve the n first letters, last(pStr,n) to get the n last ones, part(pStr,n1,n2) to construct a substring from the n1[th] letter to the n2[th] one, and, finally, CAPITALIZE(pStr) to transform it to uppercase.

The magic rule for smooth composition is to build your algorithm using pure functions. This way, the output of one function can securely form an input for the next one, without causing any side effect or any trouble in the global state.

To test this, let's put the code in Listing 7-26 in a file called fcomposed.ring.

---

[9]Remember, I usually postfix the name of the variable by p if it is used as a parameter of a function.

Listing 7-26. fcomposed.ring

```
word = "humanized"
// Testing every function alone
    ? first(word,5)          # => Human
    ? last(word,3)           # => zed
    ? part(word,3,5)         # => man
    ? CAPITALIZE(word)       # => HUMANIZED

// Now let's make a thinking by comoposing these functions

        // Give me the first letter of the last 3 letters
            ? first( last(word,3) , 1)      # => z
        // Give me the 2 to 4 part of the last 5 letters
            ? part( last(word,5) , 2, 4)    # => ize
        // Give me the enitre word but with MAN capitalized
            ? first(word,2) +
              CAPITALIZE( part(word,3,5) ) +
              last(word,4)
            # => huMANized

//*** Our functions ***

        func first(pStr,n)
            n1 = 1
            n2 = n
            return substr(pStr,n1,n2)

        func last(pStr,n)
            n1 = len(pStr) - n + 1
            n2 = n
            return substr(pStr,n1,n )

        func part(pStr, n1,n2)
            return substr( pStr,n1, n2-n1+1 )

        func CAPITALIZE(pStr)
            return UPPER(pStr)
```

Save it and run it. This is what you get:

```
human
zed
man
HUMANIZED
z
ize
huMANized
```

Play with the code of other functions; there are a lot of them!

Fabricating Functions

Yes, you can turn a corner from your program garden to a factory that generates functions dynamically. Who said that a dynamic programming language, like Ring, was a bad thing?

Usually, the shape of your function can be defined at programming time: you know exactly what name the function should have, what parameters to include in it to host its inputs, what code is written inside to compute those parameters, and what output must be returned. Let's say these are 99 percent of the cases.

But the other 1 percent will stare you in the face one day or another: you actually don't know part of your function, or its entire contents, until the program runs and you get more context from the execution environment or directly from the user. In this case, you must fabricate a function and execute it at runtime. To do so, you can rely on calling a function you construct in a variable, using the call() function as we saw before, or by using the workhorse of all functions in Ring: eval().

Suppose you want to resolve the equation y = 3 x^2 + 2x + 5. That's really easy; you write an algorithm with just one function (test this in a new file called formula. ring), as shown in Listing 7-27.

Listing 7-27. formula.ring

```
 ? f(0)
func f(x) { return 3*x*x + 2*x + 5 } # => 5
```

Then you say ? f(0) and you get 5, you say f(5) and get 90, and you say ? f(-2) and get 13.

The problem with that solution is that it is restricted to a second-order form of equations, while what you need is a free-form input of any kind of formula. Ideally, you want to make it possible for the user to specify it. In a new file called free-formula.ring, try Listing 7-28.

Listing 7-28. free-formula.ring

```
SEE "Enter formula:" + NL
GIVE formula            # The user enters the formula
fStr = "func f(x) return " + formula # function constructed
eval(fStr)              # function is dynamically executed
? f(0)
```

On the first line, the user enters the formula she wants, maybe the same as the first example: 3*x*x + 2*x + 5. On the second line, the code of the function is dynamically constructed: func f(x) return 3*x*x + 2*x + 5. On the third line, it is executed. Finally, the fourth line uses it and shows the same value: 5. With this huge difference, the user can enter whatever formula comes to mind!

Comparing Functions

Functions can be compared in Ring using the = or != operator. Let's consider the three functions shown in Listing 7-29 by calling them and comparing them (inside a new file you call fcompared.ring).

Listing 7-29. fcompared.ring

```
// Declaring functions
f1 = func { SEE "Hello!" + NL }
f2 = func { SEE "Fine?" + NL }
f3 = f1
// Calling them
call f1()
call f2()
call f3()
```

```
// Comparing them
SEE ( f1 = f2 ) + NL     # gives 0 => FALSE : they are different
SEE ( f1 = f3 ) + NL     # gives 1 => TRUE  : they are equal
SEE ( f2 = f3 )          # gives 0 => FALSE : they are different
```

Run it and get the following result:

```
Hello!
Fine?
Hello!
0
1
0
```

Let's go from functions to objects right now.

Objects and Object Orientation

A computer program consists of data and some operations on them. Object-oriented programming is a programming style that models the program world using objects. To do so, data and operations are crafted together in cohesive code blocks called *classes*. At runtime, the code describing the classes is transformed into live objects hosting data and waiting for any message other objects send. Based on the data received via those messages, the object adopts the appropriate behavior by executing the appropriate operation on the data.

Unlike a function, an object is a live and dynamic autonomous computer being. It is born (when you instantiate one using the *new* keyword), grows up (when you add new data to a *list* variable, for example, inside that object), communicates (when you call a method from an external object), and dies (when you put any other value in the variable specifying that object). Objects can inherit their core data (attributes) and behavior (methods) from parent objects (using the *from* keyword), as well as have their own specific data (attributes) and operations (methods). Meanwhile, they keep an open eye on their privacy and advocate for a sound neighborly relationship with stranger objects (by defining the private attributes and methods under the *private* region of the class). Strangers (calls from outside) are never allowed to know what is happening inside, and if they need to enter the house (by calling a method of the object or modifying one of its attributes from ouside the class using the *dot* operator), they enter from the door and not the window (by using the private attribute or method in the scope of the object, and not from outside)! When dancing together at computer runtime, objects can communicate (by method calls), and be composed (by inheritence, aggregation, composition, or concatenation).

Creating Objects from Classes

A *class* is the blueprint for an object. It guides the compiler in building the object in memory and defining its data structure and logic behavior. The data structure is designed using *attributes*, and the behavior is designed using *methods*. Attributes are a set of variables occupying the class region, just after the class name. Methods are functions acting at the scope of the object. They both represent the members of the class. In Ring, a class is declared using the class keyword, as shown in Listing 7-30 (write this to a new file called person-class.ring).

Listing 7-30. person-class.ring

```
class Person
{


name
job          # The class region, containing attributes
age


def info()
    ? "Name : " + name
    ? "Job  : " + job        # Methods region
    ? "Age  : " + age


} # NB : Class opening and closing braces are optional
```

If you try to run this code, nothing happens, because class is just a description and gives no order to Ring to execute anything. To make it come to life, we need to create an object based on that class using the new keyword. Our person-class.ring program becomes Listing 7-31.

Listing 7-31. person-class.ring

```
// Creating an object of type "person"
new Person {
        // Providing values to the object attributes
        name = "Majdi"
        job  = "Doctor"
        age  = 42
        // Calling the info() method in the object
        info()
}

// Class description
class Person
{
        name
        job
        age

        def info()
        {
            ? "Name : " + name
            ? "Job : " + job
            ? "Age : " + age
        }
}
```

Now, you can run the program and see the result:

```
Name : Majdi
Job  : Doctor
Age  : 42
```

At this level, there is nothing super interesting that makes us think that an `object` is more suitable than a `list` to do the same thing. In fact, all the code can be replaced by the code shown in Listing 7-32 (put this in a new file called `person-list.ring`).

Listing 7-32. person-list.ring

```
// Defining the list
aPerson =
[

        :name = "Majdi",
        :job = "Doctor",      # Those replace the attributes
        :age = 42,

        :info = func {
                ? "Name : " + :name
                ? "Job   : " + :job      # This replaces the method
                ? "Age   : " + :age
        }
]
// Showing the person info
f = aPerson[:info]               # This replaces the object
call f()                         # creation and method call
```

Execute. Same result:

```
Name : Majdi
Job  : Doctor
Age  : 42
```

In reality, an object offers a bunch of interesting advantages over a list. This section will present them in detail.

First, let's learn, once and for all, how an object can be initialized, how it can be accessed, and then how objects can be sent as parameters to functions and returned as values from them.

Initializing Objects

When creating objects using the new keyword, it is possible to initialize them with a given value. You already saw how to do this using the init() method when we created a user-defined type called ucdString in Chapter 2 (in Listing 2-28) to make it possible to manage Unicode text in Ring.

CHAPTER 7   FUNCTIONS, OBJECTS, AND BEYOND

Make a copy of that listing, and put it in a new file called `object-init.ring`, while adapting it as shown in Listing 7-33.

Listing 7-33. object-init.ring

```
load "guilib.ring"     # Importing the RingQt extension

// Creating the o1 object while initializing it
o1 = new ucdString("أبراس")

// Displaying the text attribute
? o1 .text

Class ucdString
    text
    oQString = new QString()

        // Object initialization method
        def init(pStr) # pStr contains text we put in 2nd line
                oQString.append(pStr) # Qt creates unicode text
                text = pStr # Attribute text is initiated
```

When you execute it, you get the name Apress written in Arabic.

Accessing Objects

Objects are accessed in Ring in two ways: by using the classical dot operator (`object.attribute` or `object.method()`) or by using braces (`{}`).

Inside the braces, `{ ... }`, we can use the object attributes and methods directly.[10] This can be done when we create the object using the new keyword or at any time using the following syntax:

```
ObjectName { # Accessing object data and methods directly }
```

Listing 7-34 shows an example (write this code to a new `object-braces1.ring` file).

---

[10]The remaining code examples in this section come from the Ring documentation.

Listing 7-34. object-braces1.ring

```
o1 = new Point
See "Object created." + NL

See "Now we access it using braces..." + NL

o1
{
    X = 5
    Y = 15
    Z = 25
    print()
}

Class Point x y z
    def print
        SEE x + NL + y + NL + z
```

Execute it so you get the following:

```
Object created.
Now we access it using braces...
5
15
25
```

We can also use braces to access objects when we call functions or methods, like in Listing 7-35 (write this code in a new object-braces2.ring file).

Listing 7-35. object-braces2.ring

```
o1 = new Point

print( o1 { x=10 y=20 z=30 } )

func print object      # can also be written func print(object)
        SEE object.x + NL +
            object.y + NL +
            object.z

Class Point x y z
```

Execute it and get:

```
10
20
30
```

Finally, we can use the code in Listing 7-36 and switch between using braces and the dot operator to access the objects (write this code inside a new `object-braces3.ring` file).

Listing 7-36. object-braces3.ring

```
o1 = new Point

o1 { x=10 y=20 z=30 }.print()
Class Point x y z
        def print
                SEE x + NL + y + NL + z
```

Execute it. You get the same result as previously:

```
10
20
30
```

Using Setters and Getters

There are two possible ways of using object attributes in our code: we can assign values to them, and we can assign them, as values, to other variables. In the first case, we say that we are *setting* them, and in the second, we say that we are *getting their value*.

Let's take a simple class `Person` with only one attribute, `name`. In the case of setting the object attributes, it looks like Listing 7-37 (use this code in a new file called `setter.ring`).

Listing 7-37. setter.ring

```
o1 = new Person
o1.name = "Selmen"       # Setting name attribute to "Selmen".
? o1.name
Class Person name
```

After being set, the name attribute is used in the line ? o1.name to show the name of Selmen.

To get the value, the code looks like Listing 7-38 (save this code in a new file called getter.ring).

Listing 7-38. getter.ring

```
o1 = new Person
cDefault = o1.name      # Getting the default value of name
                        # attribute, "Mahran".
? cDefault
Class Person name = "Mahran"
```

After getting the value of the name attribute and assigning it to the cDefault variable, that variable is used to display the name of Mahran.

This is only a part of the story, though. To give you full control over what to do when the setting and getting operations happen, Ring provides you with two nice automatic methods, called *getter* and *setter*. To illustrate them, in practice, think of the following two requirements:

- In the setter.ring file, when the name attribute is set in any corner of the program to any value other than "Selmen", Ring captures it and allows us to manage the situation.

- In the getter.ring file, every time the name attribute is assigned to a variable in the program, then Ring notifies us with a message.

To manage the first situation, we add a **set**Name() method to our Person class, and there we specify a piece of logic. The method is fired automatically by Ring every time it encounters a line of code containing **o1.name** = "Anything". To see it, in code, adjust the setter.ring file to look like Listing 7-39.

Listing 7-39. setter.ring

```
o1 = new Person

o1.name = "Selmen"        # Setting name attribute to "Selmen"
                          # => The setName() method is fired!

// ? o1.name    # Note that this line is disabled using //
               # and that printing happens inside the class

Class Person
    name
        def setName(value)      # value recieves this

            if UPPER(value) = "SELMEN"
                ? "Hello, Selmen."
            else
                ? "Hi, " + value + "!"
                ? "I was looking for Selmen, where is he?!"
            ok
```

Execute it. Observe the result.

```
Hello, Selmen.
```

In this case, the first condition of the if block inside the setName() method is verified. And then, ? "Hello, Selmen." is executed. Now change the second line to o1.name = "Mariem", and run it again. You've got it; this is what you should get:

```
Hi, Mariem!
I was looking for Selmen, where is he?!
```

By the way, I've used the UPPER() standard function to be sure Selmen has been captured in all his moods. In fact, whether we set o1.name to selmen (in lowercase), SELMEN (in uppercase), or any other combination in between (sELmen, SELmEN, etc.), they are all transformed to SELMEN by UPPER(value), and the condition is always verified.

Now, we show how we can ringify the second requirement. Go back to the getter. ring file we made previously in Listing 7-38 and adjust it as shown in Listing 7-40.

Listing 7-40. getter.ring

```
o1 = new Person

o1.name = "Mahran"     # Let's affect a value to name attribute
cString = o1.name      # Getting the value of name attribute
/*
Note that there is no printing happening here in the main
region of the program. What you will see on screen, will be
printed inside the getName() method of th Person class below.
*/

Class Person
     name

     def getName
             ? name + " is now being assigned!"
```

Immediately after parsing = o1.name in the third line of the program, Ring flies directly to the getName() method, which is the getter of the name attribute inside the Person class. The getter takes control then of the execution flow and shows the following result on the screen:

```
Mahran is now being assigned!
```

If you change the second line where the name attribute was set to o1.name = "Sonia", then the message you get on the screen changes accordingly.

```
Sonia is now being assigned!
```

There is an empirical finding I want to share it with you here: when the execution flow is interrupted in the line cString = o1.name, cString is cut off from that execution flow and left behind (Figure 7-3).

Figure 7-3. *cString is left unassigned when the getName() method is used*

To verify this by yourself, add a line at the end of the main region of the program (just before the class) and write this:

```
if cString = NULL then ? "But, cString remains NULL!" ok
```

Then run the program again and reflect on the result, as shown here:

```
Mahran is now being assigned
But, cString remains NULL!
```

What do you think of such a decision taken by Ring? Does it seem to be counterintuitive to you? Personally, I think that, unless a strong case can be made for it, this behavior should be changed so that cString receives the value assigned without disruption. Again, let's ask a question in the language's Google Group and wait for an answer.[11]

Sending and Returning Objects

Objects in Ring are sent to functions by reference, as we know already, and returned by value.[12] But this has an important exception: when there is a composition of objects (an object's attribute is a variable of type object), objects are returned by reference and not by value (for good reason, as we will discover in a minute). Let's say the same thing in code.

First things first, when an object is sent, then it's sent by reference.

Let's consider the program shown in Listing 7-41; I invite you to save it in a new file called sent-byref.ring.

Listing 7-41. sent-byref.ring

```
01 o1 = new Point { X = 10 Y = 10 }
02 ? o1
03 ? move(o1,5,5)      # o1 is sent by reference
04 ? o1
```

---

[11]This time, I'll leave it to you. So, go and subscribe to the Ring Google Group (https://tinyurl.com/w6xzz6e) and be the first to ask a question. I'll be observing the group to know who you are.

[12]By the way, the same rule applies to lists.

```
05
06 func move(po, px,py)
07          po.X += px
08          po.Y += py
09          return po
10
11 class Point X Y
```

Run it and look at the result, as shown here:

```
x: 10
y: 10

x: 15
y: 15

x: 15
y: 15
```

The first pair of values, X = 10 and Y = 10, reflects the state of the o1 object just created in the first line of the program. On line 4, this same object is sent to the move() function by reference.

On lines 7 and 8, inside the function, the X and Y attributes of o1 were changed. On line 10, its changed value has been returned to line 3 to be printed. Hence, you see the second pair: X = 15 and Y = 15.

Finally, because o1 was sent by reference, any change of the object attributes inside that function influences its initial state. Hence, you see the third pair of o1 attributes as printed on line 4: X = 15 and Y = 15.

Second, when an object is returned, then it is returned by value, except if there is a composition of objects, and the object returned is an attribute of another object. In this case, the object is returned by reference and not by value. To show it by code, let's analyze this sample I picked from the Ring documentation (reproduce it in a new file called returned-byval.ring), as shown in Listing 7-42.

Listing 7-42. returned-byval.ring

```
01 func main
02         o1 = New Screen  {
03                 addPoint() {  # Object accessed by reference
04                         x = 100
05                         y = 200
06                         z = 300
07                 }
08                 addPoint() {     # Object accessed by reference
09                         x = 50
10                         y = 150
11                         z = 250
12                 }
13         }
14     SEE o1.content[1]
15     SEE o1.content[2]
16
17 class Screen
18     content = []     # hosts a list of objects
19     def addPoint
20             content + new Point
21             return content[Len(content)] # Object returned
22                                          # by reference
23
24 class Point x=10 y=20 z=30
```

The algorithm composes a Screen object from a number of Point objects. When a Point object is returned from the addPoint function on line 21, it is returned by reference. That means any change of its attributes on lines 4 to 7, or on lines 9 to 11, will impact the original object. This dynamic has been implemented in Ring to enable declarative programming, which is the most natural way of programming by composition. The section "Inheritance and Composition" will explain what object composition is and why it is fundamental when programming with objects.

Before that, let's do a quick review of what we learned on objects so far.

A Recap: Object Structure and Class Event Mechanism

After discovering the basics and before we dig into the more advanced staff in the remainder of the section, it's the perfect time to show you two things.

- The overall structure of a class in Ring

- What I call the class event mechanism in Ring

In Ring, the complete structure of a class is given by this syntax template:

```
Class ClassName From ParentClassName # From can also be < or :
    Attributes ┐
    ...        ├ # Class region
               ┘            ┐
                            ├ # Public region
    Methods                 │
    ...                     ┘


    Private ┐
    {       │
        Attributes
        ...         ├ # Private region
        Methods
        ...
    }       ┘
```

As you can see, Ring usually puts what is important and more common in the forefront (the Public region), while putting what is secondary and exceptional at the end (Private region).

The Public region contains the attributes and methods that are visible from outside the object. Therefore, they can be accessed from anywhere in your code, after you create an object from that class, of course. While in the Private region, you put the attributes and methods that form the internal parts of the class. You can change your mind anytime, from spaghetti to shakshuka, and no one will ask you why! You'll learn more about the use of this privacy feature in the section "Securing the Object World with Encapsulation."

This template is what serves as a blueprint for designing the static facets of your object: the set of its attributes and methods and whether they should be public or private. But Ring provides you with more than this: a set of specific methods, working automatically for you, by capturing a useful set of dynamic events that can happen when you are using your class in Ring code (that's why I call them a *class event mechanism*) and for which you can write a specific behavior. Look at the list here:

- `init()`
- `operator()`
- `getAttribute()`
- `setAttribute()`
- `BraceStart()`
- `BraceEnd()`
- `BraceEvalExpr()`
- `BraceError()`

Some of these methods have been presented before; the others will be exposed later in the chapter.

Inheritance and Composition

Again, in this section, I will show you the advantage objects have over lists in modeling data requirements. The idea is to make it with `list` first, envision some changes that you need, assess the complexity that will arise, and then show how object inheritance and composition radically solve the issue.

A friend of yours, who works in the IT department of a bank, saw your code in Listing 7-32 for `person-list.ring` that you wrote at the beginning of the section and asked you to make it suitable for showing the data of the bank customers. The expected output of the program looks like this:

```
Name          : Shidong
Job           : CEO
Age           : 54
Customer ID   : C12500
Bank account  : XA12500
Address       : 20, Peace Avenue. Toronto.
```

We can immediately observe that there is a set of additional data related to the banking domain. This can be modeled in a aCustomer[] list:

```
aCustomer =
[
     :customerID = "C12500",
     :bankAccount = "XA12500",
     :address = "20, Peace Avenue. Toronto."
]
```

Make a copy of person-list.ring and call it customer-info.ring.

Intuitively, we can add the new list required by the bank (aCustomer) to the old one (aPerson), like this:

```
aPerson + aCustomer
```

The aCustomer[] list is then added as an additional item to the main list, whose structure becomes something as shown in Figure 7-4.

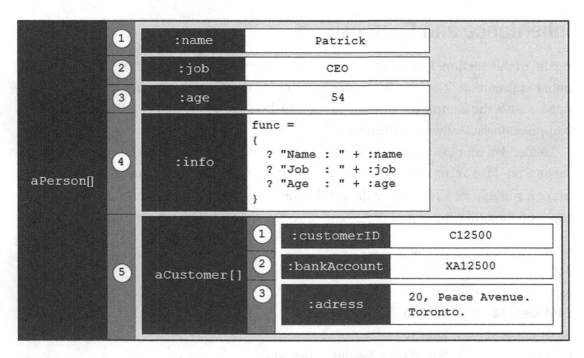

Figure 7-4. *Structure of the aPerson list in the runtime*

Our anonymous function hosted in the aPerson[ ] list is no longer suitable and needs to be extended to cover the printing of the new data hosted in the inner aCustomer[ ] list. One may say we need just to change it to the following:

```
:info func {
    ? "Name      : " + :name
    ? "Job       : " + :job
    ? "Age       : " + :age
    ? ""
    ? "Customer ID    : " + aPerson[5][:customerID]
    ? "Bank account   : " + aPerson[5][:bankAccount]
    ? "Address        : " + aPerson[5][:address]
```

Since the new item added to the aPerson list (which is the aCustomer list) can be reached by its range 5. The whole program looks like Listing 7-43.

Listing 7-43. listway1.ring

```
01 // Declaring the main list
02 aPerson =
03 [
04    :name = "Shidong",
05    :job = "CEO",
06    :age = 54,
07
08    :info = func {
09        ? "Name : " + aPerson[:name]
10        ? "Job : " + aPerson[:job]
11        ? "Age : " + aPerson[:age]
12        // These are new lines added
13        ? ""
14        ? "Customer ID       : " + aPerson[5][:customerID]
15        ? "Bank account      : " + aPerson[5][:bankAccount]
16        ? "Address           : " + aPerson[5][:address]
17    }
18 ]
19
```

```
20 // Declaring the banking list
21 aCustomer =
22 [
23    :customerID = "C12500",
24    :bankAccount = "XA12500",
25    :address = "20, Peace Avenue. Toronto."
26 ]
27
28 // Adding the two lists
29 aPerson + aCustomer
30
31 // Calling the autonomous function defined in aPerson[]
32 f = aPerson[:info]
33    call f()
```

Let's save it in a `listway1.ring` file and run it. It works, as shown here:

```
Name : Shidong
Job  : CEO
Age  : 54

Customer ID : C12500
Bank account : XA12500
Address : 20, Peace Avenue. Toronto.
```

This works, but it has a serious design problem.

Composing Objects with Inheritance

In fact, we've mixed up data from different domains by putting `address`, which is some personal data, inside the list dedicated to banking information. Your program should be redesigned so `aPerson[]` contains all the personal data and so `aCustomer[]` contains only the banking data. In the future, when you call one or another, you are sure to have semantically coherent data in the same place.

To solve the problem, we should move the `:address` element from `aCustomer[]` (line 25) and insert it inside `aPerson[]` (line 7). Don't forget to drop the comma at the end of line 24 and add a comma at the end of line 7. Try it and run the program again. This is what you get:

```
Name : Shidong
Job  : CEO
Age  : 54

Customer ID :
Bank account :
Address :
```

What happened? The instructions, inside the anonymous function, responsible for printing the new data (lines 14 to 16) have been broken by the change we just made to our code. In fact, because :address has been moved from the aCustomer[] list to the aPerson[] list, it is no longer correct to call it by saying aPerson[5][:address]. Instead, we can simply say aPerson[:address]. And because a new item has been added to the aPerson[] list, then 5 should be replaced by 6 on lines 15 and 16 so they look like Listing 7-44.

Listing 7-44. Part of listway1.ring

```
15    ? "Customer ID  : " + aPerson[6][:customerID]
16    ? "Bank account : " + aPerson[6][:bankAccount]
```

To be in harmony with the domain scopes we established according to which address belongs to the Person domain and not the Customer domain; see line 17 in Listing 7-45.

Listing 7-45. Part of listway1.ring

```
17    ? "Address     : " + aPerson[5][:address]
```

This should be deleted altogether from the aCustomer list. The address printing should be leveraged by adding a line inside the anonymous function so it looks like Listing 7-46 (the added line is in bold).

Listing 7-46. Part of listway1.ring

```
08    :info = func {
09         ? "Name : " + aPerson[:name]
10         ? "Job : " + aPerson[:job]
11         ? "Age : " + aPerson[:age]
12         ? "Address : " + aPerson[:address]
```

```
13          // Those These are new lines added
14          ? ""
15          ? "Customer ID : " + aPerson[6][:customerID]
16          ? "Bank account : " + aPerson[6][:bankAccount]
17      }
```

If you've been attentive while making the necessary changes, you'll execute the code and get this:

```
Name : Shidong
Job  : CEO
Age  : 54
Address : 20, Peace Avenue. Toronto.

Customer ID : C12500
Bank account : XA12500
```

This is fine, but at what cost?

Object orientation was invented to overcome such complications. It offers the programmer a cohesive design experience and a logical container of his assets, both data and operations: the so-called *object*. Free your mind of related to lists now, and let's solve the same problem using objects.

The first step is thinking about the model of our program. A model is a representation of the main actors of the solution (called also *entities*) and their behavior. The sole entity we have here is Person, right? That seems logical, since Customer is also a Person. But from a modeling perspective, they are two different entities, where every customer is a person but with some specific data and, maybe, specific actions.

Two entities are then necessary.

- An entity of type Person

- An entity of type Customer that is also of type Person

Translated to Ring, this is said using these two sentences (write them in a new file called objectway1.ring), as shown in Listing 7-47.

Listing 7-47. objectway1.ring

```
class Person

class Customer from Person
```

Let's add a simple code inside every class, as shown in Listing 7-48.

Listing 7-48. objectway1.ring

```
class Person
    ? "I am a person"
class Customer from Person
    ? "I am a customer"
```

Now, create the objects using the new keyword, as shown in Listing 7-49.

Listing 7-49. objectway1.ring

```
1 new person
2 ? ""     # We'll let a empty line for clarity
3 new customer
4
5 class Person
6    ? "I am a person"
7
8 class Customer from Person
9    ? "I am a customer"
```

Save the file (objectway1.ring) and execute it. The output window will show these two pieces of information:

```
I am a person

I am a person
I am a customer
```

The first one comes from line 6 in the Person class. The second comes from the accumulation of two sources: line 6 in the Person class and line 9 in the Customer class. The reason of this is the use of the from keyword in the definition of the Customer class. The from keyword means literally that all the code written for the parent class will be copied from it and pushed inside the Customer object once created.

In OOP jargon, we say that Customer inherits from Person. Inheritance solves radically our design problem and saves us all the pain we get from using lists, in this particular case.[13] Our program is clean now; see Listing 7-50.

Listing 7-50. objectway1.ring

```
01 // A customer is created
02 new customer {
03         name = "Shidong"
04         job = "CEO"
05         age = 54
06
07         customerID = "C12500"
08         bankAccount = "XA12500"
09
10         super.info() # super points to parent class Person
11         ? ""
12         info()
13 }
14
15 // Defining the parent class
16 class Person
17         name job age
18         def info()
19             ? "Name : " + name
20             ? "Job : " + job
21             ? "Age : " + age
22
23 // Defining the child class
24 class Customer from Person
```

---

[13]In other situations, lists can be even more useful than objects as a modeling tool. In particular, the data-oriented design movement, promoted mostly by game engine programming and other high-performance real-time systems, avoids objects and builds upon data structures (lists in Ring jargon) to model their software. To better understand the differences between object-oriented and data-oriented approaches, read this Medium article written by Jonathan Mines: https://tinyurl.com/yxcd7cxd.

```
25          customerID bankAccount
26          def info()
27              ? "Customer ID : " + customerID
28              ? "Bank account : " + bankAccount
```

Save, run, and see the following:

```
Name : Shidong
Job  : CEO
Age  : 54

Customer ID : C12500
Bank account : XA12500
```

Our model is built, now, upon a clean foundation. We have to separate logical domains: `Person` for any personal data and operations, and `Customer` for any banking data and operations. Yet, the two domains are automatically linked together, by inherence. Any change in one, by addition or deduction, is seamlessly reported to the other. So, unlike the list way, where any change must be propagated manually in many possible places of the code, Ring tends to protect your objects, automatically, by notifying you about what goes wrong with them. Let's experiment.

Suppose we decided to delete the `job` attribute from the `Person` class. Comment the appropriate line (line 17) by inserting `//` just before `job`. So, the line looks like Listing 7-51 (see the code in bold).

Listing 7-51. Part of objectway1.ring

```
16 class Person
17      name // job age
```

Run the program, and observe that we always have the same result. `age` is correctly printed in the Output window along with the other personal information. But, this is not the object attribute `age` that is shown here, but the `age` variable declared on line 5 inside the object scope. Because the `info()` method is part of that scope, Ring finds this `age` variable and prints its value. In other terms, if `age` is identified as an attribute of the class, then any change means a change to the object data structure. Otherwise, it is considered as a new variable declared there and used inside the object scope, like any other variable.

Now, let's push it further and comment out the age variable on line 5. Now, our code doesn't contain neither an age object attribute nor an age variable. But age is still used on line 21 inside the info() method. What is Ring's opinion? It rejects the error and protects you from shipping it when you deliver your program to your friend.

```
Line 21 Error (R24) : Using uninitialized variable : age
```

Remember when we made a little change in the list example. Ring was unable to give us any help. Object orientation is a different programming experience that comes with something you really need: peace of mind! We can even add entire new entities without any regression. The whole point here is that inheritance helps us extend our program model smoothly to cope with the new requirements we gather from the real world.

Excited, your friend asks you to help him extend the program to cover other actors, the employees. Immediately, you craft a new class in your model, Employee, that inherits naturally from Person and exposes its specific data and operations. You ask your friend two direct questions.

- What are the *data* and *operations* required for Employee?

- Can you split them into two categories, those that are specific to Employee and those that are shared with other Persons?

Your friend says Employee must carry this data: job, salary, employment date (emp_date), and hobby. Like all the other entities, the sole operation expected is to show this data using an info() method. While salary and emp_date are specific to Employee, the job and hobby entities are a matter of personal data and should be under the umbrella of the Person class.

Make a copy of the current objectway1.ring file, as shown in Listing 7-43, and create a new file called objectway2.ring. Inside the file, erase the block from line 1 to 13 related to the creation of a Customer object. Then, update the Person class to look like Listing 7-52.

Listing 7-52. objectway2.ring

```
class Person
    name job age hobby
    def info()
```

```
? "Name : " + name
? "Job : " + job
? "Age : " + age
? "Hobby : " + hobby
```

Then add the description of a new Employee class, as shown in Listing 7-53.

Listing 7-53. Part of object-way2.ring

```
// Defining a second doughter class
class Employee from Person
    salary emp_date
    def info()
        ? "Salary : " + salary
        ? "Employement date : " + emp_date
```

Finally, at the beginning of the file, create an object from Employee using the new keyword and writing inside the object braces, as shown in Listing 7-54.

Listing 7-54. Part of objectway2.ring

```
// An employee is created
new Employee {
    name = "Zoubeir"
    job = "Banker"
    age = 28
    hobby = "Swimming"

    salary = "64K"
    emp_date = "2014/10/10"

    super.info()
    ? ""
    info()
}
```

Save, run, and check out the results, as shown here:

```
Name : Zoubeir
Job : Banker
Age : 28
Hobby : Swimming

Salary : 64K
Employement date : 2014/10/10
```

Composing Objects with Aggregation

If inheritance embellishes the design of your objects, cleans them, and optimizes them, then composition turns them into clay in your hands as a software craftsperson.

Let's continue with the example of code we made in the previous section. Make a copy of object-way2.ring and call it object-way3.ring. Inside the file, delete the block related to the creation of an Employee from lines 1 to 14.

Imagine that the bank decided to connect customers to employees to develop their social relationship. Every team is composed of two customers and one employee. Quickly, we can model them by designing a new class, Team, at the end of the compose-inherit.ring file, as shown in Listing 7-55.

Listing 7-55. Part of compose-inherit.ring

```
// Composing a team of employees
Class Team
     oEmployee
     oCustomer1
     oCustomer2
```

To create a team and then show their names on the screen, use the code shown in Listing 7-56.

Listing 7-56. Part of compose-inherit.ring

```
// A team is created
oTeam1 = new Team {
     oEmployee  = new Employee { name = "Mark" }
```

```
        oCustomer1 = new Customer { name = "Matt" }
        oCustomer2 = new Customer { name = "Steve" }
}
// Displaying the team
? oTeam1.oEmployee.name
? oTeam1.oCustomer1.name
? oTeam1.oCustomer2.name
```

What we've made is a strict translation to Ring via the following two sentences:

```
A Team contains one Employee and two Customers.
Please display their names on screen!
```

Therefore, when you save the file (`compose-inherit.ring`) and execute it, you get the following:

```
Mark
Matt
Steve
```

As a programmer who thinks in objects, you'll find that a wide spectrum of real-world situations can be modeled this way, with composition. It is more natural and, perhaps, more efficient than inheritance. The particular type of composition we used here is called *aggregation*. In fact, we've aggregated objects of different identities inside another object that serves as a container for them, without altering their own identities. Still, other types of object composition exist, like concatenation and delegation. So, let's not finish the section before taking a rapid look at them.

Composing Objects with Concatenation

Concatenation turns back to adding the members of one object to the members of another, dynamically. This is a way to enrich the data structure and behavior of a given object without relying on class inheritance. The advantage is that no tight coupling exists between the parent and child objects, since everyone is totally independent from the other. This makes your objects more flexible and your software more resilient and expandable because concatenation eliminates the need for sharing the same state (same attributes) between the chain of the family tree (i.e., the chain of inherited objects).[14]

The previous example (in the `compose-inherit.ring` file) of designing an `Employee` entity by inheriting from the `Person` class can be done differently. No `from` keyword is needed, just a new object of type `Employee` that we compose, dynamically, by concatenating its main members with the members of the `Person` object. To do so, Ring provides a crucial feature: adding new members to objects at runtime using the `addAttribute()` and `addMethod()` functions.[15] Let's show how we can use the first one to concatenate the attributes of two objects.

To simplify the code, we will consider that class `Person` contains simply `class Person { name age }` and that class `Employee` contains `class Employee { salary emp_date }`. Our objective is to create an `Employee` object in which the four attributes are concatenated, without using any inheritance!

To do this, make a copy of `compose-inherit.ring` and name it `compose-concat.ring`. Inside the new file, write the code shown in Listing 7-57.

Listing 7-57. compose-concat.ring

```
// Storing the list of attributes in Person
o1 = new Person
a = attributes( o1 ) # Gives [ :name, :age ]

// Creating the Employee by concatenation
o2 = new Employee
{
    addAttributes(a)    # Person attributes are added
    ? attributes(self) # To verify the final result
}
```

---

[14]This feature of the Ring language enables what is known today as *context-oriented programming* (COT). According to `https://tinyurl.com/2ef2ly`, "Context-dependent behavior is becoming increasingly important for a wide range of application domains, from pervasive computing to common business applications. Unfortunately, mainstream programming languages do not provide mechanisms that enable software entities to adapt their behavior dynamically to the current execution context. This leads developers to adopt convoluted designs to achieve the necessary runtime flexibility."

[15]While reading the several libraries written in Ring, you will find that this concatenation feature is widely used. Understanding it here will help you better understand how those libraries work and how they have been made.

```
// The two Classes to be concatenated
class Person
    name
    age

class Employee
    salary
    em_date

    def addAttributes(a)        # The object adds new
        addAttribute(self,a)    # attributes to itself
```

That's pretty clear, isn't it? We have been able to achieve the concatenation requirement by allowing our `Employee` object to enrich itself autonomously. The method we provided, `addAttribute(self,a)`, is self-defined and can add any list of variables in `a[]` it receives into concrete attributes of the object. The same thing can be done to add new methods using the `addMethod()` function. For that, I will let you dig into the subject in the Ring documentation.[16]

Composing Objects with Delegation

Delegation is a form of composition where an object delegates part of its duties to another object. First, this is useful to avoid duplicating the same stuff inside many objects. Second, it reinforces a culture of specialization where the object does, locally, what it knows best and transfers the remaining work to a more skilled object.

As a simplified example, let's build on the previous `compose-concat.ring` file and work on a copy of it called `compose-deleg.ring`.

Suppose we want to add a feature to the `Person` object that calculates the `age` based, of course, on a birth date (`birth_date`). Because calculating age, among other calculations for dates, is a task that we want to keep separate in a specialized object, we can create a `DateCalculator` class that does the job. Our `Person` object will send a message to the `Calculator` to tell it the following: this is my date of birth; please make your calculations and send me the answer. Without further explanation, I will leave you with the code, as shown in Listing 7-58.

---

[16]http://ring-lang.sourceforge.net/doc1.11/metaprog.html?reflective#addmethod-function

Listing 7-58. compose-deleg.ring

```
// A person is created
oPerson1 = new Person {
     name = "Rafik"
     birth_date = "01/08/1976"
     age()         # This method will calculate the age
                   # but by delegating it to a specialized
                   # external object (see age() method below)
}

// Printing the person object
? oPerson1

// Defining the Person class
class Person
     name
     birth_date
     age

     def age()
          // Delegation happens here
          o1 = new DateCalculator(birth_date)
          age = o1.age()

// Defining the DateCalculator class
Class DateCalculator
     date
     age

     def init(d)
        date = d

     def age()
          n = floor( diffDays(date(),date) / 365 )
          this.age = n
          return age
```

This is the output you get when you run the program:

```
name: Rafik
birth_date: 01/08/1976
age: 43
```

Here, `name` and `birth_date` are provided natively by the `Person` object, while `age` is provided by delegation to a specialized `DateCalculator` object.

Your Recipe for Object Composition

Every seasoned programmer will give you a different point of view of which form of object composition should be a priority over the others in your object-oriented designs. My recipe to you is simple.

- Use composition by *aggregation* as much as you can.

- Use composition by *delegation* when aggregation doesn't work.

- Resort to composition by *concatenation* when neither aggregation nor delegation can do the job.

- Surrender to *inheritance* when it is inevitable.

- *Encapsulate* the internal implementation of the object.

This is the first time we are talking about object encapsulation in this book. Read the following section and you are covered.

Securing the Object World with Encapsulation

By law, the bank is constrained not to allow anyone, any system, and any code to access the data of `CustomerID`, `age`, or `bankAccount`. These must be protected programmatically.

In Listing 7-59 (save the code in a new file called `private.ring`), the three attributes coming after the keyword `private` are protected against external access, while all the other attributes remain public.

Listing 7-59. private.ring

```
// A customer is created
o1 = new Customer

// Let's access the public attributes
? o1.first_name          # Works => gives Bob
? o1.last_name           # Works => gives Dylan

// Let's access a private attribute from outside the class
? o1.customerID          # Breaks => Access denied!

// Let's access a private attribute using a method that does
// this inside the class
? o1.bankAccount()       # Works!

// Defining the Customer class
Class Customer
        // Public region of the class (accessible from anywhere)
            first_name = "Bob"
            last_name = "Dylan"

        // A public method to expose a private attribute to the
        // outside world
        def bankAccount()
            ? "From inside the class: " + bankAccount

        // The private region
        Private

        age
        customerID
        bankAccount = "XD113300"
```

Run the code and you get the following:

```
Bob
Dylan

Line 9 Error (R27) : Using private attribute from outside the class :
customerid
```

Printing the `first_name` and `last_name` public attributes happens without problem. By contrast, when the line `? o1.customerID` tries to access a private attribute from outside the class, Ring interrupts the program execution and complains by returning an R27 runtime error.

To solve this problem, comment out the line responsible for generating the error message (`// ? o1.customerID`) and then run the program again. This is what you get:

```
Bob
Dylan
From inside the class: XD113300
```

Hence, the public region is run without problem, and `Bob Dylan` is returned safe and sound. Then, the `? o1.bankAccount()` line is executed. The `bankAccount()` method is a public method of the `Person` class and therefore can be accessed from anywhere but also has the right, like any other member of the class, to access its private region. There it does its job by reading the `bankAccount` private attribute and returning its default value to the calling line: `? o1.bankAccount()`.

It's easy then to hide any data and, by analogy, any method, to limit its visibility to the scope of the object (in other words, it can't be called from the outside). But what is the true value provided other than achieving pure privacy conservation? The answer is that this forms a structural feature and a strategic pillar of object-oriented programming called *encapsulation*.

In the spirit of object-oriented design, as imagined by the fervent Alain Kay, objects do nothing more than exchange messages. There is no holy hand that flies over the program world and says to an object do this or do that. An object can be assimilated into a biological cell that evolves in the body of the program, in two dimensions, following these simple rules:

- Internally, the object does its work in total freedom, but no one in the program world should care. This part can change when necessary, extended or replaced altogether without informing anyone in the city, since there is no dependency with them at all.

- Externally, the object must share the minimum necessary information about its identity and the kind of information it is able to contribute as a citizen of the program world. When other objects need the object to send some simple information, process a calculation it is specialized in, or participate in a composition or a delegation of a given task on which it is supposed to have an added value, then those objects must send the object a message with a well-defined touchpoint such as a public method with a well-defined number of parameters.

To put it simply, the object must be encapsulated internally to be communicative externally. Encapsulation is basically the guarantee of sustainable communication between objects and the stability of the whole software.

Managing a Collection of Objects

In practice, you rarely program with a single instance of an object. In fact, the sample application you made for your banker friend should be able to deal with many people and, among them, many employees and many customers.

Real-world programs could have millions of instances of the same object moving around in the computer memory. As a programmer, you rely on your programming language to deal with the hard stuff of optimizing memory, collecting the garbage produced by the use of some objects that are still there but no longer useful, and many, many other technical components. Still, there are some practical skills you need to do by hand: constituting a list of objects, sorting them depending on the value of a given attribute, finding a particular object inside the collection, sending and receiving a collection of objects, and so on.

If you know how to use lists in Ring, then you are covered. Just put your objects in a list and then deal with them at runtime using all the functions provided. It is also possible to apply a function to all the objects (usually called the map() function). The following are some examples to show how all this works.

We want to start from a simple Employee class with just two attributes, name and salary. Then we design a class to host a collection of Employee objects. When Employee initiates, the class receives a list of objects and builds its collection internally. Then the class becomes able to do various jobs such as filtering itself according to a defined attribute, searching for an object with a given value for one of its attributes, and, finally, applying a given function to all the objects hosted in the collection.

Listing 7-60 shows the code. Read it carefully because it's very well commented. Save it to the collection.ring file.

Listing 7-60. collection.ring

```
// Constructing a list of Employee objects
a = [
    new Employee { name = "Ahlem" salary = 38000 },
    new Employee { name = "Zohra" salary = 28000 },
    new Employee { name = "Hajfa" salary = 26000 },
    new Employee { name = "Yemna" salary = 48000 },
    new Employee { name = "Najet" salary = 58000 },
    new Employee { name = "Saliha" salary = 42000 }
]

// Creating an object containing a collection of employees
_oEmployees = new Employees(a) # _ is used here as a decorator
                               # to easily identify object
                               # in code collections

// Managing the collection of objects
_oEmployees
{
        ? "Listing the object collection:" + NL
        ? getList()

        ? "Sorting the collection by name:" + NL
        ? sortBy(:name)

        ? "Sorting the collection by salary:" + NL
        ? sortBy(:salary)

        ? "Searching for the range of name 'Saliha':" + NL
        ? searchFor('Saliha',:name)

        ? "Searching for the range of salary 28000:" + NL
        ? searchFor(28000,:salary)
}
```

```
// Defining the Employee class
class Employee
    name
    salary
```

```
// Defining the Employees class (=> collection of objects)
 class Employees

    // This attribute will contain the collection of objects
    aList = []

    // This method recives a list of objects and adds them as
    // an attribute (in the collection of objects aList[])
    def init(paList)
        aList = paList

    // This method returns the collection of objects
    def getList()
        return aList

    // This method sorts the collection by attribute
    def sortBy(pAttribute)
        return sort(aList,1,pAttribute)

    // This method searchs for the value of an attribute
    def searchFor(cValue,pAttribute)
        return find(aList,cValue,1,pAttribute)
```

In the Output window, you will get the following result:

Listing the object collection:
name: Ahlem
salary: 38000.000000
name: Zohra
salary: 28000.000000
name: Hajfa
salary: 26000.000000
name: Yemna
salary: 48000.000000

name: Najet
salary: 58000.000000
name: Saliha
salary: 42000.000000

Sorting the collection by name:
name: Ahlem
salary: 38000.000000
name: Hajfa
salary: 26000.000000
name: Najet
salary: 58000.000000
name: Saliha
salary: 42000.000000
name: Yemna
salary: 48000.000000
name: Zohra
salary: 28000.000000

Sorting the collection by salary:
name: Hajfa
salary: 26000.000000
name: Zohra
salary: 28000.000000
name: Ahlem
salary: 38000.000000
name: Saliha
salary: 42000.000000
name: Yemna
salary: 48000.000000
name: Najet
salary: 58000.000000

Searching for the range of name 'Saliha':
6
Searching for the range of salary 28000:
2

You've got the list of objects in the order of their creation by code, and then you get the same list filtered by name and then by salary. Finally, you get two numbers, 6 and 2, corresponding, respectively, to the range of the name Saliha and the range of salary 28000 in the collection.

As homework, I want you to add an apply(f) method to the Employees collection. Its role is to receive a function f you declare outside the class and proceed by applying it dynamically to all the objects of the collection. This function could be, for example, something that capitalizes the names or adds 10,000 to every salary. Go back to the previous example of anonymous functions and follow the same implementation as for the map() function (see fmap.ring file in Listing 7-24).

Changing the Object Operators

Your objects, when they are carefully designed, can serve as building blocks to a pseudolanguage that reflects your personal style and copes with the specific domain you are programming in.

Suppose we have a Text class that is as simple as shown in Listing 7-61.

Listing 7-61. text.ring

```
o1 = new Text("I love you, Ring!")
? o1.content

class Text
    content

    def init(p)
        content = p
```

Save this to a text.ring file and execute it. Did you say you loved Ring? I'm so happy about that. Now, imagine (just imagine, don't execute) we were able to say this:

```
? o1 * 3     # Getting three copies of our text
```

and we get this:

```
I love you, Ring!
I love you, Ring!
I love you, Ring!
```

Or if we were able to say this:

```
? o1 / 2     # Dividing the words in two slices
```

and we get this:

```
[ "I" , "love" ]
[ "you" , "Ring" ]
```

Or, finally, if we were able to say this:

```
? o1 - ", Ring"     # Deleting ", Ring" from the text
```

we get the following:

```
I love you!
```

It's not a fantasy, though, but a feature we can easily add to our object through operator overloading. Take a look at the code in Listing 7-62 and then write it to a new file called overloading.ring.

Listing 7-62. overloading.ring

```
o1 = new text("I love you, Ring!") # sent to init() method

? o1 * 3    # * is the operator and 3 is the paramter
            # we will call them cOp and p here after

class text
    content      # the only attribute of the class

    def init(txt) # txt contains text received from line 1
        content = txt # the attribute is set with the txt text

    def operator(cOperator, nValue) # fired by * 3 in line 3

        switch cOperator  # The operator, * in our case
        on "*"
            cStr = ""
            for i=1 to nValue # text is repeated 3 times
                cStr += content + NL
```

```
        next i
    off

    return cStr # The repeated text is returned
```

Now, run the code and take a look at the result, as shown here:

```
I love you, Ring!
I love you, Ring!
I love you, Ring!
```

In fact, every class you make in Ring comes with a standard method called `operator()` that you can use to change the default meaning the language has for some logical and arithmetical operators, such as >, <, =>, +, *, /, etc. When such a method is added, then its code is executed automatically by Ring when the operator is used with the object. For example, when we say o1 * 3, then the code under `operator(cOperaotor,nValue)` where `cOperator = "*"` is executed, with `nValue` being equal to 3.

Of course, you can change 3 to any number, even 0 if you want, and it will always work as expected. Try to hack it, and when you finish, prepare yourself to taste the sugar of object braces, which are one of the killer feature of the Ring language!

Interacting with Objects Inside Braces

When you are accessing an object with two opening braces, some interesting events are automatically fired by Ring such as `braceStart()`, `braceEnd()`, `braceExprEval()`, and `braceError()` but also `getAttribute()` and `setAttribute()`. Most of them were invented to facilitate the implementation of declarative and natural programming in Ring.

Listing 7-63 (which is similar to the one we worked on in the section "Sending and Returning Objects") builds on what we learned earlier and illustrates the use of some new methods such as `braceStart()` and `braceEnd()`. Write the code in a new file called `braces.ring`, as shown in Listing 7-63.

Listing 7-63. braces.ring

```
// A new screen is composed declaratively

new Screen {      # This opening brace fires the braceStart()
                  # method in the Screen class

        addPoint() {
            X = 10
            Y = 10
            Z = 10
        }
        ? aPoints[ len(aPoints) ]     # => Shows the Point
                                      #    just added

            anything anytime          # Invokes getAnything() and
                                      # getAnytime() methods in the
                                      # Screen class

}      # This closing braces fires the braceEnd() method in
       # the Screen class

Class Screen
    aPoints = []
    anything
    anytime

        def braceStart()
            ? "Hello!" + NL

        def addPoint()
            aPoints + new Point
            return aPoints[ len(aPoints) ]

        def getAnything()
            ? "Anything!" + NL

        def getAnytime()
            ? "Anytime!" + NL
```

```
        def braceEnd()
            ? "Bye!"
class Point
        X Y Z
```

Save this in braces.ring and execute it. This is what you get:

```
Hello!

x: 10
y: 10
z: 10

Anything!

Anytime!

Bye!
```

Can you figure out the rationale behind every function used? I'm sure you can. These functions can be used in various situations but especially when it is a matter of creating programs that embrace the declarative and natural programming paradigm.

These two paradigms are built on top of object-oriented design and provide us with a unique advantage that every Ring programmer should benefit from. The following two sections ("Beyond Objects, Declarative Programming in Ring", and "Beyond Objects, Natural Programming in Ring") will show you how this works and why you should care.

Beyond Objects, Declarative Programming in Ring

Unlike classical imperative programming, where you tell the computer how it must behave to do a job, declarative programming is intended to describe what the job is, while hiding its imperative implementation from your eyes.

Let's look at a simple story to help you understand the difference, which is essential before learning how to write declarative algorithms in Ring. Here in Sousse, a beautiful touristic town in Tunisia, I help buy what we need at home to make a delicious couscous dish. To solve it imperatively, Listing 7-64 shows the pseudocode I have designed in my head (save this to a new imperative-steps.ring file).

Listing 7-64. imperative-steps.ring

```
takeTheGuffa()      # Guffa is a traditional bag made from fronds
                    # of palm tunisians use to put things in
goToTheShop()
selectThingsToBuy()
compareWithBudget()
selectAnAlternativeThing()
putThingsInGuffa()
payThemCash()
goBackToHome()
```

This is what we usually do when we opt for a bunch of procedures, functions, and objects, and then we call them in a logical temporal order to get things done. The focus here is on the process itself, so if one day I move from Sousse to live in Amsterdam, where there is no room for guffas anymore, the program becomes useless. Some of the actions, and their order, would need to be changed for cultural reasons.

Now, we will concentrate on the final result we should have: a `Guffa` class containing a well-defined list of things that are suitable for cooking a couscous but fitting into the budget I have. The pseudocode of such descriptive thinking will look something like Listing 7-65 (save it to a new `declarative-description.ring` file), as shown in Listing 7-65.

Listing 7-65. declarative-description.ring

```
Guffa {

    budget = 10000

    listOfTgings {

        Thing { name = "couscous" price = 2500 }
        Thing { name = "tomatoes" price = 1500 }
        Thing { name = "onion" price = 1200 }
        Thing { name = "salt" price = 300 }

        getTheTotalPrice()
    }
```

```
    canBye = No or Yes # depending on budget > totalPrice

    buy() # depending on the value of canBye
}
```

Once described like this, independently from any implementation detail, our program is a universal algorithm that can be executed in any corner of the world. The whole solution is contained in the Guffa { } region. Inside that region, we can specify the Guffa attributes, like the maximum budget I have, if I canBuy it, the listOfThings I can put in it, and any necessary action I may have to undertake, like buy().

Inside the listOfThings { } area, I manage the guffa content by adding new things or deleting existing ones. Every Thing { } is an inner region where we can specify its name and its price. While doing this, we can use getTheTotalPrice() to get the current listOfThings{}. Once that's done, this information will influence our decision to buy() or not our Things, depending on the result of the comparison between the total price and the maximum budget.

This is a totally different programming experience, isn't it?

Yet, this is the same experience that underlines successful technologies like the ubiquitous HTML, and more advanced languages like QML, the declarative mother tongue of the Qt framework or the elegant Ruby language or Kotlin or REBOL. So, let's look at an example of declarative code from these languages.

The first sample written in QML is shown here:

```
import QtQuick 2.9 # import from Qt 5.9

  Rectangle {
      id: canvas
      width: 250
      height: 200
      color: "blue"

      Image {
          id: logo
          source: "pics/logo.png"
          anchors.centerIn: parent
          x: canvas.height / 5
      }
  }
```

We can immediately infer what is meant by this code: it's a logo inside a rectangular container. A similar minimal effort is required for understanding the following declarative Ruby code:

```ruby
output = FancyMarkup.new.document {
  body {
    div id: "container" {
      ul class: "pretty" {
        li "Item 1", class: :active
        li "Item 2"
      }
    }
  }
}
```

This reminds us of an HTML combo list (ul) with two items (li), where the first one is activated. In Kotlin, a quiet similar declarative code may look like this:

```kotlin
val data = mapOf(1 to "one", 2 to "two")

createHTML().table {
    for ((num, string) in data) {
        tr {
            td { +"$num" }
            td { +string }
        }
    }
}
```

Yep, this describes an HTML table using the same HTML semantics: table for the table, tr for rows, and td for columns. As you see, with no skills at all in these four different programming languages, we were able to understand the code because it's written declaratively. And declarative programming, unlike imperative, mimics the way our mental perception is constructed for understanding the world.

Ring brings to you the beauty of the declarative paradigm while taking it a step further, toward more elegance and more power. Let's take a look at this code sample from the WebLib library:

```
// Declarative code in Ring : making a web page
load "weblib.ring"

func Main
  WebPage()
  {

  div
   {
    div
    {
       H1 {   text("My Web Page")   }
    }

    div
    {
       for i = 1 to 3
         div
         {
            classname = "col-sm-4"
            H3 { html("Welcome to the Ring") }
            P  { html("Using a scripting language is fun!") }
         }
       next  i
    }

   }
}
```

Clearly, this program constructs a web page with a main container (div) and two inner subcontainers. The first one includes the title My Web Page, and the second contains three copies from a subtitle and a paragraph.

Many libraries of the Ring codebase are written this way, including the extensive gaming library GameLib that we are going to learn in the next chapter. Therefore, mastering the skills of reading declarative code written in the Ring way is essential to using its most important libraries. Nevertheless, you need to experiment with your own declarative programming and master the technique of building it on top of your object-oriented code.

To do so, let's go back to our introductive `Guffa` example and transform its pseudocode to an executable Ring program. First, write the code in Listing 7-66 in a `guffa.ring` file.

Listing 7-66. guffa.ring

```
Guffa {

    budget = 10000

    listOfTgings {
            Thing { name = "couscous" price = 2500 }
            Thing { name = "tomatoes" price = 1500 }
            Thing { name = "onion" price = 1200 }
            Thing { name = "salt" price = 300 }

            getTotalPrice()
    }

    canBuy()     # Yes or No depending on budget > totalPrice

    buy()        # depending on the value of canBye
}
```

Run this and let Ring tell us the following:

```
Line 1 Error (R24) : Using uninitialized variable : guffa
```

In fact, Ring indicates where to start in implementing our declarative micro domain-specific language (DSL), not in web or game programming like we saw earlier but in Guffa programming.

Seriously, and because Ring builds declaratively on top of object-oriented programming, Guffa should be an object, or an instance of a Guffa class. Therefore, try adding the new keyword before the word Guffa at the beginning of the program, as shown here:

```
new Guffa {
```

Execute this again to get another hint from the compiler:

```
Line 1 Error (R11): error in class name, class not found!: guffa
```

It is acknowledged now by Ring that Guffa is a class, but it has not been defined yet, so let's say this at the bottom of the file:

```
class Guffa
```

Run it. The error system points to line 5 now and says the following:

```
Line 5 Error (R24) : Using uninitialized variable : listofthings
```

It's the same recipe: because we know Ring was built declaratively using objects, listOfThings should be an object. Therefore, add it as a member of the Guffa class, like this:

```
class Guffa
    new listOfThings
```

Execute this, and you get the following error:

```
Line 20 Error (R11) : error in class name, class not found! : listOfthings
```

Ring recognizes the object but complains that its class is not defined. Let's define it by adding the following at the very bottom of the program code:

```
class listOthings
```

Now Ring points back to line 5 again where it finds the following:

```
Line 5 Error (R24) : Using uninitialized variable : listOfThings
```

Inside the Guffa region, we add a new keyword before the name of the uninitialized variable listOfThings to turn it into an object, like this:

```
new Guffa {

    // ...

    new listOfThings {
            Thing { name = "couscous" price = 2500 }
            Thing { name = "tomatoes" price = 1500 }
            Thing { name = "onion" price = 1200 }
            Thing { name = "salt" price = 300 }

            getTotalPrice()
    }

    // ...
}
```

We run this and get the following:

```
Line 6 Error (R24) : Using uninitialized variable : thing
```

The Thing object encountered on line 6 has not been initialized. Like we did with the listOfThings object previously, we add a new keyword before every Thing object. So, the Guffa region looks like this:

```
new Guffa {

    // ...

    new listOfThings {
            new Thing { name = "couscous" price = 2500 }
            new Thing { name = "tomatoes" price = 1500 }
            new Thing { name = "onion" price = 1200 }
            new Thing { name = "salt" price = 300 }

            getTotalPrice()
    }

    // ...
}
```

Then, at the bottom of the program, we add an object attribute of the listOfThings class by saying new Thing. The listOfThings class now looks like this:

```
class listOfThings
    new Thing
```

Run this and see the result, as shown here:

```
Line 23 Error (R11) : error in class name, class not found! : Thing
```

The Thing class is not found. Let's define it at the bottom of the program by adding the class Thing. Execute it. Now Ring says the following:

```
Line 11 Error (R3) : Calling Function without definition !: gettotalprice
```

There is something new here! For the first time in, Ring missed a function, not a class: getTotalPrice(). Because this belongs to the listOfThings class, let's add it as a method of the class by saying def getTotalPrice(). The class becomes as follows:

```
class listOfThings
    new Thing
    def getTotalPrice()
```

Ring jumps now to line 14 and tell us to change the pseudocode there to a real code, as shown here:

```
Line 14 Error (R3) : Calling Function without definition !: canbuy
```

Let's take the opportunity to add both the canBuy() and buy() functions to the Guffa class. Here's an example:

```
class Guffa
    new listofThings
    def canBuy()
    def buy()
```

Execute. Wow, we're done: no errors at all! Let's not wait for any further messages from Ring and set all the required attributes: budget in class Guffa, and name and price in class Thing. And why not add a show() method so the content of Guffa can be seen any time? Do it and you get the updated version of the guffa.ring program shown in Listing 7-67.

Listing 7-67. guffa.ring

```
// THE DECLARATIVE LAYER OF THE PROGRAM
new Guffa {
    budget = 10000
    new listOfThings {
        new Thing { name = "couscous" price = 2500 }
        new Thing { name = "tomatoes" price = 1500 }
        new Thing { name = "onion" price = 1200 }
        new Thing { name = "salt" price = 300 }
        getTotalPrice()
    }
    canBye() # TRUE or FALSE depending on budget > totalPrice
    buy()    # depending on the value of canBye
    show()   # Shows the content of the Guffa
}

// THE IMPLEMENTATION LAYER OF THE PROGRAM
class Guffa
    oThings = new listOfThings
    def canBye()
    def buy()
    def show()

class listOfThings
    new Thing
    def getTotalPrice()

class Thing name price
```

I won't go further here in implementing the lacking functions. To see a quick result, you can just add ? name, for example, between the braces of every Thing object so the listOfThings block looks like this:

```
new listOfThings {
    new Thing { name = "couscous" price = 2500 ? name }
    new Thing { name = "tomatoes" price = 1500 ? name }
```

```
    new Thing { name = "onion" price = 1200 ? name }
    new Thing { name = "salt" price = 300 ? name }
    //...
}
```

If you do this and execute, then you get the following:

```
couscous
tomatoes
onion
salt
```

Well, the most important lesson is the understanding we gained, step-by-step, while traveling in the brain of Mahmoud Fayed as he imagined how to build declarative programming on top of object-oriented programming. His logic is straightforward: when facing a domain-specific problem (the guffa problem in our case), we undertake these three simple steps:

1. Think of the semantics of your world in term of objects.

2. Implement them imperatively in classes.

3. Leave the imperative layer behind, and use the declarative features enabled by Ring to describe the solution by composition like we did for the guffa components.

A real-world implementation of the major declarative Ring libraries relies on more elaborated techniques of composition, where the Things are stored in a collection of objects, and where every addition of a new object is returned by reference to its caller, in the declarative layer of the program, to be adjusted there. This is not new to you, though, and the new version of the Guffa program shown in Listing 7-68 should look familiar to you (write it to a new file called guffa-extended.ring).

Listing 7-68. guffa-extended.ring

```
func main
    o1 = New Guffa {
        // The following objects are accessed by reference
```

```
func main
    o1 = New Guffa {
        // The following objects are accessed by reference
        Thing(){ name = "couscous" price = 2500 }
        Thing(){ name = "tomatoes" price = 1500 }
        Thing(){ name = "onion" price = 1200 }
        Thing(){ name = "salt" price = 300 }

        show()
    }

class Guffa
    aList = []              (2)                    (3)

    def Thing
        aList + new Thing

        return aList[len(aList)]  # returned by reference 17

    def show
        for i=1 to len(aList) ? aList[i] next

class Thing name price
```

(1)

Run it and you get the following:

```
name: couscous
price: 2500

name: tomatoes
price: 1500
```

```
name: onion
price: 1200

name: salt
price: 300
```

The main enhancement resides on the simplification of the design of the data model: Guffa contains Things directly, without using an intermediate container called listOfThings like in the previous code.

Second, composing Guffa by Things happens via a method call of the main Guffa object called Thing() (arrow (1) in the previous code). That function feeds a collection of objects (aList, a member of the Guffa class) to store the memory of our Guffa (arrow (2)). Unlike the first code example, its content is not lost. Then, the last object just added to the collection is returned by reference to the declarative zone of the code (arrow (3)). There, where its scope is fully accessible between two braces, the object is adjusted declaratively.

My advice is to revise this particular sample of code and understand its dynamics, as illustrated by the three arrows at the top of Listing 7-68. Granted, this will empower you to implement the necessary imperative foundation for your declarative layer and hack, if you want, any standard Ring libraries and code.

We can even do some acrobatics by adding this marvelous feature: from an expressiveness perspective, the following parentheses (in **bold** in the code) should be avoided:

```
o1 = New Guffa {
    //...
    Thing() { name = "couscous" price = 2500 }
    Thing() { name = "tomatoes" price = 1500 }
    Thing() { name = "onion" price = 1200 }
    Thing() { name = "salt" price = 300 }
    //...
}
```

This really makes our code look more natural. And you know what? You don't need my help to do it.

But to reward you for your patience in this long chapter, this is what you should do:

1. Delete the parentheses.

2. Create a member in the Guffa class called **Thing**.

3. Rename the `Thing()` method in the class `Guffa` to **get**`Thing()`.

4. Run and observe that the result is the same.

In practice, when you are playing the role of a business analyst who talks to a customer to understand her requirements for some new software, the semantic layer forms the reference jargon of her business world. You'll design it quickly in dumb classes, and then, while sitting on your customer desk, you'll compose her business workflows collaboratively using declarative composition. Your software prototype is ready, and the first interactions of your customers will clarify further ambiguities and potential mistakes in the initial design.

Believe me, this is a key differentiator of Ring, and it's a strategic asset you should master and use to tackle complex programming problems. For once, there's a serious implementation of a domain-specific framework inside a general-purpose programming language, and you can use it when developing large industrial-grade software.[17] In fact, thousands of lines of code have been written this way inside Ring, and the web, gaming, and GUI libraries are just three examples you are already aware of.

In the next and last section on object orientation, I give you a nice illustration of how Ring excels in delivering innovation on top of objects, by discovering how natural programming, like declarative programming, has been provided to talk to our computers in pure English, Arabic, Japanese, or any other human language.

Beyond Objects, Natural Programming in Ring

When Ring was designed, a design goal was to empower both visual programming and natural language programming. In fact, writing software without code is a continuous interest of Mahmoud through his work on the PWCT technology we will talk about later in the book. Also, he strongly believes that the future of programming will go natural. Several years ago, in 2010, he made a particular innovation by developing the experimental Supernova programming language.[18]

Supernova was a kind of human-machine dialogue based on pure English. You write a program like this:

```
I want a window and two buttons
```

---

[17]I am working on a large software project and developing a declarative layer of the entire software system for an aircraft manufacturer using Ring.

[18]https://www.codeproject.com/Articles/66996/Supernova-Programming-Language

With this code, you get a window and two buttons, effectively, on your screen.

The same feature has been made possible in Ring. So, you could write code like this:

```
Please tell me something. If you don't tell me hello I will ask it one more
time and if you don't care, I will just go away. Otherwise, I will tell you
my name and ask you for yours.
```

For sure, your colleagues from other programming languages won't believe you when you say this is a piece of computer code. But you can execute it in front of them, and the program asks you the following:

```
Please tell me something...
```

Suppose you answer with the following:

```
I don't have time!
```

Then the program responds with this:

```
Tell me hello at least...
```

Now you say this:

```
No, man!
```

The program says this back to you:

```
Ok, bye.
```

But if you responded differently by saying `hello`, for example, then the program reacts friendly by saying this:

```
Oh thanks, your welcome! My name is Ringuter, and you?
```

As you see, everything is natural right inside the plain code. Coding is transformed into a conversational dialogue between you, the programmer, and the computer. Does this seem futuristic? Maybe, but one thing is certain in Ring: the future is now!

Today, the spread of AI and bot conversational applications has transformed programming toward the adoption of humanized user interfaces based on natural language processing (NLP) technologies. Writing an algorithm that understands our everyday jargon, captures the intent of what we say, and reacts sensitively depending on the context are some of the new requirements programmers are invited to solve.

But NLP used to be a complex issue and seems to be inaccessible to the ordinary programmer, yet over the capacities of the general-purpose programming language. Now Ring is changing all that.

Building a Natural Layer for Your Program

In a new natural1.ring file, write the code in Listing 7-69.

Listing 7-69. natural1.ring

```
new App
{
        I want window
        The window title = "Hello, Ring!"
}
```

If you run it, you'll get a `class not found` error, but wait. Do you remember our nullify.ring example in Chapter 2? Great. The morale of the story is that we can write any narrative in a class region, and Ring will consider its words as attributes. Accordingly, add Listing 7-70 at the bottom of the code.

Listing 7-70. Part of natural1.ring

```
class App
    I want indow
    the window title
```

Now the code compiles correctly, and an object is created with all six attributes. Make the small change in Listing 7-71 to see the content of the object (in bold).

Listing 7-71. natural1.ring

```
oApp = new App     // naming the object
{
        I want window
        The window title = "hello world"
}
? oApp            // showing the object content
```

```
class App
    I want window      # attributes of the 1st instruction
    the window title   # attributes of the 2nd instruction
```

Run and see the result:

```
i: NULL
want: NULL
window: NULL
the: NULL
window: NULL
title: Hello, Ring!
```

Matching up every "natural" word to a "formal" attribute of the class gives us the freedom to speak naturally inside Ring code. But speaking is much more than formal freedom: it's about understanding the meaning. What we need is to capture the order we give to Ring by saying a sentence of words, i.e., a chain of attributes. I, and then, want, and then window should be interpreted as a makeWindow() function, for example. Next I will show you how we can do it.

Parsing a Natural Statement Inside Your Code

The idea is to count the words until reaching the last one, window in this case, and only then the makeWindow() function is called. The question now, how can we parse the code so every word of the I want window instruction can be triggered? It's easy in Ring: using the getAttribute() and setAttribute() methods!

Look at the revised version of the program (save it to a new natural2.ring file); see Listing 7-72.

Listing 7-72. natural2.ring

```
oApp = new App
{
    I want window
    The window title = "Hello, Ring!"
}
```

```
class App
    I want a window
    the window title

    def getI()
        ? "Parsing the word 'I'"

    def getWant()
        ? "Parsing the word 'want'"

    def getWindow()
        ? "Parsing the word 'window'"

    def setTitle(value)
        ? "Setting the value of title to '"+ value + "'"
```

As you would expect, executing the code will display the following:

```
Parsing the word 'I'
Parsing the word 'want'
Parsing the word 'window'
Parsing the word 'window'
Setting the value of title to 'Hello, Ring!'
```

This kind of interactivity offered by the class event mechanism makes it easy to implement our tactic of parsing words and counting them until reaching the end of the sentence. Let's experiment it by changing the code of the App class to Listing 7-73.

Listing 7-73. natural2.ring

```
Class App
        # Attributes for the instruction "I want window"
            I want a window
            nIWantWindow = 0        # => the 1st counter

    # Attributes for the instruction Window title
    # Here we don't define the window attribute again
            title
            nWindowTitle = 0        # => The 2nd counter
```

```
# Keywords to ignore, just nullify them
        a = NULL
        the = NULL

# Counting the 1st word in the 1st instruction
def getI
        if nIWantWindow = 0
                nIWantWindow++
        ok

# Counting the 2nd word in the 1st instruction
def getWant
        if nIWantWindow = 1
                nIWantWindow++
        ok

# Executing the first instruction
# because last word is reached
def getWindow
        if nIWantWindow = 2      # LAST word reached
                nIWantWindow= 0
                SEE "Instruction 1: I want window" +NL
        Ok

        # Counting the 2nd word in the 2nd instruction
        # NB: the 1st word (want) has been counted
        if nWindowTitle = 0
                nWindowTitle++
        ok

# Executing the second instruction
# because last word is reached
def setTitle cValue
        if nWindowTitle = 1
                nWindowTitle=0
                see "Instruction 2: Window Title = " + cValue + NL
        ok
```

Execute and check out these results:

```
Instruction 1 : I want window
Instruction 2 : Window Title = Hello, Ring!
```

Remember, if a reserved Ring keyword like AND, for example, is needed to be part of the natural code, then what you need is to change it at the top of the code.

```
ChangeRingKeyword    and    _and
```

Then restore it at the end by saying this:

```
ChangeRingKeyword    _and    and
```

By analogy, you can change how Ring interprets an operator, like + for example, by using ChangeRingOperator.

Enabling the User to Provide Natural Statements

Let's work on an additional feature of our program: what if the natural code was read from an external file or entered interactively by the user? To make it simple, we will just host it in a string variable called cString and then send it to a function called myLanguage() to be executed there dynamically, with the eval() function, of course. The new version of the program becomes Listing 7-74 (save this code in a new natural3. ring file).

Listing 7-74. natural3.ring

```
func Main
{
    cProgram =
    'I want a window and the window title is "hello world"'
    myLanguage(cProgram)
}

func myLanguage cCode
    # We add to the code the instructions that change
    # keywords and operators, because eval() uses a new
    # compiler object (the original keywords and operatos)
```

```ring
cCode = '
    ChangeRingKeyword and _and
    ChangeRingOperator = is
' + cCode

new App
{
    eval(cCode)
}

class App
    # Attributes for the instruction "I want a window"
    I want a window
    nIWantWindow = 0       # => the 1st counter

    # Attributes for the instruction Window title
    # Here we don't define the window attribute again
    title
    nWindowTitle = 0       # => The 2nd counter

    # Keywords to ignore, just nullify them
    a = NULL
    the = NULL
    ChangeRingKeyword and _and
    and = NULL
    ChangeRingKeyword _and and

    # Counting the 1st word in the 1st instruction
    def getI
        if nIWantWindow = 0
        nIWantWindow++
    ok

    # Counting the 2nd word in the 1st instruction
    def getWant
        if nIWantWindow = 1
        nIWantWindow++
    ok
```

```
# Executing the first instruction
# because last word is reached
def getWindow
    if nIWantWindow = 2      # LAST word reached
    nIWantWindow= 0
    SEE "Instruction : I want window" + NL
Ok

# Counting the 2nd word in the 2nd instruction
# NB: the 1st word (want) has been counted
if nWindowTitle = 0
    nWindowTitle++
ok

# Executing the second instruction
# because last word is reached
def setTitle cValue
    if nWindowTitle = 1
    nWindowTitle=0
    SEE "Instruction : Window Title = " + cValue + NL
ok
```

Capturing Numbers in Natural Statements

More features can be included to our natural language by writing code after the opening and before the closing braces. I introduced the braceStart() and braceEnd() functions earlier, so let's discover the new braceExpEval() function. Like its sisters, this special method has been introduced to facilitate the implementation of natural programming in Ring. In particular, it enables us to capture values in the English text of our program. For example, see Listing 7-75 (save this to a new natural4.ring file).

Listing 7-75. natural4.ring

```
# Natural Code
new Natural {
    Add 2 numbers together
}
```

```
# Natural Code Implementation
class Natural
    # Keywords
    add=0 numbers=0 together=0

    # Execution
    def braceExprEval x
          ? x
```

Execute it. This is what you get:

```
0

2

0

0
```

This means that braceExprEval() evaluates every word of the natural text and returns its value. In our case, all the strings are 0 and 2 is 2, of course; see Figure 7-5.

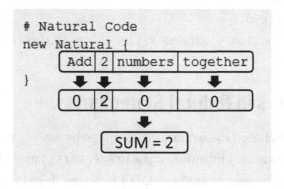

Figure 7-5. *Parsing of the natural words by braceExprEval()*

This is good because we can think of a loop iterating value times on every word, where value is the sum of all the values returned for all the words provided in our sentence (0 + 2 + 0 + 0). This iterates 2 times. Therefore, we can enhance the program to look like Listing 7-76 (put this code in a new natural5.ring file).

Listing 7-76. natural5.ring

```
# Natural Code
new Natural {
    Add 2 numbers together
}

# Natural Code Implementation
class Natural
    value

    # Keywords
    add=0 numbers=0 together=0

    # Execution
    def braceExprEval n        # => n is 2 in our case as
                               #    provided by us in the natural
                               #    sentence above

        value = n

    def getNumbers
        nSum = 0
        for i=1 to value
            ? "Enter number " + i + " : " GIVE n
            nSum += n
        next
        ? "Sum : " + nSum
```

You run it, and the program asks for two values. You give them, and you get the sum shown here:

```
Enter number 1 :
12
Enter number 2 :
14
Sum : 26
```

Change the natural statement as shown in Listing 7-77.

Listing 7-77. Part of natural5.ring

```
# Natural Code
 new Natural {
     Add 3 numbers together
 }
```

Then you run and you get the following:

```
Enter number 1 :
10
Enter number 2 :
5
Enter number 3 :
8
Sum : 23
```

The program asks you to provide three numbers and then computes their sum. You can make this program for any number you want. You only need to be natural! And if you find it a little tricky to implement, then don't worry: Ring comes with a natural library called NaturalLib that transforms the task of designing statements like this, and other more complicated like the ones we started the section with, dead simple. Unfortunately, we won't cover this nice library in this book, so please rely on yourself to learn about it from the Ring documentation.[19]

Capturing Errors Inside Natural Code

When you are living with your objects inside the braces, Ring helps you by using braceStart(), braceEnd(), braceExprEval(), but also braceError(). The last one is more than necessary to capture any error you make and decide on how you fix it before the program breaks. Listing 7-78 shows an example (test it in a new brace-error.ring file).

---

[19]http://ring-lang.sourceforge.net/doc1.11/natural.html?highlight=natural

Listing 7-78. brace-error.ring

```
new point {
    X = 10 Y = 10
    sum()
}
```

```
class Point X Y
```

Obviously, an error will be raised by the compiler, as shown here:

```
Line 3 Error (R3) : Calling Function without definition !: sum
```

To capture it, you just need to add the method in Listing 7-79 to the Point class.

Listing 7-79. Part of brace-error.ring

```
class Point X Y
    def braceError()
        ? "ERROR!"
```

When you run it, you won't have any program disruption. By contrast, the execution continues, and what you have is a polite ERROR!, nothing else. Using this technique, your potential errors when you write natural code can also be managed!

Summary

You have now the necessary knowledge to practice natural programming in Ring. Unleash your imagination and go beyond what is possible with other programming languages: add a human-machine conversation layer to your programs, use the business domain language of your customers to write code, develop an industry-scale bot for the bank of your friend, or even create a mother tongue programming language by just translating Ring keywords and operators!

Are you waiting patiently for the next chapter? I know you are. Now is your opportunity to apply all the serious stuff you have learned so far in the funny and exciting domain of game programming. Meet you there.

CHAPTER 8

Designing Games in Ring

The declarative programming of video games has not gained the interest it deserves in the computer science research community. For example, although Quasi-Engine is a Qt5-based framework that intends to be a complete multiplatform toolset to ease 2D game development, providing ready-to-use QML elements representing the basic game entities needed by most games, this project seems to be abandoned.[1] On the commercial software side, the VPlay engine (now Felgo Engine[2]) is a cross-platform development tool, based also on the Qt framework. Felgo developers use QML, the declarative tongue of Qt, along with an additional language required for scripting such as JavaScript or C++ to create mobile apps and games. Regarding general-purpose programming languages, to the best of my knowledge, I am not aware of any[3] initiative out there, in Python or Ruby or any other "competing" language, that provides a standard, free, open source, and declarative game programming engine besides Ring.

In the course of this chapter, you will learn the basics of programming games in Ring using the Ring 2D Game Engine. I'll cover the following:

- I will help you understand the conceptual foundations of game programming in general.

- I will guide you through a straight-to-the-point learning path to gain the 12 practical algorithmic skills that are necessary for making any game.

- I will show you how Ring is unique in embracing the declarative paradigm in developing games, while emphasizing the advantages and mitigating any complexity that could arise from the code deep hierarchy side effect.

---

[1]See https://github.com/INdT/Quasi-Engine. I'm not sure, but some folks on the Internet say that the team behind Quasi-Engine shifted to the proprietary Bacon2d game engine (http://bacon2d.com/).

[2]See https://felgo.com.

[3]Correct me if I'm wrong.

© Mansour Ayouni 2020

M. Ayouni, *Beginning Ring Programming*, https://doi.org/10.1007/978-1-4842-5833-0_8

The sections "Three Fundamentals of Game Programming" and "Mastering the Big Picture" will cover the foundations. The section "Twelve Practical Skills You Should Have" will cover the practical skills. In "A Complete Game in Ring," you will learn how to use the knowledge you acquired to develop a real-world game in Ring.

But before all that, I'll share my personal story with game programming. You will find an answer to the question of why I chose game programming to showcase Ring's capabilities and not any other domain such as desktop, mobile, and web. Also, you will come to understand why today's game programming still leverages the same ideas and constructs of the 1970s and 1980s such as game loop, sprites, timeframes, graphics rendering, and algorithmic mathematics.

Nine Things You Will Learn

You'll do the following in this chapter:

- Get the big picture of the game programming domain

- Discover the Ring approach to developing games declaratively

- Master the conceptual foundation of game programming

- Build the 12 technical skills necessary to programming games in Ring

- Understand the connection between the object-oriented and declarative paradigms

- Look inside the 2D Game Engine and leverage its powerful feature in designing games

- Practice programming in the context of real-time applications like video games

- Manipulate the game objects, including searching, filtering, and animating them

- Organize and refactor large game codebases

A Personal Perspective on Game Programming

So, why did I choose game programming? There are number of reasons, but first I will share my personal journey with computer programming.

The first time I saw a video game was in the 1980s when the Rural Youth Club of our village got an Atari 26000 console along with a Telefunken color TV and a handful of game cartridges. This was like a cultural big bang in the region and a deep change of how we conceived entertainment and spent our free time in the local, agricultural village. See Figure 8-1.

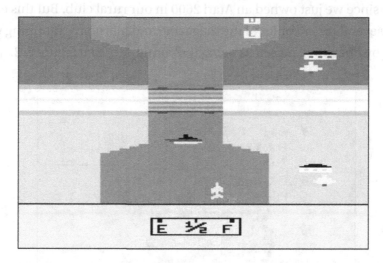

Figure 8-1. *Atari River Raid: the first video game I ever played*

Besides enjoying playing the games, I started to wonder how these games were created. There was user documentation available with the Atari console, but no one was able to understand it, even those who were studying English in high school. At that time and place, no one knew that those games were made using something called a programming language. Today, despite that Tunisia has made a remarkable jump into the digital era, many rural African societies are still struggling from the same problem.

In 1985, when I was in fourth grade, my teacher, who had just come back from France, was the first person who talked to me about personal computers and the programming revolution. That's when I discovered that the magic behind video games was no more than a list of instructions we give to the machine to be executed, and no more!

Such simple information, which might seem simple for people in other corners of the world, was like a divine revelation for me, because it led me to the light of knowledge and scientific supremacy. When I found out that people were able to control machines through a formal programming language, I decided right then to be a computer programmer.[4]

I don't remember exactly when and how I accidentally got a copy of the French *Science & Vie* magazine, but it included a computer program listing and explained how a simple air fighter game could be programmed in BASIC. The article stipulated that code must be entered into a Commodore 64 personal computer to be run. This was disappointing, since we just owned an Atari 2600 in our rural club. But this encouraged me to look for several other copies of the magazine and learn programming without a computer, just by imagining myself as being the computer![5] See Figure 8-2.

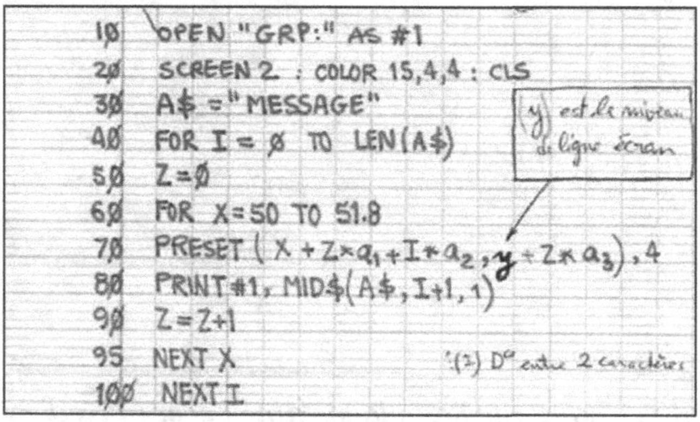

Figure 8-2. *Do you remember when I showed you this in Chapter 5? Now you better understand it*

A couple years passed with me practicing programming with pen and paper before my father gave me an unbelievable gift: an MSX personal computer and a Thomson colored TV. Inside the computer box, there were several books; one of them was an introduction to BASIC programming in Arabic, and the other was a colorful catalog of dozens of video games! See Figure 8-3.

---

[4]This is why I'm writing a book for about in programming now, after more than three decades.
[5]Now I understand how instructive this experience was to get an inside understanding of how a program works, something lacking a lot in programmers' skillsets today.

Figure 8-3. *The first book that introduced me to programming*

I was about 12 years old when my self-made, real-world programming journey began. The love of coding and deep fulfillment of writing functional programs, in many areas, made my day, every day. For sure, games were my first point of interest, but my dream of making sophisticated games was always constrained by the limits of my technical expertise. This was until I got a copy of a book called *The MSX Games Book*, written by Jim Gregory, that provided dozens of professional-grade game samples programmed in BASIC.

The book contained extensive code listings without in-depth explanations. And this left me to my destiny to try to understand what was happening in the head of professional programmers when they were designing advanced games. While entering the code into my MSX computer, I was always trying some variations of the variables used and the subroutines forming the architecture of the program. See Figure 8-4.

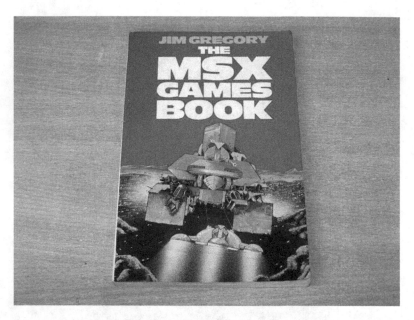

Figure 8-4. *The MSX Games Book taught me how to code many games in practice*

Thanks to such a long-term "learning by doing" process, I was able to understand some fundamental concepts that still form the basics of game programming today, like the game loop, game timing, and game sprites that we will talk about in the next section. In particular, sprites and how to craft them in the video memory of the computer using the Assembly language were a huge discovery for me. In fact, before noticing their existence, I had tried all the possible ways to code graphic objects on the screen using the standard painting instructions of BASIC but never succeeded in providing them with smooth animations and reactive behavior.

Later, I got the chance to read *25 Graphic Programs in Microsoft BASIC* by Timothy J. O'Malley, which I found on the street where old books are sold in Medina,[6] the capital Tunis. By contemplating the beauty of programs provided, I learned how to generate computer art that is mathematically defined to enrich my games, along with animation effects. The most valuable addition to my game programming skills, though, was the strategy I adopted to make platform-independent graphics so the game could run efficiently on any compatible microcomputer while getting the best graphics performance possible from the machine. And you know what? All these subjects are mainstream today, and any professional game programmer should be able to deal with them! See Figure 8-5.

---

[6]Read about the ancient Medina of Tunis on Wikipedia: https://en.wikipedia.org/wiki/
Medina_of_Tunis.

Figure 8-5. *The book 25 Graphic Programs in Microsoft BASIC taught me how to use sprites to streamline my games*

Over the years, while making other programs in several domains and many countries, I never felt the same pleasure as I get from programming games. In the course of my career, I have met hundreds of programmers from all generations. The difference between someone who has a game programming background and someone who doesn't is clear. Game programming is a serious opportunity to face some of the most complex technical challenges of today's software: real-time applications, graphics rendering, computer mathematics, big data optimization, performance monitoring, network programming, artificial intelligence, and more!

That's why I ask everyone who is planning to forge a rock-solid profile of a computer programmer to consider learning how to make games. Computer schools also need to reform their computer programming curriculum and make the switch to gaming as the default training material to help provide the industry with high-quality software engineers.

That's my personal journey into programming and why I chose the game domain to showcase Ring. So, welcome to the fascinating world of game programming in Ring!

Three Fundamentals of Game Programming

Before we delve into practice, I will briefly introduce three fundamental concepts you will find in any game programming framework: the game loop, game timing, and game engine.

Understanding these basic concepts will help you embrace the mental model of game programming, which is actually different from and somehow disruptive to the conventional programming mindset. In fact, game programming belongs to the wider area of real-time software programming that is in vogue these days.

A real-time system is a program that is running inside a continuous loop. The loop will be repeating a number of actions continuously while updating the state of the system. During each iteration, the program needs to monitor the object's activities and intercept any meaningful events coming from inside or outside the system.

In particular, game programming deals with inputs coming from the user who controls some game objects and reacts to the behavior of others. Updating the game world requires computing the new values of all the object attributes, in each iteration, and performing the necessary graphic rendering, which usually comes with a critical performance cost. Such a cost is the main source of lags and lack of responsiveness one might observe in video games. Unfortunately, this one chapter won't cover these details. Maybe in a near future, I'll be dedicating a whole book to all aspects of game programming in Ring.

Game Loop

The *game loop* is the masterpiece of any game program. Right after its setup, a game enters into a continuous iteration and keeps repeating a number of actions until the program is shut down by the player or the game has normally reached its end.

In the jargon of video games, the iteration is called a *frame*. It's executed, say, 30 or 60 times per second, and thus we say that the game is updating itself at a rate of 30 or 60 frames per seconds (FPS).

The most classical game loop takes the form of the following pseudocode:

```
While theGameIsRunning
    interceptInputs()
    updateGameWorld()
    renderGraphics()
Repeat
```

Under the umbrella of `interceptInputs()`, the program intercepts any input coming from the user (from a keyboard, mouse, or joystick, for example) or from the environment (a network message in the context of a multiplayer Internet game, for example) and identifies the attributes of the game objects that might be updated by such inputs. (If the player presses the up arrow, for example, then the player's vertical object position should be advanced to the top.)

At this particular moment, `intercepInputs()` gives control to the `updateWorld()` action that is responsible for propagating the new values across the object attributes. In reality, the game loop does not have the luxury of updating every object alone but does it for all the objects available in the gaming world in one shot, i.e., at every iteration of the loop.

Once the world game has been advanced to a new state defined by the user inputs, the whole game needs to be graphically rendered through the `renderGraphics()` action. Thus, the look and feel of every object is regenerated by the GPU[7] and displayed on the screen in a reasonable amount of time (a fraction of second) so the player sees smooth and reactive gameplay.

In more complex games requiring a lot of computation, with tons of graphics and multimedia resources to be rendered, the game loop can be parallelized and thus executed by many threads, especially when the game is intended to run on multicore computers and consoles. But this is beyond the scope of our book; it is sufficient now to base our understanding on the pseudocode of a complete standard game loop, as shown here:

```
While theGameIsRunning
    interceptInputs()
        switch keypress
        on arrowup y -= 5
        on arrowdown y += 5
        off
```

---

[7]A graphics processing unit (GPU) is a specialized electronic circuit designed to rapidly manipulate and alter memory to accelerate the creation of images in a frame buffer intended for output to a display device. GPUs are used in embedded systems, mobile phones, personal computers, workstations, and game consoles. —Wikipedia

```
updateGameWorld()
        player.y is diminushed or augmented
        foreach enemy in theGameWorld
                if enemy collides with the player
                        kill the player
            ok
        repeat

renderGraphics()
        drawGraphics()
        makeSound()
Repeat
```

In reality, the whole loop can never be executed inside one frame but usually in three or four frames. This phenomenon is known among professional game programmers as the *input lag*. This reflects the real-world delay observed between the beginning of the loop (when the user presses the top arrow) and when the result is displayed on the screen (by the `renderGraphics()` action.

To illustrate the idea visually, let's suppose that the player will press the right arrow causing the Pac-Man to walk to the right and eat one circle, as shown in Figure 8-6.

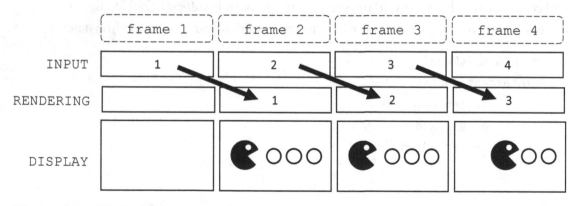

Figure 8-6. *There is an unavoidable lag of at least three frames between when the player presses a key and when the game world is rendered again*

When the game starts, the first frame is usually "wasted" in initializing the graphic resources or "remembering" the world state from the previous iteration. In frame 2, the initial world state is rendered and displayed on the screen.

During frame 2, the input of the player is intercepted. In our case, the right arrow is captured, and an order is sent to `renderGraphics()` to compute it logically inside the CPU before sending it to the GPU. This computation is done during frame 2, and only then the result (of this frame 3) is sent to the screen to be displayed during frame 4.

The main lesson we should learn here is that when our game is running at 30 FPS, then there are at least 3 frames that are lost in the input lag, leaving the remaining 27 frames to do the rest of the job required by the logical and graphical actions defined inside the game loop. This is quite common in many genres of games; in particular, when extremely high speed is required, even a lag of three or four frames becomes problematic and needs to be worked around. Again, this topic is beyond the scope of the chapter, and there is only a small probability that you will face it (unless you are planning to make an extreme 3D fighting title like *Mortal Combat* or *Street Fighter*).

This said, a particular focus should be put on time so that you know the difference between real time and game time and thus understand how the time available inside every frame is consumed and how those two perspectives of time can be synchronized no matter what processor speed our game is running on.

Game Timing

Human time is counted in seconds, while machine time is counted in processor cycles or clock ticks. As a game programmer, you need to take care of both and never forget that your main two stakeholders, the player and the machine, don't speak the same language of time!

If your game is written for a particular PC processor and looks fine moving an object in an acceptable way, then what happens if the same game is run on the more powerful processor of a multicore Xbox console, for example? Your object will move more quickly on the screen. In fact, while the real-world time remains unchanged, the Xbox will make more iterations of the game loop per second than the PC. Therefore, the object position is incremented more often, and the object moves more quickly!

To say it in pseudocode, the player who moves 5 pixels to the right in every frame when the right arrow is pressed becomes vulnerable when more frames of the loop are executed per second on a more powerful machine.

```
While theGameIsRunning
    interceptInputs()
        on arrow-right     xPos += 2
```

```
    updateGameWorld()
            player.X = xPos        # player moves 2 pixels to the
                                   # right every loop execution
    renderGraphics()
Repeat
```

If we are developing on a machine that runs at a rate of 30 FPS, for example, then the player will move 60 pixels per second, say 2 pixels in every loop iteration. On a more powerful machine that runs at a rate of 60 FPS, the player would move 120 pixels per second, resulting in abnormal movement in the gameplay.

In an extreme scenario, this discordance of time can destroy the gameplay and make your game unplayable. That's why it is common to take the elapsed real-time time between the two iterations into consideration and force the loop-updating function to respect it, no matter what horsepower the processor has. In other words, we need to think about our player's movement in terms of pixels per second and not pixels per frame. You can use a common technique called *delta time*, which is available by default in every gaming framework, including the Ring engine, to solve the problem. The standard game loop can be enhanced to incorporate the delta time factor like this:

```
t0 = time()        # get the real-time before the loop
While theGameIsRunning
    // Calculate the realtime elapsed since last frame
    realTimeElapsed = time() - t0       # in seconds
    // Convert it to gametime (in processor clocks)
    gameTimeElapsed = toGameTime( realTimeElapsed )

    // calculate the time factor (deltaTime)
    delatTime = realTimeElapsed / gameTimeElapsed
            # => this factor will ensure our loop is resilient
            #     against the variation of the number of cycles
            #     the machine undertakes per second

    interceptInputs()

    updateGameWorld()
            player.X += 5 * deltaTime
            /* Whatever the number of processor clocks is, if
```

```
                      the elapsed time corresponds to the realworld
                      Time expected by the player (and the programmer)
                      Then the player object will always move by 5px.

                      Hence if the processor is twice as quick then
                      the deltaTime (= 1/2 in this case) will
                      constraint its ability to increment the player's
                      position in every cycle by limiting it to
                      5 * 1/2 = 2.5px PER FRAME and preserve the
                      overall movement at 5px PER SECOND.
            */
        renderGraphics()
Repeat
```

As a general rule, whenever you have a game object for which you are going to update an attribute across many frames (movement, scaling, rotation, etc.), then you should write your updateGameWorld() function while considering delta time. In practice, when you are building your game on top of the Game Engine, you don't need to worry; you'll just need to specify the value of the FPS attribute of your Game object, and the Ring gaming framework does the rest. But understanding such details is fundamental for you to use the engine consciously, especially if you decide to code your game without the engine.

An additional complication we are going to end the section with relates to a subtler problem. You would think that deltaTime would be a magic solution to forge a peace charter between machine clocks and human seconds. Unfortunately, the armistice collapses anytime you resort to using a physics library or when you opt for a totally different multiplayer game arsenal. In these cases, it's quite common that the player of your game will experience an abnormal acceleration of a rocket targeting him or a higher jump in the air of the main actor than he would expect.

To solve the problem, the wide majority of game frameworks, including the Ring Engine, rely on a basic solution called *fixed time rate*, also known as *frame limiting*. The idea is to force the loop to wait for a fixed time (FixedFPS) even if all the logic and rendering has been computed.

The opposite case can also happen, when the time allotted to the loop has elapsed but the rendering of the game world is not computed. If no precautions are taken, then the rendering of the current frame will continue to be executed in the next one, and this will generate an annoying inconsistent display effect. In this case, game engines usually provide a technical solution called *frame dropping*. Despite its possible negative impact on the display of the current frame, the incomplete rendering is interrupted at the end of the frame to preserve at a minimum the consistency of displaying the next one.

I hope you are aware now of the complexity of the loop and time issue. Game engines are made to abstract these issues and work internally for us poor programmers so we can concentrate more on our game design and logic.

Game Engine

For sure, you can use Ring or any other programming language to create games without relying on any engine. I can't prevent you from embarking on such an interesting educational experience. I'll just say, based on my many years of programming hard-coded games, that what you will end up with is more or less one of these two situations: you reinvent the wheel in every new project and try to make some snippets of code as reusable as possible, maybe with some success if you are making the same genre of games; or, you end up forging your own gaming framework or even your own game engine after many years of hard work.

In this section, I will give you a high-level overview of the Ring 2D Game Engine so we can use it to develop a real-world game. In particular, I show you how Ring models the game world and its various game objects and then how the engine abstracts the complex stuff like dealing with platform-specific rendering and time synchronization issues through the use of industry-scale, well-tested C++ libraries. Finally, I will expose the key differentiator of Ring when using it to enable a completely declarative experience in programming games.

Before we start, let's ask ourselves: what are game objects, and what types do we need in our games?

Game objects shouldn't be confused with objects related to OOP. In fact, although Ring opted for object orientation to model the game world, other frameworks will use other paradigms, such as functional or pure procedural, to model the same game objects.

Game objects are whatever things should "appear" in your game, either explicitly like the player actor, the enemies, and the background environment, or implicitly like the camera you could use to change the worldview perspective and any invisible trigger you could define to use as a hint to detect a collision or suddenly show a terrifying ghost if the player reaches the trigger position.

In terms of the two basic actions of the game loop (updating the world and rendering it), these objects can be of one of three types.

- The object is rendered but never updated, like the background or a building or any other thing that is rendered once and stays static during the whole game.

- The object is rendered and updated in every iteration of the game loop, like every dynamic animated thing you could find in a game, such as the player actor, the enemies, the bonus stars, and so on.

- The object is updated but never rendered or displayed, like the triggers we talked about earlier, so only their values are monitored to make some decisions, and they never quit the boundary of the updateGameWorld() function to reach the renderGraphics() function.

That being said, how does the Ring Game Engine see the game world and hence model its objects? Well, this corresponds to the object-oriented layer of the GameLib library. It's useful then to take a look on the overall library architecture, as shown in Figure 8-7.

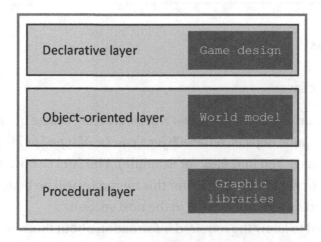

Figure 8-7. *The three layers of the Ring Game Engine*

At the top of the diagram, there is a declarative layer intended to be used by you, the programmer, to design your game. We will come back to this in a minute, in the next section. At the bottom, there is a layer responsible for effectively rendering your game's graphic objects and managing your multimedia resources.

The low-level services provided by this layer are provided by a Ring wrapper of two powerful C libraries specialized in 2D game graphics: Allegro and LibSDL. All you need to do is to call the function you need from its Ring flavor (`gl_draw_circle()`) without thinking of the potential differences between the two supported libraries and any other graphics library we could support in the future.

Allegro has been selected because it's quite simple and popular in desktop games, while LibSDL is a powerful library that is well optimized to mobile games. Because of the abstracted binding layer, you will always use the same code even if the low-level library changes.

Between the two, there is the object layer, where we can find the game engine classes structured like this[8]:

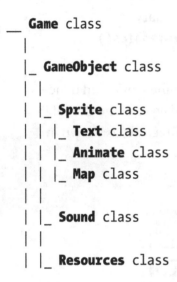

```
__  Game class
 |
 |_  GameObject class
 | |
 | |_  Sprite class
 | | |_  Text class
 | | |_  Animate class
 | | |_  Map class
 | |
 | |_  Sound class
 | |
 | |_  Resources class
```

When you program a game in Ring, you will be creating a Game instance of the Game class to host all your game objects. A GameObject can be of type Sprite, Sound, or other Resource (such as image and font files, for example). The Sprite object can also be of type Text, Animate, or Map. The rationale for this hierarchy will be better understood when we start practicing the code engine in the next section.

For now, we need to know the required information about those objects so that we understand how to use them when designing our games. To do so, let's expose the members of every class and give a short comment about every one of them.

---

[8]This can be easily identified when you open the folder `C:\Ring\ringlibs\gameengine\classes` if your Ring installation folder is `C:`, of course.

The Game Class

The following are the Game class attributes:

Attribute	Description
Title	String defining the game window's title
aObjects	List containing all the objects in the game
FPS	Number defining how many times the draw() method will be called per second on the objects of type Sprite available in the game (inside the aObjects list)
FixedFPS	Number defining how many times the animate() method will be called per second
shutdown	True/False value to end the game loop

The following are the Game class methods:

Method	Description
refresh()	Deletes all objects in the game (from the aObjects list)
settitle(cTitle)	Sets the window title using a string parameter
shutdown()	Closes the application

The following are a group of keywords defined by the Game class, as attributes, but when they are used, they automatically cause the execution of the corresponding getAttribute() method:

Keyword	Description
sprite	Creates a new Sprite object and adds it to the game objects
text	Creates a new Text object and adds it to the game objects
animate	Creates a new Animate object and adds it to the game objects
sound	Creates a new Sound object and adds it to the game objects
map	Creates a new Map object and adds it the game objects

447

The GameObject Class

The following are the GameObject class attributes:

Attributes	Description
enabled	True/False defining the state of the object (Active/Not Active)
x	Number defining the x position of the object
y	Number defining the y position of the object
width	Number defining the width of the object
height	Number defining the height of the object
nIndex	Number defining the index of the object inside the object list
animate	True/False to animate the object or force it to be fixed on the screen
move	True/False to allow the object to be movable using the keyboard or not
scaled	True/False to allow the object image to be scaled so it fits to the height and width of the object, or not
draw	Function to be called when the Game Engine is drawing the object
state	Function to be called when the Game Engine is animating the object
keypress	Function to be called when a key is pressed
mouse	Function to be called when a mouse event happens

The following are the GameObject class methods:

Method	Description
keyboard(oGame,nkey)	Checks for Keyboard events
mouse(oGame,nType, aMouseList)	Checks for mouse events
rgb(r,g,b)	Returns a new color using the RGB (Red, Green and Blue) values

The Sprite Class

Remember that this Sprite class inherits from the GameObject class.

The following are the Sprite class attributes:

Attributes	Description
image	String defining the image file name
direction	Number defining the direction of the object's animation
point	Number defining the target point of object's animation
nStep	Number defining the increment/decrement during animation
type	Number defining the object's type in the game (optional)
transparent	True/False defining whether the image is transparent

The following is the only class method available for a Sprite object:

Method	Description
Draw(oGame)	Draws the Sprite object

Text Class

Remember that this Text class inherits from its parent Sprite class.

The following are the class attributes:

Attributes	Description
size	Number defining the font size
font	String defining the font file name
text	String defining the text to be displayed
color	Number defining the color of the text

The following is the only class method available for a Text object:

Method	Description
Draw(oGame)	Draws the Text object

449

The Animate Class

Remember that this Animate class inherits from its parent Sprite class.

The following are the class attributes:

Attributes	Description
frames	Number defining the number of frames
frame	Number defining the active frame
frameWidth	Number defining the frame width
animate	True/False; activates or deactivates the animation
scaled	True/False; determines if the images of every frame is scaled to fit the width and height of the frame, or not

The following is the class method:

Method	Description
Draw(oGame)	Draws the image at a given frame number

The Sound Class

Remember that this Sound class inherits directly from the GameObject class.

The following are the Sound class attributes:

Attributes	Description
file	String; determines the sound file name and path
once	True/False; determines whether the sound is played once or in a continuous loop

The following is the only class method available on the Sound object:

Method	Description
playSound()	Plays the sound file

The Map Class

Remember that this Map class inherits from the Sprite class.

The following are the Map class attributes:

Attributes	Description
aMap	List defining the tile map content using numbers
aImages	List defining the images used for each number in the map
BlockWidth	Number defining the tile map block width (default = 32)
BlockHeight	Number defining the tile map block height (default = 32)
Animate	True/False defining the animation status of the map

The following are the Map class methods:

Method	Description
getvalue(x,y)	Returns the item value in the Map according to the visible part

This is all that you need to know so you can use the Game Engine. Some of the information provided here is obvious, and some isn't clear enough. Use this section as a reference to come back to when needed.

Right now, before we start practicing real game programming stuff, we need to look at the big picture.

Mastering the Big Picture

Game programming is an impressive endeavor. You can easily get lost in the vast number of details you need to take care of, even if you are making a small, casual, children's game. You can also find it difficult to understand how things work and how code is executed behind the scene. In this section, I will explain, as simply as possible, the high-level architecture of the technological skills you are exercising when you write games in Ring.

The first thing I need to reiterate is that, while using the Ring Game Engine and its friendly declarative paradigm, you will be writing code as clear as this:

```
new Game {
        Sprite {
                type = BACKGROUND
                image = "sky.png"
                animate = true
                state = dontAcceedFrontiers_f()
        }

        Sprite {
                type = PLAYER
                image = "plane.jpg"
                movable = true
                keypress = emitRocket_f()
        }

        for i = 1 to 3
        Enemy {
                type = ENEMY
                image = "enemy.jpg"
                animate = true
                direction = Random
                state = emitRockets()
        }
        next i
        }

        Text {
                type = SCORE
                text = "00"
        }

        Object {
                type = VIRTUAL
                state = func(Game,allObjects) {
```

```
                    oPlayer = getPlayerObject()
                    foreach obj in allObjects
                      If obj.type = ENEMY and collide(obj,oPlayer)
                            showfire(obj.x,obj.y)
                            Game.Delete(obj)
                            Game.Delete(player)
                            relpayOrQuit()
                      end
                    next
        }
        }
}

// And then you write your functions...
func dontAcceedFrontiers_f()
        // ...

func emitRocket_f()
        // ...

func getPlayerObject(oGame)
        // ...

func collide(obj1,obj2)
        // ...

func showfire(x,y)
        // ...

func replayOrQuit()
        // ...
```

It's a true design experience indeed, as stated without exaggeration in the title of the chapter.[9] Nevertheless, you should be aware that you are working over a complex technological big picture as dense as shown in Figure 8-8.

---

[9]This will be exposed in detail in the upcoming sections of the chapter.

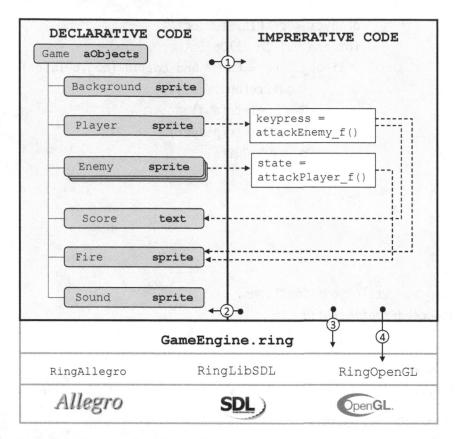

Figure 8-8. *A detailed view of the technological stack of the Ring Game Engine*

In the upper two boxes, this is where you write code. This code can be declarative, to describe the world game and establish its basic look and feel (the box to the left), or procedural. It's in this box where you write your logic using classic Ring statements inside functions. Those functions are usually exposed by the declarative layer as events you need to provide a response for, such as state, keypress, etc. (the box to the right). Under the hood, there is the Ring Engine itself, composed of the game classes you learned about in the section "Game Engine," along with some interfaces written in Ring to connect to some low-level specialized libraries (Allegro, SDL, OpenGL) and to provide their services to you via your declarative or imperative code.

As shown in the figures and the pseudocode presented previously, when you start designing your game world using the declarative constructs provided by the Ring Engine (sprite, text, map, animate, object, sound), a hierarchy of objects is constructed automatically for you by the Game Engine. Those objects remain in memory during the game and are passed to the low-level graphic layer to be rendered physically on the screen. Some sophisticated features, such as animation, for example, are also designed declaratively by specifying the object to animate, specifying the direction and speed of the animation, and then transforming the hole scene to the same low-level graphic service performed by the GPU.

When an event is defined inside the declarative code, via `keypress`, for example, then a function must be called to answer it. In general, you will be writing some imperative code to specify the behavior you expect of one or more objects in the game when a key is pressed. The sole restriction is that you should write it inside an anonymous function, because the engine has been designed this way[10] and because this is a good option to give you a window of freedom to define the behavior of your game, right inside the declarative layer of the code. But your functions can also contain declarative code to add a moving rocket, for example, when the spacebar is pressed by opening an `oGame` brace and composing the rocket `sprite` there, in pure declarative terms.

Nothing prevents you, though, from calling, by yourself, any of the services of the low-level libraries right from your imperative code. In particular, when you create an object in which you want to draw a circle, for example, then you are free to use any of the available Ring interfaces to Allegro, SDL, or OpenGL. Whatever the graphic engine used, you will find that the Ring function is always the same, `gl_draw_cricle()`, for example.

This said, you need to be careful about the number of connections established between the declarative and imperative layers, between the imperative layer and the engine layer, and between the imperative layer and the low service layer. All these are made by you while programming your game. Therefore, a vast number of bugs will be produced because of bad management of those connections or an overuse of them. At the same time, you should keep in mind that what you are designing declaratively and writing imperatively will be transformed at runtime to a live world of objects continuously updated by the game loop, as shown in Figure 8-9.

---

[10]Go back to Chapter 7 to remember what anonymous functions are used for.

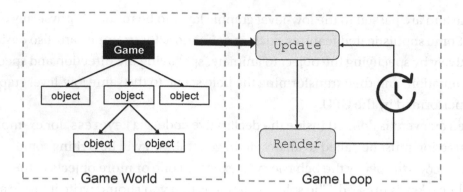

Figure 8-9. *Your declarative game design is transformed into a hierarchy of objects living in the game loop*

This is obvious in the domain of game programming, but beginners tend to forget it: you are evolving in the context of real-time applications, where every line of code you write, every object you instantiate, and every service you call will be executed inside an infinite loop, unless the program is closed or interrupted.

With this knowledge, you can now delve with confidence into the practical skills you need to develop successful games in Ring.

Twelve Practical Skills in Your Bucket

Game programming is generally perceived to be a complex domain, which is true. But things are not that complicated in Ring.

In fact, besides the theoretical background presented in the first part of this chapter and despite the abundance of material we presented in the tables, you just need 12 elementary technical skills, in practice, to program games in Ring.

Skill 1: Opening a Window to Host the Game

A game runs inside a window. So, you need a way to create a window and show it on the screen.

To do this, you can write the code shown in Listing 8-1 in a mygame.ring file that you create in a new chap8 folder.

Listing 8-1. mygame.ring

```
load "gameengine.ring"  # Give Control to the Game Engine

func main                 # Called by the Game Engine

        oGame = New Game            # Create the Game Object
        {
                title = "My First Game"
        }                           # Start the Events Loop
```

Try it to get a window at the center of the screen.

This window has been created as an instance of the Game class by using oGame = New Game. Inside the braces, nothing is provided except the title of the window (title = "My First Game"). The most important things to keep in mind, though, are the following:

- When the GameEngine.ring library is loaded, the control of the application is completely delegated to the engine. Remember, there will be a game loop to launch, an event system to activate, and a bunch of low-level stuff to do such as graphics rendering, animation, sound management, and so on.

- This means two things.

  First, you need to shift your mind from the standard programming of applications to the specific mindset of programming real-time applications and more precisely of programming games!
  Second, if you have any global variables you want to use in your code inside the game, then these globals must be defined before the engine is loaded (before Load "GameEngineLib.ring").

- The events loop is actually started by the engine when the closing brace of the oGame object is reached. This means three things.

  First, the engine will consider any attributes defined statically in the oGame region as a material it must perform to set up the game. These will be rendered once, like the background image, for example.
  Second, the engine will identify any dynamic thing you put in the oGame region, and it does the necessary processing to update it in every execution of the loop (so the animation effect, for example, can be produced).

Third, the engine will be sensing the oGame region for any event that dynamic objects could emit (a keypress on the PLAYER object, for example) and do the necessary processing to branch it to a function you provide that does the job. Then this function is called by the engine, in the same place it was called from inside the loop, in order for the game world to go forward (you'll learn about function calling in skill 5).

- Finally, there is a func main() at the beginning of the program. Be careful because this should be preserved! In fact, the game engine has been designed to take control over our code by searching for this main function. This means one thing: if main() is dropped, the engine won't be fired at all.

You learned a lot here with just five lines of code! If you are waiting for some real stuff, then here we go: let's set up the graphic ambiance of our game with a background image first.

Skill 2: Setting the Ambiance

Let's take a second to prepare the graphic and sound resources we are going to use in this exercise and then in the game project in the next section.

To do so, open the following folder in Ring: C:\Ring\Applications\StarsFighter. Copy the three following subfolders: fonts, images, and sound. Then copy them to the folder chap9 you just created in the previous section. Now we are ready to use the image file called stars.jpg as the background of our game window. Adjust the mygame. ring file (by adding the portion in bold) so it looks like Listing 8-2.

Listing 8-2. mygame.ring

```
load "gameengine.ring"
func main
    oGame = new Game
    {
        tilte = "My First Game"
        Sprite {
            file = "images/stars.jpg"
        }
    }
```

Simple, right? Oh, yes. Before we execute it, note that our code is purely declarative. We aren't coding any low-level stuff here. We're just describing what we want as a final result: a screen and an image. Execute and observe the result, as shown in Figure 8-10.

Figure 8-10. *Our ambiance: the background is moving!*

There is some odd behavior: the background is moving. How do we fix it? Well, the object is a sprite. Let's go back to "The GameObject Class" section and look for an attribute that is related to animation in the corresponding table. Look at the GameObject table. Do you think the animate attribute is the answer? I think so. Let's add a line after file = "image/stars.jpg" that contains the following statement: animate = false. Execute it again, as shown in Figure 8-11.

Figure 8-11. *Our background after being fixed*

It's wonderful. However, the name of the game is not displayed in the title of the window! Why do you think this is?

It's simply because we committed a spelling mistake; we wrote `Tilte` in lieu of `Title`. We need to be careful here; Ring won't help you by raising a syntax error because what you are entering is considered as a name of a new variable set to the `"My First Name"` value and not the `Title` attribute of the game object.

If you open the image in an image viewer, you will see that it's 1920px by 1080px wide, larger than our game window, which is 800px by 600px by default. Figure 8-12 shows the actual situation of our application.

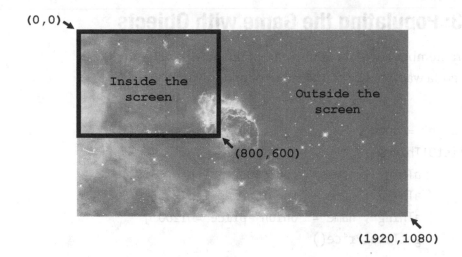

Figure 8-12. *The game window is a limited view of the game world*

Add x = -500 y = -350 after animate = false and execute again. The galaxy is nicely centered on the screen.

In addition, think of the coordinate system adopted by the Ring Engine: X and Y values begin in the top-left corner and are incremented to the right and to the bottom, respectively. In particular, and when the background image is larger than the screen like in the current configuration, one can easily simulate a world scrolling by and moving the image position in the inverse direction of the movement itself. To do this, let's tell our background to be animated again by saying this: animate = true. Run it and check it out. If you were positioned at the center of the world, in what direction are you moving?

There are several types of scrolling that games can implement, such as infinite scrolling, where the world seems to move without limits; parallax scrolling, where two background images move in different directions to simulate the feeling of depth; and four-way scrolling, where the player can move in all directions and discover the four hidden corners of the world. The latter type is usually used, in conjunction with the simulation of the zoom effect, to implement the camera movement in your games. But again, unfortunately, this basic chapter on game programming doesn't have the space to cover them in detail.

You'll learn more about animation later in the section "Skill 4: Animating Objects."

Skill 3: Populating the Game with Objects

Do you remember our guffa example from the previous chapter?

The guffa was filled by composition of things like this:

```
Guffa {
    Budget = 1000
    listOfThings {
        aThing { name = "couscous" price = 2500 }
        aThing { name = "tomatoes" price = 1500 }
        aThing { name = "onion" price = 1200 }
        getTotalPrice()
    }
}
```

Similarity, a Game object is composed of GameObjects of type sprite, text, map, sound, or drawing object. Let's experiment with them all by adding them one by one to our game world.

Adding Text

In the mygame.ring file, add the code in Listing 8-3 after the closing brace of the sprite object.

Listing 8-3. Part of mygame.ring

```
text {
    file = "fonts/pirulen.ttf"
    text = "HELLO GAME!"
}
```

Execute this. The text is moving. We confronted the same issue before with the background image. This is related to the same Sprite object (because Text is inheriting from Sprite). You fix it by adding the text braces: animate = false.

There are more Text attributes to play with; experiment with them by going back to the corresponding table in "The Text Class" section earlier. In particular, I want you to adjust the size and color attributes of the text because those two attributes will be all that we need in the course of our chapter.

Adding a Sprite

Let's add a PLAYER and three ENEMIES to the scene. Add these after the text section, as shown in Listing 8-4.

Listing 8-4. Part of mygame.ring

```
// PLAYER
Sprite
{
        type = GE_TYPE_PLAYER
        file = "images/player.png" transparent = true
        x = 350 y = 450
        scaled = true width = 100 height = 100
        animate = false move = true
}

// ENEMIES
for g = 1 to 3
        Sprite
        {
                type = GE_TYPE_ENEMY
                file = "images/enemy.png" transparent = true
                x = 120 + g*100        y = 80
                scaled = true width = 80 height = 80
                animate = false
        }
next g
```

Execute this and get the result shown in Figure 8-13.

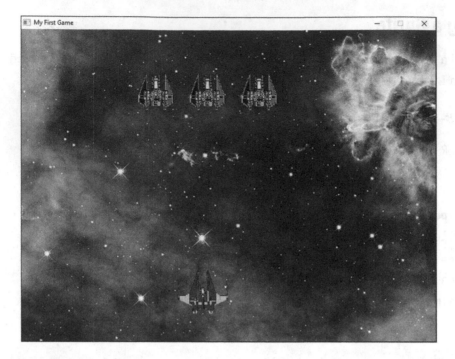

Figure 8-13. *Our world game, populated by a player and three enemies*

At this level, I want you to pay attention to two things.

First, sprites can have a value for their type attribute. This is optional but will help you in filtering your object list later when the game gets more complex. We will go back to this later in the section "Skill 6: Querying Game Objects."

Second, sprites, and any other objects, can be added by using a for loop and by taking advantage of a dose of randomness applied to their attributes. This is particularly useful and shows how flexible Ring is by inviting such imperative constructs right inside the declarative code.

Adding a Drawing

Let's draw a circle inside the game window. Add this after the ENEMIES section, as shown in Listing 8-5.

Listing 8-5. Part of mygame.ring

```
Object
{
    x = 300 y=300 width = 200 height=200

    draw = func oGame,oSelf {
        oSelf {
            gl_draw_circle(x,y,50,
            gl_map_rgb(255,255,255),5)
        }
    }
}
```

Execute it and observe a white circle at the center of the screen. This is a particular type of object we didn't included in the previous section, but here it is. You can use it to draw any simple or complex drawing you want by relying on the service of the Ring graphic library.

You might wonder if there is an exhaustive list of things you can draw using gr_draw-like functions. Open the following file:

```
C:\Ring\ringlibs\gameengine\gl_allegro.ring
```

Explore, and then test, some of the possible drawing functions available: gl_draw_point(), gl_draw_line(), gl_draw_rectangle(), gl_draw_triangle(), and more!

Adding a Sound

You need just to specify the file and whether the sound needs to play continuously or only once. Test it with the code shown in Listing 8-6.

Listing 8-6. Part of mygame.ring

```
// Sound
Sound { file = "sound/music2.wav" }
```

Now we will discover an important game object and design tool: the tile map.

Adding a Tile Map

Go to the following folder:

c:\ring\applications\flappybird3000\images

Make a copy of these three images:

fbwall.png
tbwallup.png
fbwalldown.png

Then paste them in the current folder, as shown here:

c:\ringbook\chap8\images

Tile maps are mainly used to partition the world game into several scenes that you can switch to in order to discover other corners of the game or to get to the next level of your gameplay.

The world is then divided into squares of equal size. Each square is defined by an index and can host a sprite or a part of sprite, as shown in Figure 8-14.

Figure 8-14. *A tile map from the open source tool Tiled from mapeditor.org*

In Ring, we define tile maps using the map object. If we go back to the description table of the Map class, in "The Map Class" section, then we find that it contains these attributes:

- aMap: A list defining the map content using numbers

- aImages: A list defining the images used for each square of the map

- blockWidth: A number defining the tile map block (or square) width

- blockHeight: A number defining the tile map block height

- animate: A flag defining the animation status of the map

- getValue(x,y): A method returning the block to which the point (x,y) belongs

Let's experiment some of these and try to display this map on the screen, as shown in Figure 8-15.

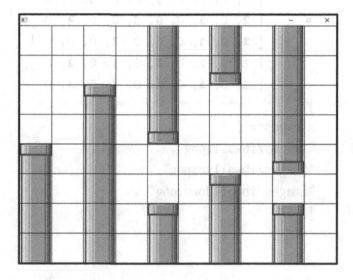

Figure 8-15. *A tile map in the game window*

Of course, the grid is an imaginary construct that helps us understand how the map object works. To implement it, we need to create an aMap list with 10 columns and 8 lines and then put every image in the corresponding block by specifying its number: 1 for fbwall.png, 2 for tbwallup.png, 3 for fbwalldown.png, and 0 for nothing. It's not programming anymore; it's painting with numbers (save this to a new mymap.ring file), as shown in Listing 8-7.

Listing 8-7. mymap.ring

```
load "gameengine.ring"

func main
    oGame = new Game
    {
        map {
            blockwidth = screen_w / 10
            blockheight = screen_h / 8

            aMap = [
                [ 0, 0, 0, 0, 1, 0, 1, 0, 1, 0 ],
                [ 0, 0, 0, 0, 1, 0, 3, 0, 1, 0 ],
                [ 0, 0, 2, 0, 1, 0, 0, 0, 1, 0 ],
                [ 0, 0, 1, 0, 3, 0, 0, 0, 1, 0 ],
                [ 2, 0, 1, 0, 0, 0, 0, 0, 3, 0 ],
                [ 1, 0, 1, 0, 0, 0, 2, 0, 0, 0 ],
                [ 1, 0, 1, 0, 2, 0, 1, 0, 2, 0 ],
                [ 1, 0, 1, 0, 1, 0, 1, 0, 1, 0 ]
            ]
            aImages = [
            "images/fbwall.png",
            "images/fbwallup.png",
            "images/fbwalldown.png"
            ]

        }
}
```

Execute this and observe the result. Perfect, isn't it? But how can we use a tile map to animate the world it represents? Wait for the section "Skill 5: Intervening in the Game State" to get the answer.

Skill 4: Animating Objects

There are many types of animations that a game can contain. Interpolated animation is where the object position is updated to simulate a movement effect, and frame-by-frame animation is where a succession of images is displayed at the same place. These are the two most common kinds of animation, and they are supported in the Ring Game Engine.

Other types of animation, such as physics and particle system animation and skeleton animation, can be added by selecting a C or C++ library (like Box2D for physics animation, for example) and binding it to Ring. In the scope of this beginner book, it's sufficient to show how the first two types work, which will be sufficient to cover any basic genre of game.

Let's begin with interpolated animation, as shown in Figure 8-16.

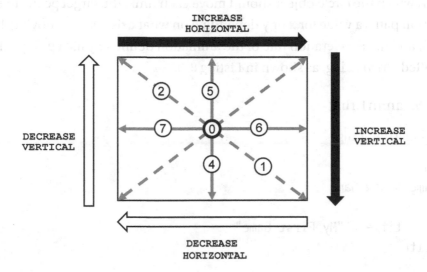

Figure 8-16. *The animation direction supported by default by the Game Engine*

If you were at center of the screen, then the your direction takes the value 0. If you move on the diagonal to the bottom (both x and y positions are increased), then it's direction 1. Its reverse direction is 2 (both x and y positions are decreased).

Now if you decide to move orthogonally following the horizontal line, then your direction is 6 if you are moving to the right (the x position is increased horizontally) and 7 if you are moving to the left (the x position is decreased horizontally). Similarly, 4 and 5 both represent your movement following a vertical line, where 4 means you are moving to the bottom (the y position is increased), and 5 means you are moving to the top.

The Ring Engine specifies these values in the following constant variables so you can use them to write expressive code:

```
GE_DIRECTION_NOMOVE = 0
GE_DIRECTION_INC = 1
GE_DIRECTION_DEC = 2
GE_DIRECTION_RANDOM = 3
GE_DIRECTION_INCVERTICAL = 4
GE_DIRECTION_DECVERTICAL = 5
GE_DIRECTION_INCHORIZONTAL = 6
GE_DIRECTION_DECHORIZONTAL = 7
```

Let's try all of them,[11] including a random one with the value 3, by adjusting the direction in which the circle object should move each time, the target `point` to reach on the animation path (a value for `x` or `y` depending on what axis you are moving, horizontal or vertical), and the acceleration rate of the animation defined by `nStep`. Try this in a new file called `anim1.ring`, as shown in Listing 8-8.

Listing 8-8. anim1.ring

```
load "gameengine.ring"

func main
        oGame = new Game
        {
                title = "My First Game"
        Sprite
        {
                type = GE_TYPE_PLAYER
                file = "images/player.png" transparent = true
                x = 300 y = 450
                scaled = true width = 100 height = 100
```

---

[11]If you are wondering why some directions are missing (in Figure 8.16 but also in the list of constants shown earlier), such as center-to-up-right and center-to-down-left, then remember this is an open source project built on a culture of collaboration. You can use this opportunity to take what you learned in the book so far and contribute by adding this feature to the Ring Game Engine. To do so, study the code of the `Sprite` class; you will find it in `c:\ring\ringlibs\gameengine\classes\gamesprite.ring`. Focus on the `animate(oGame,oSelf)` method. Change it, test it, and then contribute it by posting a message in the Google Group.

```
        animate = true
        direction = GE_DIRECTION_DECVERTICAL
        point = 0        # target point
        nStep = 2        # acceleration rate
    }
}
```

It's that easy. Try to imagine the amount of work done internally by the Ring Engine to simplify the use of animations in your game programs. In the future, more advanced animation techniques will be supported, and you can also implement your own.

Now we will explore the second type of animation: frame by frame, or *explicit animation*. To do this, we will write the necessary code to simulate an explosion. In the images folder, we have an image called fire.png, as shown in Figure 8-17.

Figure 8-17. *A spritesheet containing 13 images for the exposition animation*

You will probably recognize the steps an explosion takes; there are 13 steps here. The idea is to cut the image into 13 equal images and then display them sequentially, in the same place on the screen, to simulate the explosion. This has been a de facto technique for cinematic and cartoons animations for many years; now you can take advantage of it in your games.

This kind of sprite sheet is considered by the Ring Game Engine as a sprite composed of many sprites. This is really helpful to store all the graphics once in memory while using only the portion needed. Now, how can we turn it into a nice collision? It's simple.

For that, take a look at the Animate class in Listing 8-9 to see how we are using it to perform a frame-by-frame animation in (save it to a new file called anim2.ring).

Listing 8-9. anim2.ring

```
Load "gameengine.ring"

func main
    oGame = new Game {
        Animate
        {
```

```
            file = "images/fire.png" transparent = true
            x = 50 y = 50
            framewidth = 39.38 height = 42

            state = func oGame, oSelf {
                    oSelf {
                    if frame < 13
                            frame++
                    else
                            frame = 1
                            oGame.remove(oSelf.nIndex)
                    ok
            }} # end of oSelf and state
        } # end of animate
}
```

The Animate class of the Ring Engine asked us for the sprite sheet image file and the dimensions of one single frame. Since the fire.png image is 512px by 42px and since the number of frames is 13, then the framewidth is 512 / 13 = 30.38px. Of course, the height remains 42px. This is all that you need to say. Then the frames are advanced simply by using frame++ inside the state function.

Take this as a rule of thumb: any influence you want to have on your objects while they are animated must be written in the state function. When the explosion finishes, hence frame=1, the Animate object must be cleansed from the game memory with oGame.remove(nIndex). Agreed?

With these two types of animation, interpolated and frame-based, you are ready to design various gameplays. Advanced animation scenarios need advanced animation techniques, but those are not covered here to keep things simple.

Skill 5: Intervening in the Game State

The game state is actually formed from all the data about all the objects in the game world at a given point in time.

The state is then updated perpetually by the game loop. During its iteration, and for any active object, the Ring Engine gives you the possibility to intervene in the loop process and inject a piece of code as an anonymous function that influences the state of the game from the window of that particular object. You should be aware, though, that every line of code you put there will be impacting every frame of the game, and thus repeated indefinitely, until the game is shut down.

To show this case, we will be using the code we made for the Map in Listing 8-7, mymap.ring, and use the state attribute of the Map object to write a function that animates the tile map. In fact, decrementing the map's x coordinate by 3 pixels every loop iteration will simulate the effect of moving the whole tile map to the left. Listing 8-10 shows the corresponding code (save this in a new file called mapanim.ring).

Listing 8-10. mapanim.ring

```
load "gameengine.ring"

func main
oGame = new Game
{
    Map {
    blockwidth = 80
    blockheight = 75
    // NB : the map has been extended to 16 by 8 blcoks
    aMap = [
            [ 0, 0, 0, 0, 1, 0, 1, 0, 1, 0, 0, 1, 1, 0, 0, 1 ],
            [ 0, 0, 0, 0, 1, 0, 3, 0, 1, 0, 0, 1, 3, 0, 0, 1 ],
            [ 0, 0, 2, 0, 1, 0, 0, 0, 1, 0, 0, 3, 0, 0, 0, 3 ],
            [ 0, 0, 1, 0, 3, 0, 0, 0, 1, 0, 0, 0, 2, 0, 0, 0 ],
            [ 2, 0, 1, 0, 0, 0, 0, 0, 3, 0, 0, 2, 1, 0, 0, 0 ],
            [ 1, 0, 1, 0, 0, 0, 2, 0, 0, 0, 0, 1, 3, 0, 0, 2 ],
            [ 1, 0, 1, 0, 2, 0, 1, 0, 2, 0, 0, 3, 0, 0, 0, 1 ],
            [ 1, 0, 1, 0, 2, 0, 1, 0, 2, 0, 0, 0, 0, 0, 0, 1 ]
    ]

    aImages = [
            "images/fbwall.png",      # Represented by 1 in aMap
            "images/fbwallup.png",    # Represented by 2 in aMap
            "images/fbwalldown.png"   # Represented by 3 in aMap
    ]
```

```
    // Animation happens here
    state = func oGame,oSelf {
        oSelf {
            x -= 3
            if x < - 2100 x = 0 ok
        }
    }
    }

}
```

When the Ring Engine reads the state variable, it executes the anonymous function it contains directly in the game loop,[12] causing the oSelf object (the current Map in this case) to move to the left by decrementing its x position by 3 in every loop iteration. It's as simple as that.

Skill 6: Querying Game Objects

Your game world is made of objects. While programming, you will need a way to find a particular object or apply an action to a given family of objects.

Querying your objects depends on how they are stored in the data model of your game application. In some advanced game engines, they are stored in complex data structures such as trees and graphs, for example. Regarding the Ring Engine, a simple yet flexible solution is provided: all your objects live in the aObjects list of the current Game object. And because the list type in Ring can easily be used to model any advanced data structure, from a hash table to a matrix to a graph, then nothing prevents you from adopting a complex data representation of your game world.

This said, the plain simple aObjects list will be widely efficient to cover the majority of games you would expect from a 2D game engine. Yet its use is simple and consistent with the operations of the list type in Ring.

In practice, there are two use cases you will need: finding an object by its index and filtering the list of objects depending on their type. Read on to discover a third, interesting use case.

---

[12]The order of execution of the functions provided in the state variables of all the objects depends on the index (nIndex) of every object inside the aObjects list in the Game object.

Getting an Object by Its Index

When your objects are added declaratively to the Game container, they are automatically added to the aObjects lists of that Game object in the order of their appearance in the code.

To see this in action, let's go back to the code we wrote (in the mygame.ring file) for displaying a game world with a background, one player plane, and three enemy planes. Make a copy of it and save it to a new file called mygame-extended.ring; then adjust it to contain the code in Listing 8-11.

Listing 8-11. mygame-extended.ring

```
load "gameengine.ring"

func main
oGame = new Game {
        // BACKGROUND => Object with nIndex = 1
        Sprite {
                type = GE_TYPE_BACKGROUND
                file = "images/stars.jpg"
                scaled = true
                width = 800 height = 600
                animate = false
        }
        // PLAYER => Objec with nIndex = 2
        Sprite
        {
                type = GE_TYPE_PLAYER
                file = "images/player.png" transparent = true
                x = 350 y = 450
                scaled = true width = 100 height = 100
                animate = false move = true
        }
        // ENEMIES     => Objects with nIndex = 3, 4, and 5
        for g = 1 to 3
        Sprite
        {
                type = GE_TYPE_ENEMY
```

```
            file = "images/enemy.png" transparent = true
            x = 120 + g*100 y = 80
            scaled = true width = 80 height = 80
            animate = false
        }
    next g
}
```

While parsing this code, the Ring Engine constitutes the aObjects of the current Game object (oGame in our case) list as follows:

Index	Description
1	The sprite representing the background
2	The sprite representing the player's plane
3	The sprite representing the first enemy's plane
4	The sprite representing the second enemy's plane
5	The sprite representing the third enemy's plane

To reference any of these objects in any place inside the Game braces, you need just to use the following, for example:

```
oPlayer = oGame.aObjects[2]
oFirstEnemy = oGame.aObjects[3]
```

Then do whatever processing you want, to see whether the two objects collide for example, or simply to see whether they have the same width, by saying this:

```
If oPlayer.width = oFirstEnemy.width then { // doStaff... }
```

Generally, this is used inside the state function of a given sprite to compare some of its attributes with those of another object in the game world. We will show the practical use of this later, among other places, when we talk about collision detection.

Filtering Objects by Type

Usually, you need to verify a condition or apply an action on a bunch of objects in one shot. When a rocket is fired by the player's plane, for example, all the enemy objects need to be checked for collision in a single operation. Or, for example, when you, the player, change the configuration of the game to select a different color for a particular type of objects, then this modification is made for all the objects in the same action.

To make this happen, the aObjects list needs to be filtered based on a given value. Actually, there is no limit on what to base the filtering on, since the list can be parsed, and any attribute of its objects can be used. But, in practice, it's not convenient to use any attribute like that, because such a practice in programming games could generate a huge performance cost.

The Ring engine comes with a simple and pragmatic solution to that: you have an attribute called type of the Sprite class that you can use to base your query on (take a look back at the structure of this class in section "The Sprite Class"). By default, four types are supported.

- GE_TYPE_BACKGROUND = 1
- GE_TYPE_PLAYER = 2
- GE_TYPE_ENEMY = 3
- GE_TYPE_FIRE = 4

Nothing prevents you from adding other types. At the end, they are just numbers! But they help organize your logic and simplify the task of managing your world in real time.

To use this feature, you need to specify the type of object inside the object braces like you see in the previous code listing. Then, when you want to filter aObjects using one of these types, you just say, for example, the following:

```
for i=1 to len(oGame.aObjects)
      If aObjects[i].type = GE_TYPE_ENEMY
            attackThem()
      ok
next i
```

To add a personalized type not included by default in the engine, you can specify it as a global variable that you should write before the main function of your program, as explained before. So you say this:

```
GE_TYPE_MONSTER = 5
GE_TYPE_CITIZEN = 6
GE_TYPE_STRANGER = 7
```

And so on, and so on.

Getting an Object with Its Name

It would be nice to reference a sprite directly by using the name we give to it and not by using an agnostic index. Then we could say `monster.x` in lieu of `aObjects[7].x`, for example. This a more agile way yet more consistent than calling an object using an index that could change at any time, such as if a preceding object is removed from the world, for example.

Because the `RingEngine` library is open source, you can change the engine class's design by adding such an attribute to the `GameObject` or `Sprite` class. But this is not the best option for us as a Ring community. Any change in the codebase of the engine needs to be made in the official distribution of the language so anyone can benefit from it. When you share a copy of your game code, anyone can take it, open it in Ring Notepad, and test it with the current version of the Ring Engine.

Do you remember when we made a proposal to the Ring team about time functions in Chapter 1 and how they quickly responded? I was going to do the same thing here, but I discovered that this was already done, as shown in Figure 8-18.

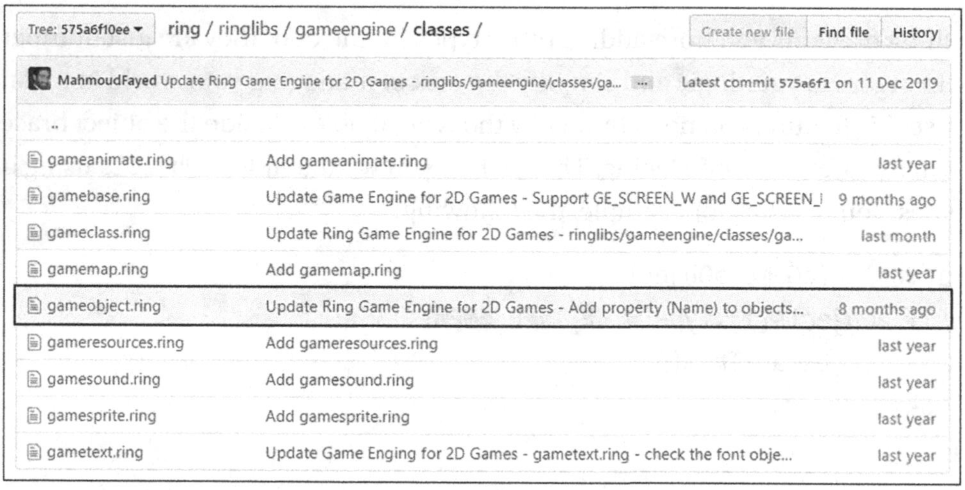

Figure 8-18. *Always keep an eye on the Ring GitHub page and see what's new*

As a Ring programmer, you should regularly visit the GitHub page of the language. There you see that daily enhancements are being made. To get the updates, you need to use the Ring package manager.[13]

---

[13]http://ring-lang.sourceforge.net/doc1.11/ringpm.html

Skill 7: Intercepting Events

During the execution of the game loop, the Ring engine will be continuously listening for any input event from the keyboard, the mouse, the touch screen, or even the network. When the event is captured, then a function provided by you, the programmer, is executed, without preventing other events or other functions from taking their turn in the execution process.

Actually, capturing events and organizing them in a complex computer program like a video game is not a simple task. Adequate design patterns, made for parallelization and synchronization, are necessary. Otherwise, the application can quickly turn into a totally nonresponsive and unusable system.

To describe this complex event management mechanism, let's look at a screen of an air fighting game, as shown in Figure 8-19.

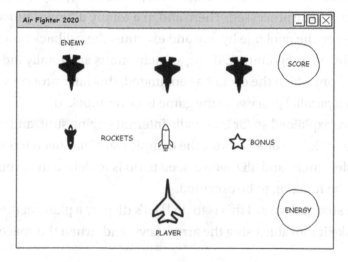

Figure 8-19. *We will be developing this prototype in the next section*

First, the game engine analyzes the game world, object by object; then harvests any event it can capture; and then stores it in a centralized pool of events in the order of their occurrence. For Figure 8-19, there are at least 10 events we can enumerate, as shown in the following list:

- The player moves around and hits the borders of the world.

- The player moves around and hits an enemy.

- The player moves around and collides with a star bonus.

- The player moves around and collides with an enemy's rocket.

- The player emits a rocket targeting enemies.

- The rocket emitted by the player hits an enemy.

- The game reaches the maximum score.

- The game reaches the minimum energy.

- The game reaches the end of the level.

- The game is shut down.

If they are to be processed sequentially one after the other, then any performance lag in the management of the current event will have a negative impact on the next one. Of course, any interruption of one node will cause an interruption of the entire chain.

To overcome such a risk, the game engine keeps recording any new event in the pool of events and asks it to be processed. Then, and in a totally different process, the engine takes the events from the pool one by one and executes the callback functions defined for each of them by the programmer. Being asynchronous and totally independent from the actual object from which the event has emanated, this later process will execute every function in a parallel process so the game is never blocked.

Everything I've explained so far is actually internal engine stuff, and, ultimately, you shouldn't care about it.[14] In other words, the complex stuff has been written for us by the Ring engine designers, and all that we need to do is to define the event on the right object and write the function to be executed.

To show how straightforward this is to do,[15] let's display a plane at the bottom center of the screen, make it movable using the arrow keys, and, when the spacebar is pressed, launch a rocket!

First we write the code that displays the plane and makes it movable by the arrow keys (save this to a new file called plane.ring), as shown in Listing 8-12.

---

[14]Unless you're like me and somewhat headstrong and decide to go into the internals of the engine, you should read about all the classes to understand them. In this case, you can find them in the c:\ring\ringlibs\ringengine\classes folder.

[15]This is not really the case with other competing game engine frameworks.

Listing 8-12. plane.ring

```
load "gameengine.ring"

func main
oGame = new Game
{

    Sprite {
            file = "images/player.png"
            scaled = true
            width = 100
            height = 100

            x = (screen_w - width) / 2
            y = screen_h - height - 50

            animate = false
            move = true          # All what is needed to make it
                                 # movable by the arrow key!
    }

}
```

Execute this and test moving the plane using the four arrow keys on your keyboard. It works fine, but something needs to be done for the object not to leave the screen. Here, we can use what we learned in the previous section and intervene in the game state to control the x and y attributes of the object.

Then we add the code shown in Listing 8-13 to the sprite code.

Listing 8-13. Part of plane.ring

```
state = func oGame, oSelf {
     oSelf {
            // Protecting the west and east borders
            if x < 0
                   x = 0
            but x > (screen_w - width)
                   x = screen_w - width
```

```
        // Protecting the north and south borders
        but y < 0
                y = 0
        but y > (screen_h - height)
                y = screen_h - height
        ok

    }
}
```

Execute this, and travel to the borders by driving the plane using the four arrow keys on the keyboard. The plane refuses to leave the game window, which is what we want. More generally, any constraint or rule or logic you want to apply on animated objects must go inside the state function.

Now we will build the second component of our game world, the rocket. It's yet another sprite we can add declaratively without any special effort. The sprite must obey these considerations:

- The sprite is fired when the spacebar is pressed.

- The sprite is animated vertically while decrementing its y attribute: GE_DIRECTION_**DEC**VERTICAL.

- The launching point must be the (x,y) position of the plane, and the target of the rocket must be in the invisible side of the upper screen.

- When the rocket exceeds the screen size, then it must be deleted from the aObjects list of the game so our game world is kept clean.

Does this seem like a lot of work? Declarative programming can turn such complex requirements into a consistent design experience. First, let's display the rocket along its animated path. Add the code in Listing 8-14 to the game container as a second sprite object of the game.

Listing 8-14. Part of plane.ring

```
Sprite {
        file = "images/rocket.png"
        transparent = true
        scaled = true
        width = 30
```

```
        height = 60
        // Storing the plane object in a variable for
        // the sake of expressiveness
        oPlayer = oGame.aObjects[1]
        // Positioning the rocket at the cannonn nozzle
        x = oPlayer.x + (oPlayer.width - width) / 2
        y = oPlayer.y - (oPlayer.height - height)
        // Don't animate it right now
        animate = false
    }
```

If this is done right, Figure 8-20 shows what you get (if not, please review the code from the beginning).

Figure 8-20. *The rocket is precisely positioned in front of the plane*

Now, we can add the animation requirement as described in the second point from the beginning of the exercise. The rocket should move vertically while decrementing its y attribute, i.e., in the direction specified by the GE_DIRECTION_DECVERTICAL constant.

Then we set animate to true at the end of the code, and we add the code in Listing 8-15.

Listing 8-15. Part of plane.ring

```
// Animating the rocket
animate = true
direction = GE_DIRECTION_DECVERTICAL
point = - height # the rocket goes out of screen
nStep = 5    # this is the acceleration rate
```

These four lines and the values they provide will cause the rocket to travel confidently following a strict path until it disappears from the game world! Run the program and observe it yourself. Don't hesitate to change nStep to 20 and then to 2 to get a sense of its impact on the movement acceleration of the rocket.

There is a warning I want to tell you about here: imagine you were in a real-world game with hundreds of rockets to be emitted by the player and also by the enemies. In the context of a multiplayer game that is run online with thousands of users, the number of rockets can be huge. In such a case, the memory of the target machine, especially when the game is played on a mobile phone, can be saturated quickly because of these unused objects that left the screen but never left their place in the memory storage.

A wise practice is to delete any object that becomes useless or unnecessary, when it explodes, for example, or leaves the screen entirely. Technically, this is as simple as deleting it from the aObject list by specifying in nIndex in the remove(nIndex) method of the Game object.

It is clear, though, that this feature must be implemented while intervening in the state of the rocket sprite and checking when it exceeds the borders. Add this to the rocket sprite code, as shown in Listing 8-16.

Listing 8-16. Part of plane.ring

```
state = func oGame, oSelf {
        oSelf {
                if y < 0
                        oGame.remove(nIndex)
                ok
                ? len(oGame.aObjects) # read hereafter
        }
}
```

Our object pool is now clean. But we need a way to debug it, right? That's why I added the ? len(oGame.aObjects) line inside the state.

As mentioned earlier, this line of code will be executed on each iteration of the game loop. So, what we get is the number of objects stored in the aObjects container at every frame of the game lifecycle. If the game loop has been executed 24 times before the rocket leaves the room, then what we get in the Output window of Ring Notepad is a list where all the numbers are 2 except the last one, 1!

This is the proof that our rocket has been deleted from aObjects. Leave this code as is. We will be deleting it later. Instead, it's time to focus on the last requirement: everything we implemented must be fired when the spacebar is pressed on the keyboard.

This is easy. We just move the code from the rocket sprite section and place it in the keypress event inside the player sprite section. In fact, the whole animation we made for the rocket must be fired up when the spacebar is pressed inside the player sprite. Therefore, the complete code of the sample will look like Listing 8-17.

Listing 8-17. plane.ring

```
load "gameengine.ring"

func main
oGame = new Game
{
     Sprite {
          file = "images/player.png"     scaled = true
          width = 100      height = 100
          x = (screen_w - width) / 2
          y = screen_h - height - 50
          animate = false move = false

          state = func oGame, oSelf { oSelf {
               if x < 0
                    x = 0
               but x > (screen_w - width)
                    x = screen_w - width
               but y < 0
                    y = 0
               but y > (screen_h - height)
                    y = screen_h - height
               ok }
          }

          keypress = func oGame, oSelf, nKey { oGame {
          Sprite {
               file = "images/rocket.png"
               transparent = true
```

```
                 scaled = true width = 30 height = 60
                 oPlayer = oGame.aObjects[1]
                 x = oPlayer.x + (oPlayer.width - width) / 2
                 y = oPlayer.y - (oPlayer.height - height)
                 // Animating the rocket
                 animate = true
                 direction = GE_DIRECTION_DECVERTICAL
                 point = - height
                 nStep = 5

                 state = func oGame, oSelf { oSelf {
                     if y < 0
                           oGame.remove(nIndex)
                     ok }
                     ? len(oGame.aObjects)
                 }
          } # closing brace for Rocket sprite
      } } # closing braces for keypress and oGame

   } # closing brace for Player sprite


} # closing brace for oGame
```

Execute the code. When the user presses the spacebar, the rocket is launched. Press it several time to launch many rockets. You'll see the list tracing the number of objects in the Output window. It's a long list, but you can scroll down to see how the number of objects varies during the loop execution. However many rockets you launched, the list ends with the number 1. This means that all the rockets that left the screen have been deleted and that the object world contains just the player sprite.

Now that we are confident with the cleansing process we put in place, let's drop the corresponding line from our code and make one more enhancement because pressing any key, not only the spacebar, will lead to the execution of the keypress function. How do we fix this?

Just after the keypress line, add the code in Listing 8-18 (the statement in bold).

Listing 8-18. Part of plane.ring

```
keypress = func oGame, oSelf, nKey { oGame {
      if nKey = KEY_SPACE
            Sprite {
            // Rocket sprite code goes here...
```

And just after the closing brace of the rocket sprite, add ok to close the if condition, as shown in Listing 8-19.

Listing 8-19. Part of plane.ring

```
      } # closing brace for Rocket sprite
ok
```

If we want to close the game once the player presses the Escape key, then we adjust the code to look like Listing 8-20.

Listing 8-20. Part of plane.ring

```
keypress = func oGame, oSelf, nKey { oGame {
      if nKey = KEY_SPACE
            Sprite {
            // Rocket sprite code goes here...
            } # closing brace for Rocket sprite
      but nKey = KEY_ESC
            oGame.shutdown()
      ok
```

Here's some useful information to end this section with: you can find all the constant variables the Ring engine uses to enhance the expressiveness of your programming experience in a C header file, called gameengine.rh, stored in the ring/ringlibs/gameengine folder.[16] While reading the file, you will see that other events are supported for mouse and finger events for the touch screens. There are plenty of code examples in the Ring documentation and dozens of open source games you can look at to learn how to use these events.

---

[16]As said earlier, the Ring Game Engine is built upon a low-level graphic service foundation, written in C, that is provided to serve as a hub between Ring and specialized libraries like Allegro and SDL.

Skill 8: Detecting Collisions

Almost all games should include a collision detection system. Two game objects collide inside the game world when their coordinates overlap. If the objects are simple enough, i.e., can be defined by a rectangular zone, their collision can be detected by writing simple conditional code. But if they are rather complex geometric shapes, a trapezoid or even a circle, then some mathematics are needed.

Almost any game object can be surrounded by a virtual rectangle that we can use to enable the detection of its collision with other objects. Let's design a simple game world containing two movable stars on a beautiful city background and then try to detect any possible collision between them (see Figure 8-21).

Figure 8-21. *Mission: detecting when the stars collide*

Before you move on, copy the images supermancity.jpg, smstar.png, and smstar2. png that you find here:

C:\ring\applications\superman2016\images

to the folder images here:

c:\ringbook\chap8

We will leave the stars nontransparent, because I want you to observe the limits of every rectangle while you are testing the star collisions. Later you can just add transparent = true to fix it.

Because this is declarative programming, you will write the code as if you were designing the game world using graphic software. You will describe how the background and the two stars appear and what behavior they have by just configuring the corresponding sprites; see Listing 8-21 (save the code in a new file called stars.ring).

Listing 8-21. stars.ring

```
load "gameengine.ring"

func main
oGame = new Game {
        // BACKGROUND
        Sprite {
                file= "images/supermancity.jpg"
                x = 0 y = 0
                scaled=true width=800 height=600
                animate = false
        }
        // RANDOMLY-MOVING STAR
        Sprite {
                file = "images/smstar.png"
                x = 300 y = 100
                width = 170      height = 167
                direction = GE_DIRECTION_RANDOM
                point = 700 nStep = 2
        }
        // MOVABLE STAR (BY ARROW KEYS)
        Sprite {
                file = "images/smstar2.png"
                x=300 y=450
                width = 170      height = 167
                animate=false move=true
        }
}
```

Run the file and be sure you get the same result as shown in Figure 8-21.

Inside the code of the movable star, precisely at the state portion of it, we will be writing the code that detects any collision with the first moving star. Algorithmically, being placed inside the state will help us monitor how both object coordinates move and check when they just touch each other. Visually speaking, we need to think of the situation as shown in Figure 8-22.

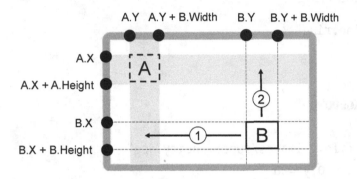

Figure 8-22. *A mental/visual approach to solve the collision problem*

To simplify our reasoning, let's suppose that object A is fixed while B is moving. By analyzing Figure 8-22, we can easily infer a visual solution to the collision problem. Hence, two conditions must be verified.

- **B** should enter the gray zone of object **A** from its vertical corridor (follow arrow 1 in Figure 8-22)

- At the same time, **B** should enter the gray zone of object **A** from its horizontal corridor (arrow 2 in Figure 8-22)

Let's verify the first condition with code. For that, I suggest you fix the moving star and change the two stars' positions to cope with the visual situation shown in Figure 8-22 (changes are in bold). When the second star enters in the collider (1) of the first star, then we can close the game. Add the code in Listing 8-22 to the second star sprite section in the stars.ring file.

Listing 8-22. stars.ring

```
state = func oGame, oSelf { oSelf {
      oTarget = oGame.aObjects[2]
      // Movable star is inside the vertical corridor
```

```
    if oTarget.y <= x and x <= oTarget.y + oTarget.width
        oGame.shutdown()
    ok
}}
```

Execute the code. Try to move the movable star to the left by pressing the left arrow key. When the start enters the collider, then the game ends. It works then! What you need to do now is to add the code of the second corridor and set the stars back to their initial configuration. In particular, we want the first one to move randomly to see how our collision algorithm performs.

I'll leave this as an exercise for you. You can also go back to the animated Map example we made previously, add a flying bird sprite 🐦 (find it at `images/fbbird.png`), and then detect any collision of the bird with the map walls. In this case, don't allow it to move.

In the "A Complete Game in Ring" section, you will find a complete implementation of everything you have learned here in terms of the collision detection and explosion effect of the Air Fighter 2020 game.

Skill 9: Implementing and Testing the Gameplay

How do you construct a score system inside your game? How do you allow the player to get from one level to another? Will your game finish at a certain point or run continuously until the player decides to leave on their own? Should the game store a high score to compare different players' performances?

These are some of the questions you are required to ask and find answers for during the phase of gameplay design. In general, the simpler the play rules are to understand, the more successful your game will be. But gameplay design is really a huge domain that needs to be approached here as simply as possible so you can get an idea about how to implement a simple score system for your game. In the "A Complete Game in Ring" section, while studying the complete code of the Air Fighter 2020 game, you will find a more consistent implementation for a level system on top of the score system of the game.

Suppose we are playing the game represented in Figure 8-23.

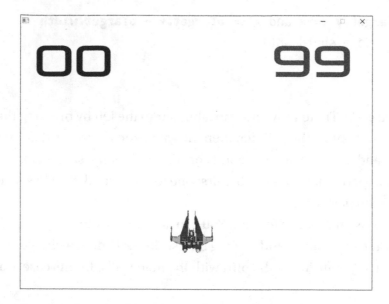

Figure 8-23. *The simplest game on Earth, made for learning how to implement score and energy features*

It is dead simple, composed of just one game player represented by the plane and two text objects. On the left, we will show the score, and on the right we will show the chronometer.

From the start, the time is counting down from 99 to 0. When the spacebar is pressed, the score is incremented by 10. If the time counter is less than 30, then the player becomes unable to harvest new score points. When the score reaches 100, then the game is idled, and no more score points can be gained. Anytime the player hits the Escape key, the game is shut down.

This gameplay is not that interesting, because there is no real competition or drama in our design, but it shows you how a wide majority of game score systems work.

Let's design the game world first. Create a new file called plane-extended.ring and start typing the code in Listing 8-23.

Listing 8-23. plane-extended.ring

```
load "gameengine.ring"

func main
oGame = new Game {
        // SCORE      => nIndex = 1
```

```
Text {
        text = "00" size = 100
        file = "fonts/pirulen.ttf"
        x = 30 y = 20
        color = GE_COLOR_BLACK
        animate = false
}

// ENERGY      => nIndex = 2
Text {
        text = "99" size = 100
        file = "fonts/pirulen.ttf"
        x = 570 y = 20
        color = GE_COLOR_BLUE
        animate = false
}

// PLAYER      => nIndex = 3
Sprite
{
        type = GE_TYPE_PLAYER
        file = "images/player.png" transparent = true
        x = 350 y = 450
        scaled = true width = 100 height = 100
        animate = false move = true
}
}
```

Run the file. It's the same as Figure 8-23!

It's clear that time winds down as the game goes on. Therefore, updating the energy
level can happen in the player's state. Add the code shown in Listing 8-24 to the player
sprite code.

Listing 8-24. Part of plane-extended.ring

```
state = func oGame,oSelf { oSelf {
        if nEnergy>0 { nEnergy-- }
        oGame.aObjects[2].text = "" + nEnergy
        if nEnergy=0 { nEnergy=0 }
}}
```

Before you execute, add these two globals at the beginning of the program file, even before giving control to the Game Engine in the line load "gameengine":

```
nEnergy = 99
nScore = 0
```

Execute it now. Time is decrementing successfully and then stops at 0. But if you find it going very quickly, you can add this at the top of the oGame class region: FixedFPS = 15 or whatever value fits to the animation speed you prefer.

Now we will focus on augmenting the score by 10 every time the spacebar is pressed. Clearly, this must happen in the keypress event under the player sprite object. Add the code shown in Listing 8-25 just after the state block.

Listing 8-25. Part of plane-extended.ring

```
keypress = func oGame,oSelf,nKey { oSelf {
        if nKey = KEY_SPACE
                if nScore <=90 { nScore += 10 }
                oGame.aObjects[1].text = "" + nScore
                if nScore = 100 { nScore = 100}
        but nKey = KEY_ESC
                oGame.shutdown()
        ok
}}
```

Once implemented, the gameplay must be tested by real players, and feedback must be collected, quantitatively and qualitatively. Professional game houses incorporate their centralized game analytics systems. Those are detailed statistics they collect from the gameplay of thousands of game sessions. Analyzing them will help the game designer understand the parts that need to be enhanced and those that are destructive to the playing experience. In our case, we will just perform a unitary test of the gameplay rules we defined at the beginning of the section and see whether they are fully supported by the code we just implemented. To do so, execute the game, and follow the steps shown here. If the rule doesn't pass, you must go back to your code to fix it before going to the next one. Here I assume all the rules were successful except the last one.

1. Do nothing; just watch the chronometer going on. At the end, it must stop at 0.

2. Press the spacebar. The score shouldn't be incremented.

3. Press the Escape key. The game should close.

4. Execute the game again and press the spacebar three to five times. The score should add 10 every time.

5. Let the time wind down to 0. Press the spacebar again. Nothing should happen on the score side.

6. Press the Escape key. The game should close.

7. Execute the game again. Press the spacebar so the score reaches 100. Be sure not to be constrained by the available time. Once the score reaches 100, the game is completely idled.

There is a bug here; did you see it? If the score reaches 100, the game is not idle because the time counter is still flowing down. To resolve this, change the condition statement in the player's state from this:

```
if nEnergy>0 { nEnergy-- }
```

to this:

```
if nEnergy>0 and nScore <100 { nEnergy-- }
```

As you can see if you test it, the problem is resolved. But another one still exists. Are you able to find it? You should try all the possible scenarios of gameplay and give it to your family members or your friends to try. If you are in a professional video game studio, you should do some gameplay testing by a dedicated team. Never deploy your game to the public without fully testing its gameplay.

We've gone on a long journey together during this book, but I can't leave you without mentioning one last bug. When the chronometer reaches 0, the spacebar still harvests points! Make an effort to reproduce the issue first and then solve it, please, before you move to the next skill I want you to master in developing games in Ring: organizing and refactoring code.

Skill 10: Organizing and Refactoring Code

As described in the section "Mastering the Big Picture," a game program written on top of the Ring Game Engine contains a declarative silhouette in which some other code, both declarative and imperative, can be injected.

Declarative programming is awesome; it makes it easy to design the game world and describe the game objects without caring about how they are implemented. Despite this, when your games evolve and your codebase grows, two major problems can quickly arise.

- Your code hosts a deep hierarchy of nested braces and becomes difficult to be modeled mentally and hard to read.

- The many calls of functions in several places and the many events may transform your application into a plate of shakshuka (or spaghetti code if you want).

In this section, we will briefly demonstrate these two problems in code and then show how organizing and the refactoring the code are the two solutions you should use to mitigate against the number-one threat of game programming: code complexity.

As you know, Ring stores the game objects in a one-dimensional list called aObjects. Every time an object is included inside the oGame braces, it is added to the list.

```
oGame = new Game {
    Object {
        // first game object
    }
    Sprite {
        // second game object
    }
    Sprite {
        // third game object
    }
    Text {
        // Fourth game object
    }
    // And so on...
}
```

At this level, whatever the size of the game world is, there is no complexity at all, since the code is organized with just two levels of indentation.

Game objects expose events, such as state, keypress, and draw. These are captured automatically by the Ring Game Engine, but the logic to be executed after the event is up to you, the programmer, to provide in the form of an anonymous function.

Writing these functions adds at least two levels of indentation, as shown here:

```
oGame = new Game {
    Object {
        // first game object
        Draw = func oGame, oSelf {
            oSelf {
                // Drawing goes here
            }
        }
    }
    Sprite {
        // second game object
        State = func oGame, oSelf {
            oSelf {
                // Animation code goes here
            }
        }
    }
    Sprite {
        // third game object
        Keypress = func oGame, oSelf, nKey {
            oSelf {
                // Keypress code goes here
            }
        }
    }
    Text {
        // Fourth game object
    }
    // And so on...
}
```

The code gets longer, but it is still informative. In practice, all the code blocks we've just added come with their own additional levels of hierarchy. For example, the code of the keypress function could look like this:

```
Sprite {
     // third game object
     Keypress = func oGame, oSelf, nKey {
          oSelf {
                    // Keypress code goes here
                    switch nKey
                         on KEY_ESC
                                   // Escape code goes here
                         on KEY_SPACE
                                   // Space code goes here
                         Other
                                   // Other code goes here
                    off
          }
     }
}
```

Put them together and observe how deep the code base is becoming. It's like a cherry on top of the cake; some of the anonymous functions you will write will come with yet another complete hierarchy of declarative code, like this, for example:

```
Sprite {
     // third game object
     Keypress = func oGame, oSelf, nKey {
          oSelf {
                    // Keypress code goes here
                    switch nKey
                         on KEY_ESC
                                   // Escape code goes here
                         on KEY_SPACE
                                   // A new object is generated
                                   oGame {
                                        Sprite {
```

```
                                    // The fifth object code
                                    // goes here
                               }
                          }
             Other
                         // Other code goes here
          off
       }
}
```

As you can see, about ten logical hierarchical levels were created; however, the human visual system can't manage more than about three at a time. In a codebase containing hundreds or even thousands of lines of code (LOC), this can become difficult to reason about, read, manage, and maintain.

It would be nice if Ring Notepad contained a side panel to show the complete hierarchy of the game in an interactive tree or provided the fancy feature of hiding and showing portions of nested code, but from such a young project, we can understand and humbly not be so demanding. Personally, I think the problem of code complexity shouldn't be delegated to any sophisticated IDE tools and should be leveraged, consciously, by the programmer at the code structure level by organizing code carefully and by refactoring it when necessary.

There is a lot to say about how you master the codebase of your game and prevent it from becoming too complex with deep hierarchies and unmanaged interconnected function calls. Here, I will give you some simple and practical tips that I usually use myself while programing with the Ring Game Engine.

At the organization side, keep the separation as clear as possible between the game loop and the rest of the program.

```
// Put any global variables in an exetrnal file
load "globals.ring"
load "gameengine.ring"

#################################################################
// This is the core of the game, kept dead simple
func main
oGame = new Game {
title = "Stars Fighter"
FPS = 60
FixedFPS = 60
```

```
play(oGame)     // This function will include the main code

}
############################################################
```

// Here goes the functions part of the program
// ...

This is where the refactoring side comes into play. Functions are, by far, your best ally to gain code expressiveness.

```
func play(oGame)
        // the world game is built here
        Sprite {
                // ...
                /*
                When a key is pressed, don't write the code
                of the anonymus function directly, call an
                external function instead:
                */
                keypress = attackEnemey_f() #_f shows it is a
                                                callback function
        }
func attackEnemy_f()
        f = func oGame, oSelf, nKey { oSelf {
                // the function code goes here
                // ...
                /*
                if a new sprite needs to be generated, then
                don't write it here, again, make a function
                call instead. Let it be as expressive as
                this one:
                */
                launchRocket(oGame,oSelf)
        // dont forget to return back the function
        return f
```

All the functions are not callbacks, though, and some of them can be employed to be fully reusable in any context. Providing an updateScore(oGame,n) function that updates the score of the game by adding n points, using a showfire(oGame,oSelf) function that shows an exposition sprite at the place of the current object and then deletes them both (the object and the explosion effect), and so on, are all possible solutions that could be refactored to enhance both the program structure and its learnability.

On a related note here, sending the oGame (and oSelf in some cases) objects as parameters of your functions transmits the game state from inside the game loop to the external function. Therefore, you will get the best of two worlds: your logic is active at the game loop level while being fabricated peacefully outside the game loop.

Once your code is organized and your game logic is refactored into well-defined expressive functions, there remains yet another complex challenge: streamlining the overlapping calls you could have between functions and deciding where you should take a given action, if many sprites are candidates to host it. As an example, when two sprites collide and an explosion must happen, in which one should we write the code of that explosion? And because all the objects of our game are not allowed to fly out of the game window, what is the specific game object that we should host the stayIn(oGame) function in?

Because this is a large issue that relates to embracing the power of design patterns for decoupling the user interface layer of your game from its logic written inside functions, I will just invite you to read three instructive articles written by Christian Hanselmann on Medium[17] about the importance of reactive programming.

Skill 11: Distributing Your Game on Many Platforms

Ring has been made, by design, to be portable on any platform.

First, the Ring compiler and virtual machine are both written in a portable ANSI C code that you can compile using Microsoft Visual C/C++, GNU C/C++, Clang, Borland C/C++, Tiny C, and so on. Hence, Ring itself, and any code you write on top of it, should run on Windows, Linux, macOS, and Android, without any problems.

Second, Ring has been designed for embeddability with any C/C++ in two directions: you can include C/C++ code inside your Ring project, or, inversely, you can include your Ring code inside a C/C++ project. In both cases, multiplatform compatibility is widely supported.

---

[17]https://tinyurl.com/ya7w4mso

Regarding the Ring 2D Game Engine, and because the low-level graphics service is delegated to external libraries like Allegro and LibSDL, then any platform supported by them is also supported by your game. I have made the necessary tests on Windows, Linux, macOS, and Android, and I expect that they also work on other platforms.

That said, Ring provides an interesting window into the world of multiplatform compatibility via RingQt, which is the Ring library that binds your Ring applications to the Qt framework. If you export your Ring code as a Qt project using the Ring2EXE tool and you open it with Qt Creator, the standard IDE of Qt, then you can build it on any platform supported by Qt.

Finally, you could ask, what about porting a game made by Ring to be playable on the Web? Interesting question. I will ask it on the Ring Google Group because I'm not sure of the answer. Here is my question to the Ring designer:

Hello Mahmoud,

What do you think is the best strategy to port a game made on top of the 2D Game Engine to be played on the Web ? In particular:

- *Do you think that adding a target compilation in Ring2EXE to the WebAssembly[18] format can be considered in the future so the games written in Ring can play as is, without any HTML burden, in the browser?*

- *If not, how can one enhance the architecture of the Ring Engine by adding an HTML rendering library like Phaser,[19] for example, along with the other supported C++ libraries, Allegro and LibSDL?*

- *In this case, how can we avoid the window class, which is made to be run on the desktop to replace the browser window?*

I know these points may require extensive answers, but some quick hints can be sufficient since I'm dealing with the subject in the chapter of the Ring book dedicated to gaming.

Thank you in advance.

---

[18]WebAssembly is an open standard that defines a portable binary code format for executable programs inside the browser. Unlike JavaScript, WebAssembly is running natively and provides better performance for 2D and 3D games.

[19]Phaser is a free software 2D game framework for making HTML5 games for desktop and mobile. You can learn more at `https://phaser.io`.

The creator of Ring responded and we can find the answers to these questions at the following link[20]: `https://tinyurl.com/whnczpf`.

Another useful detail is that Ring allows you to distribute your game as a compiled object file without source code (called `ringo`). This can be your preferable option if you want to protect the source code in a commercial version of the game. To do this, you just invoke the command line and type `ring mygame.ring -go`, where `mygame.ring` is the file name of your game project. Ring generates a `mygame.ringo` binary object file that you can execute using the command `ring mygame.ringo`. That's it.

Let's end the section with the last skill I want you to have while developing sophisticated games in Ring.

Skill 12: Monitoring Your Game Performance

As explained in the section "Game Timing," performance is a critical aspect of game programming that you should look at. Usually, any function you write in the code of your game is executed inside the game loop. Thus, the time it takes, both in the number of processor clocks and in human time (perceived by the user in seconds), should be monitored. This is your tool to demystify the potential lags you might observe in your games.

Two functions of Ring, `clock()` and `clockPerSecond()`, can be used within the boundaries of your program to improve the performance of your code. Usually, you will need to get these two basic measurements:

- The total time consumed by a complete execution of the game loop

- The time taken by a given selected region of your code

After identifying where the major time is consumed, you can add more `clock()` and `clockPerSecond()` functions[21] inside the corresponding region, until you find the particular statement that is the primary cause of the performance problem.

---

[20]In case you are offline, here is the answer from Mahmoud: Ring can be compiled to WebAssembly using Clang and Emscripten without problems. So, we have many options like using Qt (Support WebAssembly too) or RayLib. In the future, we may support RayLib in addition to Allegro and LibSDL in the Game Engine.

[21]`clock()` takes a timestamp, and `clockPerSecond()` tells how many processor clock ticks are in one second. You can learn more about them in the Ring documentation: `https://tinyurl.com/uc9ebpp`.

In practice, and because the declarative front end won't help you a lot when adopting this meticulous strategy, you need to dig into the internal code of the Ring engine. For that, open the `GameClass.ring` file from the `C:\Ring\ringlibs\gameengine\classes` folder and place your watchdogs around the three functions `startup()`, `start()`, and `drawobjs()` beginning on line 60 of the file.[22]

More generally, and if we embrace the same naming we used at the beginning of the chapter when describing the game loop functions, this is what you need to do:

```
// Monitoring the overall time taken by the loop (t)
t0 = clock()
While theGameIsRunning
      // Monitoring the time take by the input interception phase (ti)
      ti0 = clock()
      interceptInputs()
      ti = clock() - ti0

      // Monitoring the time taken by the update phase (tu)
      tu0 = clock()
      updateGameWorld()
      tu = clock() - tu0

      // Monitoring the time taken by the graphics rendering phase (tg)
      tg0 = clock()
      renderGraphics()
      tg = clock() - tg0

Repeat
t = clock() - t0
```

Execute and trace the values of your four "tees" (`t`, `ti`, `tu`, and `tg`). Start by analyzing the big picture. Then zoom in and monitor the region causing the problems. In practice, performance lags are observed in the graphic- and sound-rendering functions. But sometimes, you will face them in the input interception region if you write functions, in response to user events, that are poorly optimized for running in a real-time loop

---

[22] I advise you to capture the opportunity to focus on this class, understand its structure, and reflect on the role of every method it contains. This is the core of the Ring Engine, and its mastery will help you a lot.

context. In other cases, the root cause of the performance lag may reside in the operating system itself when it encounters a memory bottleneck. So, be careful.

For the rest, and by experience, the Ring Engine will generally perform very well in the updating region. But even there, don't be 100 percent confident, because some issues could happen, depending on the complexity of the world game you designed.

A Complete Game in Ring

This section contains an application showcasing everything you learned in this chapter. Walk through it step-by-step and line-by-line. If things get fuzzy, go back to the corresponding skill in this chapter, read that section again, and make sure you have a good understanding of the fundamental concepts and practical skills.

This game is a re-creation of a standard game delivered with Ring and that I redesigned while learning to use the Game Engine. The original game was written by the Ring creator himself and contains all the nice code gymnastics you would expect from a high-level programmer. But because my programming mind is quite basic and somehow allergic to deep hierarchies and dense cartographies of object messaging, I decided to write it again from the ground up, with the motivation to provide you with more expressive code. As a beginner, you should fall in love with the language in general and in particular with its wonderful game engine!

Hence, the following sections contain code without narration, and your challenge is to understand the code and enhance it by changing some rules of the gameplay or by forging a better structure and more expressive functions. This is something I invite you to do with other Ring applications and core components as well: hack them, change them, and understand how they work. Whatever time you invest will be more than rewarding.

Before You Make It, Play It!

Before starting to read the code provided in the next sections, open the Air Fighter game from the Ring installation folder:

```
C:\Ring\applications\starsfighter.
```

There you find the main game file called `starsfighter.ring`. Run it and start playing while reflecting on what you have learned about sprites, animation, collision, score, and so on.

After that, analyze the original source code of the game and try to understand it, as much as you can. Take note of any ambiguity you encounter and any questions you have. Then start a new file and start experimenting the following portions of code. Every section has been designed to constitute a step forward and provide you with a sense of achievement and self-esteem.

At the end of the program, I left a subtle bug I want you to discover and correct, in the contex of of advancing the gameplay from one level to another. Happy Ringling!

Loading Globals

Here is how to load globals:

```
// Globals.ring
nLevel = 1
nSession = 0

nEnemies = 0
nStars = 0
nVelocity = 0

nScore = 0
nScorePoint = 0
nMaxScore = 0
nEnergy = 0

bCanFight = True
bCeasefire = False

GE_TYPE_SCORE = 11
GE_TYPE_ENERGY = 22
GE_TYPE_REMOVE = 33
GE_TYPE_DESTROY = 44
GE_TYPE_BONUS = 55
GE_TYPE_LEVEL = 66
GE_TYPE_SESSION = 77
```

Write the Game Loop

Here is how to write the game loop:

```
load "globals.ring"
load "gameengine.ring"

func main
oGame = new Game {
        title = "Stars Fighter"
        FPS = 60
    FixedFPS = 60

        play(oGame)
}
```

Write the Game World Function

Here is how to write the game world function:

```
func play(oGame)

        oGame { init(oGame) // load the globals first
        // Start designing the world
        // BACKGROUND
        Sprite
        {
                type = GE_TYPE_BACKGROUND
                file = "images/stars.jpg"
                x = -300     y = -200
                animate = false

                state  = stayin_f()
        }
```

```
// PLAYER
Sprite
{
        type = GE_TYPE_PLAYER
        file = "images/player.png"     transparent = true
        x = 350     y = 450
        scaled = true    width = 100    height = 100
        animate = false  move = true

        keypress = attackEnemy_f()     # emits rocket
}

// ENEMIES
for g = 1 to nEnemies
Sprite
{
        type = GE_TYPE_ENEMY
        file = "images/enemy.png"     transparent = true
        x = 120 + random(100)*g + g*10     y = 80
        scaled = true    width = 80    height = 80
        animate = true
        direction = GE_DIRECTION_RANDOM

        state = attackPlayer_f()     # launches random
                                     # rockets on the player
}
next g

// LEVEL
Text {          type = GE_TYPE_LEVEL
        text = "LEVEL " + nLevel + " : " + nSession
        animate = false
        size = 24
        file = "fonts/pirulen.ttf"
        x = 20        y = 20
        color = rgb(255,255,255)
}
```

```
// SCORE
Text {         type = GE_TYPE_SCORE
      text = "00"
      animate = false
      size = 60
      file = "fonts/pirulen.ttf"
      x = 650         y = 20
      color = rgb(255,192,0)
}

// ENERGY
Text {         type = GE_TYPE_ENERGY
      text = "100"
      animate = false
      size = 40
      file = "fonts/pirulen.ttf"
      x = 670         y = 520
      color = rgb(60,255,255)
}

// SOUND
sound { file = "sound/music2.wav" }
}
```

Write the Game Initialization Function

Here is how to write the game initialization function:

```
func init(oGame)
    oGame {
          nSession++
          if nSession > 3 {
                nLevel++     //if nLevel > 3 { gameOver(oGame) }
                nSession = 1
          }
```

```
        switch nLevel
        on 1
                nEnemies = 3
                nVelocity = 5
                nStars = 3
        on 2
                nEnemies = 5
                nVelocity = 10
                nStars = 5
        on 3
                nEnemies = 7
                nVelocity = 15
                nStars = 8
        off

        nScore = 0
        nEnergy = 100
        nMaxScore = 100
        nScorePoint = nMaxScore / nEnemies

        bCanFight = True
        bCeasefire = False
    }
```

Protect the World Frontiers

Here is how to protect the world frontiers:

```
func stayin_f()     # No one is allowed to leave the world!
    f = func oGame,oSelf {
    oGame {
        for obj in aObjects
            if  obj.x <= 0
                    obj.x = 0

            but obj.x >= screen_w - obj.width
                    obj.x = screen_w - obj.width
```

```
            but obj.y <= 0
                obj.y = 0
                // When rockets exceed from the top,
                 // remove them
                if classname(obj)="sprite" and
                   obj.type=GE_TYPE_FIRE
                        remove(obj.nIndex)
                    ok

            but obj.y + obj.height >= screen_h
                obj.y = screen_h - obj.height
                // When rockets exceed from the bottom,
                // remove them
                  if classname(obj)="sprite" and
                     obj.type=GE_TYPE_FIRE
                        remove(obj.nIndex)

                 ok
            end

        end

    }}

    return f
```

Attack the Enemies

Here is how to attack the enemies:

```
func attackEnemy_f()      // WE ARE INSIDE THE PLAYER'S SCOPE

    f = func oGame,oself,nkey {

       if nkey = key_space and bCanFight = True

            // ROCKET LAUNCHED
            updateEnergy(oGame,-5)
            oGame {
                Sprite
                {
```

```
                    type = GE_TYPE_FIRE
                    file  = "images/rocket.png"
                     transparent = true
                    x = oself.x + 30       y = oself.y - 30
                    width = 30       height = 30
                    point = -30       nstep = 20
                    direction = ge_direction_decvertical

                    state = destroythem_f()
                      }
             } # oGame region is closed here

         but nkey = key_esc
                 oGame.shutdown()
         ok

   } # the f function region is closed here

   return f # the f function is returned to the caller
```

Accept to Be Attacked!

Here is how to player gets attacked:

```
func attackPlayer_f()        # WE ARE INSIDE THE ENEMEY STATE

     f = func oGame, oSelf {

     // LAUNCH ROCKETS RANDOMLY FROM ENEMEY STATE
     if random(1000/nVelocity) = 1 and bCeasefire = False
         oGame
         {
                 Sprite
                 {
                 type = GE_TYPE_FIRE
                 file  = "images/rocket2.png"
                 transparent = true
                 x = oself.x + 30
                 y = oself.y + oself.height+ 30
```

```
            width = 30
            height = 30

            point = ogame.screen_h+30
            nstep = 5
            direction = GE_DIRECTION_incVERTICAL

            state = theygotme_f()        // INSIDE ROCKET STATE
            } # the Sprite region is closed here
       } # the oGame region is closed here
    ok # the if region is closed here
} # the f function region is closed here

return f # the f function is returned to the caller
```

You're Captured, Write a Collision Function

Here is how to write a collision function:

```
func theygotme_f()        // INSIDE ENEMY'S ROCKET STATE

    f = func oGame,oSelf {
        // The player index = 2
          oPlayer =  oGame.aObjects[2]
        oRocket = oSelf

        // Detect collision
      if oPlayer.x <= oRocket.x and
          oRocket.x <= oPlayer.x + oPlayer.width and
          (oPlayer.y <= oRocket.y and
          oRocket.y <= oPlayer.y + oPlayer.height)

          oGame.remove(oRocket.nIndex)
          showfire(oGame,oRocket.x,oRocket.y)
```

```
                updateEnergy(oGame,-5)
                if nEnergy = 0
                        oGame.remove(oPlayer.nIndex)
                        bCeasefire = True
                ok

        ok
    }

    return f
```

Destroy the Enemies, Without Mercy!

Here is how to destroy the enemies:

```
func destroythem_f()        # WE ARE INSIDE THE PLAYER'S STATE!

    f = func oGame,oSelf {

    for obj in oGame.aObjects
        if classname(obj)="sprite" and
            obj.type = GE_TYPE_ENEMY

                if oself.x >= obj.x and oself.y >= obj.y and
                    oself.x <= obj.x + obj.width and
                    oself.y <= obj.y + obj.height
                        updateScore(oGame,nScorePoint)
                        // EXPLOSION
                        showfire(oGame,obj.x+40,obj.y+40)
                        // REMOVE enemy FROM OBJECT POOL
                        oGame.remove(obj.nindex)
                        exit
                ok
            ok
    next

    }

    return f
```

It Exploded, Show the Fire!

Here is how to show the fire at the position of the explosion:

```
func showfire(oGame,pnX,pnY) # WE JUST NEED THE POSITION
     oGame {
          Animate
          {
          file = "images/fire.png"       transparent = true
          x = pnX                         y = pnY
          framewidth = 39.38              height = 40

          state = func oGame, oSelf {
          oSelf {
               if frame < 13
                    frame++
               else
                    frame = 1
                    oGame.remove(oSelf.nIndex)
               ok
          }} # end of state
          } # end of animate
     }
```

Monitor Your Energy

Here is how to monitor the player's energy:

```
func updateEnergy(oGame,n)

     nEnergy += n

     if nEnergy = 0
          gameOver(oGame)
     but nEnergy <= 0
          nEnergy = 0 bCeaseFire = True
```

```
but nEnergy = 30
        bCanFight = False
        r = random(nStars)        if r=0 { r=1 }
        addBonus(oGame,r)
but nEnergy > 30
        bCanFight = True
but nEnergy > 100
        nEnergy = 100
ok

for i=1 to len(oGame.aObjects)
        if oGame.aObjects[i].type = GE_TYPE_ENERGY
                oGame.aObjects[i].text = "" + nEnergy
                exit
        end
end
```

Grow the Stars, They Are Bonuses!

Here is how to add stars randomly as bonuses in the scene:

```
func addBonus(oGame,n)
    oGame {
    for g=1 to n
    Sprite {
        type = GE_TYPE_BONUS
        file = "images/smstar.png" transparent=true
        x=300       y=200
        scaled=true width=50 height=50
        point=800 nStep=3 direction = GE_DIRECTION_RANDOM

        state = bonusCaptured_f()
    } # end of Sprite region
    next g

    } # end of oGame region
```

The Stars, Captured!

Here is how to capture stars and detect their collision with the player's aircraft:

```
func BonusCaptured_f()
    // INSIDE STARS'S STATE
    f = func oGame, oSelf {

    oGame {
        oStar = oSelf
        oPlayer = aObjects[2]

        if oPlayer.x <= oStar.x and
           oStar.x <= oPlayer.x + oPlayer.width and
           (oPlayer.y <= oStar.y and
           oStar.y <= oPlayer.y + oPlayer.height)

                    harvestBonus(oGame,oStar)
                    oGame.remove(oStar.nIndex)
                    upDateEnergy(oGame,20)
        ok # end of if region
    } # end of oGame region
    } # end of f function region

    return f
```

To Be Captured, They Must Be Harvested

Here is how to harvest stars so they move quickly out of the scene:

```
func harvestBonus(oGame,oStar)        # oStar is harvested!

    oGame {
        Sprite {
            file = "images/smstar2.png"       transparent=true
            x = oStar.x        y=oStar.y
            scaled = true
            width=oStar.width
            height=oStar.height
```

```
                point=800
                direction=GE_DIRECTION_INC      nStep = 15
        }
    }
```

Your Score, Updated

Here is how to update a score:

```
func updateScore(oGame,n)       # INSIDE PLAYER STATE
    oGame {
            nScore += n
             if nScore = nMaxScore { gameOver(oGame) }

            for obj in aObjects
                    if classname(obj)="text" and
                      obj.type = GE_TYPE_SCORE
                            s = 0 + obj.text
                            s += n
                            obj.text = "" + ceil(s)
                            exit
                    end # end if if region
            end # end of for region

    } # end of oGame region
```

Play Again or Quit?

Here is how to ask for another game:

```
func replayOrQuit_f()
    f = func oGame, OSelf, nKey {
            if nKey = KEY_ESC
                    oGame.shutdown()
```

```
        but nkey = KEY_SPACE
                oGame.refresh()
                replay(oGame)
        ok
    }

    return f
```

Sure, I Want to Play Again!

Here is how to start another game:

```
func replay(oGame)
    nScore = 0
    nEnergy = 100
    play(oGame)
```

Game Over!

Here is how to end the game:

```
func gameOver(oGame)
    oGame {
        oGame.refresh()

        // BACKGROUND
        Sprite
        {
            type = GE_TYPE_BACKGROUND
            file = "images/stars.jpg"
            x = -300      y = -200
            animate = false
        }
```

```
Text
{
text = "NEXT LEVEL?"
size = 70        color = rgb(0,0,0)
file = "fonts/pirulen.ttf"
x = 65        y = 255
animate = false
}

Text {
text = "NEXT LEVEL?"
animate = true
size = 70        color = rgb(255,255,255)
file = "fonts/pirulen.ttf"
x = 60        y = 250
animate = false

keypress = replayOrQuit_f()
}
}
```

If you have reached this point, then you deserve this gift: any game can be run in full-screen by adding this simple statement in the main function just after loading the GameEngine.ring library and before creating the Game window:

```
GE_FULLSCREEN = TRUE
```

Also, you can set GE_SCREEN_W and GE_SCREEN_H constants to whatver size you want for your game screen, before creating the game object:

```
GE_SCREEN_W = 800
GE_SCREEN_H = 600
```

Nothing is required to make your game playable using USB joysticks, controllers, and gamepads. In fact, the Game Engine maps their buttons automatically to the keyboard keys so you don't need to change anything in your code!

Beyond Gaming, Video Games Culture

I told you at the beginning of the chapter that the skills you will gain in making video games will make you a distinguished programmer. Now, at the end of the chapter, I would like to tell you that video games as a cultural medium convey a system of meaning around dreams and virtual reality, social dynamics and sociability, and immersion and interactivity. In fact, they can turn anyone from a technical gamer to a distinguished human being.

So far, games have been considered to be a symptom of addictive consumption, a destroyer of social connections, and a noisy combine harvester of family time. Gamers themselves have been regarded as second-order nocturnal citizens inhabiting their closed virtual worlds and sadly disconnected from reality.

Humanity in this digital era is seen as a victim of its own dogmas: screen time can make your eyesight worse, games can lead to attention problems, action games can turn your kids to violence, and so on.

However, in her TED talk called "Your Brain on Video Games,"[23] Daphne Bavelier, a brain scientist specializing in measuring the impact of technology on the brain, demonstrates that video games can result in better learning, more focused attention, and enhanced vision. In particular, action gamers are good at resolving visual conflicts, tracking moving objects, maintaining attention for long time, and performing multitask switching.

In addition, as promoted by Daniel Muriel and Garry Crawford in their book[24] *Video Games as Culture: Considering the Role and Importance of Video Games in Contemporary Society*, games are more than a medium; they are the cultural lens through which we get a fresh and dogma-free understanding of our social life: "Drawing on empirical data – including interviews with gamers, as well as key representatives from the video game industry, media, education, and cultural sector – authors do not only consider contemporary video game culture, but also explore how video games provide important insights into the modern nature of digital and participatory culture, patterns of consumption and identity formation, late modernity, and contemporary political rationalities."

Video games are pervasive. There is a whole set of humanity living with them and inside them, spending hundreds of thousands of hours of playtime every day, and generating a lot of feelings, actions, reflections, conversations, and contributions to the world economy. It's time to go beyond common assumptions and try to look at gaming from a totally new cultural perspective.

---

[23]https://www.youtube.com/watch?v=FktsFcooIG8
[24]https://www.taylorfrancis.com/books/9781315622743

Gaming and gamification are used today not only in entertainment but also in management, development and poverty mitigation, peace building, and conflict resolution. Hence, game worlds are designed to model the complex situation at hand and to provide an opportunity to play with some if-then scenarios to forge better understanding and decision-making.

As far as we are concerned as programmers, gamification can be used to better understand what programming really is. In fact, most of the root causes of the software crisis reside in the low-quality computer code that programmers are crafting with millions of LOC every day. This problem of quality is driven essentially by a lack of understanding of the complex nature of programming. Overly simplistic texts, the easyfication[25] of marketing discourse, and toolset- and syntax-oriented programming curriculums are contributing to this crisis and preventing the emergence of a generation of great programmers!

No one can be happy about such a situation, but this is the brutal truth of today's computer programming economy where tons of programmers are pushed into the market every day without a convenient framework of understanding and an expert-level reference of the necessary skillset.

In the next and last chapter of the book, I will provide a modest contribution to the software industry about what is lacking today in crafting great programming minds: a brand new framework for understanding and learning programming based on gamification, along with the skillset every learning program, be it institutional or personal, should target in the first place.

If you feel like you are not interested, then you can leave the book right now: you have acquired everything you need to be a good programmer in Ring. But if you think that your next goal is to evolve from a good to a great programmer, then please continue to Chapter 9.

Whatever you decide, listen to these gamers,[26] and if they convince you, then you may find meaning in becoming a culture-aware game programmer, with a strong motivation to make your next sublime video game in Ring.

---

[25]Don't look in any dictionary. This a new word I just invented as a critic of the marketing discourse in the technology domain that claims that everything is easy to learn and easy to work with!

[26]https://www.youtube.com/watch?v=E2o0e5onDtw

CHAPTER 9

A Gamified Foundation for Mastering Ring

What is the difference between a good programmer and a master programmer—a guru, we say? The answer is technical expertise.

Good programmers target a certain level of technical expertise, and when they reach that level, they are happy to stay there, either maintaining it or extending it with yet another area of expertise. They earn good salaries and deserve professional recognition, while contributing actively to the advancement of the software economy.

Master programmers are the technical experts in programming, but all technical experts are not master programmers. There is an additional dimension masters bring to the table with their skills and beliefs: they understand the complexity of programming as a sociotechnical assemblage and as a changing system, and they are here to convey a humanized message through their programming journey.

Being a master in programming is not a qualification you get from a prestigious industrial organization or a job you obtain in a world-class software company. It's a personal decision, a lifelong project you undertake so that your contribution to the human knowledge of computer programming becomes the ultimate goal for your entire life.

A master programmer isn't limited to "mastering code" but instead "masters" every aspect of the programming system in the course of their real-world, customer-facing experience with programming: requirements analysis, solution design, software architecture, code crafting and refactoring, security and performance monitoring, user interface design, change management, team conflict resolution, and many, many other skills.

Therefore, if you decide to become a programming master, prepare yourself to answer a number of questions: How can I write clean and beautiful code responsibly? How can I think algorithmically to solve problems with elegance? How should I energize my teammates to make better programs? How do I find the right equilibrium

© Mansour Ayouni 2020
M. Ayouni, *Beginning Ring Programming*, https://doi.org/10.1007/978-1-4842-5833-0_9

between passion and professionalism in my programming job? How do I understand programming itself, as a formal discipline and as a social system, and model its multidimensional nature consistently in my mind? How can I talk about programming clearly and deeply so others can escape from any kind of blind-men-and-the-elephant parable? Are there any assumptions about programming that should be challenged, any dogmas to be clarified, and any established learning paradigms to revolutionize?

The chapter is my essay on providing radical, scientifically based, and by-experience answers to these four major questions:

- Why is programming so complex, and what are the minimal expert-level skills we need to forge to master the art of crafting code?

- How can we tell the story of programming in an engaging and instructive way, and how can we better understand it?

- Are there any conceptually ludic tools that help us master the metacoding facets of programming to manage the change of computer programs and to control the performance of a programming team?

- What are the rules of thumb someone can follow to become engaged in, seriously and securely, in a programming mastery journey?

I have divided the chapter into four main sections, each related to one of these questions, and a conclusion, which contains my final words to you in the book.

The section "Programming: Toward a New Metaphor" unveils the root cause of software complexity and low-quality computer code: the predominant "construction" (or "building") metaphor. It then proposes a new framework for understating programming by embracing a gaming metaphor and explains the metaphor's rationale, expressive power, and ability to solve the accumulated drawbacks of software construction. I conclude this section with a reference skillset that any programmer should target. The skillset will serve as a basis for the learning experience in the chapter that you can use as a guideline for becoming a master of Ring, or any other programming language you prefer.

The section "Ringoria, the Programming Land of Ring" develops a complete fantasy world, called Ringorialand, based on the gaming metaphor and aligns it to the Ring programming language. Thus, the story of programming is told, maybe for the first time, by combining the rigor of systemic thinking with the magic of virtual worlds and the interactivity of gaming. You will understand not only the symbolic constructs you use every day in the programming language in a totally new way (data structures are water, functions are sand, algorithms are recipes, the computer is a millstone, delivery is a trip made by two lovers to the mountain of lights, lights are the customer requirements, and so on), but also the humanized atmosphere in which the programming project happens, the technosocial problems that arise, and the tedious software delivery workflow that is performed.

The section "In the Pocket of Every Ringler," where Ringler is the name we give to the Ring master in our fantasy world, I will show you the tools you need to know to master the facets of programming that are not related directly to code. You'll learn, among other things, how to measure changing requirements and how to assess their impact on your own performance and the overall performance of your programming team.

Finally, in the section "Rules of the Game," I give you my advice from the lessons I have learned over three decades of my relationship with programming.

Unlike the previous chapters, this one contains almost no program code, only narration. Still, it contains a lot of visuals and profound discussions about you, the programmer, and what you do, the programming. If you are not used to such discussions, this is your opportunity to take a step back from your code editor and contribute to reflections on what you are, how you code, and the way you learn.

By the end of this chapter, you will have a new set of knowledge and will be on the way to becoming a master Ringler, in other words, a master in Ring programming.[1]

---

[1] I hope you will enjoy this chapter as much as I enjoyed writing it, even if you may find it somewhat hard to understand or even profound. I decided to include it in this book because of a question from my daughter: "What are you talking about in this book, Dad? Can you tell me the story of this thing, programming?" Therefore, the map of the island later in this chapter was initially designed by my daughter Teeba and extended by myself, and the fantasy characters were composed based on the visual taste of Haneen, her sister. Cherihen, my wife, contributed by recording the song you can hear when we come to meet Princess Ringaliza, the singer of the Ringza storz. They all helped me as my first "test" readers of the story and made dozens of constructive suggestions. The chapter is therefore somewhat a family effort, and I hope you'll be an integral part of it. If you are happy with the result, use it to tell the story of programming to your kids, your computer science students, and the beginner members of your programming team.

Nine Things You Will Learn

In this chapter, you'll do the following:

- Understand the complex nature of programming

- Understand how a building/construction metaphor contributes to this complexity

- Understand how gamification enhances the process of learning programming

- Tell the story of programming using the gamified fantasy world of Ringorialand

- Get an immersive experience by looking to the Ring programming language and its components using the lens of Ringorialand

- Identify the minimal necessary skills to evolve from a good to a master programmer

- Assess the importance of visual thinking and storytelling in learning programming

- Understand the metacode's social and emotional dimensions of programming

- Design a personalized mastery-capacity building program to learn programming

Programming: Toward a New Metaphor

As a programmer, your mission is to "construct" software programs using computer code, usually as a response to a customer demand. From defining a program's goal to delivering it as an executable application, so many tasks enter into play. They are multiple, diversified, interdependent, and complex tasks. I won't tell you in a sentence what they are; the whole chapter will cover this. But I can tell you what program "construction" isn't: simply sequencing lines of code and alternating them with `if`s and `then`s and bunch of `for` and `while` loops.

Still, defining what program construction is raises a big question about the versatility of the dominant "building" metaphor used so far by the software industry to design programs and teach programming. Although a huge advancement in software quality has been made over decades, the promdiminace of the problem of poor computer code in our software projects invites us to think of a better paradigm.

First, I discuss how programming is approached nowadays and critique the dominant "building" metaphor. Then, I analyze the problem of poor computer code quality and show how it is actually enforced by the large adoption of that metaphor. I argue that the existing programming metaphor of construction is the root cause of all problems in software. Next, I propose a strategy for solving those problems, at the root level. I use a gaming metaphor for programming and demonstrate its ability to embrace the solution strategy I have designed. Finally, I conclude by sharing a target skillset of programming, called Table Complete.

A Critic of the "Construction" Metaphor

The software industry has been promoting the metaphor of program "construction" for long time. Programs are associated with buildings, programmers with builders, and program architecture with a building blueprint. Programs are thought to be formed of pieces of code like walls are formed from pieces of stones.

In his influential book *Code Complete*,[2] Steve McConnell argues that the image of "building" software is more useful than that of "writing" or "growing" software. The following list, as compiled by Christopher Ross in his excellent series of articles[3] reviewing and summarizing *Code Complete*, highlights some of the helpful similarities between building construction and software construction:

- The size of the project increases the amount of planning needed.

- The foundation and framework are developed first.

- Core structures/components are added to the frame.

---

[2]McConnell's *Code Complete* book is a bible of constructing code. I advise anyone who is serious about a programming career to put it in a privileged place on their bookshelf. Exhaustive, clear, and practical, McConnell's book has filled in many gaps in my programming skills. My critic of the construction metaphor shouldn't be understood as a message to ignore such foundational books but as a directive to find answers to some unanswered questions. I'll talk more about that later in the section where I propose you look at programming from a new perspective and later in the chapter when I explore the systemic and social nature of programming.

[3]https://tinyurl.com/y2bt2sxh

- Fine-tuning and optimization occur after the core structures are built.

- You often don't need to re-create/build things that are already built (e.g., bathroom fixtures in construction or existing libraries or interface classes in software).

- Regular inspections should occur throughout the process.

- Large projects often need to be over-engineered because the cost of failure is high.

- Similarly, the larger the project, the more elaborate the planning process and the greater the need for technical and managerial controls.

Despite the maturity and wide acceptance of this paradigm and despite the huge value that the "construction" viewpoint brings to the skills of any programmer, there is room to ask: is software really like building? I don't think so.

In its infancy, programming emerged with a more natural metaphor: writing. A programmer is a writer, and programs are written using a programming language providing the words, syntax, and semantics necessary to create a "constructive" dialogue between humans and the computer. Programming is then a synonym of creating, not structuring, and of communicating, not implementing. Such a paradigm remains vibrant nowadays but only at the algorithmic level. In fact, it proved to be inefficient in the case of large programs and industrial component-based and distributed software architectures.

In my opinion, this insufficiency isn't a result of an inherent weakness in the writing metaphor but in the amount of effort dispensed in making it useful on a large scale. Industrialization, normalization, and globalization all played a key role in changing the focus from the "writing" to "building" idea. The market economy influenced software designers who are paid to enforce externalization, reusability, and interoperability of n-tier, component-based, service-oriented, and micro-service-oriented software.

There are many issues I can cite about the building metaphor and its questionable ability to represent the complex idea of software.

- Buildings are static and don't change over time, while software does change.

- Buildings are finite product; software is never complete.

- Buildings rely on a well-defined creation process and are made from known quantifiable entrants; software relies on data that is a fuzzy thing at every level: input, processing, and output.

- A building is delivered with zero tolerance for any visible issues; no software is ever delivered totally bug-free.

- Unless the house is damaged by a force majeure, it remains fully functional 12 months per year 7 days per week; software can break anytime, every second, and usually for unpredictable reasons.

When it comes to learning programming, this is where the construction mental framework is full of weaknesses. Its main drawback is that it enforces the illusion of mastering the bull by simply maintaining its horns, osculating all the differences we mentioned earlier.

Because my mission in this book is to start you on your first steps on the path to mastering Ring, I can't leave you imprisoned in this programming as construction metaphor.

If you reflect on the previous chapters, you will find that I used the "code-as-a-construction" idea only when we worked on the modularity value of our programs (algorithm composition and program structure), especially when we streamlined the data acquisition architecture in Chapters 3 and 4.

But our focus on code construction has always been augmented by two other dimensions: "code-as-a-story," when I immersed you in the little worlds of Maiga and Foumakoye, for example, and "code-as-a-game," when I challenged you, sometimes pushed you willingly in a wrong direction, and left you to your destiny to complete some tasks.

Each of the three dimensions of the programming world ("code-as-a-structure" (or as construction if you prefer), "code-as-story," and "code-as-a-game") adds a unique value to your coding experience, respectively: modularity, expressiveness, and immersion.

These are the three values I see in modern programming, and Table 9-1 presents them from the perspective of three organic players of any computer program: code itself, the data transformed by the code, and the user as an ultimate beneficiary of that code.

Table 9-1. *Howt the Construction Metaphor Fits into a Limited Part of the Programming Landsape*

Immersion	Code-as-a-Game	Simulated Worlds	Augmented User Interfaces
Expressiveness	Code-as-a-story	Data semantics	Conversational user interfaces
Modularity	Code-as-a-construction	Data model	Graphical user interfaces
Dimension/Player	Code	Data	User

Looking to the first intersection cell (at the bottom left of the table), we immediately capture where the predominant building metaphor can really play well (in designing modular code) and where it doesn't (in all the remaining cells). For now, we need just to focus on the "Code" column and ask, what do storytelling and gaming have to do with software programming? A lot, really. In a few words, they help us design expressive and learnable code for the first, "code-as-story," and realize an engaging and immersive programming experience for the second, "code-as-a-game."

By design, a story is a narrative recall of the conflictual relations between actors, events, places, and resources during a given period of time. It has the power to represent abstract ideas in a situation and communicate valuable information by projecting the ideas inside a comprehensive and emotionally engaging scenario.

Gamification, on the other hand, is the best way to explore complex domains by experimentation and learning by doing. When it is well done, it maximizes the learner's immersion in the program world and turns the journey into a fascinating discovery and learning experience.

Clearly, learning how to program needs to be approached differently with a radically new metaphor. But this won't be useful if it is not made, by design, to overcome the drawbacks of the current one, the construction metaphor, and if it does not define a framework for solving them. The question then is, what are the problems caused by the building metaphor and how they can be solved?

The Problem of Software Construction

Poor software quality can be explained by a large number of factors. Some of them are obvious: bad user experience, unusable features, security, and performance issues, to cite just a few. If we dig a bit deeper, there is also buggy and complex code. Still all of these are more symptoms than real causes. Building our programs upon complex software architectures, inefficient data models, or vague customer requirements and unrealistic estimates is more the root cause explaining these symptoms See Figure 9-1.[4]

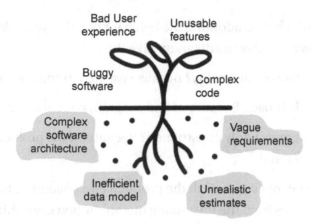

Figure 9-1. *Root causes explain the symptoms, but how can we identify them?*

In the software domain, unlike medicine, where it is easy to understand the difference between treating the symptom of pain and curing its cause, one can quickly get confused between surface causes and deeper roots. Like medicine, however, any wrong decision based on a wrong assessment puts the health of the body/software system at risk.

For many years, I have been designing problem trees in many domains (health, water scarcity, peace building, digital divide, institutional performance...) for governments and international foundations based on system thinking and the root-cause analysis (RCA) methodology.[5] This is a complex discipline that requires a deep knowledge of the domain, an evidence-based process, and many iterations of error and correction. In this section, I guide you step-by-step you through the problem tree of poor software quality, going from the problem of "bad software construction" to the root cause of "inadequate construction metaphor." Along the way, we will jump on the valuable opportunity of unveiling some of the hidden programming problems that are uncommon to talk about in the programming community but play a decisive role in the software crisis. See Figure 9-2.

---

[4]Image taken from the Noun Project web site at `https://tinyurl.com/v62ggtq`.

[5]Among other methods and tools, I use the RCA software tool from NASA (`https://nsc.nasa.gov/RCAT`) and the Apollo RCA methodology from RealityCharthing.com.

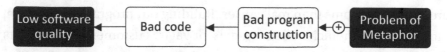

Figure 9-2. *A high-level problem tree of the software construction problem*

Going from left to right and adopting the behavior of a five-year-old child, we ask a "Why?" question in every box of the diagram. Like this:

- Why is software of low quality? Because we are writing bad code.

- Why our code is bad? Because of bad program construction.

- Why are programs badly constructed? Because of the problem of the building metaphor.

The point is that the root cause of all the problems we encounter today regarding software quality emanates from the unsuitable metaphor that everything is built on. If we don't tackle the roots of the problem by inventing a new metaphor, we will continue constructing bad code and build more low-quality software.

Let's develop the + icon in Figure 9-2 to show you the cascading route from "Bad software construction" to the root cause "Problem of metaphor." Let's ask ourselves again: why are our software creations badly constructed these days? There are five factors to answer this: misunderstanding of requirements, weak technical mastery, inability to cope with change, bad social environment, and fragile emotional readiness. See Figure 9-3.

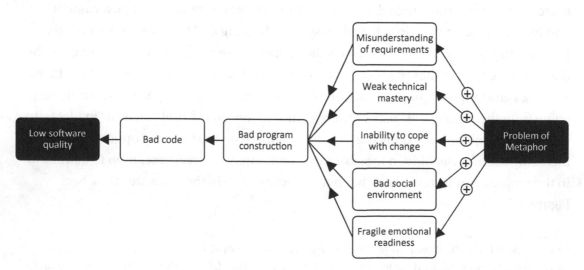

Figure 9-3. *Five factors explaining why programs are poorly constructed*

At this level, it is interesting to read the problem tree from right to left. Assuming that the problem of the construction metaphor is the source of all problems, then we can say that the building metaphor limits our ability to understand customer requirements, forge technical expertise, cope with change, ensure a sane social environment, and forge active emotional readiness for programming. Some propositions are strong enough, but some aren't yet. Never mind, as long as we are going to develop the problem tree, things will become even more straightforward.

In Figure 9-4, I show the tree view of each of the five factors, but for the sake of brevity, I will comment only on the second one, "weak technical mastery," which corresponds to the scope of this chapter and, by extension, of the entire book.

The first cause of "bad program construction" is a misunderstanding of the customers' requirements. Digging deeper into the problem tree reveals why this is the case. In particular, the building metaphor root cause is responsible for "a problem of understanding," which in turn explains all the problems in between, all the way back to "requirements misunderstanding."

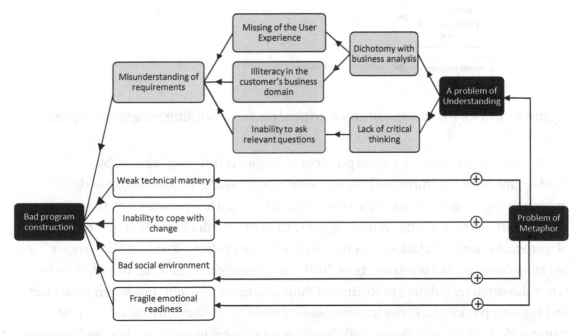

Figure 9-4. *There is a "problem of understanding" resulting from the root problem of the construction metaphor and contributing to the problem of requirements misuderstanding*

The second factor is "weak technical mastery." The problem tree in Figure 9-5 shows its five causes: unfamiliarity with modeling techniques, weakness in problem solving, poor knowledge of the programming language, lack of code expressiveness, nonmastery of programming tools, and, finally, hard-to-refactor, inflexible code.

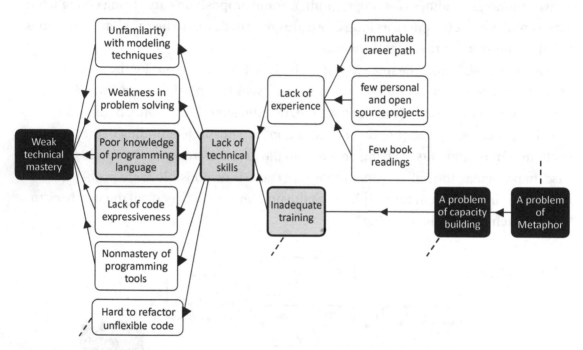

Figure 9-5. *The tree demonstrates a critical path in building programming skills.*

As you can see, there is a main problem of "capacity building" caused by (and augmenting the impact of) the root-cause problem. "Poor knowledge of the programming language" sits at the edge of the critical path represented by the thin strokes. But poor knowledge is nothing more than the result of the inadequate training of a programmer and a lack of experience in software projects. Because "Experience" is not something we can teach in a book (with rare exceptions[6]), all what we can do is to target the capacity building problem and think of a more relevant programming skillset and training paradigm. Those training assets should be as disruptive as the mental framework used for their design and should embrace new ideas other than building and constructing.

---

[6]Every idea in this book comes from real-world experience.

The last three factors are the inability to cope with change, a bad social environment, and fragile emotional readiness. See Figure 9-6.

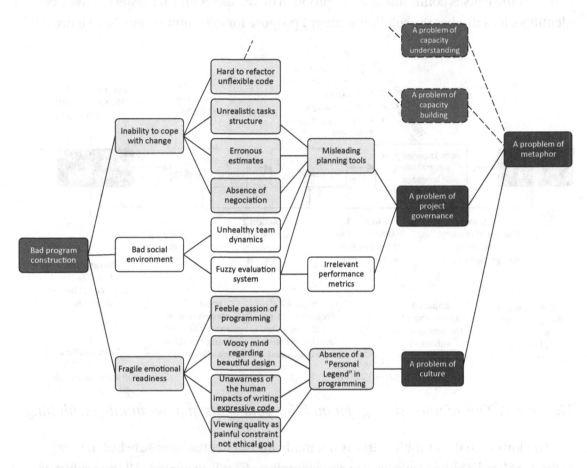

Figure 9-6. *Two supplementary descendants of the metaphor problem: culture and systemic project governance*

Just because we're not discussing all of them now doesn't mean they can be ignored. Be sure that these "soft" problems do not have "hard" impacts on your technical capacity in writing code. We will take just a second to discuss the problem of "Absence of personal legend in programming."

As defined by the Brazilian writer Paulo Coelho in his famous novel *The Alchemist*, a *personal legend* is, simply put, the act of achieving one's destiny. While personal legends differ from person to person, a personal legend is fulfilled by embarking on an educational journey and realizing the full importance of one's own significance in relation to the universe.

Design of a Solution Strategy

Now that the causes contributing to the problem of "Weak technical mastery" have been identified, let's discuss the solution strategy I propose for alleviating them. See Figure 9-7.[7]

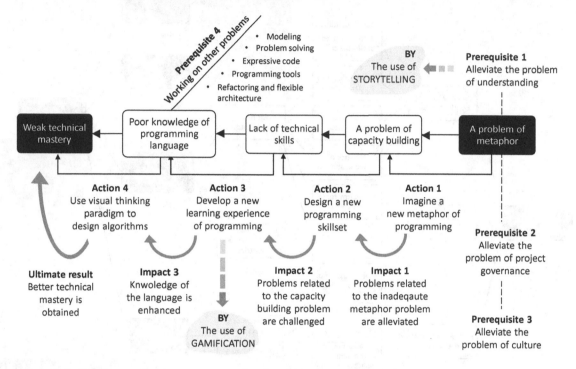

Figure 9-7. *Our solution strategy for building your skills in programming with Ring*

You know what? A problem tree is not made for intellectual pleasure but to solve at the root level. When we do so, a positive domino effect is expected. All the problems we analyzed in the section form potential points of enhancement you should target strategically with a continuous lifelong capacity-building effort.[8] In Figure 9-7, I propose that you undertake these strategic actions:

---

[7]In the jargon of international foundations, this is called a *logical framework* or simply a *logframe*. For each problem, there is strategic action (or more) with an expected impact. The accumulation of intermediary impacts leads to the ultimate result.

[8]In this chapter, I'm adopting the "strategic learner" approach, which I define as the will to profoundly master the subject of learning by understanding its multidimensional nature, rethinking its established assumptions, and innovating its paradigms, methods, content, and tools of learning. The strategic learner is aware of the effort he should invest in learning, targets higher levels of expertise, and takes advantage of the wide variety of human knowledge available in relation with the subject, directly or indirectly.

- Adopt a new metaphor, the gaming metaphor, which better represents the complex and systemic nature of computer programming.

- Work on the alleviation of all the first-class problems directly influenced by the change of metaphor including, but not limited to, the problem of capacity building.

- For the problem of capacity building, design a new skillset whose content is extracted from the articulation of problems in the problem tree and less from conventional online trainings, programming language help systems, and textbooks.

- Once the skillset is designed, develop a new learning experience based on storytelling, discovery, and gamification.

- In particular, embrace algorithmic design using a visual thinking paradigm.

This said, I will now tell you why gaming can be a better metaphor for learning programming.

Gaming as a New Metaphor for Programming

When I decided to craft a new metaphor for programming,[9] I began asking myself, what is a metaphor? And what is programming itself so I can think of a metaphor for it?

Defining the Word *Metaphor*

In Iraq, if one says to his neighbor, "What is your color today?" then the neighbor would probably respond, "I'm fine, and you?"

---

[9]...for all the good reasons we exposed in the previous section, but mainly because I feel responsible for providing the best possible learning experience for a beautiful programming language like Ring!

More to the north, in the Tea Land, a metaphoric name of the multicultural zone around the Kurdish Tigris, "it's hard to imagine breakfasts, business meetings, haggling around carpets in the traditional old market or ferries without tea. Whether you drink it in a Turkish coffee shop decorated with colored pillows or sitting on a carpet in a Kurdish house, you will always find it present."[10]

In *The Poetics*, Aristotle[11] teaches us that metaphor consists of "transporting the meaning of a different word either from genus to species or from species to genus, or by analogy." When for Cicero,[12] "If the language does not provide a term to express something, the metaphor become the tool by which we will find elsewhere what we lack."

Merriam-Webster defines a *metaphor* as "a figure of speech in which a word or phrase denoting one kind of object or action is used in place of another to suggest a likeness or analogy between them." In simple English, adds `litrarydevices.net`, "When you portray a person, place, thing, or an action as being something else, even though it is not actually that something else, you are speaking metaphorically."

In popular music, Elvis Presley describes his sweetheart as a hound dog that won't leave him alone: "You ain't nothin' but a hound dog. Quit snoopin' 'round my door." The same metaphor is used by old Arabic people when they describe a friend who is exceptionally faithful by saying "He is faithful like a dog."

Religious texts and records, from Judaism to Christianism to Islam to Buddhism, are also a rich source of metaphors. In such a critical context, whether the metaphors used to explain these reference texts are good or bad makes as a huge difference as the difference between tolerance and fanaticism and between peace and war.

---

[10]Translated from Arabic from `https://tinyurl.com/y2bwgqbn`.

[11]Aristotle (384 BC–322 BC) was a Greek philosopher during the Classical period in Ancient Greece, the founder of the Lyceum and the Peripatetic school of philosophy and Aristotelian tradition. Along with his teacher Plato, he has been called the Father of Western Philosophy. His writings cover many subjects including physics, biology, zoology, metaphysics, logic, ethics, aesthetics, poetry, theater, music, rhetoric, psychology, linguistics, economics, politics, and government. Aristotle provided a complex synthesis of the various philosophies existing prior to him, and it was from his teachings that the West inherited its intellectual lexicon, as well as problems and methods of inquiry. As a result, his philosophy has exerted a unique influence on almost every form of knowledge in the West, and it continues to be a subject of contemporary philosophical discussion.

[12]Marcus Tullius Cicero (106 BC–43 BC) was a Roman statesman, orator, lawyer, and philosopher who introduced the Romans to the chief schools of Greek philosophy and created a Latin philosophical vocabulary such us evidentia, humanitas, qualitas, quantitas, and essential. —Wikipedia

In the Arabic language, there is an interesting family of "Majaaz" (metaphor) called "Mursal" (expanded) because the relation between the word we spell and the meaning we have in our head for it is a logically typed relation. The following are some examples of these relations that will serve as a helper inspiration in designing our upcoming new metaphor:

- Partial metaphor, if the spoken word is part of the target meaning. Example: "We sent an eye to observe the enemy." What is sent is a whole person, not only his eye.

- Total metaphor, if the first is containing the second. Example: "India performed a water revolution in irrigation by harvesting the rain." It is impossible to harvest all the rain but only a portion of it.

- Causal, if the first is a cause of the second. Example: "I own a small tearoom. Every morning I open the door of gain." When I go at work, I open the door and wait for customers so I can make money.

In cognitive linguistics, conceptual metaphors refer to the understanding of a conceptual domain in terms of another. The two famous examples usually cited here are the metaphor of money used to express time ("You spent all the time I gave you") and the metaphor of directionality to express quantity ("Prices are rising in crazy jumps in Tunisia in 2019!").

Building on this wide variety of instructive material, we can forge a definition that is suitable for our own purpose of finding a representative metaphor for programming. Thus, we define *metaphor* as a symbolic representation of a complex real-world system that is simple enough to help us understand its main structure and functions, learn them, and reason about them. Concretely, this symbolic representation is a mapping between two conceptual domains, "programming" and "gaming" in our case, conveying a meaning to every source element in terms of its corresponding target element. A subset of the symbolic mapping we will use to develop the "gaming" metaphor in the next part of the chapter will be introduced here, just to stimulate your sense of imagination, as shown in Table 9-2.

Table 9-2. *A Sample Mapping Between Programing and the Gaming Metaphor*

Programming	Gaming
Programming domain	Game theme
Programming rules	Game mechanics
Programming	Playing
Programming experience	Gameplay
Data	Water
Functions	Sand
Computer	Millstone

A complete picture of the new metaphor will be presented later in the chapter so you can see what relates data to water and functions to sand. Next, we tackle a more difficult subject: defining programming!

Defining *Programming*

As you probably know, *programming* is the activity of making programs. A program, in any domain, is a structured plan to define the scope of work, the logical steps necessary for its completion, and the time it takes to execute it. In Tunisia, we usually ask a friend, "What is your program for tonight?" to see if we can go together to a public café and watch a match of the Tunisian football team. In computer science, a program is the plan in a programming language so the machine can follow it to transform some data inputs to new data outputs.

This is the ubiquitous definition of programming you will find everywhere, with more or less deviation. Still, it is a simplistic definition hiding the cognitive, social, and emotional aspects of programming as a human activity.[13] Defining programming in a way that reveals its complexity and its sensitivity to human mental capacity, physical fatigue, management decisions, a programmer's emotional readiness, and team social dynamics is an obligation in crafting any successful metaphor.

---

[13]I am pleading for a programming science discipline that is independent from computer science and that focuses on the systemic nature of programming and reveals the impact of its social and emotional dynamics on the performance of programmers and the quality of software.

Based on my hand-on experience in various software projects, programming, as a whole system, resembles Figure 9-8.

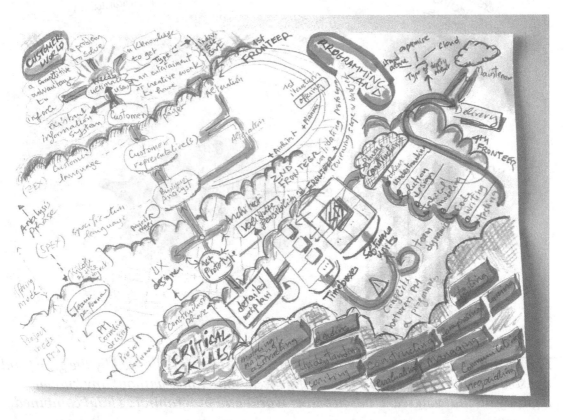

Figure 9-8. *The complexity of programming domain: several frontiers between the customer world and the programming land and inside the programming land itself, many actors and types of activities, many social dynamics, and a number of critical skills!*

If this has given you a visual shock, then you've captured the first dimension of programming: complexity!

The picture isn't that difficult to comprehend, though. In intentionally simplistic words and a few mechanical steps, Figure 9-9 shows what I suggest you keep in mind for now.

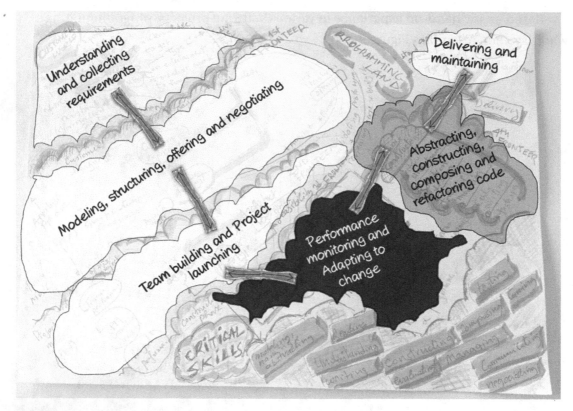

Figure 9-9. *The scope of this book, writing code itself, is delimited by the gray (and not so dark) lake to the right, but is influenced, sometimes without any known logic, by all that you see in the customer world and programming land combined*

I left the skills zone at the bottom uncommented because it will be the subject of our concluding section. Now, let's ask ourselves an innocent question: where are the complexity zones situated in Figure 9-9? Everywhere. Some of the places are more prone to generate trouble than others, especially at the Heartland (dark) area of "performance monitoring and adapting to change."

In geostrategy, we learn from Mackinder[14] that the Heartland (a landlocked region of central Eurasia) is the most important territory on Earth. The power that controls it, in the 20th century, will dominate the world. Similarly, mustering change in programming is what determines its failure or success. The first was complexity; change is then the second dimension of programming.

---

[14]Mackinder, a English geographer (1861–1947), known as the father of geopolitics.

If you take a look back at our problem tree in the first section, an inability to cope with change is caused by inflexible and hard to refactor code but mainly by misleading planning tools. In concrete words, when there is a mapping between the time structure of your programming tasks (timeboxes in Figure 9-10) and the structure of written code (software units in the same figure), all the unwanted guests are welcomed to your programming party.

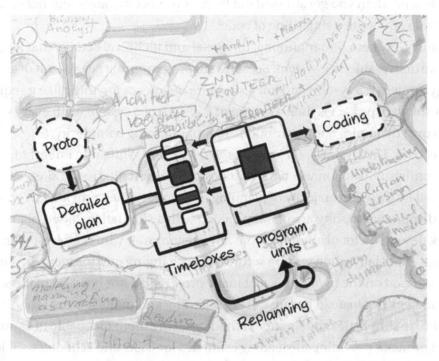

Figure 9-10. *The source of struggle in software projects is planning: planning tools suppose a simplistic relation between a unit of work and a containing timebox, which is never verified, because the same unit of work jumps by force of circumstances inside many timeboxes*

As a programmer who is paid to provide concrete code, you are all the time under the pressure of a bunch of "corrective" decisions of your initial plan (replanning in Figure 9-10) because a new requirement has emerged, a quality issue became intolerable, or a member of the team has suddenly retired.[15]

---

[15]The last time this happened to me was in 2018, when I was about to sign a big contract with a private school in Tunisia and received a message on Facebook about a developer retiring.

A serious problem we have in our software domain is that project planning is based on the same mental constructs of the 1950s supposing that a project can be modeled by a plan and the plan itself materialized by a Gantt chart. This is something you can't change, as a programmer, since nobody will take you seriously these days when criticizing PMP,[16] Scrum,[17] or even Microsoft Project. Still, you need to be aware of the problem because you want to face it when you lose your peace of mind during an electric team meeting or when you get stressed out by your project manager and become unable to concentrate and write a single line of code!

Software is a system. Programming, the social and technical activity that leads to the software deliverable, is a system. So, software programming is a system of a system. By analogy, project is a system and not a structure of tasks or anything like a sequential process. A software project is then a system of a system of a system, with every system hosting its own dynamics and contributing to programming complexity.

In their book *The Dynamic Progress Method*,[18] J. Chris White and Robert M. Sholtes went from criticism to action when they proposed an alternative to the classic CPM[19] method used by the wide majority of planning tools today. They provided us with a systemized approach to software planning along with a simulation-based planning tool. Their work deserves a lot of attention from any programmer who is interested in coping with change, especially when writing software in a changing environment. In a nutshell, their idea is based on the hypothesis that many projects fail not because of the skills of project managers but instead because of the planning and management tools they use. These tools use simplistic models and methods, making them incapable of capturing reality and prone to providing misleading estimates for costs and schedules. "It is like aiming a gun through a fuzzy scope; the chances of hitting the target are very slim." Figure 9-11 illustrates the project system as modeled by the authors.[20]

---

[16]PMP: Project Management Professional certification delivered by the Project Management Institute (pmi.org).

[17]Scrum: An iterative project management method defining roles, events, and rules that bind them together.

[18]The book based on their research is called *Agent-Based Simulation for Project Management*; see `http://tinyurl.com/y4bk3hhh`.

[19]The critical path method (CPM) is used to plan a project by defining each necessary step in it and estimating how long each will take. The goal is to prevent the kind of bottlenecks that can plague any complex plan, according to F. John Reh, in TheBalance (`https://tinyurl.com/yxczthlo`).

[20]Many thanks to Chris White for kindly allowing us to use his visual.

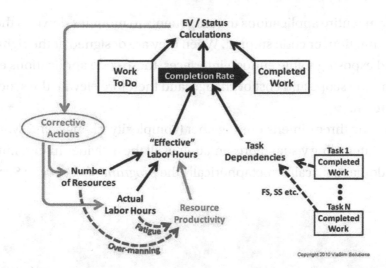

Figure 9-11. *A systemic representation of a software project. Management decisions and resource fatigue affect programming completion rate as well as classic task dependencies prone by CPM tools like Microsoft Project*

At this point, let's summarize: unlike *metaphor*, the term *programming* is hard to define. The simplistic definitions largely available today are not satisfying. A deeper look at programming as a system is necessary. This led us to discover the two first dimensions of programming: complexity and change.

The third dimension is synergy. The Cambridge Dictionary defines *synergy* as "the combined power of a group of things when they are working together that is greater than the total power achieved by each working separately." The online dictionary illustrates the subject with this particular sentence: "Teamwork at its best results in a synergy that can be very productive."

What makes a programming team work in synergy? It's the ability for them to share programming resources and reuse the same code at many places in their program. Shared resources and reusable resources are the answer.

Programmatically speaking, the most fundamental shared resource is the program architecture. It is formed from the descriptive models of the program covering its data, logic, and user interface aspects. These models define the foundation of any programming activity and impact the other two dimensions of programming: if the architecture is poorly designed, the software gains in complexity won't be able to cope with change. On top of the architecture, the reusable resources in programming are applications, from entire applications to components to modules down to the minimal reusable class, function, or code snippet. When they are designed at the right level of abstraction and exposing stable enough interfaces, these code applications enable reusability, limit the scope and cost of change, and therefore elevate the synergy of the programming team.

Considering the three dimensions together (complexity, change, and synergy), we can imagine an interesting visual representation of all the activities intervening in the programming domain. I'll call it metaphorically the *programming cube*."[21] See Figure 9-12.

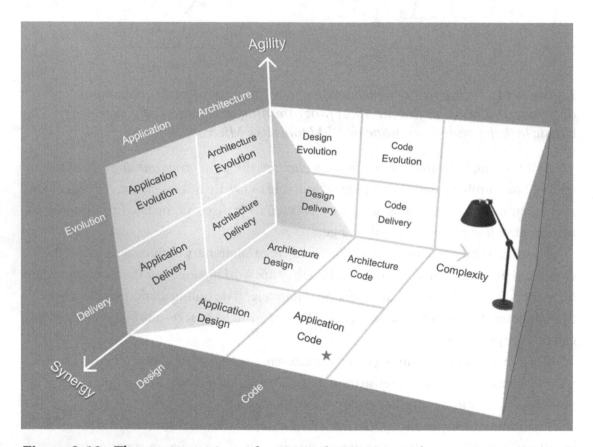

Figure 9-12. *The programming cube: a 360-degree vision of your mission as a programmer*

---

[21]I was inspired to design this visualization by the Enterprise Cube proposed by the CISAR foundation in France in their effort to model the enterprise system. See www.ceisar.org.

For the anecdote, if someone tells you she will finish a course in programming in only 21 days, then all that she will get is a microscopic ★ in the right-bottom cell of the cube.[22] This is not the case with this book, where your programming skills are taken seriously. What you will get is not a total coverage of all the cells of the cube, though, but two major things.

- A good understanding of the complexity of programming and the realistic problems you will encounter every day

- A good mastery of the foundational skills of the art and technique of writing code

It has become clear now that the building metaphor is too simple to model programming complexity. It does not have the required conceptual plasticity to cope with the extremism of its change, the synergy of its resources, and the social choreography of its team dynamic.

What about gaming?

Gaming, as a Programming Metaphor

In a forum in a corner of the Internet,[23] a programmer with the nickname Wallslide posted a story: "Last night I was in my research lab working on a very stubborn bit of software. Things were going my way, and I was feeling pumped up about it. When a lab mate asked what was going on, I explained how I was 'winning' and was surprised when he failed to understand my attitude. I guess I had assumed that people view coding in the same way that I do (I've never really thought about it before). When I'm coding, I feel that I am doing battle with some entity that is trying to prevent me from accomplishing my goal. Each bug that I catch is a thrust, and each unexpected exception is something that I have to parry. It's a very personal and exciting sort of challenge for me to code an application because of the metaphor I use. My lab mate said that he thinks of programs as something that he breeds and that he's the cultivator of the program, gently guiding it toward the endpoint. Another friend describes his programming as 'bending.' He pictures Lego-like pieces on sticks that he then bends together to create his program."

---

[22]This might also be the case of people who think they are programmers because they added a line on their CV with the name of one of a trendy web or mobile programming framework.

[23]https://arstechnica.com/civis/viewtopic.php?t=80085

Then the programmer asked, "What sort of metaphors do you guys have for your programs?"

The following were some of the interesting answers:

- "As a metaphor, I regard programming as constructing a complex machine with lots of axles and gears but without a noisy engine" (by Warmachine).

- "A fair amount of the time, I feel like I'm doing a similar task over and over. Variations of a theme. But when I have interesting problems (or weird bugs), I find it to be like a puzzle or a maze. I feel so good when I discover the answer or am able to fit the pieces together to solve my problem" (by ChrisKa).

- "Are we talking programming or debugging? Programming is like building—you can't 'win' at building. Debugging is like sleuthing—I suppose you can "win" by solving the case" (by R. Daneel Olivaw).

- "Programming is artisanship in the same way as any sort of craftsman does" (by Warrens).

This discussion demonstrates that the lambda programmer is highly conscious of the problem of metaphor but the software industry and research community tend to completely ignore it. In this section, I make my contribution to the discussion. I start by defining what gaming is, and then I explain its symbolic mapping to programming.

Gaming can be defined as the activity of making games, the experience of playing games, or the business of selling games.

A game is a social, intellectual, or physical interaction, made for fun, between two players or more, with one of them at least being a human who competes against a goal in respect to a well-defined and accepted set of rules inside a real or unreal gamified[24] environment.

A game is defined by its theme, story, characters, mechanics, and gameplay.

- The theme represents the background context, in other words, the historical, geographical, and cultural layers the game is happening on.

- The story is the narrative of the game.

---

[24]*Gamification* is the process of applying the game metaphor to a target domain, like programming in our case, so it becomes playable.

- The characters are the actors and creatures carrying out the story of the game.

- The mechanics set the rules of the game.

- The gameplay is the gaming experience of the player of the game toward an ultimate goal.

In programming, the theme is the customer context, the story is the requirement, the characters are the members of the programming team, the mechanics are the functional and technical rules, and the gameplay is the programmer's experience in writing code. The latter includes the algorithmic thinking adopted to solve the problem, the interaction of the programmer with the development environment, and the programmer's interactions with the team.

Like programming, playing happens inside a complex system, the game world. Like with a programmer, the main mission of the player is adaptation to change. Like a programming process, playing relies on a stepped roadmap toward a final goal. Like the human dynamics inside a programming team, gaming establishes a social framework of interactions. Finally, like a programming project, achievement of the game depends on two main factors: the mission complexity and the player performance. When used as a metaphor for programming, gaming is immediately ready for representing every one of the similarities mentioned.

Unlike programming, though, gaming is basically fun,[25] highly interactive, and mentally immersive. To reach its goal, the player usually makes errors to discover the wrong path and adapt its tactic accordingly. Those are missing places in the programming land, and using gaming as a programming metaphor is an opportunity to discover them.

Gaming is a metaphor for programming. But more interestingly, gaming is a metaphor for learning and living.

In an article entitled "The necessity of failure: Gaming as a metaphor for learning and living," published in 2014 in the *Sydney Morning Herald*, James Dominguez explains, "Like most Japanese logic puzzles, the key to success is not just filling in correct answers, but also to eliminate the incorrect ones. While some solutions are obvious, others require the player to make an assumption, follow it a couple of steps, discover that it's incorrect, and then mark it as a wrong move."

---

[25]Programming used to be fun in the pre-IDE age. That's my point of view, not a scientific truth. What brought me to Ring is the renaissance of that ancient feeling of having fun when writing code. This feeling is also the motivation for writing this book.

Dominguez adds, "There is a deeper parallel here, though, beyond logic puzzles and video games. In life, during our seven or eight decades on this earth (good luck permitting), this is precisely how we learn, how we discover new things, and find better ways to do old things."

Like gaming, programming should be an activity for learning and living.

Gaming has the ability to "say" what has been said before using the construction metaphor and tell us the story of what has never been told. More importantly, gaming, being complex itself and built by design for reactivity and adaptation to change, is the best convenient medium for learning a complex and changing system like programming.

Now that I have established the new metaphor, there is a chance to wear the gaming glasses and see programming in a completely new[26] way.

Programming, Redefined!

Close your eyes. You are teleported to a fantasy world called Ringorialand.

Now, open your eyes.[27]

Programming is providing lights to someone in need. Lights are extracted from stars. Stars are generated by mixing water and sand, according to a well-defined recipe, inside a magic millstone, called Ringuter.

This is done by a Ringler. The programmer is the Ringler. Recipes are the programs. They define what kind and quantity of water and sand must be used, how they are composed, and how much rotation they need in the millstone. Every time the same recipe is operated in the same kind of millstone, the same kind of stars are generated.

In this land, customers have representatives: miners.

Every recipe comes in response to a customer's request of one and only one type of light. If many types are requested from the miner, then probably he didn't own a clear vision of his real customer need. In all cases, different types of lights must correspond to different recipes. Finally, complex or unknown types of lights are approached by the use of a magical type called "light of lights."

The reliance on the complex "light of lights" must be avoided by the medium Ringler to the extent possible. Otherwise, a chewed Ringler, under the commands of Ringshtein the Alchemist, must be invited to help the team.

---

[26]There will be new words in the next paragraphs you have never heard before. Read ahead and try to imagine their symbolic meaning. When you read the section "Ringoria, the Programming Land of Ring," they all become familiar.

[27]I know you didn't obey, but that's OK.

It is important to understand that what is delivered by the Ringling team is not the lights but the recipes. The Ringorialand standard is to test the generated stars and lights inside the kingdom, before delivering the recipe to miners, just to ensure the quality of the Ringorian work.

The delivery of recipes is a social, emotional, and technical experience. The Ringling team must include in their recipe not only how the stars were "cooked" in the Ringuter but also how they are transported to be thrown on the summit of a mountain called the Cap of Lights.

Ringoria, as an exporting nation, is paid with miner's gold when the delivery of recipes to these miners is accomplished. But a Ringler is not given his part of the gold until the generated light succeeds in providing the final customer with the ultimate value he needs: recovering from an illness in case he asked for a Light of Health, augmenting wealth in the case of the Light of Gold, getting a new knowledge in case of Light of Wisdom, and enjoying a better life in case he requested a Light of Happiness.

Delivery is a mean to an ultimate goal: customer success. For the Ringlers, the cooking of a quality recipe, which made quality stars and generated quality lights, is not the end of the story. Ringlers are not evaluated only for the quality of recipes they make but also for the success provided to final customers who use their recipe. Ringopus, the protecting octopus of Ringoria, controls the quality of recipes inside the frontiers of the island. As for the dragon Ringza and when programs go live in the customer land, he flies there and reports to the Ringling team whether or not their customer is made successful, in other words, whether or not their delivery has been successful!

Customers are supposed to receive a genuine and unaltered copy of the recipe written in the Ringza language. Then they must operate it on a compatible millstone with the original one made in Ringoria. They can make it by their own or ask for an ambassador service, a member of the Ringling team, who travels to their foreign land and assists them in the process of getting their stars, or getting their lights.

Miners are not the customers. They are the representative of negotiators and the payers on behalf of the final customers.

The Ringling team is led by Ringson, the powerful admiral. Customer requirements are gathered by Ringayar the poet, a kind of business analyst. The user experience is designed by Princess Ringaliza. The program architecture is a matter of alchemy, the exclusive job of Ringshtein. Queen Ringafoye has the final word in accepting a new customer, launching a new programming mission, validating the deliverable, solving conflicts, and distributing the earned gold.

Finally, programming happens in a programming land, by an elite people called *programmers*, using a common programming language, and depending on a nation-wide law everyone respects. To know programming, one needs to know the following:

- The land, including its frontiers, landscape, main places, and secret positions

- The people of that land, including their culture, personal profiles, and social classes

- The language they use for communicating their thoughts in solving problems

- The laws that govern their daily life

These points will be covered one by one in the next sections.

We are playing, but it's a serious game[28] with a well-defined skillset we aim to achieve. In the next section, I will define the scope, depth, and structure of the skillset necessary for mastering a programming language like Ring.

A Target Skillset of Our Gamified Learning Experience

Here I revisit the programming cube developed earlier in the chapter and show you where we are going to put our efforts in only one subset of what is required to mastering programming in Ring. Precisely, our focus is set on Code and Design from the Complexity axis and on Application and Architecture from the Synergy axis, with a limited consideration of Code Evolution from the Agility axis. See Figure 9-13.

---

[28]Serious games are "games that do not have entertainment, enjoyment, or fun as their primarily purpose" (Michael and Chen, 2005). Learn more about the concept and its historic origins here: `https://tinyurl.com/y3jkbrqf`.

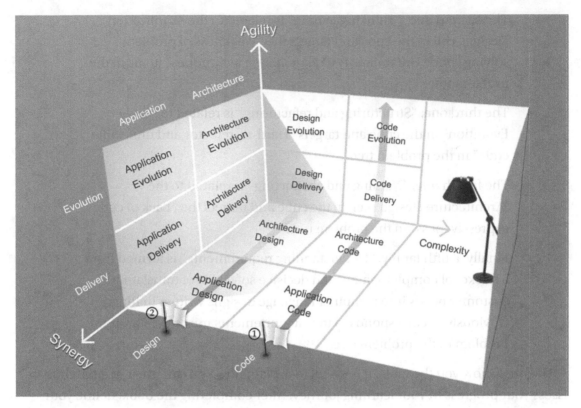

Figure 9-13. *The programming cube: priorities of our learning experience in this chapter*

The flags show the two main perspectives we are going to focus on. The arrow transverses the technical subjects we will cover, and the intensity of its color represents the strength of that focus.

In Table 9-3, which I'll call "Table Complete,"[29] I show you the list of programming skills we are going to build our gaming system around. These are the most basic skills with the most impact on helping you forge a real mastery of Ring. They are divided into five groups, each of them related to a particular cell of the programming cube and targeting a particular problem of the problem tree.

- The first one, "Mastering Ring" is related to the "Application Code" cell in the cube and targets the "Poor knowledge of the programming language" in the problem tree.

---

[29]After the *Code Complete* book mentioned earlier

- The second one, "Thinking in Ring" is related to the "Application Design" cell in the cube and targets the "Weakness of problem solving" and "Unfamiliarity with modeling techniques" items in the problem tree.

- The third one, "Structuring and refactoring" is related to "Code Evolution" in the cube and targets "Hard-to-refactor and unflexible code" in the problem tree.

- The fourth one, "Naming and abstracting" is related to the "Architecture Design" cell in the cube and targets the "Lack of code expressiveness" in the problem tree.

- Finally, a fifth family, "Understanding requirements," is formed from a bucket of complementary and decisive soft skills of translating customer needs into computer language designs written in Ring. Obviously, it corresponds to the "Requirements misunderstanding" problem in the problem tree.

Before I show you the table, it is useful to explain how you can use it as a baseline to assess your progress in your learning journey. After completing the book, define your actual level in each skills area by filling in one of the three circles in the "Before" column.

- Leave them like this ●●● if you feel you have no mastery at all.

- Leave them like this ●●● if you have basic understanding but no practical experience.

- Leave them like this ●●● if you have done it once and can use it in writing your real-world programs.

- Finally, leave them like this ●●● if you think you are a real ninja and have a full mastery of the subject.

Anytime in the future when you feel you have made significant progress, go back to the table and record it in the "After" column. By the way, you will notice I filled in the table for an imaginary programmer who used the table before and after reading this book. But this is just an illustration; feel free to modify them yourself.

Say hello to your Table Complete.

Table 9-3. *Table Complete*

Goal	Learning units	Your level	
		Before	**After**
I: Mastering Ring language *Success factor:* **Your knowledge of the language**	1. Mastering types	●●●	●●●
	2. Mastering operators	●●●	●●●
	3. Mastering standard functions	●●●	●●●
	4. Mastering objects	●●●	●●●
	5. Mastering functions	●●●	●●●
	6. Mastering variables scope and parameter passing	●●●	●●●
	7. Understanding time and space complexity	●●●	●●●
	8. Using the language libraries	●●●	●●●
	9. Using C/C++ extensions	●●●	●●●
	10. Mastering the errors and exceptions system	●●●	●●●
II: Thinking in code *Success factor:* **Your ability to solve problems**	11. Finding the root cause of a problem	●●●	●●●
	12. Adopting a solving strategy	●●●	●●●
	13. Selecting an efficient algorithm	●●●	●●●
	14. Designing an efficient data model	●●●	●●●
	15. Understanding legacy code	●●●	●●●
III: Structuring and refactoring *Success factor:* **Your ability to embrace the craftsperson culture**	16. Understanding program structure	●●●	●●●
	17. Designing a changeable architecture (designing for change)	●●●	●●●
	18. Analyzing impact of code change	●●●	●●●
	19. Negotiating change of code structure	●●●	●●●
	20. Delivering in a changing environment	●●●	●●●

(*continued*)

Table 9-3. (*continued*)

Goal	Learning units	Your level	
		Before	After
VI: Naming and abstracting *Success factor:* **Your ability to forge design models**	21. Naming variables, functions, parameters, classes, packages, libraries and program files	●●●	●●●
	22. Designing at the right level of abstraction	●●●	●●●
	23. Hiding complexity with encapsulation	●●●	●●●
	24. Embracing declarative and natural programming	●●●	●●●
V: Understanding requirements *Success factor:* **Your ability to translate user requirements to computer language words**	25. Gathering requirements in a declarative way (describing the what, not the how)	●●●	●●●
	26. Asking the right questions to educate customer and preserve focus	●●●	●●●
	27. Drafting program prototypes	●●●	●●●
VI: Managing change *Success factor:* **Your ability to mentally represent programming as a gaming system**	28. Negotiating exceeding of scope	●●●	●●●
	29. Designing the work breakdown structure (WBS) of the required work	●●●	●●●
	30. Identifying technical risks and demonstrating technical feasibility	●●●	●●●
	31. Estimating required time and efforts and providing alternatives	●●●	●●●
VII: Empowering people *Success factor:* **Your ability to forge a magnetic personality by ethically caring of the success of your teammates**	32. Sharing programming knowledge	●●●	●●●

You may agree that exposing all these skills in a narrative way will lead us to another 900+ pages of *Code Complete*. That's why gamification and storytelling come into rescue to give us an bird's-eye view of the complex land of programming. Hence, the remaining part of the chapter will tell you the story of the complete gamified fantasy world I designed for you to learn Ring.

Ringoria, the Programming Land of Ring

In 1200 BCE, there was a sovereign kingdom located in the Deep Sea on a well-protected island called Ringorialand, or more simply Ringoria.

The island is inhabited by a special kind of people, called Ringorians, whose sole mission is to transform sand and water into holy lights. Those lights are sold to foreign miners for gold.

Ringorians demonstrate religious commitment to making nice work and have a strong attachment to beauty as their very first reason of existence. They believe in God Ringaros, the unique, ultimate, harmonious, and invisible power of the whole universe. They host his love in their hearts and bring his words to their minds.

Ringoria was led by King Ringamesh for more than 300 years using a strict law called the Roadmap of King Ringamesh. He left the world and delegated the kingdom to his wife Ringafoye whose mission is to ensure the roadmap is respected by every citizen, at every moment, in any context. She has the exclusive power of promoting a common Ringorian to become a Ringler by putting a ring on his finger. Only a Ringler is allowed to participate in the teams negotiating with miners, entering the castle, and operating the Ringuter.

The force of law is enforced by Admiral Ringson (son of Ringafoye), who is a symbol of power and has full control over the kingdom. The beauty of everything done in Ringoria is illustrated by the beautiful voice of Princess Ringaliza, sister of Ringson. Ringayar, the poet, lives an impossible love story with Ringaliza because the royal family is against him. Ringshtein the Alchemist, the inventor of the Ringuter, is the most protected person in the kingdom. Under his supervision, Ringlers operate the Ringuter to transform sand and water into brilliant stars, called *storz*. Those storz form the substance from which lights are generated by throwing them, by Ringayar and Ringaliza, on a mountain called Cap of Lights.

The Ringorialand Map

The only available map of Ringoria was left to us by an unknown historian who documented a lot of valuable information about this mysterious land. In this section, I take you on a trip to discover the map and its most relevant places, objects, and characters, and how they map to the real world of the Ring programming language. See Figure 9-14.

Figure 9-14. *Map of Ringorialand with ten relevant indications*

At the center of the island there is the royal floating Castle (1) sitting magically on a lake of pure water called Watermania (2). To the right, there is a stockroom (3) where lights, foods, and arms are preserved. Farther right, you find the Bay of Sand (4), the main source of sand used in conjuction with Watermania's water to make stars. To the north of the island, there is a mountain called Cap of Lights where lights are actually generated (5). To the south, there is a watchtour used exclusively by Ringuards, the military force of Ringoria. To the west-north, there are fleets used by Ringlers during their travels to negotiate deals with miners (7). To the west-south, there is the neighbour island of Xtensia (8), a friendly agricultural nation providing Ringoria with "fruits of power" from its trees irrigated with Rinogorian lights. An octopus called Ringapus (9) is swimming all the time around the island; he never sleeps, and he reports every event, of any kind, to the Castle. Between the Castle and the Cap of Lights and just before the northern bridge, you notice a large and secret area only Ringorians know about. At the surface there is a training camp, and deeper in the ground there is an Underground Station. Keep it secret, though!

To the north again, in the plain sight, there is a dragon (10) called Ringza, the voice of wisdom. Right now, Ringza is flying abroad in a mission you will discover later in the chapter; that's why you don't see it on the map. Ringza is the protector of the native language all Ringorians use. In particular, Ringlers use it to write their recipes while operating the Ringuter. The language is named Ringza after the dragon's name. In the real world, Ringza is the Ring programming language.

As for Xos the enemy, it's always invisible, and there is no way to paint it on the map. You'll learn more about him later.

Ringoria, you've got it, is the programming world of Ring.

The Floating Castle

The floating Castle is the command center of the kingdom. It is floating due to a well-defined law of water physics[30] invented by Ringshtein. Built from a special clay imported from the Kingdom of Tombuktu 7,000 miles away, the building is waterproof and can't be crumbled by wind or burned by fire. See Figure 9-15.

---

[30]The Chinese sage Lao Tzu stated the paradox of water in his ancient text *Tao Te Ching* by saying: "There is nothing softer and weaker than water, and yet there is nothing better for attacking hard and strong things." Find out more in this Live Science article called "The Surprisingly Strange Physics of Water": https://tinyurl.com/y5845eot.

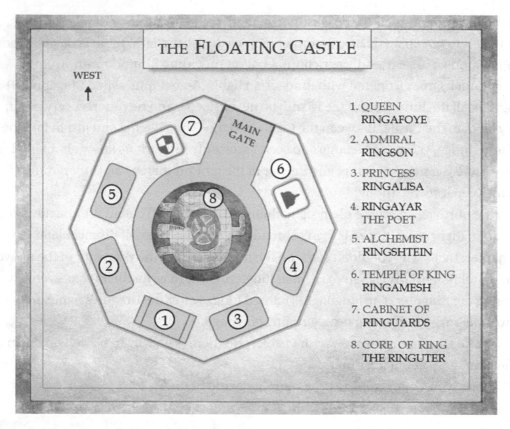

Figure 9-15. *The Castle is the command center of all Ringoria*

The Castle is the most protected place out there (7) because it hosts the memory of King Ringamesh (6) and the department of the Queen (1) and her team (2, 3, 4, and 5). At the core of the Castle, there is a special kind of millstone: a Ringuter (8).

In programming, the Castle and its occupants can be thought as a programming team in a software company. Queen Ringafoye is the CEO, Ringson is the project manager, Ringayar is the business analyst, Ringaliza is the user experience designer, and Ringshtein is the software architect. The computer is the Ringuter, and the programmer is you, the Ringler!

Watermania

Watermania is not a conventional lake. Here all the items that Ringlers need in their recipes are designed from a special kind of water. See Figure 9-16.

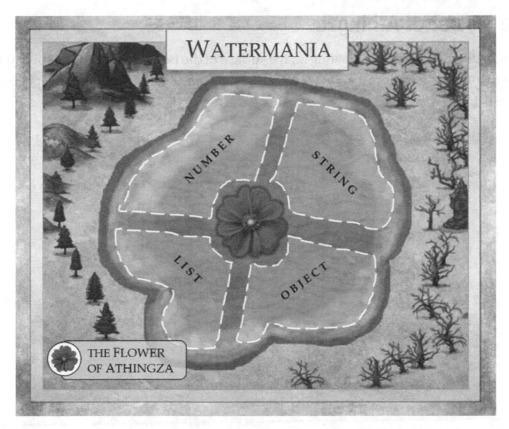

Figure 9-16. *Watermania: four types of pure water in Ringorialand*

It is formed of four water isthmuses[31] and a central floating flower, called the Flower of Athingza, carefully cached under the foundation of the Castle. This is where the Ringlers make their composition of water (names) and add it to the selection of sand (behavior) they import from the Bay of Sand.

In Ring, these are the four basic data types that form the substance from which other data types can be designed. The fluid nature of water resembles the same fluid nature of data in software programs. The Flower of Athingza assists the Ringlers in making elegant designs of their recipes.

---

[31]An isthmus is a narrow piece of land connecting two large areas across an expanse of water by which they are otherwise separated. For Watermania, I've taken inspiration from Coran: "[25.53] It was He who let forth the two seas, this one is palatably sweet and this salt, a bitter taste, and He set a barrier between them."

The Flower of Athingza

Athingza is a magical flower floating on the surface of the lake, but for Ringshtein and his team of Ringlers, it is more a framework for making names and designing concepts. See Figure 9-17.

Figure 9-17. *The Flower of Athingza: the modeling arm of the Ringler*

They use it for guideline when they merge water types to create new names and when they add sand to water to add a behavior to these names. Names and behaviors are the main components of the SPEX substance, which forms the first entry to the Ringuter.

In programming, designing an efficient and well-planned data model is a decisive factor in the success of any program.

The Bay of Sand

Four types of sand are available in the Bay of Sand. Every type has a particular role to play in the overall composition made inside the Castle. See Figure 9-18.

Figure 9-18. *Types of sand in the Bay of Sand: 1. Keywords, 2. Operators, 3. Standard functions, and 4. Ring libraries*

In Ring, these types of sand are the brute substance and main features of the language: operators, keywords, standard functions, and Ring libraries. They must be very well understood to use them when needed. For example, a programmer who isn't aware of the existence of a standard function multiplying two matrices[32] can waste a valuable amount of time developing it from scratch.

---

[32]Take a look at the MatrixMulti() function in the documentation of Ring (https://tinyurl.com/yxssfdlg).

In the world of Ringorialand, you are not allowed to pick a particular type if you are not familiar with it. A minimal knowledge is then required. Otherwise, you will be invited to go to the Royal Library to read and then to the Training Camp to develop your skills.

The Ringuter

The Ringuter is not a dead old millstone. It's a magical creature (4)!

In addition to the "Water and sand" entry (1), the Ringuter is fed with zex and spex (2), a kind of document written in the Ringza language describing the needs of the miners in terms of lights, and tex and yex (3), the technical designs, also written in Ringza, of the Ringuting recipe (7).

Its main output is not ground wheat but brilliant stars called *strorz* (6). Ringshtein and his team of Ringlers document every Ringuting operation they make on a separate piece of leather called Recipe (7).

Every recipe, when it proves to be successful, must be sent to be archived in the Royal Library sitting in the Underground Station. See Figure 9-19.[33]

---

[33]Do you want to see a real millstone (they are still in use in my rural village)? Here is an article containing a photo of a millstone from the region of Gafsa at the center of Tunisia: https://tinyurl.com/y6nscehl.

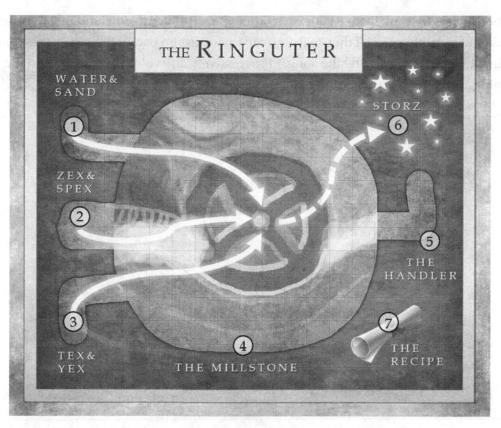

Figure 9-19. *Ringuter millstone, computer of the Ringorian age*

In programming, Ringuter is the computer, the machine that executes code and transforms data. Any programmer of a high-level language like Ring needs to have a basic knowledge of how a computer works. At the same time, a good understanding of the concept of time and space complexity is necessary.[34] Every successful Ringuting operation makes you earn the esteem of Queen Ringafoye in person. The queen is free to decide whether you are rewarded or not at all, when, and how.

The Cap of Lights

After the storz are generated from the Ringuter, Ringayar writes a poem, and Ringaliza transforms it into a song. They take a horse with a torch and travel to the mountain. It takes them seven days and seven nights before they arrive. There they pray, purify their

---

[34]This is why we included a related skill in Table 9-3.

hearts, and feel they are in love with each other and with the world. Suddenly they hear a profound horrible voice! If they feal any fear, they must go back. Otherwise, they start reading the poem and singing the song.[35] Progressively, the voice dissepears, and the Cap of Lights generates the required lights. See Figure 9-20.

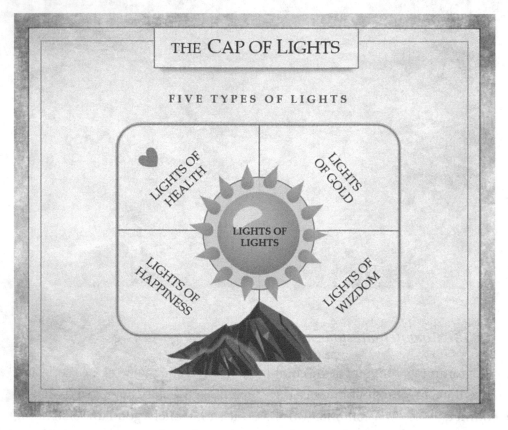

Figure 9-20. *Customer needs on the Cap of Lights: four lights and the Light of Lights*

In programming, lights represent the ultimate customer needs. In my experience, this is the most misunderstood piece by programmers. Usually, what is required from the customer is never met by the delivered software. Here I suggest a semantic framework to master the understanding of customer requirements.

---

[35]You want to hear a song of Ringaliza in front of the mountain? Here it is: https://tinyurl.com/y43rene4.

In the real world, a customer comes to you, the programmer, with one of these five needs:

- A problem he needs to solve; your answer is a light of health

- A competitive advantage he needs to enhance; your answer is a light of gold

- A new expertise he needs to acquire; your answer is a light of wisdom

- A need of entertainment; your answer is a light of happiness

- A combination of those; your answer will be a light of lights

There is a lot to say about the alchemy of designing data and code models, but remember, we won't be able to learn everything in one book. The basics are covered, though, in your Table Complete (see Table 9-3) in the fourth category, "Naming and abstructing." There are four skills we will use.

- 11: Naming things

- 12: Designing at the right level of abstraction

- 13: Hiding complexity

- 14: Embracing declarative and natural paradigms

As introduced earlier, the Flower of Athingza will be of great help to the smart Ringler in structuring his efforts in designing efficient data models.

The Training Camp

The secret zone in the north of the island is a Training Camp. Ringoria keeps it secret from foreigners because this is a matter of national security. It's where magical skills are acquired. Ringlers go the Training Camp to enhance their knowledge and gain Knowledge Points (KPs). See Figure 9-21.

Figure 9-21. *The Training Camp of Ringoria: nine steps and three levels of difficulty*

In programming, training is the fuel of a programmer's career, a lifelong exercise with a strategic importance. Programmers train themselves to get new skills or fill a skill gap.

The Training Camp is organized into nine steps and three levels of difficulty. If you are the Ringler, then you can use it in two principal ways.

- Checking their instant lights. The Training Camp is used to assess your knowledge of the Ring keywords, standard functions, and basic algorithms. You'll get an instant light when you reach level 9.

- Assessing your performance in each area of your Table Complete so you get the required skills to reach the next level.

In practice, when you are playing with Ring in your programming career, Admiral Ringson will be orienting you to this Training Camp every time he identifies a weakness in your skills. Sometimes, I advise you to go there on your own will before you are captured by Ringson crusty eyes!

The Underground Station

Under the Training Camp, there is an Underground Station accessible to Ringlers only, specifically to the leadership and to its working staff. It contains a rich library of books called the Royal Library and a room for reading. This is the knowledge and research center of Ringoria. Those who work there write books, and those who don't are visiting Ringlers who may stay several days reading. Furthermore, the station is intended to educate them on patriotism and religious confession. See Figure 9-22.

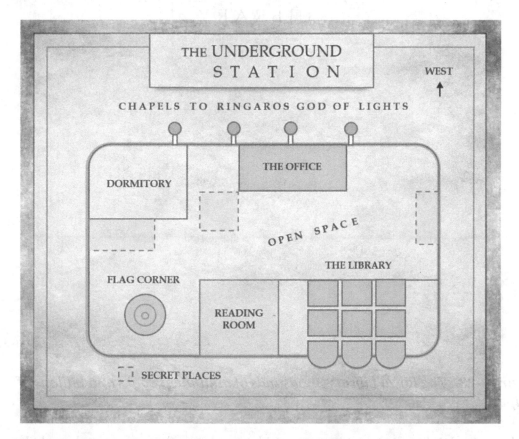

Figure 9-22. *The Underground Station under the Training Camp*

In programming, the most important piece of this Underground Station is the Royal Library, presented in the next section.

During your programming life, you are invited to do a lot of reading. You should take the reading activity as serious as possible and work hard to build a Royal Library of your programming world.

The Royal Library

The Royal Library is the home of knowledge and the intellectual heritage of Ringoria. The building hosts more than 7,000 books and 77,000 recipes collected by the Ringorian people over the years. See Figure 9-23.

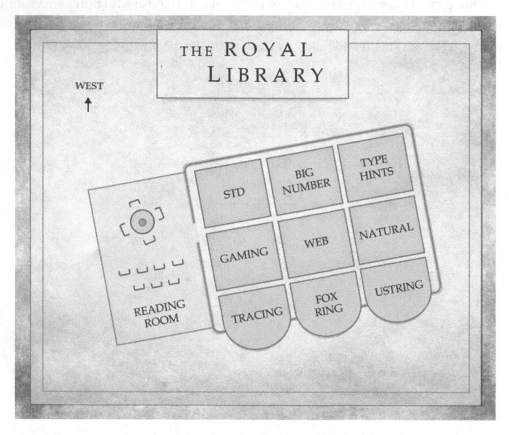

Figure 9-23. *The Royal Library: thousands of millinuem books and billions of recipes*

For every book you read and every new idea you learn, there are some knowledge lights you earn. Reading is also a provider of intellectual happiness and emotional performance. You'll learn more about how you are going to monitor your four types of performance (emotional, social, technical, and economical) when we touch on the Iron Compass[36] in the next section.

---

[36]In programming, the Iron Compass is your dashboard containing key performance indicators (KPIs) about your current programming project.

In Ring, the different departments of the Royal Library correspond to the libraries written in the Ring language and cover the following domains:

- Standard functions of the language

- 2D and 3D gaming engine

- Web programming

- Natural programming

- Tracing

- . Type hints

- Big number

- Fox Ring

That's the end of the trip. You are at the homeland now, under the sunny sky of Ringoria, breathing its earth fragrance and enjoying its clean nature. Ringoria is the most outstanding programming land you ever dreamed of.

Next, you will discover the tools every Ringler must have right in his pocket to never be lost in the hectic and changing programming world of Ringorialand: what are they, how they can be used, and what they are useful for.

In the Pocket of Every Ringler

Ringling is hard. Programming is hard.

It's hard because of the changes: changing requirements, changing data models, changing code architecture, changing teams, changing underlining deployment infrastructure, and changing changes.[37]

Programmers feel like they are walking on moving ground. They need to be directed, monitored, and "project managed." In particular, the descipline of project management in the software domain has created a vicious dichotomy between coding and managing change. Project managers usually don't understand the constraints of code, and programmers feel they are not concerned with estimates, planning, risk mitigation, and conflict resolution.

---

[37]I agree this is an exaggeration. I'm sorry.

This needs to change, and change needs to become a substance of programming exactly like code and language syntax. Managing change in programming must be in the skillset of every programmer. Remember our problem tree and how "Inability to cope with change" was one of the main causes of bad quality of code?

In the following sections, I give you the necessary tools for use during your Ringling journey. Understanding those tools will develop your awareness and makes you a better programmer. In practice, you get the following:

- A dashboard of your performance as an individual and of the performance of the mission you are working on. In Ringoria, it gives you directions via the Iron Compass.

- An overview of your most valuable skills in programming and how they compare in time and between colleagues. In Ringoria, this is the Ringometer.

- An analysis of the network of social relations between you and your teammates. Ringorians call this the Sociogram.

- The typical persona of every member of the team so you know how to deal with every one of them. Here you will discover the teamcards."

- A representation of the achievement of the programming team in terms of time, cost, and quality. In Ringoria, we talk of the triangle of team achievement (TTA) or simply "the Titiey."

- A cartography of the events occurring in the program being developed. In Ringoria, this is the Spectrogram reflecting the heat map of everything happening around the island as captured by Ringapus.

Next, I provide a visual illustration of every tool and discuss why programmers should care.

An Iron Compass

Programmers who used to work with me know me for saying "Raise your head from the dunes of code, look high to the stars, take a deep breath, and find where you are on the globe!" Coding is a detail-oriented technical job where every word counts. It takes our brain, eyes, and fingers during hours, days, and months.[38] It is easy to get overwhelmed even in 100 lines of code. Many of us don't resist the temptation to jump, as quickly as possible, to the keyboard and see our variables arising and our ifs and thens flourishing on the wall like climbing herbs.[39]

The destiny of every programmer on the programming team is left in the hands of, sometimes, slightly incompetent project managers. They think for programmers, monitor their performance for them, and make decisions for them. Worst of all, programmers have little access to the final user for whom they are asked to make a successful product, and usually, they don't meet the user at all. Unconsciously, they develop an illusive elusive of the user based on the requirements collected by slightly incompetent business analysts.

If you aspire to become a Ringler, a great programmer of Ring, then you should consider taking your destiny into your own hands. You are a programmer, so you are a sailor on a program ship in a hectic programming sea. There will be sunny days but rainy nights, flying birds but hungry sharks. Sailors on whom we can rely must be armed with the necessary tools to see their destination ahead, evaluate their progress in time and space, and be aware of any bad relation, when it emerges inside their micro-society of sailors, inside their team of programmers. In project management, we always hear the hype of dashboard, dashboard, dashboard! But when it comes to giving us programmers a simple thing with meaningful indicators to save our lives, it is hard to find a useful one. In Figure 9-24 I present you with my set of visuals you should track, by yourself, when writing code, so you are never misoriented.

---

[38]In reality, it takes us from our entire lives, our families, and our duties as social beings.

[39]This code fanaticism is the worst quality you could find in a programmer. He is the one who can't wait to show his impatience and tells you with a displeasing eye: "Enough theories, man, let me write code!" Probably you are dealing with someone who is unable to craft a design, establish a clean architecture, and think strategically about how to create a good solution for the problem at hand.

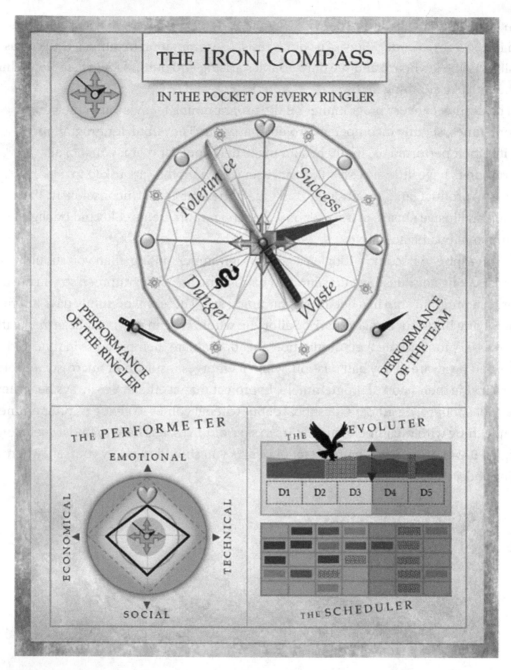

Figure 9-24. *Four visuals to situate you, programmer, in the programming land*

The first visual, ⚕, the Iron Compass, tells you where your programming performance is directed: to success, failure, or in between. You may be in a situation of wasting your energy or, more often, in a tolerance zone, where you are not that efficient, but let's say that's OK. Follow the sword to read your situation, and follow the feather (🖋) to read it in context, compared to the performance of the programming team.

The second visual in the bottom-left corner, called the Performeter, will help you to better understand the composition of your performance. This radar of four rays reflects your personal performance as a combination of four types of performances: emotional, social, technical, and economical.

To the right, you meet the Evoluter. There you see the evolution of your performance over time, compared to the performance of the entire team. Finally, in the Scheduler, you see your programming tasks (past, present, and future) inside a calendar.

Simple, right?

Indeed, always take the time to ask yourself questions like these: What is my performance in writing code? How does it contribute to the collective performance of the team? How can I explain my performance? How does all this progress over time? What are the tasks involved in my programming work and how they are planned?

A Ringometer

Like a chronometer that measures time, the Ringmeter measures your skills.

Programmer skills and programming performance seem to be linearly related: the more you get skilled, the more you are performant. This is not as simple as one could think, and most of the time, this is simply wrong. You will understand this when we will unveil the dynamic nature of this fascinating relathionship later in the chapter.[40] Such a fuzziness invites us, as programmers, to have a clear framework of assessing our skills. Again, the best possible visual we can use is a radar; this time it has five rays, corresponding each to a skills family from the Table Complete shown in Table 9-3. See Figure 9-25.

---

[40]In the section "You Are the Ringler."

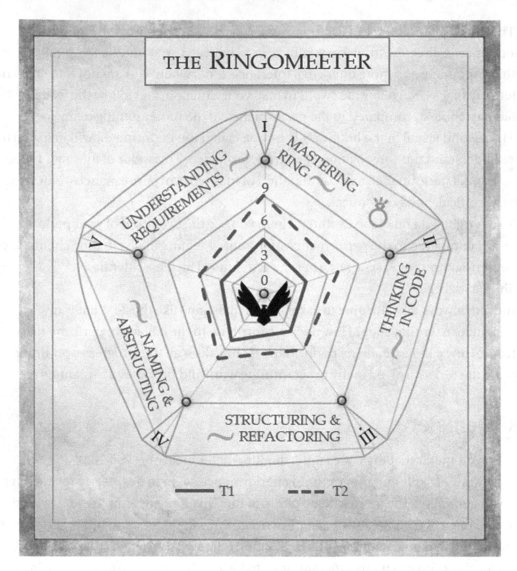

Figure 9-25. *A five-ray radar to assess your programming skills and how they progress from instant T1 to instant T2 and how they differ between a mission T1 and a mission T2*

You can agree on any number of rays and any family of skills you put on your radar. For now, while you are learning the language with me in the book, keep it as is so we can assess your progress on every family of skills in the Table Complete (Table 9-3).

A Sociogram

In my experience, the social dimension of programming is the most important factor influencing the performance of programmers individually and as a team.

Unfortunately, this is an absent dimension in todays project management dashboards. Instead, people dynamics are evaluated implicitly and only by the personal perception their project manager will have. If you used to be employed as a programmer, then I know how you felt if you were a victim of a displaced decision based not fairly on your technical performance but because the hierarchy thought you were a troublemaker on the team.

To be frank, this happens a lot. More frankly, it is human nature, and it is unavoidable. That's why everyone needs a Sociogram. See Figure 9-26.

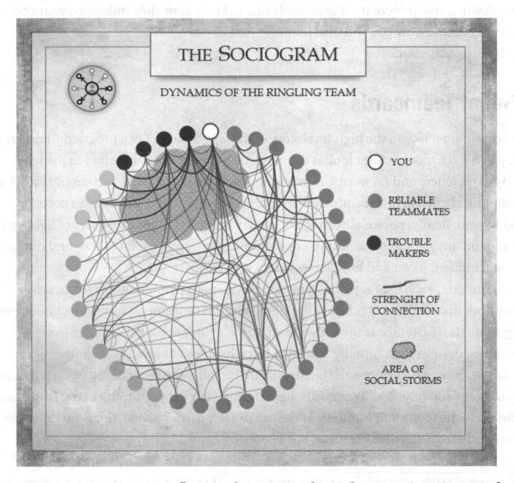

Figure 9-26. *A Sociogram reflecting the nature of social connections in one of my previous programming teams*

Draw a circle at the center of the page and a smaller circle for every teammate all over the circumference (you are one of them). Fill them with a gradient color to classify them on a continuum of reliable people you can look to and troublemakers you should avoid. Then draw a line between every two people describing the strength of their connection. If you think they are friends, then the line is dark. If they are not socially related, the link is gray.

You end up with a funny shape stimulating a sideways smile, but wait, this is a serious game. If you don't master the moving ground of the social connections between the members of the programming team, then your performance is impacted, whatever your technical skills are. The Sociogram can show you who are your friends and who are not. Excuse me for this vulgarity; it is less my will to be vulgar than it is the vulgarity of the real world.

In Ringoria, while you play, you will face similar situations. And anytime a team is created, you must analyze their teamcards first to know how they influence your coding performance and how you will deal them.

Did I say teamcards?

A Set of Teamcards

The Sociogram tells you the high-level story of the "social sauce" of a programming team. Still, you need to take a closer look at the personal profile of every member in the team.

By experience, and far from any psycholodgical paranoia, what you should look for as influenical criteria in a teammate are technical competence, maturity in decision-making, and, finally, personality magnetism. Try them. They are three rays of light you can spot on any person to get a kind of personality pattern: a useful tool to find out how they will influence you and how you can deal with them.

In Ringoria, each character has a personality pattern printed on his teamcard. Remember that Queen Ringafoye is the CEO, Admiral Ringson is your project manager, Ringshtein the Alchemist is the software architect, Princess Ringalise is the user experience designer, and, finally, Ringayar is the business analyst.

Take a minute to look at each teamcard and imagine the personality of each member of your team and how you'll play with them during your programming carer. Don't pay attention to the icons and numbers at the top of each card. Instead, focus on the three sliders and on the line linking them. See Figure 9-27.[41]

---

[41]The pictures of the team were made with the online tool Character Creator (https://charactercreator.org).

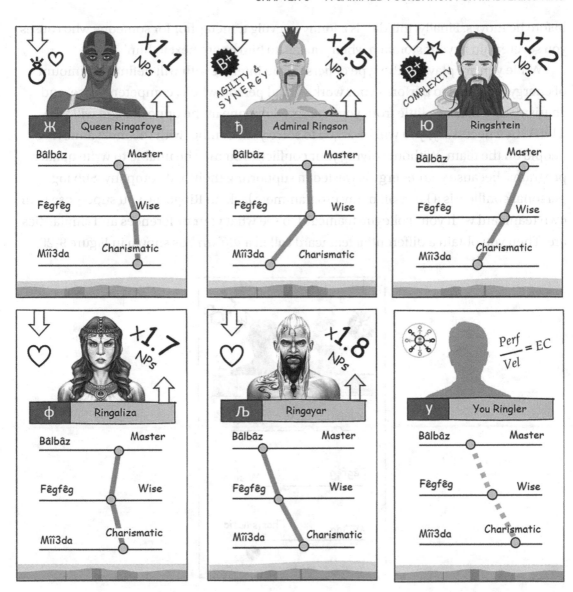

Figure 9-27. *Teamcards showing the personality pattern of every teammate*

The first slider is related to the level of technical capacity. The person is competent (Master) or not (Bâlbâz). The second shows the level of maturity of the person in making decisions. The person is wise or not (Fêgfêg). Finally, the third slider says something about the personality magnetism of your teammate. He is then charismatic or not at all (Mîîda). In the Tunisian dialect, balbâz means someone who is really chaotic in terms of his quality of work. Fêgfêg is used to describe someone who is hasty and never take his time to think

579

before he moves. Finally, mîîîda[42] is a funny but vulgar metaphor for someone who causes you severe pain in your stomach when you talk to him or are next to him!

While you are playing, the type of person you interact with will define the amount of energy you need to perform your work. A kind person who is competent, wise, and charismatic will take a little from your energy. Someone at the opposite end will take a lot. When necessary, you will be asked to solve your conflict with the most annoying people on the team. Without solving your conflicts, you may be unable to write quality programs, because your energy is wasted in supporting their bad company. Solving personal conflicts is a key skill many programmers lack. In Ringoria, you superpose your own teamcard with your collegue teamcard to see what your differences and similarities are. Then you obtain a differential teamcard called a *diffcard*, as shown in Figure 9-28.

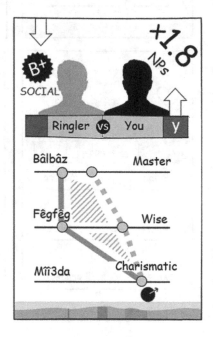

Figure 9-28. *A diffcard comparing your performance to the performance of one of your collegues*

You can see that you are somehow different in terms of technical competence and very different in terms of maturity of decision-making, but you both have a captivating personality. Your charisma, if it were real, would help you find a common ground to talk about your differences and forge the conditions of your mutual respect.

---

[42]*Mîîda* is stomach in Tunisian dialect closely related to the word *maiida* in Arabic.

A Mission "Titiey"

You've got your Iron Compass, which is your performance; its strengths and weaknesses don't cause any surprises to you. And you've got your Ringometer: your skills are assessed, and you know what you should enhance. Finally, you've got your Sociogram and a bunch of teamcards: your team dynamics are governed as they should be. Do you think you are ready now to tackle a real-world programming mission?

Not yet, dear friend. You have another flood of complexity, coming from the programming mission itself. In project management, the Golden Triangle is used to represent the three most important objectives of a project: time, quality, and cost. The Titiey is the Ringorian copy of the Golden Triangle with a focus on team achievement and not on the final software product itself. See Figure 9-29.

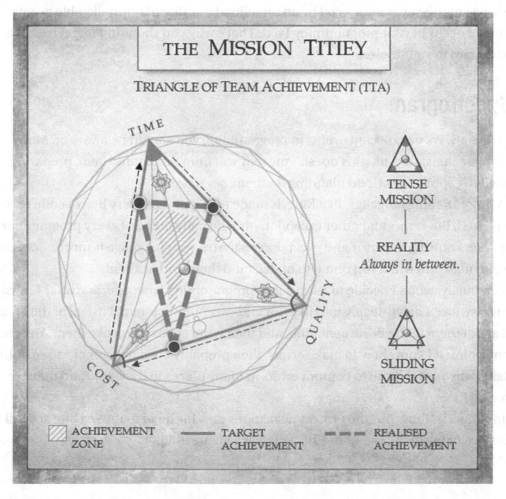

Figure 9-29. *The Golden Triangle of your programming mission*

A mission is either tight or sliding depending on whether the initial values of the objectives (time, quality, and cost) are negotiable or not. Always, your customers will insist on getting 100 percent of the required quality, exactly at the planned time and exactly with the estimated budget. I swear, this is exactly 100 percent impossible. If you are in such a configuration, then the atmosphere of work will be electric, and the quality of code will suffer a lot. That's why you should estimate it right and, in case of any difference, negotiate, and negotiate, and negotiate!

At the other extreme, your mission is sliding, and no objectives are clearly defined. If you are a research lab with an open budget, then it may be OK; otherwise, you should stop the hemorrhage as quickly as you can.

While you are playing with code in a large programming project, the complexity of your mission's Titiey will impact the level of your performance. But this is only part of the story; complexity is reinforced by an undefined number of unpredictable events that could occur in your programming land. That's why you shouldn't forget to add a Spectrogram to your toolset.

A Spectrogram

There are always unexpected events in programming you should be aware of. Most of them are inevitable, but this doesn't prevent you from predicting them, preparing yourself to capture them, and planning for them.

A programming language, like Ring, is made to respond to every line of code exactly as expected. But errors and other exceptions are the daily bread of every programmer. Therefore, knowing the error and exception system of your language is more necessary to avoid bugs, and when you don't, to understand them and fix them.

Personally, when I decide to learn a new programming language, and after I learn its basic syntax, I delve deeply into its error and exceptions system. I list all of the errors, read about them in the documentation, and then write code to provoke them. You can see my point: if I know how to make errors, then probably I will never make them. This explains why I guided you to commit errors in many places in the book, and then we corrected them.

In Ringoria, Ringapus the protecting octopus dips his head in the sea and sees all the events occurring in the island in a heat map like Figure 9-30.

Figure 9-30. *Ringoria threats as captured by Ringapus*

For you as a Ringler, this means you are invited to take urgent action to limit the effect of a threat (in dark on the map) or avoid another from happening.

That said, you now have all the elements of the fantasy world explained, and their relation to programming clarified. It lacks, of course, how are you going to play with them and what learning path you are going to traverse, but this is a matter of personal legend you will make by your own, when you engage in a profound and long-term learning experience of programming.

Nonetheless, in the next section, I try to give you a push to show you the way.

Rules of the Game

Your ultimate goal as a citizen of Ringoria is to become a Ringler, a master programmer. This will be possible by traversing many trainings (some will be hard) and traversing real-world situations (some will be complex).

When you play, you try to get the best score of Knowledge Points (KPs) and Experience Points (XPs) to enhance your social class. Your social class in Ringoria is defined by the type of ring you wear. There are three types of rings: iron for any Ringorian, silver for Ringuards, and gold for Ringlers.

To succeed in your life of Ringler, there are five rules you should respect, as listed here:

- The first one is "Believe in Ringaros!" and is a kind of ethical reference for the Ringler to adhere to.

- The second, "Roadmap of King Ringamesh," after God Ringaros' words, is the operational law guiding your programming workflow every time you are tackling a new programming project.

- The third is "Ringza by Heart, Ringza by Hand!" is your entry door to mustering the technicalities of the Ring language.

- The fourth, "Harvest the Rings," describes the deep incentives you should look for in your programming journey to cope with the mindset of a real programming master.

- The fifth is "You are the Ringler!" This isn't really a rule but a kind of "ontological" package containing many rules all centered on you, the programmer. These rules show tactics you should deploy to master the game of programming and become a strong but happy Ringler!

In the following sections, I will describe these rules one by one. Read them carefully.

Believe in Ringaros

Programming is a fruit cocktail of code, culture, ethics, and beliefs. All programmers should develop their own framework of positive values, over the years, by distilling a lesson from every programming experience. Otherwise, she better does this when she looks for another job.

Programming is hard, that's true. But it is a human intellectual activity with a powerful impact for social change. I'm not talking theory here; my own "personal legend"[43] is a humble demonstration of how programming can empower lives and change their destiny, from poverty to dignity and from a disarmed individual in a disconnected rural village to an active citizen in the wider village of the connected world. It's not about coding, but meeting different people from different cultures around coding. From Niamey to Miami, from Paris to Montreal, and from Mosco to Cairo, I have sisters and brothers who I never could have been able to know without writing code.

When your main profession doesn't convey a meaning for your existence, then how can you develop a passion for it? In turn, how can you deploy your energy to make it perfect, useful, and beautiful?

This section is a call to anyone who plans to bind their life to programming to choose the right door for the beginning of the journey: passion. Before struggling with building any technical skill, find a meaning, develop a feeling, and shape a destination. All the rest, including high salaries, is just a detail.

In Ringoria, there is a strong belief in God Ringaros, symbol of divine beauty and enlightening intelligence. There are four commandments of his that all Ringorians adhere to. Figure 9-31 shows the oldest paper from the Royal Library, scripted in old Egyptian hieroglyphic writing,[44] containing the four commandments.

---

[43]Go back to my comment on the problem "Lack of personal legend in programming" in the problem tree earlier in the chapter.

[44]I typed the text of the four commandments in this online hieroglyphic typewriter: `https://tinyurl.com/yynvoeuu`.

THE FOUR COMMANDMENTS OF GOD RINGOAROS

GREETINGS

1   BE CLEAN

2   BE STRONG

3   BE WISE

4   BE BEAUTIFUL

Figure 9-31.   The four commandments of God Ringaros

Ringlers need to be clean, strong, wise, and beautiful while writing Ringza recipes. These values obey an incremental logic that every work "Made in Ringoria" must satisfy. This means you can never pretend you are a successful Ringler when your code is strong but not clean. Similarly, you won't have the right to complain when your recipe is refused because it doesn't demonstrate an acceptable level of wisdom, even if it is clean and strong. Finally, the master of all other values is beauty. If your clean design, strong thinking, and clear wisdom do not collaborate to make a final beautiful result, then you were just wasting your time, just wasting your energy.

Back to the funny dance of definitions: what does every value mean?

Be Clean

In programming, clean design is a hot topic these days. Uncle Bob[45] has put a lot of effort into promoting the culture of clean code and clean architecture. "Clean" output comes from a programmer willing to work with code as a true craftsperson. "There are two parts to learning craftsmanship: knowledge and work. You must gain the knowledge of principles, patterns, practices, and heuristics that a craftsman knows, and you must also grind that knowledge into your fingers, eyes, and gut by working hard and practicing." See Figure 9-32.

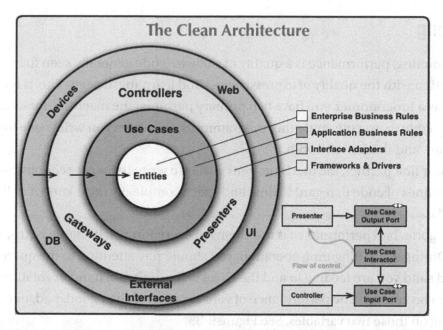

Figure 9-32. *The clean code architecture as proposed by Uncle Bob*

Clean code is an enabler of software change. To demonstrate that, Martin makes an interesting differentiation between code scope and code shape. Scope is naturally changing because the requirements change. But the shape of software code, including

---

[45]Robert C. Martin (nicknamed Uncle Bob) is a well-known advocate for the software craftsmanship movement and author of the *Clean Code, Clean Coder,* and *Clean Architecture* books. He polished his ideas about clean achitecture back in 2012 in a blog post (https://tinyurl.com/qcugmkx): "By separating the software into layers, and conforming to the Dependency Rule, you will create a system that is intrinsically testable, with all the benefits that implies. When any of the external parts of the system become obsolete, like the database, or the web framework, you can replace those obsolete elements with a minimum of fuss."

the code itself and its architecture, is usually hard and costly to change. If this is the case in your current software project, then probably your code is not that clean. Programmers must be educated to write clean code, so "the difficulty of changing a code is proportional only to the scope of change, not to the shape of change."

In every piece of code written for this book and every problem situation, there was a strong commitment to writing clean code, providing real-world knowledge and experiences, and designing for change. In some particular cases, like in Chapters 2 and 3, we were implementing Uncle Bob's clean architecture recipe, while simplifying it and adapting it to our context.

Be Strong

In programming, performance is a quality of software code generally seen to be in contradiction with the quality of expressiveness and learnable design. This is relevant because, as a programmer, you have two primary partners: the machine, for which your write code to execute, and other programmers, for whom you write code to read, understand, and think in and with.

For your first partner, the machine, your goal is to write the most economically optimized lines of code in regard to time and space complexity (also known as Big-O notation[46]).

In Ringoria, bad performance is the enemy of every Ringler. Its name is Xos, the Enemy. During every Ringuting operation, you should pay attention to the quantity of water and sand you are feeding in and the necessary number of handler rotations for the entrants to be ground. The performance of your Ringuter is then good, bad, or terrible depending on those two variables. See Figure 9-33.

---

[46]Wikipedia defines Big-O notation as a mathematical notation that describes the limiting behavior of a function when the argument tends toward a particular value or infinity. In computer science, Big-O notation is used to classify algorithms according to how their running time or space requirements grow as the input size grows. For a more pragmatic introduction, read this excellent article by Justin Abrahms: https://tinyurl.com/o4dcj86.

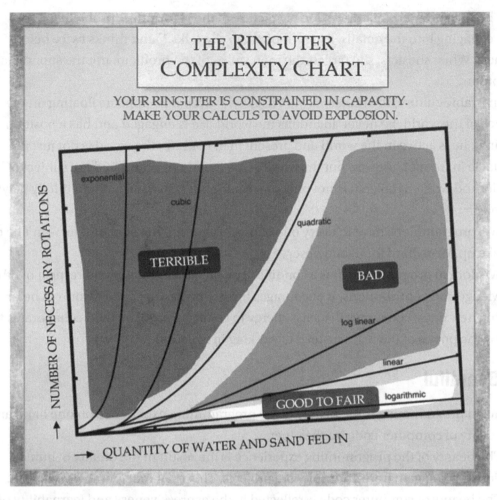

Figure 9-33. *Big-O notation in terms of Ringuting*

While playing, you will learn how to calculate the time and space complexity of your code using Big-O notation. Be careful, because if the performance is bad, then the Ringuter gives off a smoke, and if it is terrible, it explodes!

Be Wise

As defined in the *Pathfinder* role-playing game reference book, wisdom is a combination of "willpower, common sense, awareness, and intuition" that conveys personality magnetism and special ability of advisory and intellectual authority.

The wise programmer draws the big picture of the algorithmic problem at hand before digging into the details, listens more than she talks,[47] and thinks twice before she acts. When she acts, she targets the root causes of the problem, not the superficial symptoms.

In Arabic culture, the Hakeem (the Wise) say, "Even if he appears floating on the surface of the world, he never abandons the world. He is engaged and has a position within it, he is active in the world and present in it. For him, the world is not just a spectacle in front of his eyes, but the world is the theater of action and the subject of his activity and work ... Hakeem is not only a spectator but also a full actor faithfully playing his role."[48]

We, programmers, have in every one of us a "sleeping" Hakeem. But he won't be easy to wake up. Work hard for it, and deserve it.

Wisdom in programming has a condition: intellectual modesty and respect of others' knowledge and contributions. It encourages the use of existing code resources before making new ones, consumes the least energy to resolve a problem, and collaborates to deploy the power of the team instead of working in isolation.

Be Beautiful

Beauty in programming is the beauty of the programming experience on one hand and the beauty of computer code on the other.

The beauty of the programming experience is the result of the quality of human relationship you gain from your software projects. This is an indisputable condition.

The beauty of computer code is reflected in the expressiveness and learnability of that code.

I can't but agree with Bret Victor[49] who thinks that programming "is a way of thinking, not a rote skill." But people can't capture what you are thinking about in your code if it is not that visible. To say it in a short sentence, "People understand what they can see." Thus, the goal of a "programming system should be encouraging powerful ways of thinking" while "enabling programmers to see and understand the execution of their programs." In fact, Ringza, the algorithmic language we are using in Ringorialand, is an

---

[47]The Dalaî Lama says: "When you speak, you just repeat what you already know. But if you listen, you can surely learn something new."

[48]Translated to English from `https://tinyurl.com/y6ddhrmn`

[49]We cited Bret in Chapter 5 and introduced him to you there. Here I cite him again.

illustration of the power of visual thinking when writing computer code. From the real world, we adopted an open source visual programming language called Drakon[50] to be our friend in crafting visible thoughts and translating them without hassle to beautiful Ring code. You'll learn more about this in the "Ringza is a Visual Language of Thinking" section.

The Holy Book of Ringoria

As like any religious civilization, Ringoria has a holy book. This forms the symbolic reference from which moral values and operational laws are inspired. The book is written in a poetic style, is sometimes ambiguous, but has a lot of structuring messages for the life of a programmer to be peaceful, happy, and successful.

Figure 9-34 and Figure 9-35 are the two first pages I invite you to read. There will be no explanation right now since we will later invite every idea in its most convenient context. Some of them were elaborated on earlier, and it will be your challenge to identify them on your own. In the game, when I ask you a question and you find the answer in the Holy Book of Ringoria, you get an Advantage. An Advantage lets you be the winner if you are competing with another Ringler and you get the same score. For fun, if you prefer, I have prepared a recording of this text.[51] Listen and then try to find a possible connection between what you heard and the world of programming. The more you raise questions, the better your learning experience will be. In the next two pages, you will leave this Apress book and land in the Ringoria Holy Book.

---

[50]Explore the Drakon visual language project at drakon-editor.sourceforge.net.
[51]https://tinyurl.com/y4nbouhc

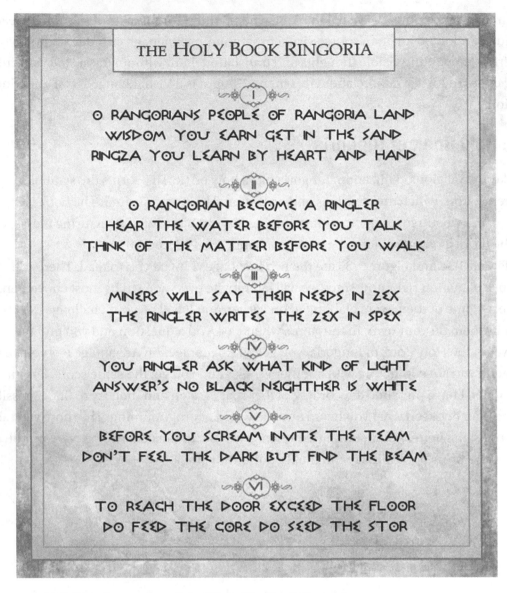

THE HOLY BOOK RINGORIA

I

O RANGORIANS PEOPLE OF RANGORIA LAND
WISDOM YOU EARN GET IN THE SAND
RINGZA YOU LEARN BY HEART AND HAND

II

O RANGORIAN BECOME A RINGLER
HEAR THE WATER BEFORE YOU TALK
THINK OF THE MATTER BEFORE YOU WALK

III

MINERS WILL SAY THEIR NEEDS IN ZEX
THE RINGLER WRITES THE ZEX IN SPEX

IV

YOU RINGLER ASK WHAT KIND OF LIGHT
ANSWER'S NO BLACK NEIGHTHER IS WHITE

V

BEFORE YOU SCREAM INVITE THE TEAM
DON'T FEEL THE DARK BUT FIND THE BEAM

VI

TO REACH THE DOOR EXCEED THE FLOOR
DO FEED THE CORE DO SEED THE STOR

Figure 9-34. *The first page of the Holy Book of Ringoria*

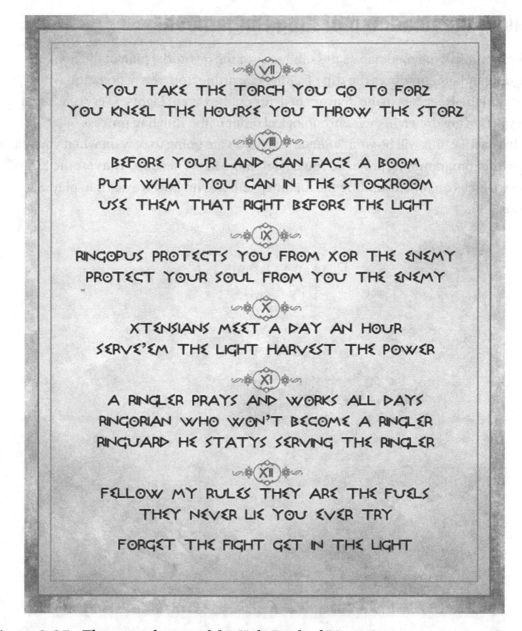

Figure 9-35. *The second page of the Holy Book of Ringoria*

Follow the Roadmap of King Ringamesh

You can think of the roadmap as the silhouette or the territorial plan of the map of Ringorialand. It reproduces the trip of a Ringler starting from the negotiation with miners in the Deep Sea to the delivery of lights on the Cap of Lights. Every place and every action are drawn in their chronological order of the Ringling process.

In practice, this will be your "mental" table you are going to play on when you make real-world programming projects. You'll learn more in the section "Harvest the Rings." Here we focus on understanding the roadmap and less on how we use it to play. See Figure 9-36.

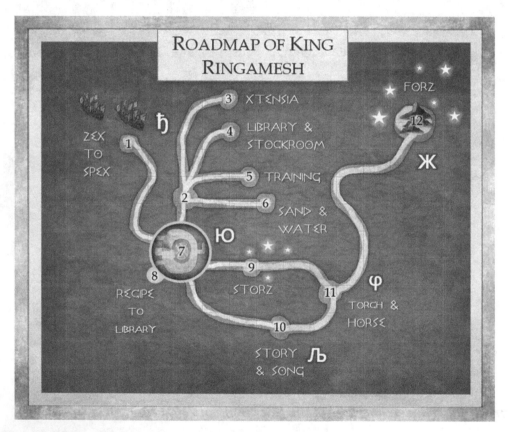

Figure 9-36. *Roadmap of King Ringamesh: the lights in 12 steps*

The roadmap can also be seen as the operational law that implements the spirit of the Holy Book in practical terms. It has the power of law, and Ringson uses it as a reference to force anyone to accomplish their duties. For example, while you are playing, if it turns out that you do not have the necessary score to enter the Castle to use the Ringuter (7), Ringson can order you to go for training and maybe to do other small duties around the kingdom. These trainings and experiences combined could elevate your score so you can enter the Castle the next time you try.

The following are the 12 steps of the roadmap:

1. Zex is transformed to spex: the customer needs are documented as requirements.

2. An analysis is made to define if there is...

3. A need of importing some power from Xtensia: decide on the potential use of external libraries to Ring written in C/C++

4. Any existing reusable recipes archived in the Royal Library or even some compatible lights (copies of the delivered programs) previously stocked in the Stockroom

5. A need of new trainings to build the skills required by the mission in hand

6. An analysis is made to define the type and composition of water and sand to be used in the Ringuter: data structures are designed and Ring functions to be used are defined.

7. All the other entrants are prepared and fed into the Ringuter: specification of requirements (Spex), technical architecture (Tex), and user experience (Yex). The correct number of rotations of the Ringuter to grind all this is defined.

8. A copy of the recipe is archived in the Royal Library.

9. If Ringuting is done right, storz are generated: in programming this is coding.

10. A story is written about the storz, and a melody is composed: in programming this is documentation.

11. A horse and torch are taken to bring the storz; the poem and the melody and go to the Cap of Lights: in programming this is delivery.

12. If Ringifying is done right (successful program delivery), lights are generated: in programming this is customer feedback.

These steps form a happy path you will probably never meet in real life. In fact, there will be a lot of deviations, exceptional events, and unexpected and sometimes unpleasant surprises. When programming for real, expect the state of your programming world, and therefore the steps of your particular roadmap, to differ. Ringlers take change into consideration in everything they do. They are realistic and work toward a moving goal using the tools we learned to stay in control.

Ringza by Heart, Ringza by Hand!

Ringza is a dragon. Ringza is the voice of wisdom. Ringza is the language. Three in one, and for a reason: there is a dose of constructive ambiguity in talking about this spectacular thing, a programming language.

God Ringaros called Ringorians to respect him in two things: learning the language by heart and using it in practice every single day. To illustrate that, the Holy Book of Ringoria comes with two beautiful word clouds.[52]

Ringza by Heart

Right to the cloud. See Figure 9-37.[53]

---

[52]The word clouds were generated with the online tool `wordart.com`.
[53]The number could change in next versions, of course.

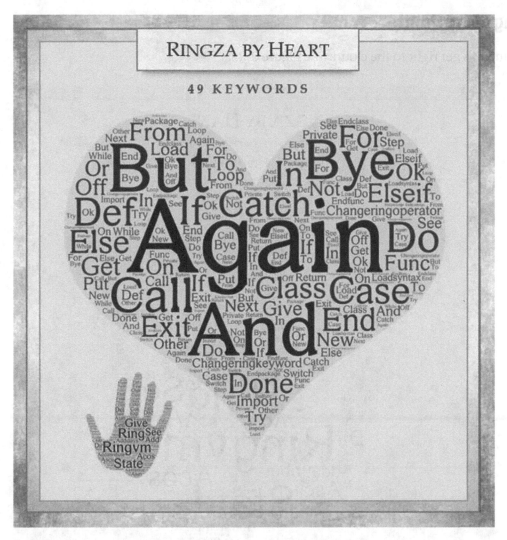

Figure 9-37. *In Ring, there are 49 keywords you should learn by heart*

The language keywords can be learned by consulting the documentation and studying the rich set of examples coming from the Ring language. They are basic features with immediate result, so discovering what they do is instantaneous. Only one or two lines of codes are generally what you need to get it working.[54]

While playing, you won't be forgiven when you don't know one of them.

---

[54]Refer to the section "Documentation and Help System" in Chapter 1.

Ringza by Hand

Again, let's get right to the cloud. See Figure 9-38.

Figure 9-38. *In Ring, there are 208 standard functions you should use in practice*

Your knowledge of the 49 keywords of the Ring language won't be all that you need. Hands-on experience with the basic 208 functions is required. These functions are organized in libraries (Royal Library), and the Ringler finds them on the bookshelf of the Royal Library. Learning them by example is always the best thing. For that, the Ring documentation provides instructive tutorials; go through them and practice. This will elevate your Knowledge Points and therefore your overall score.

Ringza Is a Visual Language of Thinking

Visualization is a powerful tool of thinking. When we were children, we drew all the time. As we go to school and engage in studying, the numbers, formulas, and texts take over and occupy our world. Dan Roam, a leading visual thinker, was right to say it in few words: "The battle today is for attention. Whether it's online, in a meeting room, or during a pitch, the audience is captured from the first moment you pick up a pen and start drawing."[55] In his book called *Draw To Win*,[56] Dan explains how "recent estimates from the visual neurosciences indicate that vision likely accounts for close to two-thirds of your total brain activity. Roughly one-third of your brain's neurons are dedicated to visual processing, and another third are occupied by vision combined with other sensory processing. That leaves one-third of your brain for everything else." Visualizing is more than drawing pictures; it is "thinking with your mind's eye." To make it happen, Dan proposes a visual language of six shapes that mimics how our brain visual system works. See Figure 9-39.

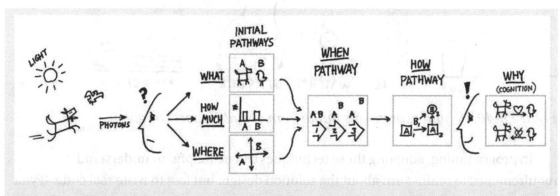

This is a simplified schematic of how the vision system works: through a series of discrete steps, each of which takes place in specific order and in specific parts of the brain, light becomes meaning.

Figure 9-39. *Visual thinking creates light when it becomes meaning!*

[55]https://www.youtube.com/watch?v=GwhpLHpDUug
[56]Thanks to Mongi Ayouni who lent me a copy of the book.

In their book *Gamestorming: A Playbook for Innovators*, Dave Gray, Sunny Brown, and James Macanufo show how visual thinking techniques can improve collaboration and communication. Thus, they say, "Yes, reading, writing, and arithmetic were instrumental in many of these monumental achievements. The written word and mathematics are both powerful tools. They are languages that we can use to make conceptual models, think about the world, and convey complex ideas to each other. But there is another language that's equally powerful, and we don't teach it in schools—at least, not consistently and not very well. It's called visual language, and it's the language we use to make ideas visual and explicit."

The three authors propose what they call the "visual alphabet," a kind of proto-alphabet of visual shapes that you can use to construct any kind of visual. In addition to letters and numbers, those glyphs are • , | , ∧, ∩, ⊃, ○, ◦, △, □, ◻, and ☺. They show how these basic constructs can be combined, like words in a natural sentence, to produce more elaborated visual expressions like the ones shown in Figure 9-40.

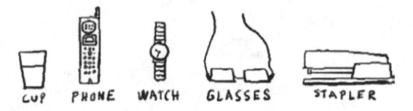

Figure 9-40. *Visual expressions made from visual "letters" or glyphs*

In programming, adopting these techniques can be helpful to understand requirements, to brainstorm about the solution design, but less to write real code. If you turn to Wikipedia and ask for a definition of visual programming, then you'll get this: "In computing, a visual programming language (VPL) is any programming language that lets users create programs by manipulating program elements graphically rather than by specifying them textually."

I can underline at least three weaknesses in such a definition:

- First, it is about a visual programming language and not visual programming as a thinking exercise.

- Second, visual programming is scaled down to the mechanical process of "manipulating" visual elements and not thinking through them.

- Third, visual is assumed to be the rival of textual.

A lot has been done during the last 30 years or so to make programming go visual. But here we are: nothing has changed, and the substance of programming remains a brute-textual code.

I believe text, in programming, will continue to be there for a long time and that text, in programming, is somehow misunderstood. Its open structure and liquid semantics nourish the illusion that the complexity of our computer programs comes from the text itself. The truth is, complexity is not in the text but in our weak mastery of expressing our ideas in the text. Thus, let's be fair: the problem is us, the programmers, not the textual code.

Research literature in visual programming is unanimous on the idea that being bidimensional makes text inherently unexpressive. However, if we think about it more closely, we should find that the inverse is true. Take a look at Figure 9-41.

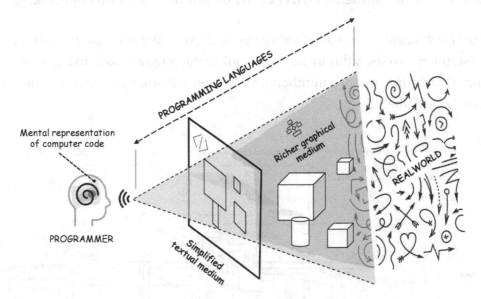

Figure 9-41. *Mental versus textual versus graphical representation of computer code*

Text plays the role of a simplification layer of the more complex real world we are striving to represent in our code. Being bidimensional leaves more room for our brains to reflect on it with the least possible quantity of noise. Thinking in code needs a clear mental representation where at the same time no one knows exactly how our neurons collaborate to understand a problem or find a solution for it. Despite this, we all agree that thinking happens here ☺, and the mental representation we feed in our brains, whether it be text or graphics, is not the most important part of it. The smaller and clearer this part is, the more energy is allocated by our brain to thinking. The larger it is, the harder it is for the brain to work efficiently and creatively! See Figure 9-42.

Figure 9-42. *Visual burden weighs heavily on our mental ability of thinking*

Visual programming can sometimes go extreme in its ability to invent problems for obvious solutions. To show this by example, look at the program code in Figure 9-43 for computing the factorial of a number in an ancient 3D-oriented visual programming language called Cube.

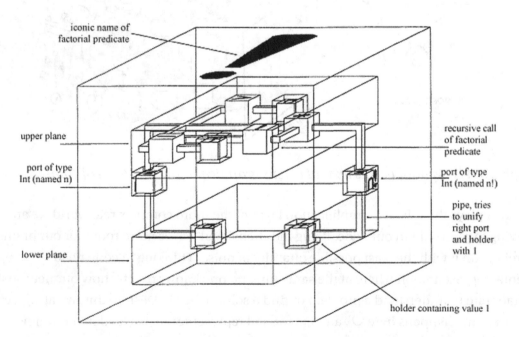

Figure 9-43. *A factorial "written" in the Cube language*

This is something we can write textually in Ring code like this: factorial(5). Even if we write it from scratch, it will be something like this:

```
f=5 // I will calculate the factorial of 5
for i=f to 2 step-1 // for each number from 5 to 2
        f = f * (i-1) // I multiply recursively by next number
next I // When finshed I get the factorial(5) in f
```

The previous Ring code is telling us the story of how a factorial is calculated, something difficult to say in pictures and impossible to say in a cube!

Therefore, the problem with the current visual programming approaches is that they put the burden on the programmer's brain with their richer graphical medium. In fact, visually oriented programming environments tend to accumulate what they lose from abandoning text with what they bring as a visual complexity. That's why programmers resist to make the shift and prefer coming back quickly to their notepads to stay in the care of their plain-old text code.

This wasn't the case in the very beginning (the 1960s to 1980s) when the visual programming movement gave us beautiful tools and paradigms. So you are aware of their contributions to alleviate the complexity of programming, I will show some snapshots of their creations. See Figure 9-44, Figure 9-45, Figure 9-46, and Figure 9-47.

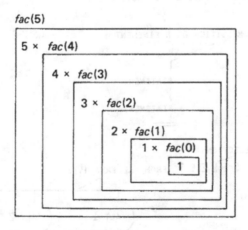

Figure 9-44. *A visual program of factorial(5) recursion frames. From Bauer (1982)*

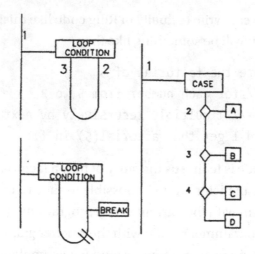

Figure 9-45. *Visual representation of loop and case branching Rothon diagram. From Brown (1983)*

--- / ---

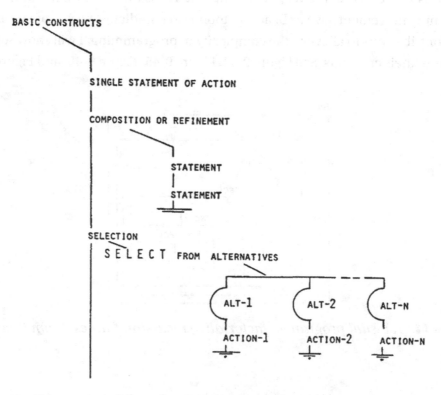

Figure 9-46. *Dimensional flowchart. From Witty (1977)*

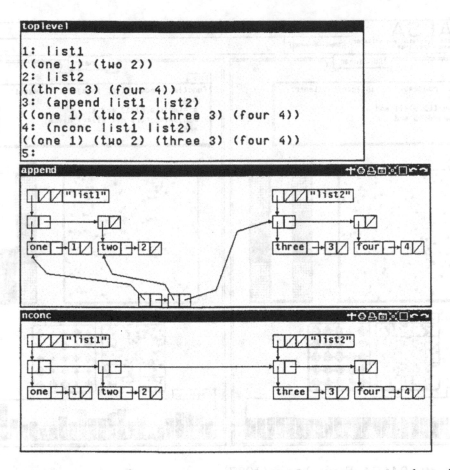

Figure 9-47. *Text to visual programming with Castle. From Boecker (1986)*

Finally,[57] I would add this "impressive piece of visual programming software, using both topological and metric conventions in representing program activity. Many of the output of the system are histogram-like in nature, intending to demonstrate the differences in effectiveness between alternate algorithms." The tool was invented by Brown and called BALSA. See Figure 9-48.

---

[57]I took these examples from an interesting book available at https://web.stevens.edu/ jnickerson/ch2.pdf. The book seems to be written by Jeffrey Nickerson from the Stevens Institute of Technology. I don't have the title of the book yet. I've contacted the author on LinkedIn, waiting for a response.

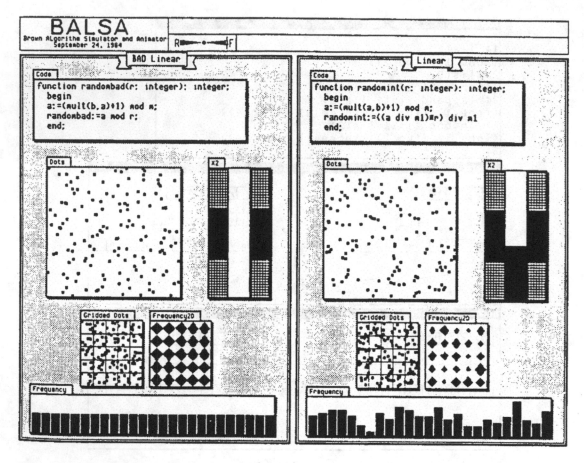

Figure 9-48. *BALSA. From Brown (1987)*

In 1986, Professor Vladimir Parondzhanov from the Russian Federal Space Agency started the creation of a visual language for algorithmic thinking with a clear goal: bringing clarity and learnability to the huge and complex source code of the VKK Space Orbiter program, implicating more than 20,000 people who need to communicate and share code. Vladimir built Drakon around three principles.

- The language is graphical but copes with the textual structure of code.

- It is hierarchical and preserves the natural human visual habits.

- The code is flowing in only one direction, most important things first, without any use of arrows between shapes and noisy visual constructs.

I discovered Drakon when it was released to the public as open source in 2011. Since then, I've used it to design complex algorithms and make them learnable by others. And when it comes to teaching programming, it has proven to be a useful tool to visualize basic algorithms in an instructive way. Furthermore, working with Drakon in mind, whatever your programming language is, can help you write expressive and clean code.

As I told you in Chapter 5, when I first discovered Drakon, there was one feature of the language that changed my way of writing code. The simple fact of imposing a direction on the flow of thinking from top to bottom and then from left to right ensures clear code. See Figure 9-49.

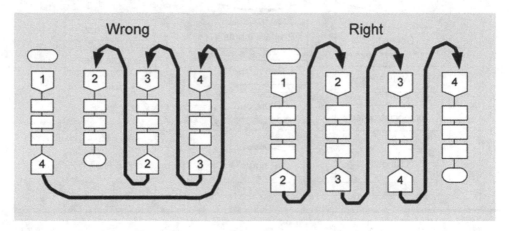

Figure 9-49. *Drakon imposes a rigorous direction on the flow of your train of thought*

In our fantasy world of programming, Drakon is nothing but Ringza, the national language of Ringoria. In Figure 9-50, I've expressed the logical steps of the Roadmap of King Ringamesh using the Drakon notation.

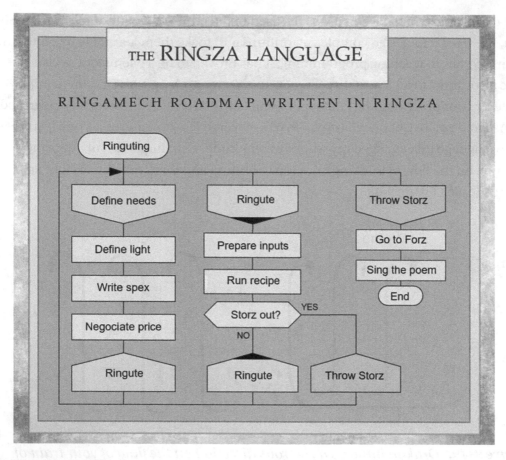

Figure 9-50. *A Ringza recipe: what we described in many pages fits into a single Drakon diagram*

As we did in Chapter 5 many times, before you jump into writing code, design your algorithmic solution visually using Drakon and then translate it seamlessly to Ring. This will lead you, naturally, to develop your visual thinking reflexes and produce better code. Over many years, I have been using the same process to teach other programming languages as well, and it has proven to be very rewarding.

Do you know that Ring was developed using a visual programming language? It is open source, called PWCT,[58] and created by Ring designer Mahmoud Fayed. See Figure 9-51.

---

[58]http://doublesvsoop.sourceforge.net

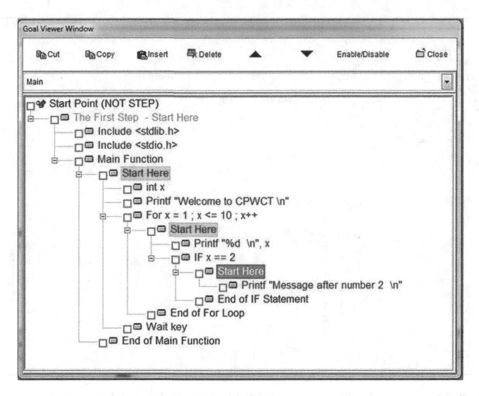

Figure 9-51. *A sample program in PWCT*

Like with Drakon, the language vision is to keep the same text-editing habits while structuring the entry of each line of code using data forms to prevent syntax errors. It is a multiparadigm language with code generated in several languages including C, Python, C#, Harbor, and Supernova (an ancestor language to Ring specializing in natural programming). The most important features of PWCT in my opinion are these two: playing programs as movies to learn how to create them step-by-step, and running programs from the past to get a better understanding of what is going on.

Finally, Figure 9-52 shows how to visually solve a complex algorithmic problem with text parsing and extracting. Yes, these visuals were my sole possible way of deconstructing the problem into manageable parts by my mind and hence find an effective solution to the problem.

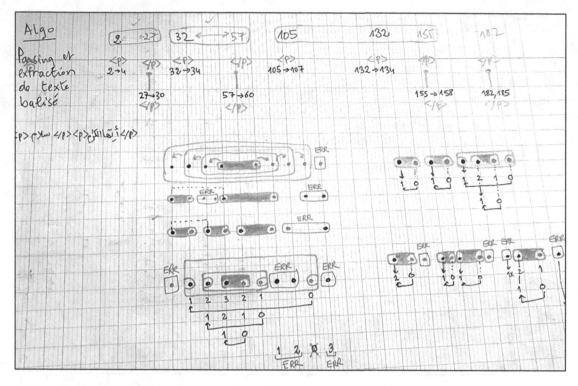

Figure 9-52. *A sample of how visual thinking can help us solve complex algorithmic problems*

Now it is time to show you, in more detail, the scope of the learning experience you are going to have and the scoring system we will be using in the game.

To the stars, Sir Harvester!

Harvest the Stars, Design a Learning Path

Because you decided to become a Ringler, you will be learning Ring while you are reading, telling stories, and playing with real-world programming missions, right? If you are lucky, then you will be harvesting stars, in the course of your learning career, by earning Knowledge Points and Experience Points. But this will come at a cost: consuming a portion of your energy. Your energy is measured in Energy Points (EPs).[59]

---

[59]I have designed a complete scoring system that I will leave for the future: my next book in programming games in Ring, where we will develop the Ringorialand game together, I hope, step-by-step.

Your learning path to become a master programmer is composed of three levels of three steps each. This corresponds to the nine steps of the Training Camp with its three levels of difficulty.[60] Depending on the number of stars harvested, you wear an iron, silver, or gold ring, respectively after completion of the first, second, and third levels. And who offers you the rings? Ringafoye the Queen, in person.

As explained, your level is the expression of your "social class" in Ringoria. You start as a foreigner who must learn the Ringza language to get citizenship and become a Ringorian. During this phase, most of your time is spent acquiring the basics of Ring that you can find in a book like this, in the documentation center of Ring, and from the mouths of experienced Ring programmers who you can reach easily in the Ring Google Group.

Then you knock at the door of the second level and work hard to become a Ringuard who deserves the silver ring. There you will learn data structures and the error system of Ring, and you fulfill your duties of using them in real programs. A duty is an exercise you find in any programming tutorial of any programming language, in designing data structures, and in managing code errors.

If this second level is achieved, then you start your ultimate journey of becoming a Ringler targeting the gold ring. During this third and last level, you play with missions to solve a selection of fundamental algorithmic problems in Ring. Such problems can be found in many programming books[61] dealing with fundamental algorithms. Pick them, understand them, and remake them in Ring.

While you are designing your learning experience, you should target only a subset of the 32 skills of Table Complete at any period of time. In Figure 9-53, I illustrate a sample learning path, inferred from the content of this book, where every chapter is represented by its number in a column of the table. You can plan out your time over a period of nine months, one month per chapter.

---

[60]You will see in a minute that this also corresponds to the nine chapters of the book.

[61]The book I advise you to base your training on is *How to Solve It by Computers* by R.G. Dromey.

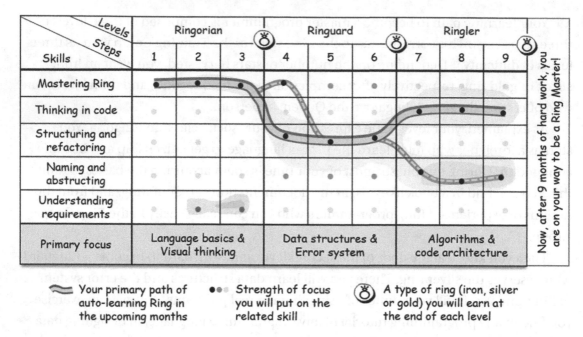

Skills \ Levels/Steps	Ringorian			🏆	Ringuard			🏆	Ringler			🏆	Now, after 9 months of hard work, you are on your way to be a Ring Master!
	1	2	3	4	5	6	7	8	9				
Mastering Ring	●	●	●	●	●	●	●	●	●				
Thinking in code	●	●	●	●	●	●	●	●	●				
Structuring and refactoring	●	●	●	●	●	●	●	●	●				
Naming and abstracting	●	●	●	●	●	●	●	●	●				
Understanding requirements	●	●	●	●	●	●	●	●	●				
Primary focus	Language basics & Visual thinking				Data structures & Error system				Algorithms & code architecture				

〰️ Your primary path of auto-learning Ring in the upcoming months   ●●● Strength of focus you will put on the related skill   🏆 A type of ring (iron, silver or gold) you will earn at the end of each level

Figure 9-53. *Your learning path of the Ring language in nine months based on the nine chapters of this book*

In this particular learning experience, the first level is limited to getting the basics and, therefore, accumulating Knowledge Points. For the two other levels, where you will face real-world problems in real-world programming projects, you are rewarded in Experience Points. Always remember, you must gather a number of KPs and XPs to gain stars. Both knowledge and experience are compulsory.

When nine months have passed (it could be shorter or longer; it's up to you), you can evaluate yourself using the Table Complete, and then start again, designing a new learning experience with a different path that explores new areas of the table you didn't visit yet. Repeat it again, and again, and never feel exhausted. You will end up addicted to learning, a cornerstone of programming mastery!

That said, you need to pay attention to one aspect nearly all the programming curriculums tend to ignore: performance in programming is not limited to achieving high results but includes minimizing the energy you should deploy.[62] While training yourself and playing the game of programming, you should find an equilibrium between what you gain and the cost of that gain. This should become clearer when we put everything aside and talk about you, programmer: you are the Ringler!

---

[62]Programmers are notoriously lazy, aren't they?

You Are the Ringler!

You are a programmer; you've got a set of skills. Those skills form the essense of your energy. You use it to perform software solutions by writing computer code, in Ring or any other programming language. Your ultimate achievement is the value your user will get from the software.

Schematically speaking, programming, from the programmer's perspective, can be described as shown in Figure 9-54.

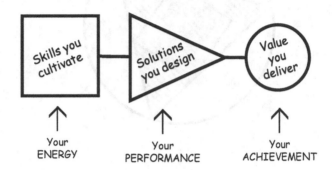

Figure 9-54. *Programming, from the programmer perspective*

In the real world, the three graphic shapes □, ▷, and ◯ are not sequentially organized like in Figure 9-54. Energy, performance, and value are always interrelated in unpredictable ways. They "work" together, mutually influence each other, and supercharge their respective impact.

To the best of my knowledge, computer science literature doesn't pay enough attention, if any at all, to the critical necessity of understanding these three "shapes" and analyzing the dynamic relation between them. All that we find are some basic and sometimes fuzzy concepts from the agile movement and the project management standards. The point is that the triplet {□, ▷, ◯}[63] forms the cornerstone of our gamification system. Therefore, they must be defined.

The first idea I want you to internalize inside your programmer brain is `<success/>`. You write programs to make your users successful. Remember, programming is providing light to those who are in need. Success must be your ultimate goal of any programming experience. Therefore, your energy must be deployed for success, your performance should enable you to reach success, and the value of your code needs to embrace what is required by your customer success!

---

[63]I repeat the shapes many times so you can memorize them.

In Figure 9-55, I evoke the Iron Compass.

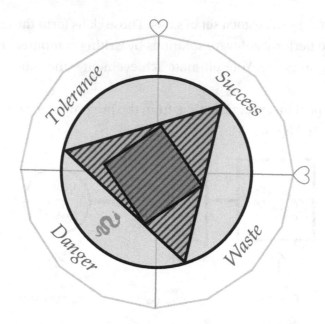

Figure 9-55. *The programmer combines their energy, performance, and the value put in the code to make the user successful*

Of course, success can be hard to obtain. Many programming projects fail, and many seeds of energy are wasted on every programmer's desk. To cope with what we called in the first section the dynamic nature of programming, the □─▷─○ diagram can be revisited to show factors influencing every one of the three shapes. Knowing them is essential in your gameplay, because they are candidates to inevitably consume your energy if you don't control them.

Factors are represented by arrows directed to the shape they are supposed to influence. If the impact is assumed positive, then you see a ⊕ sign. Otherwise, the impact is negative, and you see a ⊖ sign instead. Finally, all the factors are impossible to include in our gaming system, or it will be unplayable. Therefore, we restrict ourselves only to some of them (in black in Figure 9-56).

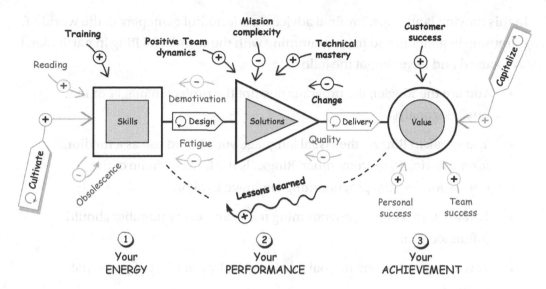

Figure 9-56. *A systemic view of the programming activity*

In the course of your programming career, you will be put in real-world situations[64] where programming is influenced by the following list of factors:

- **Training**: As an augmenting factor of the level of your skills

- **Positive team dynamics**: As an augmenting factor of your solution design

- **Mission complexity**: As a diminishing factor of your solution design

- **Technical mastery**: As an augmenting factor of your solution design

- **Customer success**: As an augmenting factor of your delivered value

- **Lessons learned**: As an augmenting factor of your skills

---

[64]The quasi-totality of the code samples you saw in this book were inspired from real-world situations I worked on in real-life projects.

In this moving landscape, my final advice for successful gameplay in the world of programming in general, and in programming with the wonderful Ring in particular, is to stay focused and never forget the following:

- You are the Ringler, the programmer, not the project manager or the business analyst.

- You speak in Ringza, the visual language you should use as a medium for mastering Ring (remember, Ringza is the fantasy name of the open source visual programming language Drakon).

- You work solo or in a programming team, and every member should influence you.

- You engage for a moving goal that is naturally a subject of perpetual change.

- You consume an energy: your skills are your energy.

- You create your performance: your performance is your vital "signal of existence."

- You deliver Ringza recipes: you write computer code.

- You fight against Xos the Enemy by designing secure and performant code.

- Negotiation is your weapon: to be a good programmer, you must negotiate before you write code. To be able to negotiate, you need a way to measure everything!

Voilà! It's the end of chapter; thank you for your patience.

Conclusion

Last week, I visited Avionav,[65] the construction company of the first Tunisian aircraft, to show them how Ring could be an option for their software development. Foued Kamel, who is the company's CEO, told me that the biggest obstacle they faced to realize their dream was themselves!

---

[65]https://avionav.net

Foued explained that engaging themselves in a closed market, restricted to developed countries, wasn't harder than the psychological decision to overcome their initial hesitation and belief they were able to do it. And they did it. Avionav designs the best aircrafts worldwide in its market segment, with customers from both the United States and China. Today, they are working to disrupt the market with an open business model to make the same happen for any other developing country that decides to develop its own aircrafts. The same should happen to everyone who dreams of becoming a master programmer.

In this chapter, I told you the truth: programming is hard, complex, and largely misunderstood. There is a kind of definitional fuzziness, combined with a dogmatic forced marriage with the so-called "building" metaphor, that is augmented by an extreme market and employability orientation, which makes programming education unsuitable for forging solid skills.

There is a problem then that we should fix at the root level. The chapter demonstrated it is a problem of metaphor. A solution is worth proposing, and the chapter designed a complete solution based on a gaming metaphor. Gaming better describes programming than any building in any city in the world. Its systemic, dynamic, and social nature gives your programming incredible value via a learning-by-playing models. It unveils some of the secrets of the world-class programmers you might find at Google, Apple, and Microsoft. It is serious gaming, though, with a well-defined skillset and a clear learning path you will be traversing in your shiny programming career.

This final chapter helped us rethink the definition of programming and told its story, maybe for the first time, via the rigor of system thinking and the magic of gamified worlds.

Like Foued and his friends, you should overcome any hesitation you have. Read the chapter again if it seems daunting at first. Understand the world of Ringoria, zenga zenga,[66] and live with its characters, one by one. Walk with them, read with them, Ringute with them, and dream with them. Focus on the skills you'll get and how you get them. Finally, close your eyes[67] and say, "I'll become a Ringler, a world-class programmer, and like the guys at Avionav, I'll craft my aircraft and let it fly, very, very high!"

---

[66]From the Libyan dialect, this means place by place.

[67]You must do it this time. Promise?

APPENDIX A

A Dialogue with Mahmoud Fayed

This appendix contains some of quality technical discussions I have had with Mahmoud Fayed, the creator of Ring, and with Bert Mariani, an active member of the Ring community and the technical reviewer of this book, on the Ring Google Group and on other mediums (slightly edited for the book). Some sections introduce details that haven't been covered in the book, while others further expand on what you already know. They helped me personally to better understand the language, so I insisted on sharing them with you.

The most important reason I've included these discussions in the book is to share Mahmoud's personality and his vision of programming. His responses contain expert know-how, philosophical reflection on the nature of programming, and Mahmoud's emotional connections to Ring and other projects.

You will find answers on how Ring was named, how it compares to other languages in the eyes of its creator, why some obvious features like the Array data type doesn't exist, how this can impact the performance of Ring programs, why Mahmoud Fayed is so responsive to answering questions and fixing bugs, how he kindly deals with critics, and many other interesting subjects.

I hope you'll find this appendix interesting to read and instructive in the same time. If you still have questions, then don't hesitate to go to the Ring Google Group and ask them.

Network Programming in Ring

Mansour: I read once that you were thinking of building a framework for network programming on top of Ring. Can you please give me a snapshot of that vision, its philosophy and main features (parallel, agent-based, IoT, wireless sensor networks, blockchain), and if it is on your roadmap for upcoming releases?

© Mansour Ayouni 2020

M. Ayouni, *Beginning Ring Programming*, https://doi.org/10.1007/978-1-4842-5833-0

Mahmoud: Netowork Programming is part of my plan for the future of Ring (the work has not been started yet because I'm working on other things). The idea is to work more on some of my ideas from the past (a super server programming paradigm) and improve Ring based on the current trends of the technology.

The super server programming paradigm is one of my ideas from 2007 and is implemented in the Programming Without Coding Technology (PWCT[1]) software. It needs a lot of improvements to be less complex and more suitable for modern technology.[2]

Composition over Inheritance

Mansour: By closely studying the programming style adopted for writing Ring, Ring libraries, and Ring tools, we can find a predominant use of the composition over inheritance principle.

Many famous technology houses (such as Qt in designing Qt3D, for example[3]) are making the move toward less class inheritance and more concatenation of the properties of the object at runtime. In Ring, this is possible through the use of the `AddMethod()` and `AddAttribute()` metaprogramming functions (we already covered this subject in Chapter 7, and you can see the documentation[4] for more information).

Now, can you tell me why this was a design choice you made in Ring? Why do you think this is useful? What advice can you give to Ring programmers in this regard?

Mahmoud: At the Ring language level:

- Ring is a multiparadigm language. Don't force a specific programming paradigm or make some methods or techniques more favorable than others.

- The Ring design is based on flexibility. The programmer decides what he wants to do. He is responsible for picking the right solution.

---

[1]http://doublesvsoop.sourceforge.net
[2]http://doublesvsoop.sourceforge.net/pwcthelp/features/programmingparadigm.htm
[3]https://www.kdab.com/overview-qt3d-2-0-part-1
[4]http://ring-lang.sourceforge.net/doc1.12/metaprog.html

For me as a programmer:

- I prefer selecting the simplest solution for the problem. For example, if the problem could be solved using (procedural programming), then I will solve it that way, and I may not touch classes or object-oriented programming.

- With respect to composition over inheritance, composition is more flexible and makes it easy to apply changes, while inheritance gives a lot of control when we have a clear idea about the system.

Many problems are better tackled using composition, while others are better solved using inheritance. If the case is in between, then my decision depends on the situation.[5]

In most cases, if I'm solving an old problem for me (I know the solution and I am aware of the final picture of the design), then I will use inheritance without problems, but I will not overuse it to avoid complexity. But if I'm developing something that could be changed too much and I need to support these changes in the future with few side effects, then I prefer composition.

Parallelization in Ring

Mansour: How can we run two Ring functions in parallel asynchronously? Is this possible within the language, or should we rely on external libraries?

Mahmoud: The Ring VM is designed to support threads through external libraries. So, we can have a flexible system that could support different thread functions provided by different libraries such as Allegro, Qt, Libuv, etc.

It's in my plan to write a standard thread library for Ring in the future. For now, it's recommended to use the threads functions provided by `gamelib.ring` (RingAllegro[6]).

A Language Copying Ring

Mansour: I came across this language today:
`http://dragon.suasive.in`

---

[5]https://en.wikipedia.org/wiki/Composition_over_inheritance
[6]http://ring-lang.sourceforge.net/doc1.11/allegro.html#using-threads

It's published by a young Indian, and it is copying Ring I think. Are you aware of it?

Mahmoud: Yes, it's developed by Aavesh from India, and he contacted me through Facebook two weeks ago to check it out.

Mansour: Great! Ring can be a mother of other languages then. This is something we could promote I think because no other language has such a "big heart."

Ring Data Type System

Mansour: Are there any resources out there about the internals of the Ring data type system? I'm particularly concerned with questions like these:

- How are the high level Ring types (take `Number` as an example) are implemented in low-level C types? What was your strategy for implicitly converting between Ring and C so we can gain the most efficient implementation? Where does this happen exactly in the language codebase?

- Since Ring doesn't have a `Float` type and similar advanced features, what are your guidelines for efficiently using Ring with such values?

- Are types in Ring relying internally on a `class` hierarchy (like `Int` in Java) or are they stand-alone types (like `Int` in Swift)?

- What are the reasons behind the `string` type implemented in 8 bits? What are the advantages compared to a larger implementation in 16 bits like the majority of other languages?

Mahmoud: Check this chapter: `http://ring-lang.net/doc1.10/generalinfo.html`. As a general rule, You don't need to think about `Int` or `Float` or `Double` when writing Ring code. Instead, think in a high-level way (`Numbers`). To answer your questions:

1. Ring always use the `Double` data type to represent *numbers* for Ring programs.

2. The `Int` data type is used only by internal Ring functions (VM-related functions) but not for Ring programs.

3. There are some functions that do arithmetic operations using the unsigned Int (Unsigned() function).

4. The string data type uses 8 bits for each character. It's good to work on binary data directly when each character represents 1 byte.

These are the main rules applied by Ring for very high-level programming. By using the Ring API and writing C/C++ extensions, you can have full control when you need it.

Bert: How is an array addressed? Does it use integer numbers?[7]

Mahmoud: In Ring, the Lists are represented using a *linked list*, and each node in this list contains the item and two pointers for the next and previous items.

Also, the list may contain an *array* or *hash table* for optimization and for quickly finding items.

When we access an *item* in the list, Ring searches for this item.

Linked lists are slower than using arrays, but it's more flexible; that's why Ring uses them.

In the future, for performance, we may add a Ring extension written in C/C++ that deals with arrays (not linked lists).

Note   I will work on improving Ring performance without adding too much complexity to the implementation code, which I want to keep simple and easy to understand.

Also, I have many plans for improving the performance that will be easily applied in the future.

Bert: Thank you for the explanation and future plans. When the Sudoku program runs 400 times faster in C code than Ring and when the Mandelbrot program runs 1,000 to 2,000 times faster in C code than Ring, then arrays and integers, which are standard in all other languages, need to be seriously considered and implemented in Ring.

If a program can be developed rapidly but it takes forever to run, it will not be used. Frankly, it is a serious drawback!

Mahmoud: For now, Ring 1.11 (under development) is faster than Ring 1.10 by a small percentage (25 percent). In the future, a lot of nice optimizations will be applied on Ring VM code (during the next Ring releases) to increase the performance.

---

[7]Bert Mariani: a member of the Ring community and the technical reviewer of the book.

About the Ring Compiler and VM

Mansour: I have a bunch of questions this time:

1. When you decided to write Ring, why didn't you use an established compiler like LLVM instead writing it from scratch in an ANSI C–based code?

2. What are the motivations and the problems for LLVM-like options?

3. What are the most important advantages for us as Ring developers to have our own compiler and VM?

4. Are there any risks behind that?

Mahmoud:

1. "When you decided to write Ring, why didn't you use an established compiler like LLVM instead writing it from scratch in an ANSI C–based code?"

Ring is designed to be a dynamic language, and these languages include features that need an interpreter or a virtual machine. But also, to achieve these goals:

- The ability to run large programs quickly (a fast compile time)

- A small size to be embedded in other applications (if we need that)

- The ability to execute code at runtime (`eval()` function and related features)

- Garbage collector (with a bunch of creative new ideas specific to Ring)

2. "What are the motivations in one hand and the problems in LLVM-like option in other hand?"

LLVM constitutes a large dependency that we can avoid.

The Ring compiler and the VM equals 20,000 lines of C code. The binary file is less than 500 KB.

Small and simple code is better and leads to more stability and easy maintainability.

A lot of popular and similar programming languages such as Lua, Perl, Tcl, Python, PHP, Ruby, etc., started with an implementation written in the C language. (We did the same thing, but with a small implementation as Lua but more language features than Python and Ruby.)

3. "What are the most important advantages for us as Ring developers to have our own compiler and VM?"

The implementation matches the design. We have a compiler *written for* this language and a VM that *is designed* for it too.

Ring includes some features that don't exist in other programming language, as listed here:

- Syntax flexibility

- Accessing objects using braces

- Class region, natural programming, declarative approach

- Special garbage collector (suitable for games; doesn't stop the world)

The implementation of such features becomes simpler when you have full control over the compiler and VM source code.

4. Are there any risks behind that?

There are no risks for this because:

- It's written in ANSI C, and we have a C compiler for each popular platform.

- It's small implementation of 20,000 lines of C code (from 2013), which has been tested for years!

- We have a visual implementation (using PWCT) so we can easily understand the details.

- It's well documented, and it's free and open source.

In the future, we could have a Ring to C translator to keep the Ring compiler (but avoid the Ring VM) to get high performance during runtime in sections that don't need the dynamic language features (like the eval() function).

Most programming languages start with (one implementation) and then many other implementations could appear from the community in the future.

Mansour: That's a nice answer yet really instructive! In particular, one line stimulated my curiosity to know more:

- Special garbage collector (suitable for games; doesn't stop the world)

Can you tell me more about how the Ring Game Engine plays better than game engines written in other languages in terms of garbage collection?

Mahmoud: The Ring garbage collector uses escape analysis and reference counting.

See this page on Wikipedia: `https://en.wikipedia.org/wiki/Escape_analysis`. Concentrate on the section "Converting heap allocations to stack allocations" and this quote:

> *"If an object is allocated in a subroutine and a pointer to the object never escapes, the object may be a candidate for stack allocation instead of heap allocation. In garbage-collected languages, this can reduce how often the collector needs to run."*

In Ring, the language itself is designed to support this idea:

- **Lexical scoping**: When we create a variable using the assignment operator, the variable belongs to the current scope.

- **Assignment operator copy variables by value (not by reference)**: The destination variable has its own scope and gets a complete copy of the source variable, with no references activated by Ring for this operation (so we don't need to track or garbage-collect anything).

When we call functions, we pass lists and objects *by reference*. After the end of each function, the reference can be destroyed automatically without caring about deleting the original object, because *we already know* that it belongs to the caller.

These rules let us know each ownership for each piece of data, and we share memory through passing lists and objects to functions by reference or through classes that return references to list items as you describe in the book. This is how the Ring Game Engine for 2D games work, but also how the Objects Library is designed to simplify the development of GUI applications using `RingQt`.[8]

---

[8]`http://ring-lang.sourceforge.net/doc1.12/ringqtobjects.html`

So, as a Ring programmer, you know exactly the lifetime of each variable you use, you know when the variable will be created and when it will be deleted, and you can delete the variable (remove it from memory) using the assignment operator.

These are some of the advantages:

- The memory is under the programmer control.

- You get a constant response time, which is very nice for games!

This simple design will help when we create a Ring to C language translator; no complex garbage collector is required.

To demonstrate that the memory is actually under the programmer control (by allocating and deleting memory using the assignment operator as we said), look at this example:

```
v = Space(1024)   # Creates a string of 1 KB inside v string
v = NULL          # v is now an empty string: Memory is just deleted
```

Most of Ring objects (List items, Strings, Numbers, etc.) are small objects (with a small size). What we have then, in our Ring programs, is a memory pool that allocates many small objects and allows us to use them without the need to go to the operating system and ask for memory each time. Read this:

https://en.wikipedia.org/wiki/Memory_pool

Again, you can read about all of this in Ring documentation:

http://ring-lang.sourceforge.net/doc1.12/generalinfo.html

In particular, this section from the documentation is nice:

> *"Remember that Ring encourage us to avoid using references, and the Assignment Operator will copy lists by value, so Ring usage of reference counting is very limited to special cases and in most cases the Escape Analysis is enough which is very fast. Starting from Ring 1.9 we extended the Reference Counting support to Ring Extensions and low level C pointers. So we don't have to care about using fclose() when we use fopen() for example. and the same for other extensions like RingODBC, RingSQLite, RingMySQL, RingQt, etc. All of the allocated resources will be cleaned by the Garbage Collector when we finish using them (when we actually loose the very last reference)."*

So, the Ring language is designed to provide automatic memory management but with a simple garbage collector and with the memory still under the programmer control.

When the Default Value of NULL Is Changed

Mansour: By default, NULL is an empty `string`, so if we say the following:

```
v = ""
if isNull(v){ ? "It's null" else ? "It's not null" }
```

we get the following: `It's null.`

And if we put any other value in v, like this:

```
v="anything"
```

we get the following: `It's not null.`

All this is good. But what if we change the default value of the NULL variable itself, like this:

```
NULL = "anything"
if isNull(NULL) {   ?"It's null" else? "It's not null" }
```

what is expected is to have "`It's not null`", right?

But what we have is...*nothing*!

Is that an internal bug of how `isNull()` is implemented? Or there is something wrong in my questioning?

Mahmoud: First, the function `IsNull()` is not related to the NULL variable in any way with respect to the function implementation. But they share the concept. The empty string `""` is a NULL value, and `IsNull()` checks whether the value is an *empty* `string`. The variable NULL contains the empty string `""` at the beginning.

Second, Ring doesn't contain constants; all what we have is *variables*.

NULL, NL, TAB, etc., are variables. (You can *change* them!) But you don't have to do this the way you did in your example.

Third, you can change them only if you need and for a good reason, like so:

```
NULL = ""        # Obvious in any situation
```

or like so:

```
NULL = "NULL"    # Useful when you dealt with SQL data
```

or like so:

```
NL = CHAR(13)    # Performs a Carriage Return
```

or like so:

```
NL = CHAR(13) + CHAR(10)   # Performs a Carriage Return + a Line Feed
```

or like so:

```
NL = WindowsNL() # Performs a New Line in Windows operating system
```

Mansour: Thank you for this clarification, Mahmoud; that's very useful indeed.

Mahmoud: As an extension to my previous answer, if you want to change the behavior of the `IsNull()` function with respect to the changes in the `NULL` variable, then consider that Ring supports *redefining* functions that are implemented in C code to be written in Ring code!

Here's an example:

```
NULL = "anything"
if isNull(NULL) {  ? "It's null" else ? "It's not null" }

func isNULL(value)
    if value = NULL or trim(value) = "" or UPPER(trim(value)) = "NULL"
        return TRUE
    ok
    return FALSE
```

Here's the output: `It's null.`

Mansour: This is phenomenal! I didn't expect that it was possible to overload the functions made in C directly in Ring. I see better now why flexibility is not a risk but belongs to the deep spirit of the language that gives this unprecedented level of freedom.

Speed of Ring List vs. C Code Array

Bert: When we write a simple program using a two-dimension array of 500×500 and then loop over every cell in the array 1,000 times, the C code was about 800 times faster!

On a human scale, something that takes 1 minute would take 14 hours to complete. Here is the Ring code:

```
// Ring version: takes 832 seconds
load "stdlib.ring"
a2D = newList(500,500)
```

```
See "Calculate Performance" + nl
See "Test Ring using list2D: 500 x 500 Loop 1000"+nl+nl

t1 = clock()
for cycle = 1 to 1000
    k = 1
    for i = 1 to 500
        for j = 1 to 500
            k = (i -1) * i +j
            a2D[i][j] = k
            k++
        next
    next
next

t2 = clock()
t3 = (t2 - t1) / 1000
See "Clock: "+cycle +" "+ t3 +" k: "+ k +nl
```

This is the C version of the program:

```
// C version : takes 0.76 to 1.25 seconds
#include <iostream>
#include <ctime>
#include <cmath>

int main()
{
    int     i, j, k, m, time_req ;
    int     a[500][500];
    clock_t t1, t2, t3;

    printf("500x500x1000 Takes ~ 1 sec \n\n");

    t1 = clock();
    for (m = 0; m < 1000; m++)
    {
        for (i = 0; i < 500; i++)
        {
```

```
        for (j = 0; j < 500; j++)
        {
            k = (i + 1) * i + j + 1;
            a[i][j] = k;
        }
    }
}

t2 = clock();
t3 = t2 - t1;
printf("Fin Value: %d %d  %d  %d  clock: %f \n", m , i, j,
a[i - 1][j - 1], ((float) t3 / CLOCKS_PER_SEC)  );

return 0;
}
```

Mahmoud: The C code is simple and could be added to Ring programs as an extension written in C when we need that. The point is that instead of repeating the C language features and adding them to the Ring language, we just use the C language when we need to write something that works with high performance.

In the future, when we develop a Ring2C translator, we will get better performance for all applications (not only applications that deal with arrays).

But performance comes later, after productivity. In this stage of Ring development, we focus on productivity.

Mansour: In a complex project like a programming language, it's almost impossible to tackle simplicity, flexibility, and productivity at the same time as performance.

A Ring key differentiator resides in the new programming experience it provides us with a spirit of computational thinking, not just crafting code. The connection it enables between structural, object-oriented, functional, declarative, and natural, all in one place, is a unique feature we are all proud of.

But this comes with a cost: some of the performance issues can't be managed at this young age of the language. The C and C++ extensions are there to give us an alternative when we need a bare-metal powerhouse. I suggest then to be patient and embrace the agenda Mahmoud is working on for the future.

Bert: Computer hardware easily and naturally handles arrays, which are just contiguous memory locations containing data. The basic instructions are to load and store from memory to the register. There are also index registers to point to memory locations.

A computer's arithmetic logic unit (ALU) is based on integers (floating points are a software routine). Assembler is the most efficient programming language to use. All modern high-level language should be able to handle arrays easily, naturally, and quickly. It should be part of the basic functionality, just like adding and subtracting.

In my opinion, the goal is not to call C code but to have the language implement the data structure naturally and natively. The speed of the hardware should be exploited properly.

Nobody will use a program that was easily and quickly developed but runs incredibly slowly!

In a human perspective, the Olympic 100 meters is run in 10 seconds, the marathon 40,000 meters in 2.5 hours. Users expect programs will give them the answer in a minute, not next week. When the result is 1000:1, then there is something seriously wrong.

Arrays are among the oldest and most important data structures and are used by almost every program. They are also used to implement many other data structures, such as lists and strings. They effectively exploit the addressing logic of computers. In most modern computers, the memory is a one-dimensional array of words, whose indices are their addresses.

Mansour: What you say is interesting. I just want to emphasize that, in practice, arrays are not more performant than linked lists in every context. If you get large data as items of the set or if you are randomly adding or deleting items, then, generally, linked lists are a better choice.

You are right when you explain that microprocessors have been made, historically, to perform better on contiguous arrays and integers than float numbers and linked lists, but this concern has actually been covered by the new architectures of CPUs (and GPUs alike) that are available today, which all include native facilities to grab arithmetic calculations of float numbers, nearly at the same performance of native integers.

The true discussion, then, needs to be focused on how programmers design their code for performance, by avoiding any cache misses their data structures and data operations would provide. Understanding how caches work (at their three levels L1, L2, and L3) and what best practices the programmer needs to adopt in designing his lists and writing his iterations over them is something that makes a huge difference: I mean that one programmer can create very bad performance with a native array, and another can make the same work with better performance using a linked list.

In my book *Beginning Ring*, unfortunately, I didn't find a window to talk about this... maybe in a future book about *Advanced Ring*. In the meantime, I suggest you take a look at this article:

```
https://dzone.com/articles/performance-of-array-vs-linked-list-on-modern-comp
```

Bert: Thanks for the link. Yes, agreed. When insertions and deletions are to be make, the property of linked list is an advantage. But, when dealing with a fixed size and format of elements, the property of arrays has an advantage. Arrays should be implemented as arrays. Arrays should *not* be implemented as linked lists!

Mansour: I took five minutes this morning to try to optimize the code you wrote in Ring. Originally, your code took 658.78s on my laptop. Too long I agree. A rapid refactoring of just *two lines* of code gave me a gain of 72 percent in raw performance (from 658.78s to just 185.67s), as shown here:

```
load "stdlib.ring"

a2D = newList(500,500)

See "Calculate Performance" + nl
See "Test Ring using list2D: 500 x 500 Loop 1000"+nl+nl

t1 = clock()

for cycle = 1 to 1000

    for i = 1 to 500

        k = (i-1) * i + 1 # I've added this line

        for j = 1 to 500
            // k = (i -1) * i +j
            // k = ((i -1) * i) + j + 1
            a2D[i][j] = k + j   # I've changed the formula
                                # from multipliation to addition
            // k++ # Unnecessarry incrementation
                    # replaced by + j in the formula above

        next j

    next i

next cycle
```

```
t2 = clock()
t3 = (t2 - t1) / 1000
See "Clock: "+cycle +" "+ t3 +" k: "+ k +nl
```

Usually, the programmer can find a way to optimize slow code by thinking differently in the logic adopted. But, there are other paths of optimization that can have a dramatic, positive impact when we totally change the design of the solution. I didn't find time to make it here, but in similar situations, there is a window for other gains in adopting additional options.

- Making some data preparation (initial calculations made outside the main loop) and data set redesign (the matrix is transformed to a list of vectors) so the number of nested loops goes down from three to two, or even one

- Clustering the hole data scope (500×500×1000) and performing the looping on a chunk of it every time, in a sequential manner

- Using metaprogramming in situations where formulas can replace loops (this is what we call *strength reduction*,[9] but it requires some mathematical pattern-matching or RegExp skills that could complicate your code)

Finally, it is important to know that the performance we gain on the program execution speed usually requires more space in memory for the algorithmic gymnastics we use. Therefore, an equilibrium must be found between what is possible and what is acceptable by the users of our program.

A deep reflection about algorithm optimization can be found here:

```
https://www.toptal.com/full-stack/code-optimization
```

Level Designer in Ring Games

Mansour: I noticed that you already created a maze designer, in the `maze.ring` game, so we can visually design a maze without writing code (WYSIWYG), as shown in Figure A-1.

---

[9]https://en.wikipedia.org/wiki/Program_optimization#Strength_reduction

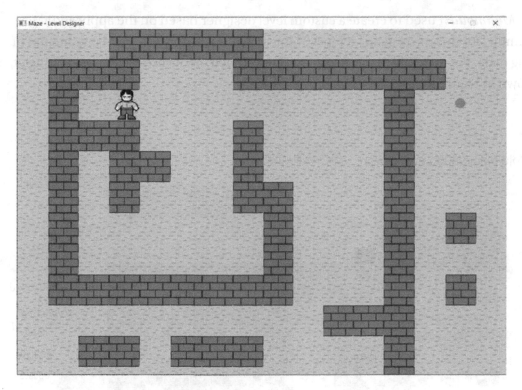

Figure A-1. *The visual level designer in the Maze game*

For those who need it, you can find the source code of the maze designer in these two files:

```
c:/ring/applications/maze/designer.ring
c:/ring/applications/maze/level.ring
```

To use it, we copy the file `designer.ring` and `level.ring` to the `maze` game folder, and then we run `designer.ring`. We can click a cell to change it to another cell that we want (of type Player, Door, Empty, or Wall). The designer works on the file `level.ring` that contains the list representing the level design. When we update the map in the designer, the `level.ring` file is updated automatically. When we finish the design, we copy the list from `level.ring` to `Maze.ring`.

I find this idea of including a visual designer for game levels amazing! Maybe you think of it as an abstract feature of the Ring Game Engine that anyone can use off the shelf with their new games.

Mahmoud: I used to create a custom level designer based on the application. For example, for this maze game, it's just 37 lines (without empty lines and comments) of Ring code. For the Gold Magic 800 game, I developed the level designer using RingQt, as shown in Figure A-2.

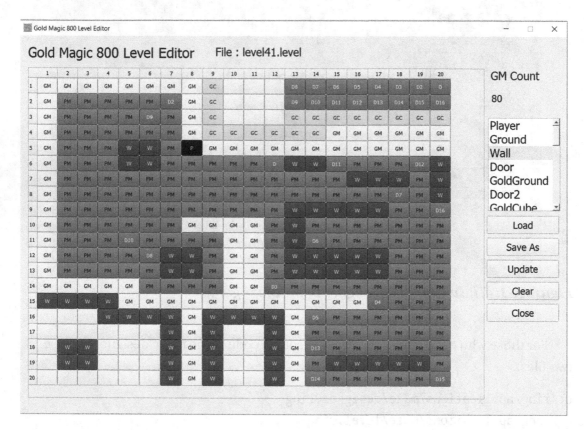

Figure A-2. *A level designer of the Gold Magic 800 game made with RingQt*

You can find the game here:

```
ring/applications/goldmagic800
```

Advice on the Use of Operator Overloading

Mansour: Disclaimer: I'm aware that \ (and not /) is not an operator in Ring, but this explanation will clarify my concern. In the Arabic text library I'm working on, one can say this:

```
load "arbStringLib.ring"
o1 = new arbString("قفْ للمُعلِّم وفّه التّبجيلا")
? o1 / 2
```

So, he gets the text subdivided into two items of the following list:

["وفّه التّبجيلا" , "قفْ للمُعلِّم"]

But also, if we want to subdivide the text between two people, طيبة and حنين (the Arabic names of my two daughters, Teeba and Haneen), then we write this:

```
? o1 / ["طيبة","حنين"]
```

So, the main text is subdivided between the two names طيبة and حنين and we have as a result the following (note that names appear on the right of each substring):

["طيبة : قفْ للمُعلِّم" ,
 "حنين : وفّه التّبجيلا"]

In the same way, and by using \ instead of /, like this:

```
? o1 \ ["طيبة","حنين"]
```

We can get the names on the left of the main strings, as shown here:

["قفْ للمُعلِّم : طيبة" ,
 "وفّه التّبجيلا : حنين"]

So the difference between using / or \ is to put the names on the right or on the left depending on the orientation of the character. To make this happen, I used operator overloading. But for \, this is impossible because this is not a numeric operator. I used this single line to activate the overloading on that character:

```
ChangeRingOperator | \
```

---

[10]For non-Arabic readers, you don't need to understand the text. Take it just as a string that we play with by subdividing into two and then over two people. For your consideration, the text is an abstract from a famous poem that calls for respecting teachers.

And in the overloaded code, I used | like this:

```
class arbString
    //...

    def operator(pOp,value)
        if pOp = "|"
        // split the string using \ here
        // ...
```

Now this is where I need your advice.

While my solution is working perfectly, I'm not very comfortable with the idea of changing the operator, mainly because it will limit the coherence of the library when it is used in other Ring code made by other developers who may use the logical operator | instead of the classical OR.

Is there any other strategy that is better than mine?

Mahmoud: There's no problem in changing a Ring operator, but you have to change it back again to avoid any problem when someone uses the original operators in other locations in the code.

You have to determine what you want to do:

- **A Ring library**: In this case, don't change the language. Just use the language features (the same keywords and operators).

- **A domain-specific language**: In this case, feel free to change anything because it will be used in special context under your control.

Look at this example that changes the Ring operators, then uses `eval()`, and then restores the original operators again:

```
http://ring-lang.sourceforge.net/doc1.10/natural.html#using-eval-with-our-
natural-code
```

Numeric Overflow Error

Mansour: In the Arabic string library I'm working on, I will allow programmer to compare strings as naturally as saying the following, for example:

```
if  oString1  >  "sometext"{ // dosomething }
```

To make this possible, I've played on operator overloading like this:

```
load "guilib.ring"
o1 = new arabicString("مصر هي أم الدنيا")
? o1 > "مصر"

class arabicString

        oQString = new QString()
        func init(pStr)
            oQString.append(pStr)

        def operator(pOp,pStr)
            if pOp = ">"
                    if arbCompare(pStr) = "more"
                            return TRUE
                    else
                            return FALSE
                    ok
            ok

        def arbCompare(pStr)
            switch oQString.compare(pStr,0)
            on 0     cRes = "equal"
            on -1    cRes = "less"
            on 1     cRes = "more"
            other    cRes = "diff"
            off
            return cRes
```

Everything goes well, and the result I get from this code sample is an obvious and correct 1 (→ cRes = "more"), until I extend the number of characters of the string to more than 8, as shown here:

```
? o1 > "مصر هي أم"
```

Then the following error message is generated:

```
Line 4 Error (R18) : Numeric Overflow!
```

Are there any details related to the Ring internal functioning that causes this? Is any adjustment necessary on the Qt side to correct the issue?

Mahmoud: In Ring, the > and < operators convert strings to numbers directly when getting the parameters. This (weakly typed) behavior is added for easy development when these operators are used with numbers.

During the conversion process from a string to a number, Ring checks for numeric overflow. This is why you get the error message shown in Figure A-3.

🔒 GitHub, Inc. (US) │ https://**github.com**/ring-lang/ring/blob/master/src/ring_vmexpr.c

```
447     }
448
449     void ring_vm_greater ( VM *pVM )
450     {
451             double nNum1=0,nNum2=0   ;
452             String *cStr1   ;
453             if ( RING_VM_STACK_ISNUMBER ) {
454                     nNum1 = RING_VM_STACK_READN ;
455                     RING_VM_STACK_POP ;
456                     if ( RING_VM_STACK_ISNUMBER ) {
457                             nNum2 = RING_VM_STACK_READN ;
458                     }
459                     else if ( RING_VM_STACK_ISSTRING ) {
460                             nNum2 = ring_vm_stringtonum(pVM,RING_VM_STACK_READC);
461                     }
462                     else if ( RING_VM_STACK_ISPOINTER ) {
463                             ring_vm_expr_npoo(pVM,">",nNum1);
464                             return ;
465                     }
466             }
```

Figure A-3. *In operator overloading, Ring automatically converts parameters from strings to numbers!*[10]

In the future, we could change this behavior and avoid it when we have operator overloading; I will check on that.

---

[11]As you will see, this has been fixed.

For now, compare things from the same type, and think about the implementation of something like this:

```
o1 = new arabicString("مصر هي أم الدنيا")
? o1 > new arabicString("مصر هي أم")
```

Mansour: I'll do so, although it remains restrictive to the level of expressiveness I want to achieve. Thank you, Mahmoud.

Mahmoud: After reviewing your post again, I considered it as a bug report. When we have operator overloading, Ring must avoid converting the `String` to a `Number` for `>` operator and similar operators too.

It has been fixed in this commit: `https://tinyurl.com/rq3xvjk`.

Now your code works as expected, as shown in Figure A-4.

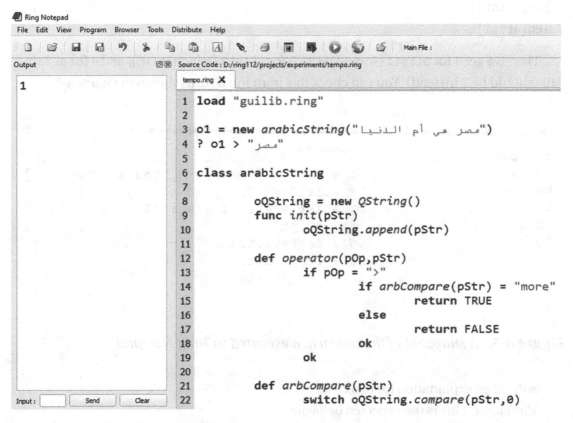

Figure A-4. Now, it's fixed, and Ring doesn't convert strings to numbers in operator overloading!

Thanks for the report. Keep up the good work.

Mansour: I'm glad you've considered the point.

A Strange Behavior in len( ) of Lists

Mansour: Let's talk to Ring and say the following:

```
load "stdlib.ring"
aList1 = ["mansour","teeba","haneen"]
aList2 = ["10","20","30"]
aList = aList1 + aList2
? aList
? len(aList1)
? len(aList2)
? len(aList)
```

Then we get 4 for aList1 (should be 3), 3 for aList2 (which is OK), and 4 for aList (this should be 7 instead). You can check this from the IDE, as shown in Figure A-5.

```
Output                              ⊗⊠   Source Code : D:/ring112/projects/experiments/tempo.ring

                                         tempo.ring  ✕
mansour
teeba                               1  aList1 = ["mansour","teeba","haneen"]
haneen                              2  aList2 = ["10","20","30"]
10                                  3  aList = aList1 + aList2
20                                  4  ? aList
30                                  5  ? Len(aList1)
                                    6  ? Len(aList2)
4                                   7  ? Len(aList)
3                                   8
4                                   9
```

Figure A-5. *A snapshot of the code when executed in Ring Notepad*

Is there an explanation for this case?

Mahmoud: This is the expected behavior.

In Ring, the + operator is defined for lists as follows:

```
List + Something ---> Add this (Something) to the List
```

Check out this line of your code:

```
aList = aList1 + aList2
```

Look at the following:

```
aList1 + aList2
```

This means the following:

```
Add the list (aList2) as an Item to the List (aList1)
```

So, `aList1` will contains four items. Then this `list` will be copied to `aList`. So, `aList` will contain four items too.

Your Approach to Testing

Mansour: When I was writing the book, I was learning the internals of the language by consulting the `c:\ring\tests` folder in the installation folder of Ring.

In a previous discussion, you said that, in developing Ring:

- You test everything.

- You write tests before code.

- You use automated testing.

- You rely a lot on manual testing.

Also, I remarked that you don't use the `Assert()` function a lot, but you write normal code that uses the functions with expressive real-world examples.

Can you please give us more details about your recipes in testing? And tell us your advice for making quality programs? And tell us if other types of testing (security checks, performance loading, etc.) are covered in the Ring codebase?

That's a lot of questions, but I know you will be both concise and accurate in answering them.

Mahmoud: Like programming, testing requires a mix of science, art, and technology. But it's more art than science or technology. When I think about testing, I remember the following basic idea in programming:

```
(Input) ---> (Process) ---> (Output)
```

During testing, you have to think carefully about these three stages:

1. For the input, you have three common strategies, shown here:

   - Accept only the correct input, reject the bad input, and display error message.

   - Accept any input, extract the correct input, or transform the input to correct input. Don't display error messages.

   - Provide the correct input to the software through input files or source code (we don't get input from the user).

2. For the process:

   - We think about it as a black box that we need to test.

3. For the output:

   - We need to know the input that produced this output.

     → *So that we can repeat the process.*

   - We need to check whether the output is correct.

     → *A change in the input will lead to a change in the output (maybe we made a mistake in the input itself).*

   - We need to think about related cases.

     → *Maybe we will discover a special case of the error that is different from the original one.*

This will let us think about the nature of the user interface of the application:

- Text-based user interface
- Graphical user interface
- Web application

and whether we have (real-time) operations or not! Are we testing a game or an application? Are we using threads? Think about the things that have an important effect on the environment!

All of these considerations, together, let us put together a testing plan where we need to test, as shown here:

- Each unit alone

- Each subsystem (after units integration)

- The complete system

The selection between the following is based on what we will test, as shown here:

- **Automatic testing**: Very fast and accurate

- **Manual testing**: Slow, advanced (lets us try new things), and uses human intelligence

I used to automate things as much as possible, but also I use manual testing as much as I can.

When developing the software, I do the following:

1. I may use a `Print` statement and `Assert` to check things quickly while typing the code.

2. I use automatic testing to test each unit alone to be sure that it produces the correct output for different cases.

I run all of the tests after each update to the code.

1. I use manual testing after all of this.

2. Sometimes I use the debugger. But in most cases, I don't use it.

The Secret Behind Mahmoud's Responsiveness

Mansour: I used to be a member of other open source projects, and some of them were backed by lucrative companies and had dozens of active programmers full-time on them.

But they never reached the level of responsiveness I observe here when I ask a question or report a bug. My question is twofold.

- How can you so quickly identify any problem in a codebase of 20,000 lines of code? And is it the visual representation of Ring inside the PWCT tool that helps you do that?

- Do you think that the same reactiveness can be maintained when the community becomes larger in the future?

Mahmoud: Thanks for your kind words. The secrets are always time management and quality management. With respect to quality management, Ring codebase really consists of different subprojects in different layers.

- The first layer (the compiler plus the virtual machine) is 20,000 lines of code, written in the C language (generated using PWCT).

- The second layer consists of extensions of C/C++. Some extensions are large; for example, RingQt is around 200,000 lines of code.

- The third layer consists of libraries written in Ring.

- An additional layer consists of tests, samples, and applications written in Ring.

I think we have around 500,000 lines of code. But they are organized in a way that keeps them as simple as much as possible. Here are some examples:

- I spent around two years writing the first 5,000 lines of the Ring compiler and the virtual machine to be sure that I can easily maintain them in the future.

- The Ring extensions in (C/C++) were generated using a simple code generator (written in Ring) and configuration files. Most problems could be solved through the generator (around 1,500 lines of Ring code) and configuration files.

This leads to simple extensions development.

From the beginning, I wrote tests and used testing automation to check the quality after each update to the source code. We have many Ring samples and applications written by Gal and Bert. I run most of them before any Ring release and after any critical update. Besides automatic testing, I use manual testing a lot.

The point is that with simple design, automatic and manual testing, good documentation, a nice team, and careful development, we can be effective in managing complexity in large projects.

With respect to time management, I used to work from four to six hours every day (the time that I focus on my programming tasks). Since I like programming and I control what I program, I consider this time as fun time. Then I use the other hours in the day to do other activities that are fun to me too (I like reading, playing chess, communicating with people through Facebook and the Ring Google Group, walking, drinking coffee while watching TV, and so on).

If you check my Facebook page, when I write a post, it's common to have from 100 to 300 comments. I used to reply to each of the comments, and many people have asked how I could do this. Here's my answer:

- It's fun for me.

- I like writing (not just code).

- I type very fast without looking at the keyboard and without moving my fingers from specific keys.

For me, I write more than I talk, and it's one of my favorite activities.
Regarding how I quickly identify a problem in a codebase of 20,000+ lines of code, well:

- I have dealt with this codebase every day, for many years, so I remember each part of it.

- PWCT lets me enjoy programming because I felt like I *designed* my software instead of writing it.

I like writing code a lot, but the point of PWCT is to free me to forget the syntax of the programming language so I can focus on the algorithms. This is important because I jump between many languages and I want to be productive as much as possible.

As for your question about whether I can maintain the same *responsiveness when the community becomes larger*, my answer is yes, because we will have more resources.

- More experience from solving problems

- Better documentation, samples, and applications

- More questions answered along the way

On Facebook, I have answered tens of thousands of messages (most of them are questions about programming in general). So, I have private documents that form a FAQ that help me answer questions.

In the Ring Google Group, we have documentation and many answers we can reuse. Also, other members like you, Gal, Bert, and the Ring team help in this process. Thanks to all of you for spreading the word.

Mansour: This makes it so clear to me why Ring is a success and will be a great success in the future. The things you mentioned are the kind of skills any great programmer should aim for and work on, with passion and patience, but also with respect to the technology and the people who use it. This is one of your assets.

In your book *The Deeper Secrets of Programming* (in Arabic), I liked when you made the analogy between rain and code and between the divinity and software abstraction and many other ideas that relate technology to philosophy and coding to meaning.

So, you have my respect and consideration for your person, your values, and your projects. May your life be all happiness and success.

The Story Behind the Name of Ring

Mansour: Can you tell me the story of the name Ring?

Mahmoud: I wanted a name that satisfies three conditions.

- Something that hasn't been used before

- Something that is short (up to four letters), which is nice for the source code and file name extensions

- Something that reflects the spirit of the language

I started the design and the implementation of the language in September 2013, but the language name was selected in April 2015. For me, it was like I had a language that could work on many platforms, be used in many types of applications, and support many programming paradigms.

So, Ring = one ring to rule them all (from the *Lord of the Rings* movie).

Since Ring is a simple and easy-to-use language, some developers in the Middle East looked at the name and said it reminds them of the Ring of Solomon, which gives power to programmers.

Ring vs. Python

Mansour: How do you see the competitive advantages of Ring compared to Python?

   Mahmoud:

- Since Ring is a young language, we have more space for innovation. Also, we have learned a lot from other languages.

- Ring is similar to scripting languages like Python and Ruby, but also it learns a lot from other languages too. Ring is distributed as a package with an IDE similar to Visual Basic. This, in addition to syntax flexibility features, provides a simpler and nice tool for beginners.

- Ring's standard support for declarative programming and natural language programming (and in the next future for visual programming through PWCT) opens more directions for better abstraction levels than we have in modern languages that are designed for developing applications.

Ring in 10 Years

Mansour: How do you see Ring in 10 years from now?

   Mahmoud: I think it will be bigger and will provide standard support for many programming domains through frameworks that use declarative and natural language programming.

   Ring is not just a language; it's designed to be a complete programming package for applications to be used by people looking for the maximum level of productivity.

Monetizing PWCT

Mansour: Why didn't you consider monetizing the extraordinary PWCT success (23+ million download and 270,000+ users on GitHub)?

   Mahmoud: I plan to do this for PWCT 2.0.

Ring Foundation

Mansour: Are there any plans to launch a Ring foundation and look for funding for it to guarantee the sustainability of the project and increase its acceptance by the industrial world?

Mahmoud: We already have a software company that will be used as the provider of the PWCT 2.0 software. But for Ring, the current open source model satisfies our needs; most of the Ring team members have stable incomes and contribute their time, effort, and knowledge. Also, we don't accept donations because we don't need it in the current stage of development.

Ring vs. PWCT

Mansour: What is nearest to your heart: Ring or PWCT?

Mahmoud: I really don't know. I have asked myself this question many times during the last few years! That's why I'm developing both of them. I get different feelings and different results when I write Ring code than when I develop using visual programming. By using both ways, I can develop the same thing, but the time, concentration, and feelings will be different based on the task.

In general, I think I prefer PWCT in these two cases:

- When I want to design a solution while I'm developing it (I'm thinking while doing something practical)

- When I want to focus only on the problem and forget the language and the syntax completely

This works for me when I developed the Ring compiler and VM using PWCT based on the C language.

When I work using Ring:

- It's already very fun to write code. I used to do that for many years!

- The speed and flexibility in modifying textual source code encourage me to write more code.

Your Final Word to the Reader

Mansour: Do you have a final word to day to the reader of this book?

Mahmoud: New programming languages are a chance to invest your time and creative ideas in improving the software development world. This can be done at many levels, including developing new libraries and frameworks that open new levels of productivity.

Ring is good at designing new development tools (generators, frameworks, tools, etc.), so use Ring to develop the next big thing in the framework world, and you will be proud of yourself!

Index

© Mansour Ayouni 2020
M. Ayouni, *Beginning Ring Programming*, https://doi.org/10.1007/978-1-4842-5833-0

H

I, J

K

L

M

Printed in the United States
By Bookmasters